JESUS WAS NOT
A MODERN DAY CHRISTIAN

How Christianity Has Made Idols

and How to Return to Truth

Rachel Amidei

This book formatting template was made by Derek Murphy of Creativindie Design.

Editing by Jessicah Lahitou

For information contact :
(racheljprojects@gmail.com)
rachela.substack.com

Book and Cover design by Designer – Anna Grissom

10 9 8 7 6 5 4 3 2 1

CONTENTS

To my dearest children, you have been a gift and a reward from Adonai. I wrote this for you to know the things I didn't know and to see Scripture in all of its miraculous wonder.

INTRO

Revelation 2:4 "But I have this against you, you have abandoned your first love."

IT'S BEEN QUITE DIFFICULT WRITING THIS SERIES. I've wavered over the years between anger at the lies I ingested growing up in the American Church to grief over the loss of knowledge among sincere and kind congregants and pastors. I feel the heart of a great Heavenly Father afflicted for His children.

The lost knowledge and power of the Western Church has resulted in splitting, fracturing, and a declining position in culture. My passion for restoration of G-d's Word to this Church has spilled over into discussions, pushing some friends away and bringing new ones near.

And many days, I hate that. I hate that these concepts I'm passionate about, so foundational to the early Church, are now considered battlegrounds capable of killing off friendships. But as we approach what seems to be a more authoritarian globe, closer to the shutting of mouths and the cancelling of ideas, closer to hatred and bitterness being the root of all motives, closer to isolation, it feels as if bold voices have a choice to make.

Tell the truth, or join the ranks. I've often been the different voice. I cannot find a good reason to change now.

This book began before 2020. Before Coronavirus isolated us from one another. Before chaos broke out across major cities in protest over the death of George Floyd. Before violence, vandalism, looting and destruction became a daily video post and one of the most prevalent news stories. Before most people were well educated on human trafficking and sexual slavery in the US. Before the meteoric rise in a new plethora of Marxist theories including Critical Race Theory, exposing itself with polarizing grandeur.

As these intense political forces and scathing revelations come to light, it is odd looking back and feeling that the Church in The West needed reform long before these issues. But it did.

In fact the reform it needed would have been a hedge against the now.

It often feels as if the Church here is heading towards a "dark ages" of sorts. The truth squandered for comfortable Christianity, and obedience to Yeshua plagiarized as legalism, Churches have plunged themselves into quite the bog of cultural relevance. The Church has been diluted and divested of its cultural influence in the few hundred years this country has been in existence. Today it often resembles a pale, weak, hypocritical and unethical ghost of its former self, already riddled with errors and intent on keeping them.

Yet, G-d loves it. G-d looks for His people in all corners of the earth and here I'm convinced many whole-heartedly love G-d back. Love. This love will win all things in the end. A love that binds us to each other, love that will conquer evil and love that will save us. It is love, in reality, that all of this is about. And I find that it is our understanding of love that seems to be a central problem with the church in America. Our definitions of love have produced thousands of denominations and ways of following G-d. Argument after argument and split after split.

I've spent a lot of my adult life evaluating love. What are its meanings, its consequences, and how should we define it? The word itself seems to have been stripped of deep or clear definition. I know, without a doubt, I spent my 20's thinking I loved different men, when I really didn't. On the other hand, there were things I did truly love, like my son.

After a difficult first marriage fraught with cheating, addiction, fear and loneliness, I hit 28 years of age with no clear conceptualization of love whatsoever, except through the tireless work and effort I put into my son. I spent and overspent money, time energy, and emotion to be the mom I thought he needed. I worked tirelessly to make up for the divorce he was experiencing, to give him direction and teach him truth. I read book after book about what he was experiencing. I walked him to the park, shared endless hours at the museum, baseball practices, school, church and extra work on academics.

I know the trend of successes we've seen in him will continue. And not because of how I've felt when I've raised him. It is because he has been raised by (not just me) but people who have spent time and energy and money "loving" on him: A love that can be quantified by actions on a day-to-day basis.

Given the extraordinary lengths of effort and work we put into our children, how can we then continue to define love as a feeling? A feeling!?! The deep need we have for love to be overwhelming, true, expansionary, rooted and life changing defined as something wispy, flimsy, prone to change at the drop of a hat or the drop of a hormone. Falling in and out of love with each other as if it was ever really love in the first place.

Perhaps it is my experience or perhaps it is my study of the Bible, but I've come to discover that feelings aren't facts and feelings alone aren't love. They may lead to love. They may help in love. And yes, I understand, feelings can promote emotionally driven deeds. Although, not all of them good. Just look at Romeo and Juliet! Immature love is as prone to disaster as to success.

But these feelings do not define love anymore than the cover of a book defines its contents. It seems to be a glorification of self-centered emotions that has led us to such a degraded cultural understanding of love. We have forgotten what the Bible really says. "To love the Lord is to obey His commands." Love was always meant to be a verb. It is always about what we do, not necessarily always about how we feel about it. It is almost always better to do the right thing and feel resentful than to do the wrong thing while feeling elated. Actions speak louder than words and actions have greater consequences both positive and negative. If you've lived here on this earth for a while, you've likely noticed that.

Not that the Bible excuses a bad attitude. And G-d judges our hearts quite evidently. But the Bible doesn't put a whole lot of stock into what you feel about its Commands. One reason may be the importance of a testimony of G-dly activity versus internal happiness. The heart has only one way to display its intent.

Case in point, Cain and Able.

Here, two brothers, who, before the Law was written down, both knew to bring G-d a sacrifice or offering in the form of the "first fruits" of what they worked. A first fruit represented the best of their crops, sheep, etc. And both did indeed bring a sacrifice.

Since they both brought something it could be argued that G-d saw their hearts and, though Cain brought an offering, his heart wasn't right so Cain didn't quite make the cut.

There is truth in this, but one doesn't need to be a heart reader to know that his offering was not the best of his crop! Anybody with two eyes (or even a nose) would have been able to evaluate that Cain didn't bring what was asked of him. A quick overview of the best of Cain's crop compared to what he brought would have sufficed. No heart evaluation needed.

What if Cain had begrudgingly brought his best? Not sure. We can't know. All we know is that his actions were proof of his heart's condition. He brought what he wanted to bring when he wanted to bring it and was angry that G-d didn't approve. He brought something on His terms, defying G-d's terms. His actions did not align with G-d's commands. His actions revealed his heart's position.

And this defines humanity.

You believe your car will carry you safely to work, so you get in it. You believe that your work will pay you at the end of two weeks, so you work. And if you really believe that G-d is love, you study the information this G-d has given to us on how to live. And the next step is to live it.

Yes, the heart condition is the root of everything. But actions are the proof.

Christians love to say, "G-d judges the heart." Indeed! If our hearts believed in this big powerful G-d, wouldn't we care about what His letter to us actually says? Would we read it passively? Would we only engage with it on the Sundays we went to church? Would we dismiss the first parts of it because they make us uncomfortable? Our hearts are dictating a lot of things, but love for G-d may not be one of them. Love always requires action. To love the Lord is to be like David; to meditate on his Laws and precepts, and to call them "perfect" and "life", and then to walk in them.

Not because they are salvation. They are not. We engage with them, we obey them, because our Father has asked us to.

My heart brims over with adoration and joyful hope most days when I engage with my children. Yes, some days, as is likely true for all parents, I wonder at my parenting skills. So, please don't take my exuberance as a dismissal of all things challenging in parenting. But these people are so precious to me that I smile about them even as I write. With everything in me I want to teach them how to avoid the pitfalls of life, the pains I've dredged myself through and the horrors of self-hatred. So I teach them. I write to them, so to speak, in more ways than one. I desire to be an example to them.

G-d is better at this than we are. He looks on proclaiming His great love for us, exclaiming how wonderful we are created to be. We are His creation! He desperately reaches out through nature, and revelation, and through the most clarifying and confirmable part, through His letter to us.

The pain and suffering and horror of Yeshua's death and the glory in His resurrection make flimsy uses of the word, "love", egregious. We exhibit our love back to Him in obedience, not for salvation, not because He forces us, but because we love Him in return; because the G-d who died, who rose again, who has pursued us relentlessly, has asked us to. We cannot get past His sacrifice, His rescue, His salvation. We are wrecked by His goodness and desperate to follow Him to the very ends of the age.

At least, this level of relationship resembles unity with G-d and exhibits the ideal in personal and national linkage with Him.

Studying His word has been the light unto my path in the deepest and truest sense. I can test the spirit that speaks to me, I can confirm the nature before me and vice versa, and I can know what to do when nature and revelation seem to be silent. I'm the most blessed of humans to have access to this letter from on High and to be able to study it. What a gorgeous moment in history and location! A person, a woman, has the time, education, cultural support, publishing industry, Rocky Mountain views, and early morning quiet times to seek out the G-d of the universe!

We are bestowed an extravagant gift. The world isn't getting any younger or kinder. It needs our joy, our peace, and our "love". If knowledge put into action is power, think what the combination of knowledge, action and the power of the Holy Spirit can produce! We've seen it on the earth before. The movement of Yeshua and His followers immediately after changed the entire world. It changed time, knowledge, compassion and revelation. It broke systems of government and religion.

That power did not dissipate. We expelled it with our ignorance, our compromises and our desire for comfort and entertainment. We abolished it with our redefining of the word, *love*, with the emergence of doctrines and demands that are man-made. We have taken away the power of action and replaced it with flimsy and overused terminology about a feeling.

However, I'm encouraged by the people I meet whose eyes are opening to Scripture and whose hearts are turning to love as G-d defines it. Things are changing and it's time we understand why that change is required. The Biblical foundation for that change, and what awaits us on other side makes the journey into discovery of truth and obedience worthwhile.

I've been discovering these tenets alongside other brilliant mentors and teachers. I don't know every answer, I won't get everything 100% right, and I definitely won't delve into every angle and mystery that G-d has in His word. That's what makes reading the Bible so beautiful. It's new with additional meaning every time. It's why we can and should go back day after day and eat of its bread and drink of its water. "Man does not live on bread alone" indeed! "But on every word that comes from the mouth of God!"

Yeshua tells us that, "all the Law and the prophets hang on these two commands, to Love the Lord with all your heart and to love others." (Matt 22:36-39) Many people believe that this means we have a new command and that command is just to love. There is no place in Scripture where Jesus calls this "new" by the assumed definition. You can find this command of loving in Leviticus 19:18, all the way at the beginning. Just because it was the first time Jesus was teaching it to his disciples doesn't mean it was a new command.

Furthermore, this isn't a command to just love with some gut instinct. It is actually the opposite. Jesus just told us that all of G-d's Laws are love. They are each and every one of them about loving G-d and loving others. Want to know how to love G-d? Look to the Law (Torah). Want to know how to love others? Look to the Law. And by this "word that comes from the mouth of God" we should live and be free.

So, what does Scripture tell us "love" means? We must go to what Yeshua teaches about his own Word. We must study the beginning and look to its definitions, instructions and values. It's time to take love seriously. This is the only hope for the future of the church, the people of G-d.

I know I've already said some things here that have taken my readers aback. A few may already claim offense. I know this based on the many conversations I've had with people over the years about these topics.

I'm not writing these essays to get into arguments. I'm writing this as a *result* of those arguments. Conversations and even debates I've had with others and with myself. Upon a good, deep look at Scripture, there is more than enough proof that we have abandoned G-d's ideas about church and discipleship. This book provides an opportunity for further thought and discussion about where we have gone astray and the necessary fixes. Just as the church in Acts did, we should wrestle with these ideas together.

If you interpret me as harsh or overly direct, know I'm fully aware that this is my style. I'm unapologetic about the realities of my findings. I'm less concerned about offending people and more concerned that I've offered the truth with concise clarity and a hope that it will bring light. But I must add, from the bottom of my heart, my openness is rooted in care and compassion for the many Believers who feel lost with Scripture, who can't break themselves out of addiction, who are overwhelmed by their past, or who have lost connection to the power of their ministries.

I've been there.

It has been G-d's truths that broke me out.

Ideas too often offend as we let our pride get in the way. I learned the hard way long ago that pride is a horrific taskmaster. Keeping the walls of pride only destroys our ability to follow Yeshua into our destinies. Don't be like the old Rachel.

Just as the Bible exhorts us, we must test our ideas, test the spirits, to see if they are in alignment with G-d's truths.

No doubt I'm as fallible as the next person. Where I get things wrong I pray I will make adjustments. The failings of many great teachers serve as warning posts for anyone attempting to preach the gospel. Great spiritual danger lies in teaching the Bible as it puts the teacher in a position to be judged by more than just people, but by G-d Himself. The last thing we need is another wolf

in sheep's clothing leading people astray. The last thing we need is another truth mixed with a lie.

The desire for truth will lead to wonderful places when you are willing to put aside sentimentalities and ego trips.

I truly believe if you look for the truth, you may find it and along with it, something you didn't know. For the average American Christian, I believe you will find much you didn't know in what I'm about to share. For the wizened mature Believer, perhaps you will be able to use this to form conversations with others.

Abandon former sentiment not rooted in Scripture. Put aside man-made ideas.

But don't abandon your reason, logic, and Holy Spirit led vision.

THE COST TO HUMBLY FOLLOW CHRIST

In every great business a cost/benefit analysis of some sort takes place. What's the ROI? How long will it take?

There is never really a question that the business start up won't cost something. Nobody thinks zero time, zero money, and zero talent is a great equation for success.

There is always a cost.

Yet, so many of my 20's and 30's were spent in easy Christianity. Sunday after Sunday I was soothed by "Jesus loves me just as I am", sermons. What a relief when pastors would say it didn't matter what I had done.

-I'd cheated on my husband
-I'd lied
-I'd spent years hating my body and my life

But week in and out the message stayed the same. G-d loved me. That's it. Apparently that met all the requirements of knowledge a Believer needs. Not only that, the sparkly packaging of great music and slick videos sandwiching the easy to swallow morsel of simple doctrine made it all the more fun. It's vague but attractive, and really, who could reject a message dressed so enticingly?!

Or so obviously?

G-d's love for us is true and evident in every breath we have. Realistically, the very existence of sunshine, trees, food, sleep, flowers, mountains, and capacity for human kindness are evidence of the love and goodness of G-d. Our ability to care about each other, to take care of a home, to work for something in the future, these qualities came from somewhere. They came from our Creator. Creation itself sings of the goodness of a G-d. His works proclaim His majesty AND His love.

What troubles me is that Sunday after Sunday so many pastors refuse to make it past the obvious. Maybe once in a while this sermon is necessary. After all, humans miss even the most obvious of signs and sometimes we need that very basic alphabet that each baby Christian must comprehend.

But it's not rare. It's the boring weekly reality. Many pastors won't preach past a kindergarten level of thinking.

In the meantime, people like my former self, are caged. Locked in prisons of their own making, every Sunday they are told G-d loves them right where they are. Right in their rotten, stinking, death producing squalor. Don't worry about that pesky little hard ask. The one that says, get up and carry your cross. Just stay in the pit and let G-d "love" you from there.

Adults with kindergarten level skills are tragedies. I was once that calamity. Walking around like a grown up, spiritually tragic, desperately lost.

Luke 14:25 – 34 "Large crowds were traveling with Jesus, and turning to them he said; 'If anyone comes to me and does not hate his father and mother, his wife and children, his brothers and sisters – yes, even his own life – he cannot be my disciple. And anyone who does not carry his cross and follow me cannot be my disciple. Suppose one of you wants to build a tower. Will he not first sit down and estimate the cost to see if he has enough money to complete it? For if he lays the foundation and is not able to finish it, everyone who sees it will ridicule him, saying, 'This fellow began to build and was not able to finish.

Or suppose a king is about to go to war against another king. Will he not first sit down and consider whether he is able with ten thousand men to oppose the one coming against him with twenty thousand? If he is not able, he will send a delegation while the other is still a long way off and will ask for terms of peace. In the same way, any of you who does not give up everything he has cannot be my disciple."

"Salt is good, but if it loses its saltiness, how can it be made salty again? It is fit neither for the soil nor for the manure pile; it is thrown out. He who has ears to hear, let him hear."

Huh.

When is the last time a pastor warned your congregation that to follow Jesus was going to be the greatest sacrifice they would ever make? THEN, when you are ready, go ahead and take that next step.

Yet here, Yeshua questions, don't you prepare to build a tower? Don't you take into account the cost of a war? How can we not take into account the cost of following Jesus before we take that step? Before we ask others to take that step?

Is it because we have forgotten there is a cost at all?

In The Cost of Discipleship, Dietrich Bonhoeffer says this,

"Costly grace is the gospel which must be sought again and again and again, the gift which must be asked for, the door at which a man must knock. Such grace is costly because it calls us to follow, and it is grace because it calls us to follow Jesus Christ. It is costly because it costs a man his life, and it is grace because it gives a man the only true life. It is costly because it condemns sin, and grace because it justifies the sinner. Above all, it is costly because it cost God the life of his Son: 'Ye were bought at a price', and what has cost God much cannot be cheap for us. Above all, it is grace because God did not reckon his Son too dear a price to pay for our life, but delivered him up for us. Costly grace is the Incarnation of God."

There is no FREE gift of salvation. It cost our Savior His life. It will cost us ours. To our great benefit. For as Bonhoeffer so beautifully notes, following G-d will make us into great, true, grown up people. We will become like our Savior and will be made fit for His Kingdom.

Yet, on Sunday morning opposing proclamations abound.

Even for those who teach that we must lay down our lives, they may intend it in the most selfish or simple sense. It often means, "Give us some money." Or "Be nice to people." Or "Go on a mission trip every once in a while." Or, "Don't be too political." Sometimes they even mean, "don't hurt other people's feelings with too much truth."

The true cost of following Yeshua is death. You die. There is no promise of gold, or riches. Though G-d desires to bless you, those blessing may look different than the cultural currents. Once again, the truth's covering seems ugly and hard. But at its center there is gold.

Yes, following Yeshua will cost something. Your ego must go. Your previous behaviors may need adjusting or even an ending. Your obedience is called forth. Your oath is taken, your allegiance proclaimed.

You DO NOT GET TO STAY THE SAME!

For in choosing the deadness of your old life you will lose your saltiness. To keep your saltiness you are to boldly proclaim G-d's truth. You will be mocked and rejected as Noah, Moses, Elijah, Paul, John the Baptist, Yeshua and so many others were. In telling the TRUTH, you will not be pleasing to some people. You may not attract a huge throng of followers or become famous or rich.

You die.

Every day, every moment, the DNA of the first Adam has to go. You have to be remade. You are being restructured to match up to your calling. That calling is resurrection and NEW CREATION.

You're going to piss people off. You're going to seem like a threat. You're going to become a joke to others. You're popularity or status may change.

You die.

You don't get to pick and choose how YOU want to follow the King. You don't get to write the contract and hand it to Him. He has already written it. He has defined how you are to become like Him. What He looks like and acts like and sounds like. He is Yeshua. He is from the beginning. He celebrates the Feast Days. He eats Kosher. He is a healer, a provider, a giver, a bold truth-teller. He cares for the widow and the orphan. He calls out when lies are spread about His word. He stands boldly against cultural evils, but FOR the people whom He loves. He died.

You die.

Salvation is not a breathtaking prayer and "Nice" feeling. It is a heart-broken, grasping, shaking, terrifying need for G-d that lands you on your knees and bids you to change everything in you. It is repentance. It is desperation for the King who can call you into your destiny and change the hell that resides with you apart from Him.

He is bondage undone. Chains broken. Gratitude, honor, awe, and surrender. He is a violent end to parts of you that were in opposition to Him.

You may need to "cut off the hand" or "gauge out the eye" that is causing you to continue to act in ways opposed to Him.

In Luke 15, Jesus tells the parable of the lost sheep. He ends it by saying, "I tell you that in the same way there will be more rejoicing in heaven over the sinner who repents than over ninety-nine righteous persons who do not need to repent."

What brings rejoicing? It is repentance. It is the sinner on their knees ready to leave their SIN at the cross and turn away from it. Ready to CHANGE!

There is not one salvation story in Scripture that is apart from this concept. The prodigal son turns from his slavery and pig slop to just SERVE in His father's house. He is humble and repentant. He flees the sin of his past to die to himself in his Father's household. The ego is gone. The love of his sin has ended.

The children of Israel must cover their doorposts in blood and make bread in haste, ready to leave and go wherever they are called. Their salvation comes with a task. They go into the desert and receive G-d's Kingdom principles. They must agree to those principles before they become G-d's church. Their agreement solidifies the story we still tell today.

The disciples were each asked to leave behind their old life, their enterprises and families. They had to sacrifice something to follow Yeshua. Despite it being a great honor in their day, they had to be willing to leave behind what they knew for something they did not know. They would have to change.

Can you think of even one founder of our Faith who was not called into action, even extreme and difficult action, in order to enter into our Heavenly Father's Kingdom?

In the long history of Scripture, we are told that nothing that is worthy is free. Anything great is going to cost something. It is the way of the world. As Bonhoeffer says, grace is that we get to follow Yeshua. Who will not take from us anything that is not returned 100 fold. For there is nothing we can really give to G-d that He needs. His desire is for our love and relationship with Him. That relationship is built through His sacrifice and our response. For if he died and was resurrected, when we die,

WE are resurrected.

The good news is not completed yet. Sin and death still hold a pungent and painful force. We can still choose separation from G-d. But for those of us willing to follow Yeshua to the cross, we will also discover life on the other side. There cannot be resurrection without death.

We have to die.

So that we can live.

Yes, I know you've heard this. But have we honestly considered it's meaning?

As I sit and write these words, I am also burdened by what more needs changing in my heart. But the burden is mixed with excitement. I have learned that each new change leads to new freedom, less stress, more confidence in my Savior, and more purpose. Purpose out of truth so deeply embedded in me that it feels like the foundations of my heart are being fortified. The strength that comes from following Yeshua resembles no other strength. It is not my own. It lives and breathes, full and filled full of meaning.

I am not ashamed of the gospel of Christ. I am more myself in Him than I ever was before.

What fear is there in change when you learn what a treasure that change uncovers? The cost is worth the goal.

There remains a disturbing side to abandoning the costly change.

In Scripture, people are often compared to plants. The spiritual realm is the field, etc. Trees serve as beautiful and tragic pictures of people and nations and also help us to understand the difference between true followers of Yeshua and fakers.

Matthew 7:19 - 23 "Every tree that does not bear good fruit is cut down and thrown into the fire. Thus, by their fruit you will recognize them. Not everyone who says to me, 'Lord, Lord' will enter into the kingdom of Heaven, but only the one who does the will of my Father in Heaven. Many will say to me on that day, 'Lord, Lord, did we not prophecy in your name and in your name drive out demons and in your name perform many miracles?' Then I will tell them plainly, 'I never knew you. Get away from me you lawless ones!'"

Well, that's a fun story. Not terrifying at all.

Yeshua goes on to talk about building your house on a rock versus sand. Which one crumbles? Well, the one on the sand of course. So how to build that house on a rock? Hmmmm. Didn't he just say it?

The relationship with Yeshua that is built solidly is built on, bum, bum buuuuuummmmm… !!! **Doing** the will of the Father.

You cannot be lawless. You must carry G-d's Law with you. You must abide in it.

You must take up your cross.

We have discussed so much about the Law. So far I have gushed about (my version of gushing I suppose) the personal freedom and beauty, the fruit, produced out of observing the Sabbath, attending to G-d's appointed times, enacting mercy, taking care of the widow and orphan etc.

The blessings are real.

But nobody should ever tell you obedience is easy. At the beginning real obedience presents quite the challenge. It gets easier as your faith builds.

I turn down work, I get quizzed over not eating pork or shellfish, I get absolutely excoriated by family when I reject particular holidays, I lose people when I share my concerns for souls stuck in sexual sin. I'm not culturally trendy. (Shocking I'm sure.) Despite some social pressures, my sacrifice so far has been easy compared to what is coming.

For the people who will see Yeshua's return, true discipleship will mean rejecting the entire monetary, community system. Not getting the Mark of the Beast poses incredible risk. It costs something. The allegiance of the End Times Believer may cost them their lives.

What horrors of culture are due to the current weakness of doctrine that promotes only salvation and never discipleship?

Why do we spurn the costs here and now when our spiritual muscles so desperately need the workout? Building our strength grants us access to impossible things being made possible. Only the strong of the faith will welcome the sight of Yeshua coming on the clouds. What hope have we if we do not embrace the cost?

Always and forever I will teach that salvation is by Yeshua and Yeshua alone. His salvation has been made abundantly complete. In His death and resurrections we have access.

We have a choice. Take the narrow way, the gate that is Christ, or reject Him.

But, if we accept Him if we accept Yeshua, *Salvation* (His name actually means "salvation" in Hebrew), there are attributes of Heavenly Citizenship He has asked us to adopt. They become part of our testimony, our love for each other, and our uniqueness.

The gospel promises that in the end, we will gain life and life abundantly. The family will be fully reunited, our home restored, our futures secure, our testimony shining, and our relationship with G-d no longer through a veil. We will clearly see and understand. Tears gone. Joy restored. Fear banished. Faith fully realized.

It is a good ending.

But to be the hero, we are called to do the hard work. We are like Frodo Baggins with all the moral victories, lessons and evil-crushing determination we can muster. Small, hidden, quiet, unseen, struggling, pressing forward, penitent at times, joyful at others, focused, parched, confused, afraid, bold, unsung, unheard of, looked down upon, persecuted, flawed, and yet, exactly what the world needs.

No, I don't believe G-d desires you to be miserable here on this earth. He knows well that the second you choose to follow Him, shredding the sin in your life carries plenty of difficulty. Whatever struggles may come beyond that are part of the system of the world, spiritual realm and natural consequences. G-d desires to bless you. He knows the quickest route to being blessed in His Kingdom is to abide in the Kingdom ways here and now.

Here and now, where it is hard.

I'm not sharing very much that is my own. These truths are old, time tested and founded in the beginning. My goal is to use Scripture to define and discern itself. I want people to see that what they really need is the Bible. G-d gave us the words He gave because that is all we needed to understand Him and His world. We don't need nice stories, self-help series or Ted-Talks sermons when we rely upon the complexity, depth, beauty and treasure of the Word of G-d. Sure those external experiences can be nice, and yes, we must be in community with our ideas and our faith.

But your faith is not, CANNOT, be reliant upon another individual.

All that will matter is what is between you and Adonai. What have you learned of Him, what do you know of His Word and have you become a doer of His things, not just a hearer?

Fall in love with the truth.

Fall in love with obedience.

Fall in love with the G-d of the Bible. The real one.

Find G-d's definition of love and what it means to love Him and His creation while we have the chance.

Be made whole. Find *SHALOM. (Peace and wholeness)*

This book is a pursuit of the love of G-d and the costly change we as individuals and as a Church must evaluate if we are going to call ourselves Kingdom Citizens.

Those who seek will find when they seek with their whole hearts. G-d ensures that the sincere seeker will find a treasure and we can rely on the promises of our Savior. Thank you for taking this journey with me. There is not a day that goes by that I'm not thankful for every way in which G-d has enabled me to write this.

Chapter 1

DEFINING TERMS

CULTURAL CONDITIONING SIGNIFICANTLY impacts human experience and the filters with which we approach our worldviews. Whether through the sensitivities of the palate or the familiarities of music patterns, we tend to prefer experiences from our rearing. The culture we live in affects the people we become.

I'm convinced that upon embracing Yeshua and accepting the Holy Spirit, G-d intends to condition us to His culture. The requirements of Heavenly citizenship often differ greatly from our cultural ideas and therefore we SHOULD be creating a unique and "holy" citizenry. But this is very often NOT an overnight transformation.

In fact, that transformation may not be happening much at all across Western culture. The tenets of Yeshua seem to be lost in comfortable, culturally relevant messaging and adoption of only the transformations that keep church email servers as empty of complaints as possible.

In speaking with many Believers regarding the facets of this series of essays, I find a cultural conditioning to American Western Christianity rooted to the very sinew of our theology. We don't just have on sunglasses; we literally have doctrinal filters sewn into our eyeballs. It is easy to read and re-read passages assuming their meaning based on our upbringing while missing words that are actually sitting there, right on the page.

I know, because I've done it.

And in the course of reading this Bible with less filters and more knowledge, phrases and meanings pop out that I was literally blind to prior to G-d's transformative work in my heart.

I suppose G-d took the wreckage of my life and used it to replace my eyes and give me new sight. It was through a complete crushing that G-d rebuilt me and opened my mind anew to His culture and the Yeshua that really lived, not the version I "hoped" had walked the earth.

The world I was thrown into about a decade ago, as my dear friend Marcel Murray introduced me to a deeper understanding of the Scriptural environment, was as foreign as the landscape of another planet. In the process G-d vastly shifted my terminology.

I had known Christian-ese quite well.

But the world of Scripture didn't use that language and so the steep learning curve I experienced was inevitable.

I've learned that the adoption of the terms I'm introducing here over the years has become second-hand to me, but certainly sometimes throws others off. I do my best NOT to do this to people, but some of the terms are just essentials. They are 101 for getting through specific ideas that this book will discuss and how Scripture describes and defines itself. I don't use ALL of these, or if I do, not often. But if you see them, now you know.

To many, this book will sound "Messianic" or "Hebrew Roots". If you must define it for the sake of simplicity, be my guest. But what I desire to share has less to do with denominations and much more to do with

Scriptural understanding. If we are to return to truth, if we are to be unified, it must be around, what we all agree, has been given to us by G-d Himself. We must come back to the Bible. Plain and simple. That the Bible provides the information that I'm sharing cannot be attributed to any modern denomination. We must each be willing to ask G-d what is true and to look for it with humility.

Now to some terms that may help the reader better comprehend this book.

TERMINOLOGY

ALEPH BET = This is the Hebrew Alpha Bet

ANCIENT NEAR EAST = Includes the Mesopotamian areas. Considered the Cradle of Civilization, locations included Israel, Syria, Turkey, Egypt, Iraq and a few others. Named this way because of their proximity to the West, these areas are the locations where Biblical activity takes place.

BRIT CHADASHA = The New Testament

CLEAN vs. UNCLEAN = Clean and unclean are not always words in the Old Testament that have to do with sin. Very often they just mean that one is good for food, one is not, one is ok to enter the temple, one is not, one does not have germs and one does. It can even mean that one is representative of life and one is representative of death. This often has NOTHING to do with righteous or sinful proclamations. It can mean that something is holy and something is simply normal (not holy or set apart). This is imperative to understand when reading the Torah.

COMMANDMENTS = Almost always referring to G-d's Laws found in the first 5 books of the Bible, or Torah.

DUALISM = The belief that material and spiritual reality are completely separate. Fallen body versus perfected Spirit. This view is in opposition to an integrated human form, body mind and spirit, and is therefore in opposition to verses discussing loving G-d with heart, mind, body, etc.

This ideology can also encompass beliefs that good and evil are equally balanced. But I tend to use the first definition when referring to dualism in these essays.

GEMATRIA = Meanings derived from the use of numbers in Scripture.

GNOSTICISM = A popular belief system during the church in Acts, antithetical to Biblical teaching. Gnosticism taught that understanding of G-d was through "special" knowledge. Mysticism and esoteric knowledge was key. This ideology believed that every single physical thing had a spiritual counterpart and ONLY the spiritual counterpart was valuable. The physical body was degraded and only the spirit of man could be good. A physical resurrection was antithetical to Gnostic ideology.

HOLY = Set Apart (Literally picked out of a bunch and put aside, separated from the regular and normal)

LAW = G-d's Teaching and Instruction. The first 5 books of the Bible.

MESSIANIC/HEBREW ROOTS = The group of people that believe all the Laws are still in effect while still accepting Yeshua as the Messiah.

THE MISHNAH= Collection of the Jewish oral tradition

MITZVOT = G-d's 613 Laws found in the Torah

MO-EDIM = The set apart, commanded, appointed times of the Lord. These are found in Exodus 20 and Leviticus 23 as well as other locations throughout Scripture. They include Sabbath, Passover, Firstfruits, Feast of Weeks, Yom Teruah, Shavuot (Pentacost), Yom Kippur (Day of Atonement), and Sukkot (Feast of Booths, Feast of Tabernacles) The "holidays" of the Lord, if you will.

RABBI = Teacher

RIGHTEOUS = Morally aligned with G-d. Right standing before the Lord.

SABBATH = The 7th day of the week from sundown on Friday to sundown on Saturday. The weekly Sabbath and concept for Sabbaths is described in Exodus 20.

SEPTUAGINT = Greek version of the Hebrew Bible

SHOFAR= Ancient trumpet made from the horn of an animal.

THE TALMUD = History of Jewish religion, including laws and beliefs. This is extra-Biblical.

TANAKH = The Old Testament

TORAH = The first 5 books of the Bible. Genesis, Exodus, Leviticus, Numbers, Deuteronomy. (SO much easier to write 'Torah', when these 5 books are what I'm referencing.) The number 5 associated with these 5 books carries its own meanings that we discuss. The reality is that ALL Of Scripture can be considered Torah, but I use this term for referencing the first 5 books in Scripture.

THE WORD = The Law and the Prophets, Yeshua himself.

NAMES OF G-d

ADONAI = Lord, or Master

G-D = Why do I put the dash? This dash reminds me, and hopefully my readers, that the One I'm referring to is the G-d of the Bible, of

Abraham, Isaac and Jacob. There are many gods on the earth. This one is the one we find in Scripture. The dash also represents the parts of Him that are unknowable and beyond our analysis or wisdom. Our limited nature cannot fathom the fullness of the Spirit of G-d.

HASHEM = "The Name". This is a way to say G-d without attempting the 4 letter name of G-d, "YHVH". This name has intimations of fatherhood. It's calling out "dad" in a Hebraic sense, while also recognizing the authority of G-d.

YAHWEH = Another representation of the actual name of G-d. Improperly pronounced but representing the name of the all-knowing Great Spirit that we see in Scripture.

YESHUA (H) = The one that Christians call Jesus. The name Yeshua means "salvation" in Hebrew. The Jews literally called out to salvation to save them. I call upon the name salvation in my prayers now and I use His name because His name embodies His character. He IS the Savior.

I'll additionally note that I use many different translations of Scripture throughout these essays. We all use different translations and exposure to some of these styles gives a well-roundedness to our getting used to the language of Scripture. I attempt to stay away from some of the more recent translations that I find to be using language too far from original meaning and intention.

My readers may wonder why I focus on certain topics and not others in this series.

For example, why not more focus on the commands to feed the poor, take care of the widow and orphan etc.? This is a good question. So let me answer before you ask.

I know you already have no problem with those commands of G-d. Who in the world does not want to feed the poor or take care of the abandoned and lonely? This is foundational to most normal people. And yes, the Church had better start doing a better job with these and with forming community in general. We were not meant to attend Church in a vacuum. We were not meant to isolate in narcissistic living while ignoring the state of those who sit in pews and chairs right next to us. Scripture is communal at every turn. Your church community is your family and your neighborhood is your mission field.

But, while my readers may not realize that these services to others are Commands and not requests of our Heavenly Father, they will likely have no objection to these acts of obedience.

Please, do not take the absence of some of G-d's Laws as an approval for forgetting them. The most important of G-d's things has to do with the "weightier" matters of justice and mercy. Caring for our fellow man through acts of justice and kindness are essential traits and a far higher call than this series has time to address.

The areas I tend to focus on in my essays are a mixture of commands that (as they all do) have to do with loving G-d and loving others, but which are not so popular, well known or understood in Christianity any longer. I also address new issues that have come up recently that the Church MUST take on but has seemed to dawdle around instead.

I address these in order to prove to you, my reader, that G-d's Laws, all of them, are good for teaching and instruction. And that we have abandoned observance and integration of Laws that we can actually enact due to historical influences and lack of knowledge. I address the ones the Church has gotten rid of to attempt to woo the Believer back into obedient relationship and repentant submission.

I also address our standing as Holy Spirit bearers in the face of a cultural onslaught. The return of knowledge of G-d's Laws, the integration of those things and the doctrines with which we approach cultural shifts are bonded. If you understand the principles in the Law, you will find a solid rock beneath your feet as the tumultuous seas and sands of cultural idols drift and crumble all about you.

Repentance brings healing and alignment and empowerment to the ministry of the body. Obedience is relational and without it, we have no evidence of oneness with Yeshua.

My hope is to show you these things. Not out of spite or judgment, but out of a sincere belief that the Great Commission to go and make disciples teaching them to obey is a call for all of us, including little old me.

I tend to come back to the same concepts over and over with each new chapter. This is how I learned and had these ideas become part of my vernacular. It is also a testament to how many of these ideas are the DNA of principles spanning a gamut of topics. Some may be bothered by the repetition, but for those whose encounters with this information are new, I hope it provides help in memory and application.

I've been blessed with a unique education and experience in this regard. I felt called to write this book first and foremost for my children. To undo the damage that culture has wrought on the Church and to assist in a way of looking at Scripture that is TRULY life changing and empowering.

To read the Word as it is and to understand it contextually, socially, logically, metaphorically, symbolically and spiritually really does produce life.

I've never loved reading Scripture more, and I've never felt more unity with the Lord. Life has appeared where previously none existed.

Because of a few wonderful teachers dedicated to truth, the light bulbs and fireworks and deep heart and mind change that Yeshua promises now occur in my times with the Lord and in my reading of His Word.

Combining my new knowledge with submission and obedience has produced something unspeakably real in my heart. Healing. Fearlessness. Forgiveness. Peace.

Wholeness.

I know the Holy Spirit desires this fulfilled presence in each and every Believer that they may walk in confident reliance upon G-d and continual knowledge that the life we see is just the beginning of life itself.

I sense the immense treasure the Church has lost through doctrines and theologies twisted by inaccuracies and fallacies. A dark shadow has loomed larger over the Western Church threatening to crush it in the weight of lawlessness and man-made religion.

I also know that the Church of Yeshua cannot be crushed completely. He has promised restoration, renewal, and life to those who seek Him.

And here you are, reading this. You are seeking. No doubt Yeshua will reveal Himself one way or another. Where even one seeks out humble pursuit of G-d, hope can still flourish. There is great hope in our Messiah. Let's get to know Him better.

Chapter 2

SYMPTOMS OF A PROBLEM

THE FAMILY

I'VE SPENT MUCH OF MY ADULT life on stages. Standing in front of people singing and playing piano and guitar to entertain, to bless, and when at church, mostly to encourage praise. After the applause, accolades, or moments of worship, I realize (at first in dismay, and now with understanding) that I'm still in my own skin. No enthusiastic clapping, not even the most vociferous sing-along or participatory note has changed my me-ness.

I am this human and I will forever be this human.

When I'm on stage, it's me there. When I go home, my thoughts and self-worth follow along. I cannot escape my own skin to become someone else, and the things that saturate me with a sense of purpose are not always what I had assumed they would be. Setting aside G-d's transformative work in my heart and the beauty and treasure in actually following Him, daily life is not always a mountaintop experience. I find this true in most people.

Yet, of all the roles I've played, there remains one wholly and uniquely different. One that keeps me going: mother.

Despite my misery during pregnancy, having children changed me sufficiently to actually *do* something new, to make every kind of shift and move, every kind of sacrifice. And all this new work and toil was just so I could remain with them more often; laugh with them, play with them, and teach them. Loving these children feels like the essence of life itself.

To love as a family is an incomparable joy and fulfillment. It is singular in its beauty and purposefulness, short of loving the Heavenly Father. It isn't the total fullness of what I have to offer, but it is such a deeply personal offering that it shapes my heart and makes my me-ness special. Two people call me mother. This is extraordinary.

G-d seems to want this depth applied to His Kingdom. We are to love each other as brothers and sisters, to serve and love G-d as good children. A whole and fortified family remains the ideal social unit and the ideal Biblical outcome for all G-d's Kingdom. One, unified, united, powerful. Family defines in a way so little else can. Regrettably, I fear we have failed more often than we have succeeded at our familial calling.

Families divided don't just fall, they wreck. I know all too well the pain of divorce and the shredding of the soul and spirit that occurs in each family member who has to undergo that process. Both spouses and children suffer. No matter how easy or low-stress the divorce, it often remains torturous and viciously destructive.

The Church family is perhaps even more wrecked and shredded than we realize. Judaism too often keeps its deep and life-changing knowledge of the Scripture to itself (short of a few standouts), Christianity has dispersed into at least 33,000 denominations fighting over who can take communion in church and which political party is more like Jesus, Catholicism has protected its predatory priests who targeted children with their abuse, and has embraced its pagan roots more and more with each passing year. We are divided, weak, and in some cases, clearly on the side of the forces that enact destruction. It's painful to us and to our Heavenly Father.

Adonai, as always, is calling His church back and has given us clues about His nature throughout the earth to observe and confirm the truths to which He is calling us.

But in order to come back, we must put family first. We must understand the gravity of just how far we may be from the established rule of our Father's house. How do we get family right? These irreplaceable social units represent and embody the root of health and wellbeing of the Church and society. So we must understand what it takes to be healthy and re-learn what it means to be a healthy family unit according to G-d's Kingdom.

Let's investigate our unique differences and celebrate them, while understanding that G-d has an ideal picture of male and female and family that we must embrace in order to comprehend His ultimate goals. The attempts to devour male and female and to lie about their existence and importance have led to depression, confusion, and a society whose basic framework has been weakened. The family is essential in the Bible and the family includes the male and female body and spirit. There is wholeness in this set up. To believe contrarily is to believe a lie. Lovingly, we must correct the disparate path we have taken from Scripture in this regard.

Defining family gives us a key to the unity of G-d throughout Scripture, from Genesis to Revelation. Without definition, we likely have no idea what G-d has, is and will do.

MALE AND FEMALE

Family begins with a union of two. In the Bible, we see G-d set up His ideal family as the union of adult male and adult female in both body and spirit. There is no doubt that the entire story of the Bible is about family and G-d's relationship with His family. From the very beginning of Genesis, there is clarity about how the theme of this story will unravel.

To the great dismay of some Biblical sects and atheists alike, the Bible is not primarily about the origins of the Universe or how long the earth had existed before this creation. In fact, the Hebrew Bible does not even begin to play with the age of rocks or water or what happened before the story of mankind. It seems clear that those stories are closed to us and are not to be conjectured about religiously.

Rather, this Word is about family, G-d's family and how He brings His house together. Even in the very first letter of the Bible in Genesis, we are given clues and direction as to the focus of the Biblical story.

In order to dig into these clues, it is helpful to understand Hebrew just a bit better.

The Hebrew language and alpha bet (Aleph Bet) function quite differently than our English language. Each letter has distinct meanings, assigned numerical values, and connection to concepts that are attached to those numerical values. So, let's look at the first letter of Scripture, the Bet. ב

To Biblical Hebrew scholars, the first letter of the Bible is essentially important, and logically it would make more sense for it to start with the first letter of the Hebrew Alpha Bet, the 'Aleph'. So, why the Bet?

The Bet has a numerical value of two, which can represent all of the parts of creation that come in pairs; this world and the world to come, man and woman, G-d and His House, the waters above and the waters below, and wisdom and understanding, the two foundational pieces of the Bible and creation itself. The Bet is a picture of two becoming one or at the very list a division of something. The pictograph (earliest use) for Bet is that of a tent or house, pointing to representation of G-d's house.

Additionally, Hebrew reads from right to left, so what we see here is a letter that is closed on the right side but open on the left. Some scholars conjecture that this means that the story before the story of man is closed to us. Perhaps we are not to religiously ponder about what G-d made before it, for how long and what happened to it. No, this story is not a history of the universe. It is the story of mankind and G-d.

Which is not to say that the Bible isn't historically and scientifically accurate. It is. In fact, the very creation story is scientifically proven. In order to create the universe and the life that we observe, certain things must be present. These include matter, energy and water — all of which show up in astoundingly perfect order in the Biblical creation story.

Much of science and the Bible are certainly not at odds, despite what scientific and Biblical communities may claim. The universe and its parts could be millions of years old and the story of this version of mankind could be about 6,000 years old and it all aligns beautifully. Ages may have happened before the story of man and G-d, but the Bible is silent on those details.

This gives us the freedom to hear scientists out when they discuss the age of the universe or the scientific perspective of the beginning of time. We believe G-d was there. We believe He provided the building blocks for everything. Outside of that, we just don't know. Honestly, neither do they. Back to the point.

My favorite reason for the Bet holding the first position in Scripture is that the Bet is a picture of the Son of G-d. The word for "create" in Hebrew is *bara,* and the Aramaic word for "son" is *bar.*

If we separate the letters within the word for *bara,* we will have *bar Aleph (the "a" at the end of bara)* where Aleph means father. So "bara" points to the concept of Son of the Father (Aleph). Thus the scripture could read: "In the beginning was the Son of Aleph." G-d created. Yeshua created. The son builds the universe.

In the very beginning we see a house, a family, and the starting of a family including human beings. The Bible is a story about the most tightly knit unit of relationship in society.

When Yeshua says that he came only for the lost House of Israel (Matthew 15:24), we gloss over it. But this House of Israel clues us in to the entire story from Genesis to Revelation, and reveals G-d's insistence that family is everything.

G-d set up the nation of Israel — the people who agreed to be obedient and useful — to bring the entire earth into familial relationship with Himself. Although Israel often failed, G-d loved and still loves and honors Israel. Here in Matthew 15, Yeshua tells us who He came to gather. It is Israel.

But now, wait. Who is Israel?

After the death of King Solomon, the nation of Israel was divided into two. Eventually, the tribes of Judah and Benjamin made up the Southern Kingdom and the other ten tribes made up the Northern Kingdom. Both of these Kingdoms rebelled against the Lord, but the Northern tribes were especially egregious in accepting and worshiping foreign gods. The House of Israel was eventually given a divorce decree by G-d and scattered.

Assyria conquered the Northern kingdom in 722 BCE and carried away the ten tribes into all the earth who became lost and unknown. Yeshua came to fulfill the prophecy that,

> "In that day the Lord will reach out his hand a second time to reclaim the surviving remnant of his people from Assyria, from Lower Egypt, from Upper Egypt, from Cush, from Elam, from Babylonia, from Hamath and from the islands of the Mediterranean. He will raise a banner for the nations and gather the exiles of Israel; he will assemble the scattered people of Judah from the four quarters of the earth" (Isaiah 11:11-12)

These scattered forgot who they were. Even now, many have no idea they belong to the original tribes. Yeshua came to bring them back into familial relationship, back into the status of tribes and people of Israel.

But G-d's plan was even more expansionary. The Holy Spirit comes in Acts and reveals to Peter that the gospel is for all the nations as well. Not just for the original House of Israel and Judah, but for each soul. There are adoptions coming. Adoptions into the House of Israel. G-d is claiming His spiritual family.

Familial relationship to the Lord is not about the physical, but the spiritual seed of G-d, those who experience a rebirth into G-d's Kingdom. Yeshua's work is about reclaiming His family and adding more by adoption as well.

Yeshua, the groom, came to gather his bride, the Church. The bride that was split into two houses, the House of Judah and the House of Israel. And we are all to become one. One family.

Embedded into the form and function of the family is the male and female, the two sets of characteristics and spirits that come together to make perfect relationship and the foundation for familial success. The very first moments of creation speak to this picture of masculine and feminine making up wholeness in the earth and universe as G-d creates from within the existence of both masculine and feminine as they exist within His/Her being!

I must stop here for a moment. This will be the last time I use "Her" to refer to G-d. Not because G-d is not feminine, but because He, His and Him are terms that can be applied to all mankind in English and throughout English history this has been a perfectly acceptable way to represent everyone. When we say mankind, we are not supposed to exclude the feminine, etc.

This is not a problem all other languages have, but it is one we have to deal with in English. G-d has many Hebrew names, some are masculine and some are feminine. In English, we cannot tell the differences. I tend to agree that the translation should say He when referencing G-d given the psychological differences and needs between man and woman. However, that is not the purpose of this study.

So, when I say He, Him, His etc. in referring to G-d, please remember this includes the masculine and feminine Great Spirit who is not definable by those terms either, but whom we must reference as best we can in these discussions. And I suppose it is an appropriate aside since we are discussing male and female in this chapter.

Perhaps it is essential to explain these things in this day and age given how quick we are to become offended at even the slightest inference of exclusion. And perhaps because, in most cultures, the feminine certainly has been written out, not written about, undermined, or just plain oppressed. Unfortunately, these human faults cloud how we discuss the Biblical text and give us a poor understanding of just how exalted the feminine was in the Old Testament.

In fact, it is hard to think of other religious works that have as many feminine heroines as the Biblical Old Testament does. At a time when many women were objects of desire or property only, the Bible exalts women as equal to men in the eyes of G-d. As G-d contemplated making Eve, He said, "It is not good for man to be alone. I will make him a helper who is his equal." (Genesis 2:18) We must remember, then, that the male form of he and his and man and mankind includes women. Moving on.

So, how do we know that G-d is about the combination of masculine and feminine and exalts both equally and requires both to create life?

We see the male and female embedded into not just human creation or animal, but into all of creation itself. It is found in the heart of the Hebrew words used to describe much of creation. As previously stated, unlike English, Hebrew words are assigned a masculine or feminine form. (Hence, "Sons" of G-d used in scripture could often be stated as "children" of G-d). "Sons" is used in our English translation because the Hebrew word for children is masculine and English translators thought this would work best.

Lots of other languages have these gender assignments as well, but it is tough to understand this in the English. When G-d separates the waters above from waters below, the waters above are masculine and the waters below are feminine. The sun in Genesis is masculine while the moon often implies the feminine. Wisdom in the Old Testament is consistently referred to as a woman, a female, and related to the Holy Spirit in the New Testament imbuing Wisdom to G-d's children. G-d calls Eve Adam's equal when He creates her. The very first letter of scripture in Hebrew, the Bet, represents a house. Only with male and female can the house be built and the commandment to "be fruitful and multiply" carried out.

Life comes through the combination of masculine and feminine. Male and female. And they are defined AS SUCH!

Let's go back to Genesis 2:18. "Then the God Yhwh said, 'It is not good for the Man to be alone; I will make him an עזר(Ezer) כנגדו(Kinegdo).'"

Here we have in English, "I will make him a 'helper'(ezer)." Which is indeed a correct translation, but usually when this word is used throughout the rest of Scripture, it is used to indicate help or actions that are *saving in nature.* It is in reference to something greater than the one being helped. You see it in Deuteronomy 33:7:

"Hear Yhwh, the voice of Yehudah and may you restore him to his people. May his own hands be enough. And may you be a "helper" against his foes."

Or Psalms 121:1-2: "I turn my eyes to the mountains. From where will my 'help' come? My 'help' is from Yhwh, maker of heaven and earth."

Instead of thinking that G-d created a creature below Adam in the form of Eve, we should more readily think that G-d created a creature to SAVE Adam. Perhaps from loneliness, or perhaps from what G-d did not consider to be "good" in Adam's solitary nature. Either way, Eve is an equal, a necessary figure, and the apex of the creation.

The second part of the phrase, Kinegdo, is translated as "fitting for him" or something close to that in English. However, in the Hebrew it is much closer to "opposite to" or "equivalent to him."

Words matter. Words change over time, as do cultures, and so getting back to the original intent of the words helps us to see the original intention of the Creator. It is my contention that man and woman were created perfectly and completely equal, with differing qualities that, in

G-d's view, are completely equal. And Scripture seems to bear that out when we take a closer look.

But we don't seem to see this equal treatment of features today. It is hilarious and painful that in the same breath cultural elites will critique the Bible for its lack of female empowerment and then go on to denigrate female qualities and abolish even the word "woman" from terminology.

Intuition is just as important as factual reasoning, but in a culture like ours, it is not often granted its due. For instance, women raising young children, generally speaking, is powerful. Women intuitively know to talk directly to their children and are therefore more capable of spurring early language learning in babies and toddlers. But when you ask young women what they "aspire" to become the answer of "a mother" is not acceptable.

And a man who is fully appreciative of women, so much so that he opens the door for them, is often called a sexist, because somehow society cannot admit that women are, in general, not as strong as men. We have lost the important concept that perhaps men showing deference to women is an act of protection that men are called to. These degradations of the natural capabilities of both men and women, in favor of the current cultural Kool-Aid, ruin the vision of equality that G-d granted both. These poor interpretations of beautiful characteristics degrade the relationship between men and women.

Not that history has been kind to women. The last to receive the right to vote in America and historically unable to own land, work, or contribute led to a rightful revolution where women demanded and achieved equal footing under the law. But it seems those achievements reached a pinnacle and are now being eaten away by a different beast altogether. Not a patriarchal one. A self-destructive evil has come to destroy the equality and beauty of womanhood.

Culture has shifted mightily. I, in my very old Millennial status, did not grow up without the blessings of voting rights and property rights. I did not have to fight the battles my forebears did. Our battles are different and we must address the exact ones we are fighting today. How do we get true equality without degrading our differences?

G-d in his wisdom shows us the picture of perfect relationship for mankind in Adam and Eve in the garden. An adult male united to an adult female on equal footing. This uniting represents wholeness. And that wholeness is reflected in all of the natural male and female elements already mentioned in creation as well.

Just as the waters above and the waters below provide for a perfect global environment for life, so both male and female are important and essential features to wholeness in family life. Sometimes we have to live without one or the other; the world isn't perfect. But striving for male and female union, just as we strive for righteous living in general, is an important part of the journey to understanding G-d's intentions for family.

We've all seen the difficult statistics on fatherless homes. According to the US Department of Health[i]:

- 63% of youth suicides are from fatherless homes, 5x the average.
- 90% of all homeless and runaway children are from fatherless homes, 32x the average.
- 80% of rapists with anger problems come from fatherless homes.

The **statistics**[ii] continue with predictably **depressing results**[iii]. Motherless children tend to have more problems in social relationships, negative feelings, emotional imbalances, and health issues as well.

The reality across the studies is that moms and dads are essential to the raising of balanced and healthy children on the whole. G-d knows this because He created it. For reasons that maybe only G-d fully understands, we need the connection to our mothers and fathers as we grow. We need a female and a male guiding and supporting us. If we continue to ignore the psychological and physical benefits of female and male union, we will continue to fight an uphill battle in raising healthy adults.

Since we are discussing male and female, I suppose nowadays a definition of those terms is necessary. The world often defines them as pretty much whichever one you feel like you are. In my view, the idea that something as foundational as an x or y chromosome can be messed with, based on a mental dissociation with your own body, is not only antithetical to science but also to intellectual integrity.

Male or female is decided by which chromosomes you have. Simple and very much unchangeable. People believe all sorts of things about themselves that may or may not be true.

But we are not called to affirm lies in others.

Someone may be born a man and "feel" like a woman all day long, but that does not make him a woman. This recognition is not only scientific, it is, indeed, G-dly.

King David speaks of being knit together in his mother's womb. We are crafted by a great, Creator. For the vast, vast majority of humanity, we come into the world male or female without choice in the matter. G-d knows what He is doing better than we do. We must first make this humble admission.

Of course, wherever G-d has created something wonderful, something exists to twist and pervert it. Enemies of the definition and healthy union of male and female exist now, and have indeed always existed.

PORNOGRAPHY IN RELATIONSHIP

Among others, one of the great destroyers of intimacy is pornography, and it has lately become a dragon in G-d's church. It has devoured female and male spirit alike. Its sinister and easily hidden draw has entrapped the young and conquered the old.

There was recently an article by the ***Babylon Bee***[iv] (a tongue-in-cheek Christian "news" site that operates much like *The Onion*) in which the author makes fun of the Christian man who doesn't want to admit that he watches *Game of Thrones*. The title reads, "Christian looking forward to 7the Season of Acting Like He Doesn't Watch Game of Thrones."

Sadly, I think the article hit the nail on the head.

Game of Thrones, an incredibly violent and **fairly pornographic**[v] TV show, took the world by storm a few years ago. I don't really know many people, Christian or not, who haven't watched it. I do know that I couldn't seem to get through much of it. I tried one episode and felt sick. *(More On This in My Technology Essay)*

I wondered: How can we protect young men from pornography when we all welcome it into our homes as long as the story attached is riveting enough?

The answer is: of course, we can't. We have failed our young men and young women alike in this area.

Pornography degrades both men and women. With no upside.

Can you think of any valuable reason to view it? Can it make you a better person? A better lover? (Those young people that think it can, boy are you in for a rude awakening) A better friend? A better follower of Christ? A better student? A better thinker? No. It will not accomplish even one of these things. But what it *does* do according to Kirk Samuels, Counselor, Minister and author of For Your Eyes Only and John Deyoung, Founder of Shiftai an organization helping to battle sexual trafficking)…

-**Causes addiction in men so severe that they are sometimes no longer able to perform sexually with their own spouse.** When watching porn, the brain releases high levels of the chemical, dopamine (among others that include oxytocin and vasopressin), dopamine is the same chemical that is released when cocaine is used. This makes it highly addictive. In the process of addiction, many men need more and more intense pornography to produce the same outcomes, or "high." More pictures, more violence, etc. There is no woman on the planet that can keep up with the rate of images that a video can. No woman can make that high happen for a man who is used to hundreds of images and views within a few minutes. According to physiology teacher, **Gary Wilson**[vi], in a very popular TEDx Talks[vii], this causes men to bond with porn instead of a person.

-**The addiction can break a woman's spirit.** Woman after woman has shared their broken hearts over their husband's addiction to pornography. Why aren't they enough? Aren't they sexy enough? Aren't they desirable enough? Of course they are! Porn is just too addictive and too accessible. If porn causes a bond that a person can't break into, this leaves the spouse feeling outside of the relationship, because they are. The porn addict is in a relationship with porn, not with their spouse.

-Uses and abuses women and men and children who may need help. We have a bit of an idea how many men and women who make porn are **drug addicted or sexually trafficked**[viii]. It's not good. We don't have a good idea where these people came from, how they grew up, or if they will live much longer. But we do know that these people are often used by an industry that globally provides trillions of images available online. The 'least of these' are being abused for viewing pleasure. Which leads me to my last point.

-Porn makes us a selfish society. We are willing to put our marriages and families at risk, our youth at risk and our conscience on the back-burner, all to fulfill a momentary sexual desire. We are willing to watch other, too often abused individuals in order to get off. This makes defending the sanctity of male and female all but impossible. We have become almost purely instinctual.

And for some reason, we've all decided we can live with this.

We live with it at great cost.

Pornography is not the only enemy of male and female value and therefore wreckage in a family. Sad to say, I believe modern feminism and the LGBTQ+ agenda have wrecked the celebration of male and female differences.

GENDER CONFUSION

We've created an unfair space for both men and women. We have told them that their unhappiness or challenges in life could be that they were born into the wrong body. Their gender doesn't match. A deadly message with heartbreaking outcomes.

Those who identify as transgender women are now being allowed to compete against biological women in all sorts of sporting events. I even found an article titled, "**Female Athletes Crushed by Women Who Were Once Men**.[ix]" Once again in the gender wars, women lose and women lose big time. "Crushed." *Ouch.*

While many are coming out against such social injustice, the powers that be seem too afraid to stand up to OR provide help for the transgender community and fix this for the sake of women and men alike. Women were the last to get the right to vote, are still the most abused community globally, and here in the United States, the gender rights movements are only continually pushing more abuse of women — whether it be transgender women in female sports, or the idea the abortion as a "good" for women.

But the realities for both women and the transgendered community are much harsher in everyday life than the sports arena. We see **stories**[x] of pediatricians and medical professionals advocating for children to go through sex-change treatments cutting off their breasts and getting harsh hormone treatments (Irreversible Damage by Abigail Shrier is a good source for these tales) surgically removing penises, and so on.

In my adolescence, we were told to love the bodies we were given. Don't look down on people because they are male, female, fat, skinny, short, tall, fair or dark. If someone had an eating disorder, it was called out for the psychologically damaging condition it was. When models got too thin and the example that was set was unattainable, journalists began to question the trend and question what it was doing to men and women alike regarding physical expectations. By 2012 **articles**[xi] about eating disorders were gaining traction. The industry could no longer put only waifs on the covers of magazines and expect parental or teen approval.

And now, with growing alacrity and acceptance, the politically correct approve of self-mutilation in the name of gender rights, gender fluidity, and whatever other terms they like to stick on it.

But really, on paper, isn't this abuse?

It's abusive to cut off parts of your body that are working just fine because you don't identify with them. In fact, isn't that a form of body dysmorphia? When an underweight anorexic looks in the mirror and sees a fat person, aren't they psychologically damaged? Living in a non-reality? And we try to help them.

Because we want them to be whole and happy.

So, who is helping those who hate their own breasts or penises? Who is trying to help them be whole and happy?

In her recent book, *Irreversible Damage*[xii], Abigail Shrier, explores the world of transgender rights through the eyes of girls and women. What do women go through in the process of transitioning? Are they happier or better off at the end of the process? Her book has been widely panned by many on the Left, but she does quite a thorough reporting job — looking at case after case of females transitioning to male, and speaking with many doctors across a span of political ideologies.

She mentions that transitioning women can never actually achieve full male status. Not only at the chromosomal level, but even in body chemistry. Women's bone structure is different and the way a woman is formed is too separate from the male structure to ever achieve a perfect transition. And so, despite the painful hormones and brutal surgeries, the outcome is that there cannot be wholeness or happiness. Often the result is more disappointment and depression. And we encourage this tragedy?

It is by now well-documented that the rates of depression and attempted suicide in the transgender community are astoundingly high. (**Amercian Academy of Pediatrics, 2018**[xiii]: Many articles attribute this to something called "minority stress." Basically, it's the idea that they do not get as much familial help and support from the community and therefore are more depressed. And truly, this could be a central, if not *the* central, contributing factor to their psychological distress. But can I push back a little?

In this day and age we live in the most open and openly accepting society regarding gender fluidity probably in human history. So, why has an unbelievable 41 percent of the transgendered community attempted suicide? Lots of people face societal pressure, hatred, stress, and rejection. Humanity exists with more pain and loss than perfection. These are common pressures and challenges.

As a musician, I get at least three "no thanks" every day. Maybe once a week, I'll hear a "yes." I'm in a constant cycle of rejection. Rejection of something really personal — my art. And yet, I've had no desire to leave my life because of it. And yes, familial rejection is a particular hurt, but is familial abuse an outcome of transgender choices or more of a cause? The challenge of analyzing gender confusion, denial, and ensuing psychological stresses adds up very quickly.

Gender is so close to us, so important, so directional for us, perhaps messing with it causes a complete psychological breakdown.

Psychologist Jordan Peterson argues that it is important to have a place in society that functions to promote whole and real community, healthy family, and to present one's self in a framework that society can interact with. (One **example interview**[xiv] with Peterson)

Transgendered people likely struggle with these aspects of living. Not because society is so horrific, but because a transgendered person transitioning will lose their ability to have children, and perhaps cannot find enough commonality with the average person who desires family and acceptable integration of body, mind and spirit. And so, the question must be what is worse; being uncomfortable but reasonably acceptable to society and having a chance at family, or being slightly more comfortable but completely at odds with society for no great higher reason?

I'd say the latter is worse.

Maybe the way I grew up was right. (Despite my exposure to the anorexic modeling realm) Or perhaps we just need to agree to it, now, here in the present. We are supposed to accept how we came into this world and love ourselves and our bodies as they are. Health of mind, body and spirit are higher aspirations than social popularity or politically correct sacrifices. Our bodies are a temple. Our minds can encompass more than obsession with physical appearances. Our spirits are bigger and meant to be more free than sexual or gender identity could ever even begin to accomplish. Acceptance may be the beginning of wholeness. I was created here, now, with a gender and a destiny that I did not write myself. I can attempt to rearrange it if I so wish, but I could also try living it.

We cannot escape our bodies and there is not evidence that abusing the body due to that conundrum is doing anyone any good. In the meantime, transgenderism is a guarantee for psychological struggle. No parent should be pushing it on his or her child or re-enforcing it. It's child abuse.

In 2008, **NPR interviewed**[xv] Dr. Zucker, a gender identity specialist in Canada who has treated children for many years. His answers regarding what is happening to children in this age of gender fluidity are quite revealing. Here is an illumanting excerpt from that interview:

"What do you think of the alternative approach — the approach that allows kids to transition to the opposite sex at an early age?"

"In the last few years, what one is starting to hear about at conferences is this group of therapists and parents who will conceptualize young children as having transgender or gender variant identity. There are some parents and therapists suggesting that the best way to help these kids is to encourage an early gender role change.

So, I've seen reports of parents enrolling their 5-year-old biological male child in kindergarten as a girl, for example. That's a very different therapeutic approach than the one I take.

The therapists supporting a child's transition early, I have characterized them in a half serious way as liberal essentialists. On the surface, the approach comes across as very humanistic, liberal, accepting, tolerant of diversity. But I think the hidden assumption is that they believe the child's cross-gender identity is entirely caused by biological factors. That's why I call them essentialists.

Liberals have always been critical of biological reductionism, but here they embrace it. I think that conceptual approach is astonishingly naive and simplistic, and I think it's wrong. I would predict if we followed kids, longitudinally, who are being told "do what you want" — or encouraging early gender role change — they would be much more likely in adolescence or adulthood to go through hormonal and surgical sex change than kids being seen in a psychotherapeutic way, and even probably than kids where people don't do anything active."

"What you're saying is that this approach essentially tracks them into a transgender identity?"

"That would be my prediction, yes."

We are pushing transgender-ism on children. Pushing them into a life with much higher depression and suicide rates. This should be called a tragedy.

Too many call it progress.

Had I grown up in today's era, no doubt my tomboy nature, love of the outdoors and baseball, and my hatred of dresses would have signaled to all the adults that I identified as male. The stereotypes released in all their glory. Only males like those things, my parents would have heard. And somebody would have asked if I felt like a boy. And maybe I would have in that moment. And then they would have sent me to specialists to see if I needed a change.

And they would have ruined my life.

I love being a woman. I love my husband. I love having children. I would have lost everything.

G-d proclaims in Genesis that male and female are "good". But our pride interjects to argue with the G-d of Creation. Humility paves the way to wisdom and understanding. Pride paves the way to destruction.

Today we need to stop worrying about our individual brand of female. Maybe you love football, maybe you hate dresses. Stop worrying about your individual brand of male! Maybe you are an artist, a painter, a poet. Stop worrying about how society views men and masculinity. In the name of love and tolerance, we have given up ground to the enemy and we are being punished for it. Be male, be female, with all the variety that exists within those chromosomal differences, but accept that you were made one or the other.

No doubt, we need to love all people, no matter where they are in their spiritual journey. The commands of kindness are not discriminatory. However, we don't need to confuse ourselves or the next generation about what G-d calls "good" in regards to His creativity and gender. As Brad Scott of Wildbranch Ministries has quipped, "God made male and female, not heterosexual and homosexual." I will add that transgenderism makes no appearance at creation either.

There are men and there are women, an x or a y chromosome. True science remains factual and helpful for all people. True scientific observation and inquiry make for healthier humans.

And for believers, the Bible is clear: men and women, distinct and equal, make for life. And G-d calls them very good.

MODERN FEMINISM

And the end of the feminine.

"A woman with a voice is, by definition, a strong woman."
Melinda Gates

Hm. Well, no, being able to babble audibly is not strength.

I suppose we must start by defining what the word "strong" means. If strength is influence, perhaps Mrs. Gates has a leg to stand on; but if strength means resolve, purpose, meaning, health and mental clarity, well… she has not quite landed the plane.

Let's start with one of the more recent public feminist undertakings. The "Me Too" movement, energized by high profile cases of sexual assault and abuse, could have been a powerful agent of meaningful change. Helpful to the many women who have been abused and sexually assaulted by men, these women have often been afraid to speak up. And they have had every right to fear because society too often did not listen or believe their tales (just look to the many women who accused Bill Clinton of sexual misconduct).

There is something wonderful about a group of people who can come together over a shared experience to pave the way for something better. This is especially true for women, given the global and historical abuse of this demographic.

But as usual, Me Too followed the course of so many other feminist operations and turned into a charade with too much overreach and overreaction, equating violent assault with micro-aggressions. We are back to something less than feminine empowerment and more about progressivism.

The concept of equality has spiraled into obsession over women's reproductive organs, sexual preferences, and an aversion to motherhood. We have chosen body parts instead of intellectual equality. A terrible choice since yes, women's bodies are different than men's.

It is forever true that women are the only half of the population that can have children. But the sacredness and beauty of motherhood and family life has been denigrated by women who insist that, in order to be equal, women have to be just like men.

I think the power and beauty of women is that they are not like men, and vice

versa. But celebration of diversity cannot co-exist with modern feminist theology.

To take one example, "Free the nipple" and associated naked marches down city streets throughout the country act as strange signposts that modern feminism is in denial about what defines power. But as much as they need to make men and women fluid entities, men and women are markedly different, both in body and perspectives.

Don't men have to cover up their penises? Why do we hate this so much? Isn't indecent exposure a crime because we value the innocence of our children and the dignity, not to mention sanitary prudence, of covering up body parts whose functions are limited to sexuality or waste elimination? And in the case of breasts, their highest functionality lies in feeding babies, something that happens both publicly and privately with very little fuss. Random exposure of this body part fails in both decency and functionality. Men don't have breasts, women do.

This push for more exposure is a continual push for women to be more like men.

We are told to be just like men, yet we hear constant complaining about men: man-splaining, sexual aggression, competitiveness, etc.

You cannot have it both ways.

You cannot hate men and also need to be like them and accomplish any meaningful positive progress. In some ways, all this self-obsessed whining about our different body parts boils down to one thing. Self-hatred. If women actually accepted their bodies, that would certainly mean that women would value them enough to use them appropriately, get naked in public sparingly (if ever), and share their bodies with men only in the most committed and healthy of contexts.

It would also mean women would accept their extraordinary differences from men as valuable, essential, and meaningful to society. It is not women's ability to have sex however they want that gives them power. But the ability to say "no"- now that is a whopper of a power-move. Women could and should use this word more often. But instead, feminism posits that women benefit from approaching sex more like men do.

Feminism abuses female sexuality with as much disdain as mentally unhealthy males have throughout history. It is the same cage, different format, Stockholm Syndrome. Just when we thought we were free from obsessing about our sexuality. Free from the objectification. The feminists became the abusers.

It must be ceded that women throughout history have always been able to have sex. Hence, the propagation of the human species. Yes, often women have been treated abhorrently in the sexual process, raped, abused, used, and degraded. But outside of those contexts, it is likely that if a woman really wanted to have sex, she could and can likely find a non-violent way to do so with a partner who is willing in the United States of America.

It has been a great disservice to women to teach that sexual freedom equates to some sort of empowerment.

Many non-empowered women have had sex throughout history. It did not make them more powerful and, in some cases, it left them far less powerful than where they were previously.

Female power is not tied up in having sex however and with whomever you like. It can be a powerful experience, it can be life-giving, but it is not what makes us human, nor is it a good explanation of value, especially in the absence of having children. Neither Mother Theresa nor Margaret Thatcher were powerful or valuable because they were having sex (or not) or because they "had a voice". They were powerful because they existed as the rare humans who embraced their G-d-given bodies and talents and successfully produced incredible outcomes. They changed things.

We should never be tricked into thinking that free sexuality will make women better off. It won't and it only feeds into the male fantasy that the nymphomaniac, newly empowered female may just spend a reckless night with him.

And the pursuit of free sexuality has created a much graver problem.

Abortion. Abortion is the feminist route to equality, because now women can also have sex how and when they want to (task no. 1 for feminism) without consequences (task no. 1 for bad men).

But this route to equality is also a lie.

Abortion is hugely consequential, not only to the life lost but to the mother's body and psyche. I've known multiple women who had abortions and afterwards began to have nightmares, anxiety, and eventually intense emotional pain when they did decide to have children. They recognized what could have been and the life that had previously existed inside them. The life they snuffed out. This psychological horror has been sold to women as equality.

It is strange that those who most enthusiastically align themselves with women's rights and health care also advocate late term abortion. Medically speaking, it is one of the most dangerous procedures you can do on a pregnant woman. It quite literally puts her life at risk. In contrast, a C-section at that time in the pregnancy is far less risky, far quicker, and could often preserve the baby.

Information squashed by the politically correct.

Feminist propaganda often results in breaking women, not building them up. Whether or not the feminists understand this, spiritually, the lies of modern feminism create a lonely and psychologically unsound trap. Feminism degrades the feminine intuition, nurturing, communication skills, teaching ability, keen vision, and power to reign in men's worst traits that make females so strong, vibrant, and important.

Today we have women who need to be like men and we call it feminism.

Women will never be equal to men regarding the outcomes of their sexuality or body. The consequences for women are higher. It is a plain fact. To deny it is foolishness. And that denial is harming men and women and the relationship G-d intended for them.

A 2011 article from the ***Daily Mail***[xvi] quotes a study published in the British Journal of Psychiatry. The research found that those who undergo abortion face nearly double the risk of mental health difficulties compared with others, and that one in ten of all mental health problems in women was a result of abortion. The article goes on to note that this study is causing the psychiatric community to take a closer look at abortion as a cause of depression, alcoholism, suicide, and other mental disturbances.

While there are vast possible physical side effects from abortion, including cancer, infertility, sexual dysfunction, and death (which rarely shows up in the discourse), what has been discussed even less is the long-term psychological damage.

The feminist calls this healthcare.

Abortion has become such a lightning rod for women's equality that you are hard-pressed to find a politician, even a pro-life one, who is willing to call any form of abortion murder or killing. It has become such a highly politicized issue that it has scared off those who secretly believe that all human life should be given a chance — no matter how small or in what location that life may be.

Whether an accident, a rape, or an intentional pregnancy, the stated goal of pro-choice proponents is that women should have a choice about the continuation of an unintended (and sometimes intended) pregnancy. And many of the most prominent politicians believe the choice should be extended all the way up until birth. Just look at the many **politicians**[xvii] who voted against a ban on partial birth abortion! The list includes prominent Dems like Barbara Boxer, Diane Feinstein, Chuck Schumer, and of course, Hillary Clinton, etc.

Despite Democrat's claim that late term abortion is necessary if something happens to the baby or mother, they ignore the clear science that abortion at that stage is far riskier for the mother than a c-section. Additionally sane doctors choose c-sections in those cases to protect mother and possibly save the life of the child. In fact, late term abortions are never medically necessary according to **Dr. Mary Davenport OBGYN and Dr. Murphy Goodwin**[xviii].

One quote from Dr. Murphy states, "many abortion referrals based on maternal health situations reflect sheer ignorance from the referring physicians. Typically, they are medical specialists who lack experience treating women with high-risk pregnancies."

Despite the sciencitific and the moral arrow pointing in the opposite direction, the push for abortion rights in America is extreme.

Why is this choice to kill so important?

Because young women have been fed the lie that sex should have no consequences and that, if they do get pregnant, they may be too poor, too stupid, or too inconvenienced to deal with the pregnancy at hand. This vicious falsehood has been funneled most enthusiastically to Black women.

Lest we forget, the founder of **Planned Parenthood, Margaret Sanger**[xix] was a racist, so-called feminist who pushed for abortion clinics in Black communities, hoping to convince Black women to get rid of their children and reduce the Black population. This nefarious plan has worked, to the great detriment of our nation and the Black community.

Today, 40 percent of pregnancies in the Black community are terminated through abortion. The Black population in America would be twice as large if the eugenicists like Margaret Sanger had not been so very successful. TWICE as large! Think of it.

Black Americans today represent 13 percent of the population. Yet Black people have been here almost as long as any other non-native racial group. What a loss! And if you don't believe me, I'd encourage a watch of **Ma-afa 21**[xx] one of the most thorough documentaries on the history of abortion in the United States. My tears at the end of the film hardened my resolve to tell the truth about this issue.

The abortion industry has found most of its success by preying on fear. Fear of economic hardship, lack of ingenuity, lack of time, lack of resources, lack of support. Fear that the mother and sometimes father just can't have a child.

If this is feminism, we should throw it out, right along with Margaret Sanger.

Any movement that tells women that they *can't* is not a valid empowerment movement. Fear tells you the odds are against you. Empowerment says, "You are stronger than you know." Fear focuses on failure. Empowerment focuses on victory. And yes, churches need to help the poor and young and afraid achieve that victory. But, no amount of assistance or lack thereof will change the morality or consequences of killing a child.

And does love get to enter the stage at some point?

What sort of behavior does love encourage? Is abortion love? Is reckless sexual activity love? Have we thought much about this? For a society all about "the love", I've yet to see good evidence that abortion is loving.

But life, the struggle for life, in those stories love abounds.

There are groups who are showing that just getting a sonogram shifts course for many women seeking abortion. The view of an actual forming baby inside the womb is a powerful testament to the humanity and individuality of the child growing inside a mother. And the moment a mother sees her child, well, many women fall in love. Love is inspired. Love and, of course, truth inspires life-giving choice.

Perhaps this is why support for abortion is declining. A **Marist poll**[xxi] released in February 2019 showed a double-digit shift towards a more pro-life stance amongst those polled. It is now as likely to find a pro-life person as a pro-choice person.

The shift has been credited to the aggressive Democratic position pushing late-term abortion, which the majority of Americans are against. Most normal people agree that a viable baby should be given a chance to live. I use the word "normal" for a reason. Maybe not always in human history, but in American society, we have traditionally believed that babies were precious and deserved to survive. Our Constitution protects that very right. It's still in our blood to not kill our children. Much to the dismay of the Left. Is that harsh? Maybe. OKAY…

In any event, the courts and media have decided culturally that women can have lots of sex, and wreck their bodies and minds to get rid of the consequences, and we call this freedom and feminism. We call it good. We call it opportunity. We call it equality.

I call it evil.

There is nothing "sexy" about this issue. If women's sexuality is tied to snuffing out life, our version of equality is best described as a dumpster fire. But somehow, this connection fails to be made in the cultural debate.

Abortion is ugly, traumatizing, painful, medical, cold, fear-based, and restrictive. It restricts life, restricts growth, restricts love, restricts openness to the whim of chance. It is controlling, harsh, and costly. Not words I would associate with feminism or feminine traits.

In fact, it sounds very much like a legitimate definition of toxic masculinity. Can't you see it? Controlling, harsh, restrictive, closed, money-based, crude? When you think of how to describe "toxic masculinity", these words are what come to mind. Sure, I'm just stream of consciousness here. Just free association. Still, I don't like the connection.

THE BEAUTY AND POWER OF MOTHERHOOD

In turning the feminist orthodoxy on its head, I believe the ability to carry and sustain another human life should help us see women in more of a heroic light.

And this is an area wherein women and men are vastly different and it's undeniable: women can have babies. Without a man, they can't make babies, but women are the incubators, sustainers, and life-givers for the next generations.

In no way can, or should, women have to become like men to be equal to them. Not only because it steals the beautiful feminine from females, but because it's actually impossible and dangerous to sustaining humanity. We see in Genesis that G-d commands us to "be fruitful and multiply." Without females acting as females, this is not a command that can be obeyed.

And let's talk realistically here: it takes a lot more sacrifice from a female to have a baby and become a mother than it does for a father to become a father.

Women have to face the realities of parenthood within their own bodies. This forced submission to the role of mother within the act of the life-giving process allows for some hard-earned lessons and opportunities for growth. It is an ineffable connection with that new human, recognition that intuition is real and essential, and that motherhood will require sacrifice.

Fathers have to learn these things differently. Mothers have the opportunity to really grasp it over the nine months that they carry these little humans. And in order to do it well, mothers have to face reality fairly quickly.

The second I learned I was pregnant, so many parts of my life changed. Food and drink for one — no caffeine, no alcohol, healthier food, less stress, and nausea management tools. More sleep was non-negotiable and more emotional discipline was required if I wanted to keep my dignity amidst the major hormone swings.

And I had normal pregnancies.

Not to mention the constant worry that one wrong choice, one contaminated piece of food, bout of flu, you name it, could destroy this life you are so excited to meet but can't yet see. The constant battle of hope versus worry, and hormones versus logic, and self-esteem versus the mirror as your body changes with or without your input, all in the first nine months of this little person's life.

(And of course, the most gorgeous, younger, not pregnant women always come out of the woodwork to torture you or flirt with your husband during those months.)

You haven't even met these little people causing such a commotion, and yet they change everything. Pregnant women get prepped for sacrifice and love like no other. Mothers who carry and birth their children have to come to grips with the physical and psychological tolls. Of course, it's all worth it. More than that, it's a gift… but it doesn't come easily.

Yet, it prepares women uniquely for the instinctual and important role of caretaking of a tiny, inexperienced human.

Women can attempt to try to make up for this reality with government-sponsored contraception or abortion. But it does not eliminate the consequences women bear for the sexual act, both physically and psychologically. At the end of an abortion, is it growth of instinct and love of life that has occurred? Or has something less productive taken place.

Giving women their due means recognizing the gift of all that femaleness offers. To destroy it in order to make women more like men or indistinguishable hurts all of humanity. We need strong women, just as we need strong men.

If we lose the feminine to the masculine in the search for equality, where will we end up?

Beauty has a function, we have just forgotten about it. Beauty inspires, transcends the perfunctory, and encourages the brave. The delicate and intricate form G-d put into women is not without its use. Beyond childbearing, the artistry is obvious. And yes, of course, we can all agree that art is subjective, but undoubtedly beautiful women have been the subjects of painters of old and photographers of new.

The dark side of that coin is obvious, hyper sexualized and objectified women do not inspire much more than a sexual response.

But what about the positive in female beauty and intricacy? What about the men who go to battle with their lover's face in mind and fight to return to it? And where will we go if women are not the height of creation as G-d tells us they were, but are de-platformed, so to speak, into the realms of gender fluidity and over-simplified equality. Is this progress? Is this a benefit?

What about the feminine view? It is often different, not just because women can switch between both sides of their brains much faster than men, but because the female eye can pick up detail quicker as well. What the female perceives about a room, a group of people, and her own children will differ vastly from what a man perceives. This gift informs the female intuition and clarifies relationship. This is valuable. It's built in for a reason and our Creator does not make mistakes. Women will have a different view and thank goodness they will! Yet difference does not mean unequal.

The Proverbs 31 woman exemplifies a wonderful mother, respected and respectful wife, a business owner and a master of real estate. There is nothing "lesser" about her. Her ideal remains almost impossible to attain, yet Proverbs reveals the creative genius of G-d in His creation of woman.

Women possess qualities we should not suppress or dispose of so easily. We should not be so quick to make women into men.

The Male PROBLEM

The progressive movement has not asked for healthier, stronger, and better men. It has asked that men remove themselves from the equation entirely. More women need to be hired in the workplace (even when women aren't applying), more women need to go to college, more women need to have a voice and if that means more qualified men take a backseat, SO BE IT! The least desirable hire in society is a straight male, especially of European decent.

In reality, we know this isn't equality. It is also unhealthy for society. We miss out on what men have to offer when we lie about what they contribute.

Good men protect women, good men stay married and stay involved in their children's lives, good men have an innate desire to take care of their families, and these good men are not being trained or brought up. They are being abolished and ignored.

The term Toxic Masculinity has come into vogue in recent years. When I Google the definition, here is what I get: "a set of attitudes and ways of behaving stereotypically associated with or expected of men, regarded as having a negative impact on men and on society as a whole."

Well, I see a giant sea of issues here. Do you see them? Which behaviors are "stereotypical"? Who defines if they are negative or positive? Which behaviors are expected?

If we are talking about clinical narcissism (more often attributed to men), who in the world "expects" that of men? When did it become stereotypical? If this is what they mean by toxic masculinity, then I get it.

But it's not what they often mean.

Too often the pejoratives are directed at men with opinions they don't like. Men who don't want to dress like women and don't believe that trans-genderism should be pushed on children. Men who don't gladly give up their jobs for women. Men who don't fall all over themselves to be politically correct.

It is not a good way to discern the men behaving well from men who aren't.

So, what does the Bible say about Biblical masculinity?

In Genesis 2, Adam is told to name the animals and work to "keep" the garden. He is given thought-intensive and labor-intensive work to do. In thoughtfulness and with effort, Adam is told to provide and protect.

Make sure things are running smoothly. Gather the fruits of labor and make sure the garden is kept well and kept safe.

The word used here for "keep" means to guard and protect. Adam is a warrior making sure that all things are safe in the garden. (Adam fails at this, as we see later with the admittance of a serpent into the garden.)

In Ephesians 5:25, men are told to love their wives as Christ loved the church. This is sacrificial love, servanthood sort of love. Patience, kindness, faithfulness, and pursuit. Christ came for his church. Yes, men are supposed to pursue women. This is innate and important.

We have another Biblical example of manhood. In 1 Kings 2:1-3, Kind David tells his son, Solomon to:

> "Be thou strong therefore, and shew thyself a man; And keep the charge of the LORD thy God, to walk in his ways, to keep his statutes, and his commandments, and his judgments, and his testimonies, as it is written in the law of Moses, that thou mayest prosper in all that thou doest, and whithersoever thou turnest thyself:"

According to David, to be a man you must keep G-d's Commands as is written in the Law of Moses. Be strong! Be resolute and firm in your belief in G-d's ways and do not depart from them.

It is interesting that David goes straight to the Word of G-d as the guide for being a good man. A good man is strong. Not in physical strength only, not in power or money, but in following G-d's Laws.

Does culture today even allow for this? Following G-d's Laws means rejecting sexual confusion, rejecting sex outside of marriage, rejecting drunkenness and foolishness, rejecting abortion, rejecting *pornography*. It means embracing the Appointed Days of the Lord, taking care of the widow and orphan and the poor, keeping the Sabbath, and loving your neighbor. This is strength and it is what makes a good man.

It is so crucial we understand that David likely had an incredible grasp on manhood. He himself escaped the evil advances of enemies and fought alongside his 37 "mighty men." These mighty men of David did INCREDIBLE things in battle. The Bible describes them almost as superheroes. They are mentioned by name in 2 Samuel 23 because of their great physical feats and their devotion to David. These are truly strong men.

But of all that was important in battle and strength, David told his son that G-d defines manhood spiritually. Have we degraded this definition?

- Our culture does not encourage the spiritual, mental, or emotional strength of men.
- Through pornography we have stolen the importance of the male pursuit of the female.
- Through abortion we have stolen the responsibility for and fathering of children.
- Through gender fluidity and sexual confusion, we have stolen the physical and mental strength of men and women as well as their defining and attributes and ability to have children of their own.
- Through approval of drunkenness and childishness we have stolen the emotional strength that men need in order to develop the characteristics of caretaker, defender, and pursuer.

We have taken from men their responsibility to love and protect their wives as Christ has the church. We have literally obliterated the metaphor that men are supposed to be like Christ.

Nowadays, men turn to drugs, alcohol, pornography and gender/sex transformations in order to medicate spiritual holes, or to feel necessary, important, and appreciated by society.

This is shameful. We need great men. We need great fathers. And it starts with the Bible.

Great men don't have to be gun-carrying, fist-fighting, loud or large to be manly. The real test of a man is his character as Scripture defines it.

A great man lives well by doing righteousness and justice. By pursuing his G-d, his wife, and his endeavors with a pure heart. He protects and defends what is good. By standing firm in G-dliness, he thwarts the attacks of the evil one and teaches his children to do the same.

Great men are not confused about definitions of manhood. They know that hard workers, driven pursuers, husbands, fathers, and servants of G-d make amazing warriors. In the discussion about improving society, men cannot be left behind nor should they be relegated to gender fluid chaos.

Ancient Problems

I just finished a fantastic book (Corrupting The Image)[xxii] by Douglas Hamp, Pastor of the Messianic Congregation we attend. In it, he describes the history of gods and goddesses that dominated past cultures. These entities are all tied to Enlil, the actual ancient name of Satan.

One of the images of gods often depicted is a woman. Sometimes called Ishtar or the Queen of Heaven, she was characterized as young, fertile, never pregnant, always beautiful. She had no children so she could keep her figure.

Many of the ancient gods were pansexual or bi-sexual in nature. So much about beauty, sexuality, youth. A responsibility-free lifestyle. Free living, free sexuality, free loving. This is what many of the gods encouraged.

We haven't changed. Satan knows exactly how to ensnare us. He has been doing it for millennia.

Family destruction has come in all forms and exists today through a brutal detachment to responsibility. In allowing ourselves and our children to mentally and/or physically mutilate their G-d given destinies, we keep the truth from prospering in our homes and culture. Christian adults must choose to pursue G-d and family above all other pulls.

A present parent will change everything for a child. A loving, committed marriage can provide health and happiness and a chance at surviving culture for the young heart.

It isn't a perfect answer. It won't work 100 percent of the time. Our children are not extensions of us. They are independent creatures with minds and choices to make all on their own.

But if we don't fix the family, we won't even have the chance to fix our future.

Yeshua is the bridegroom and His Church is the bride. Healthy relationship provides our families with G-d like qualities. Conversely, if your father on earth abuses or neglects you, your Father in Heaven seems like a monster. We see G-d as we see our parents far too often. While G-d intends to break us from this trap, it is human and hard to overcome.

We need good men. We need good women. And we need family.

The Curse of Disobedience

Between Matthew 24 and Matthew 25 we find Yeshua describing the surprise moment of His second coming. He warns that disobedience can cause people to miss His return and not be admitted into the wedding feast. Those who are followers of Yeshua, not merely admirers, are found to be ready at His second coming: true warnings indeed.

Much of this essay has been focused on gender and sex roles in the human family. They are the foundation for the continuation of life, the picture of the family and the picture of G-d in relationship, so they deserve thought and reverence in our walks with G-d. Without this understanding, the Bride of Christ cannot know her destiny. How many more fundamental Biblical issues will we get wrong when we confuse gender and sex? (For a deeper understanding of Family and the Kingdom of G-d, I'd recommend Dinah Dye's book, *The Temple Revealed in Creation.)*[xxiii]

But this is not the only important reason to call the Church back into Biblical truth. We see time and again, Israel (we) disobeyed G-d with horrific consequences. That spiritual pattern repeats. G-d does not always save us from the consequences of being disobedient, and over the long-term our iniquities can literally banish us from closeness with G-d.

Instead of walking with the Lord, we stumble across shaky ground on our own. Just as Israel's Northern Kingdom was taken captive by Babylon, so we become captive to our own sins, the world, and to the very modern iteration of Babylon we see today.

Christ came to free us from our sin. Disobedience results in bondage to that sin. And sin comes with consequences.

Conversely, obedience brings blessings. While it cannot save us, it can empower our joy, our hope, our faith, and our ministries. It can change our course and put us on a path to righteousness. And it is proof that we not only truly love G-d, but that we *know* Him.

1 John 5:3 tells us that to love the Lord is to obey His commands. Exodus 20 tells us that certain acts of obedience are a sign that we are G-d's people. (Keeping the Sabbath being one of them.)

Our light in the world is reliant upon signs that direct people to Who we belong to. If we belong to the King, we do what the King has instructed. If we belong to the world, we will look no different than the world.

This is the conundrum I see the Church in today. In areas important and trivial, obvious and obscured, we look a lot like the world.

Whether it's the programming we watch, the politicians we vote for, the food we eat, the words we use, the workweek we choose, or the family life we lead, Believers and non-believers are starting to look exactly alike.

The best way to look different than the world is to actually obey the Instructions of G-d. These are found in the first five books of the Bible, The Torah. If you follow these instructions, you will differ from your neighbor in a tangible and observable way. You will also love your neighbor like never before.

You will love according to the definition G-d has provided.

It's time for the church to rediscover its roots, its first love, and return to G-d's Kingdom principles. We must decide we want to be part of G-d's family, His lineage. To be the Bride of Christ requires something of us. It has been a long time coming. The time is here and now.

It will take a perspective shift, a re-education: a renewed commitment to Biblical and historical accuracy. It will take a change of heart.

But it's worth it. Our physical and spiritual families are at stake.

"I will ponder the way that is blameless. Oh when will you come to me? I will walk with integrity of heart within my house; I will not set before my eyes anything that is worthless. I hate the works of those who fall away; it shall not cling to me. A perverse heart shall be far from me; I will know nothing of evil." (Psalms 101: 2-4)

Chapter 3

THE REAL JESUS

Hebrews 11:6 "But without faith it is impossible to please God: for he that cometh to God must believe that He is, and that He is a rewarder of them that **diligently seek Him**."

FOR AS LONG AS I CAN REMEMBER, I have loved to read. I've found my own imagination far craftier and invigorating than most movie renditions of books and stories (or maybe I just prefer my own interpretation that much). There is a special magnificence about beautiful language put together in just the right way, revealing ultimate truths about all of us through the unique journey of a particular character.

As a child, my go-tos included the *Anne of Green Gables* series, *Little Women*, and the adventures of Laura Ingalls. I'd eventually graduate on to C.S. Lewis and Tolkien, Jane Austen, and Shakespeare. I'd lay on my bedroom floor, lamenting over Othello or laughing when Jo March cut her hair in order to sell it, pretending not to care, but unable to escape her own private battle with vanity.

As with any good story, these characters start in one situation and end in a completely different mindset, place, or position. The significance of the transformative work, the foreshadowing and connections, the path and process are meticulously laid out, word by word. This process helps the reader understand the intricacies of the characters and the beauty, heartache, challenge, and hope in the events that take place.

Without the genesis firmly established and an adept author's ability in weaving story, these characters and places would not pack the potent punch that hooks us. The stories start at the beginning. We read from the start so we can be enveloped in the author's world and understand the details of the characters and plot.

What would happen to our understanding if we started the story in the middle? Let's say, for instance, we join Frodo on his journey to Mordor right after Gandalf fights the Balrog and falls to, what they all believe, is his death. Yes, what if you had not the slightest idea who Gandalf was, or what it meant to be a Hobbit, or what the ring was, or Sam's loyalty to Frodo, or well...you see my point. So much would be missing.

Sure, through the rest of the story, you may learn a lot, really enjoy it in fact, start to understand the relationships, etc. But you would have no real picture or appreciation of the Shire, the lush green beauty of the place they were hoping to preserve. You would not know Gandalf's importance to their quest and so when he appears later, he would seem as a brand new character. Even worse, you may misinterpret the characters and their importance. Alternatively, if you happened to start all the way back at *The Hobbit*, you would fully understand Gollum: the tortured, impressively complex individual who both loves and hates the ring and how he became such a pitiable creature. You would know how long Gollum had existed.

And if you just entered the story halfway through the *Lord of the Rings* trilogy, Gollum's character could seem outrageously creepy, strange beyond belief, some other-worldly alien who popped onto the scene, randomly obsessed with the ring, inhuman.

This would happen time and again if you continued to approach books from their middle chapters. Character development, plot, foreshadowing, thematic emphases — they would all be lost and you would be busy filling in the gaps with your own ideas. This would be problematic enough with books that you read for intellectual enrichment or entertainment.

But what happens when we do this with the Bible? Start at the middle. No context, no background, no foundation.

I should point out, we do EXACTLY this with the Bible… almost always. And what holes have we filled in with our own imaginations, what misinterpretations have we promulgated as a result of telling almost all new Believers to go ahead and start reading at the book of Matthew? "Just jump into the New Testament," we say! "This is where you understand Jesus!"

And yes, yes of course you can understand so much about Yeshua just by starting SOMEWHERE in Scripture. However…

In John 5:45-47, Jesus pointedly states that in order to believe Him, you have to believe Moses. The same Moses who wrote the first five books of the Bible. The beginning. That foundation defines Yeshua and assists in confirming Yeshua's G-d status.

The beginning is the essential element to knowing Jesus. He says it himself. But we've rarely heeded His remarks. The 21st-century church seems far more interested in creating our own story, relying on our own imaginations. Our own god?

It is in the beginning where we find G-d's character, pieces of His nature, and the Laws He hands to a people of His choosing (and their choosing. They did say yes to Him at Sinai after all). We see the story of His relationship with His people, His love and frustration with them. The picture of Christ in Moses as Moses intercedes on those people's behalf. The salvation of that people from slavery into freedom and the cost of that work.

We get the underpinnings of humanity and individual human character, why sin separates and divides and destroys, how G-d makes plans for the ultimate restoration of His creation. We find His love for each thing He has created and His insistence that humans take care of it and co-create with Him. We begin to see that the seed of G-d is not a seed of physical DNA but spiritual, as brothers like Jacob and Esau, Cain and Abel, Isaac and Ishmael take opposing paths.

To understand Yeshua, we must understand what He stood for, what He did, His character, and how that changed things. What *was* He doing and what *is* He doing now?

The intention of G-d's heart and the shaping of ensuing events happened right at the beginning, in the very first words. And Jesus was there, authoring it all, putting himself into it.

Do you see Him? Many Believers don't. They look at the Bible after reading the New Testament, and when they get to the Old Testament, they think they've encountered a completely alternate being. They envision one god in the Old Testament who is grumpy, old, angry, vengeful, violent and obsessed with rules. The second god shows up in the New Testament. This one is sweet, kind, squishy, probably with a beard, blue eyes, and soft-spoken. (Thanks, Hollywood.)

The squishy god comes to save us from the scary god. Squishy god gets rid of the rules and really has to go through it in order to help all these people he loves. Vengeful god accepts squishy god's gift and the story ends with everyone in a bright shining, gold-filled Heaven where we all do whatever it is that pleases us. Sigh, the end.

As Jim Carey's version of The Grinch would say, "Wrong-O!"

But, be honest: isn't this really how most Believers have viewed Scripture? If people really believed G-d is one throughout scripture, why such terror over reading the Old Testament, specifically the Law? Why the sole focus on the four Gospels and the later books Paul wrote? (Poor, misinterpreted, brilliant Paul. We will get to him later.) Sure, some will read the Psalms a few times, learn the most tertiary versions of Noah's ark, Adam and Eve, David and Goliath, maybe Joseph and possibly Queen Esther.

But how about good old Leviticus? Who's up for it? Anyone?

And what about the deep theological conundrums this dualistic view of G-d creates? Is it possible that G-d authored all the Laws that He gave His people and then sent Himself to save us from the supposed "curse" of those very Laws? Is there any realm where that logic works? Does that sort of story plant distrust in G-d's perfection, holiness, and well, overall planning strategy? Anyone with a couple of brain cells will answer yes to that last question.

Yes, I believe that a god who has to save us from his own rules may have messed up to begin with. Yes, I'm not sure I can trust a god who has to change the plans in the middle of the story.

And, yes, I think the idea that G-d came to save us from Himself is intellectually repugnant.

Realistically, in order to believe in the goodness and brilliance of our Heavenly Father, we have to believe that there is something more to G-d's Law than the cursory reads we've given it. The Ten Commandments and other Laws that were given to Moses and the nation of Israel have purpose and meaning, and since sin still exists, they clearly still apply.

And, yes, it takes some wisdom, study, and work to dig in to those Laws. Some of them only apply if you are in the land of Israel. Some only apply to Levitical priests. Some only apply when there is an official temple. Some are only for women. Some are only for men. Not all 613 laws apply to everyone in every location at every time. BUT, some do.

It's those 'some' that we CAN apply that would make quite a difference for the Believer today. Interestingly, the Laws of Yahweh STILL remain separate and holy from how other religious and secular systems work. G-d's things are absolutely His. In following them, a natural separation becomes clear and apparent, and yes, blessings follow. Peace, family, righteousness, a love of nature and creation, a love of others, a better understanding of caretaking, a deeper understanding of work. These are just a few of the blessings that begin to transform us as we follow the Creator's instructions.

If you wanted to learn to play the piano, you would ask, "how" do I do this? If we want to follow our Rabbi, we must ask in this same spirit. How? The answer is to observe His behavior, read His Word, and obey it.

What do we know about Yeshua and how do we apply it? Where have we gotten Him right and where have we gone astray?

We follow because we have chosen to, because we love Him, because He has saved us. "But how", remains the divisive question. Where do we stand as a Church in the call to follow our Rabbi? How do we follow in alignment with Him and not with our own man-made version of Him?

What did Yeshua do and show us that can help us answer this question?

WHERE WE OFTEN GET YESHUA RIGHT

The American Church, for the most part, does indeed recognize Jesus for His most basic and important qualities. He is G-d! And He comes to us in human form clearly and miraculously in the New Testament as a servant. We recognize that this coming of His is, as ancient Hebrew Rabbis would say, Messiah-Ben-Josef, the suffering servant in His first coming. I've never attended a Christian church that does not recognize these basics about Christ.

Jesus described the law and prophets as being about loving G-d and loving others. So we understand that 1) to love the Lord is to obey His commands, and, 2) all the Law can be summed up under two ideas, loving God and loving others.

Modern-day Believers want to focus on love of G-d and others in service, sacrifice, kindness, mercy, and charitable action. Decidedly, this particular conception has helped create some beautiful ministries and generous behaviors that speak to Heaven on Earth. I credit Christianity for gearing itself towards community service and leaning towards love for our fellow man. It is commendable and beautiful in an ever more self-centered generation.

Christianity has also recognized the need to die to self. Even when the direction might be misguided, Christianity seems to hold an understanding that there are natural human traits that need to be tamed and perfected. Malice, selfishness, vengefulness, violence, dishonesty, gossip, love of money, pride, these and other toxic human behaviors are roundly worked on in the Christian community. I've heard sermon after sermon on the above behaviors and firmly believe that the Christians I know perceive that humans are naturally both good and evil. The evil inclination being an easy one to feed and sustain here on earth, we need to dispense with evil and learn to fill ourselves with good. And yes, this takes training, learning, and discipline. American Christianity has certainly targeted some of the flaws in human nature with a mind towards repentance in those areas.

American Christianity also seems to quite enjoy musical offerings to the Lord, using that time for praise and highly valuing those moments in service after service. Music has seemed to provide a foundation for the "loving G-d" part of worship.

This quick coverage represents the vagueness with which Christianity has approached these ideas. By vague, I mean mostly using Paul to discuss what obedience and love of G-d looks like. And Paul doesn't go into detail because I firmly believe that Paul assumes Believers have read the Torah already and understand the foundation OR that they will be attending synagogue each week to learn the Torah as discussed in Acts 15:21.

At the time, Paul assumed correctly. Over time, Paul's hopes for G-d's people have certainly taken a back seat. Traded for an obsession over a few of his letters to some churches who needed cultural and spiritual direction.

Well, Paul, much of the teaching of Torah that you were familiar with has been lost. Let's fix this, shall we?

THE JESUS WE HAVE MISSED

The Yeshua we seem to miss fulfills the culmination of BOTH parts of the Law. Loving others AND loving G-d. This loving G-d part reveals itself in mutiple ways in Scripture. By helping the poor and needy, Yeshua says we are helping Him. But there are other Laws that we miss that leave us in a position where we steal from G-d that which belongs to Him and we miss out on intimate relationship with our Heavenly Father.

Let me preface by saying this: what we are getting wrong is not totally our fault. We have been left uneducated. Even our seminaries do not teach the most ancient views of Scripture. They prefer to stay with Catholic doctrine or a metamorphosis of it, which is new in comparison to the deep and old principles taught in Genesis through Deuteronomy. They prefer students learn Greek, while often leaving behind Hebrew.

We have less information.

The problem is that, without obedience to the Torah, we are guessing at what loving G-d and others looks like. Some churches believe it means allowing those living in sin against G-d to be in leadership. Some churches believe that this "love" means you are free to do things that "feel" like love without any Scriptural foundation, they then attach these behaviors to Scripture instead of looking to Scripture to dictate our behavior.

But here's one upside: we have hope that we may be in the times prophesied by Scripture! Times when the word of Adonai would go out again and that it would be understood. Where a pure language is returned to the people and where knowledge is rediscovered and taught. G-d is awakening His people to His truth so that we have the tools to stand where once we might have fallen.

What follows is less of a judgment and more of a request. As John (the Baptist) appealed to the people of his day, "Repent! (Teshuvah!) For the Kingdom of Heaven is at hand." And surely it is.

It should come as no surprise that we are missing Yeshua in the very location we fear to look, the Torah. So, let's discover Him there. How can we join Him in this great story and truly understand what it means to know Him?

In Deuteronomy 13 the nation of Israel is given a test to decipher a real prophet from a false one.

> **13** If there arise among you a prophet, or a dreamer of dreams, and giveth thee a sign or a wonder, [2] And the sign or the wonder come to pass, whereof he spake unto thee, saying, Let us go after other gods, which thou hast not known, and let us serve them; [3] Thou shalt not hearken unto the words of that prophet, or that dreamer of dreams: for the Lord your God proveth you, to know whether ye love the Lord your God with all your heart and with all your soul. [4] Ye shall walk after the Lord your God, and fear him, and keep his commandments, and obey his voice, and ye shall serve him, and cleave unto him.

Here we see the Lord telling the people that we are to follow His Commandments — as in, the ones given at the beginning. We are to obey His voice and cling only to the things of G-d. Those who come and teach against the Commands, those who come and speak against what G-d has given at the beginning, these are false prophets.

It is time to return to what G-d gave at the beginning, which was Yeshua Himself. He was there and He embodied the Commands and spoke them. We turn back to Him in turning back to these things. This is a step in our repentance and also a step towards ultimate blessing and deeper relationship.

Now, a quick reminder should set my reader at ease. Hebrews 10:4 "It is impossible for the blood of bulls and goats to take away sins." Romans 4:13 "It was not through the law that Abraham and his offspring received the promise that he would be heir of the world, but through the righteousness that comes by faith."

Time and again Scripture will remind us that the Law never provided a route to salvation. For the forefather of our faith and for us today, perfect law keeping cannot give you access to eternity. That is not the purpose of the law nor is there a route within the law to make that possible. We don't obey the Lord for salvation.

After having dozens of conversations with Believers over the years, this one point becomes a stumbling block like clockwork. We have been so encoded with the fear of legalism that we attach any extra love of obedience to it. But that is fruitless. Keeping the Law cannot save you.

With that firmly in place, here are some of the things that have been lost in our walk with G-d, but in hope and joy may we unit with them now because of our love for our Savior.

THE SABBATH

Exodus 20:8 – 11 "Remember the Sabbath day, to keep it holy.
9 Six days shalt thou labour, and do all thy work:
10 But the seventh day is the Sabbath of the Lord thy God: in it thou shalt not do any work, thou, nor thy son, nor thy daughter, thy manservant, nor thy maidservant, nor thy cattle, nor thy stranger that is within thy gates:
11 For in six days the Lord made heaven and earth, the sea, and all that in them is, and rested the seventh day: wherefore the Lord blessed the Sabbath day, and hallowed it."

Traditionally observed as the 4th commandment of the 10 Commandments, the Sabbath day is first described specifically enough that we understand it clearly. The 7th day of the week is THE day that G-d set aside. It is forbidden for us to do our regular work that day or to allow anyone in our household to work. We are also told not to make anyone else or any creature work.

For as far back as human history is documented, all sorts of days/times/calendars have changed. Even today, Messianics and Jews debate about which dates belong to which Feast Days. When do they actually occur given changes to the calendar?

However, one thing has never changed through most cultures: the days of the week. Even though dates, numbers, and months have changed, from the beginning, a 7-day week has remained. We can be confident the Sabbath can still be kept accurately and that means it is on the 7th day.

Genesis 1:3 tells us that G-d created "evening and morning, the first day." The Bible begins with evening as the start to the day and so Jews throughout history observe that the new day starts at sundown. Allowing the Bible to define itself in this regard helps us clear up any misunderstandings about when Sabbath starts. It starts each Friday evening at sundown and it ends each Saturday evening at sundown.

And of course, this is a sensible way to keep days historically. Before our digital clocks, how in the world would the average person be able to know when midnight hit? They likely aren't awake for it. Throughout the vast majority of human history, people have had to live by the seasons and cycles of nature. The 24-hour day is given in its most recognizable state and allows for anyone to calculate the start and end of a day without technology.

It's kind of like an instruction manual. Let's say you have Knob 'A' on a piece of stereo equipment. The instruction manual tells you that Knob A controls the loudness of the instrument. Now you know what Knob A means with this particular item. Other items in your home may have Knob A, but that knob may do something completely different.

The Bible is the instruction manual and Knob A, in this case, is the 24-hour day. At the very beginning, Knob A (a day) is defined as beginning in the evening. This particular knob has seven settings. Roll through to the 7th and you will find that the Sabbath (the 7th-day setting) starts at sundown on Friday. (The Bible at the beginning just numbers the days, calling them 1 – 7. It isn't until later that Scripture adopts the Greek names of each day as Sunday through Saturday.)

In Genesis, G-d describes a 'day' as one rotation around the sun. Twenty-four hours. In order for a day to become symbolic, a day must first be understood and defined. Something cannot become a symbol until we understand its original form. The original form of a day in Scripture is sundown to sundown.

(Symbolic meanings associated with "day" do emerge later. Days in other parts of Scripture are related to "ages". And if you study Scripture, the 7-day, or age, cycle is very much related to the seven "ages". It is no wonder that it is believed that Christ will reign during the 7th millennium. The 7th day rest is fulfilled in the millennium where Yeshua reigns on earth.)

So we have the Sabbath, defined by scripture as the 7th day. We are not to work or make any other being work. But what, really, is the point of the Sabbath? What are we to do?

We are to practice rest.

Do we see Christ invoking this rest?

In Matthew 4:23, 9:35, Mark 6:2, Luke 4:16, as well as other verses, you see Jesus entering the synagogue to teach on the Sabbath. In John 15:10, Jesus says, "If you keep my commandments, you abide in my love; even as I have kept my father's commandments and abide in his love."

There are literally no examples in Scripture where Yeshua did not keep the Sabbath or where you will find him teaching against it. Although He was falsely accused of breaking the Sabbath by healing, He easily refutes the claim by discussing the widely held understanding that helping an ox out of a pit is considered good work to do on the Sabbath. (Luke 14:5) Doing good is always welcome in G-d's kingdom, and that includes healing people.

Yeshua makes the claim that He is "Lord of the Sabbath," which implies at the least that He is the definer and holder of the meaning of the day. And, of course, He teaches what obedience really means. The spirit of obedience aligns with the Law.

The intention is to rest and focus on the Lord, but not at the expense of the lives of humans and animals. If an animal is in trouble, you rescue it. If a person needs healing, you heal them. The concept is simple. Doing Heavenly good on the Sabbath is as welcome that day as any other day, and possibly even moreso given that our focus should be rooted in Heaven on the Sabbath.

In Matthew 5, Jesus teaches that anyone who breaks the least of G-d's commandments and teaches others to do so will be considered least in the kingdom of Heaven. He continually encourages his disciples and others to obey the Torah. It is found time and again throughout his teachings. (Matthew 8, John 5:45-47, John 7, Matthew 5, Mark 7:1-12, the list is much longer than this)

Beyond that, Yeshua must have kept the Sabbath. If not, He would have been found as a sinner both in the kingdom of men and of G-d. This would have disqualified Him from being the Messiah. G-d is perfect — He keeps His own Commandments perfectly. We needed a perfect sacrifice, and we have one in Christ. Not only did He teach on the Sabbath in the traditional Synagogue on the 7th day of the week, He taught us to follow Him. We are to celebrate the Sabbath on the 7th day of the week like Yeshua. (More in my essay, *The Big Ten)*

Hebrews 4:1-10 seems to discuss both an understanding of continuing to keep the Sabbath now and the future "day" of rest we will all enter when Yeshua reigns on the earth. (The day being like 1,000 years) Yeshua fully embodies Sabbath keeping both in our weekdays and in the long span of G-d's plan for all time.

THE FEAST DAYS and MO-EDIM

The Mo-Edim (i.e. *appointed times* in English) are the Biblical days G-d has called us to celebrate or observe. Some of the Appointed Times are Feast Days, so naturally on those days, eating is involved. But some of the Appointed Times do not have a feast attached to their observance. In other words: all Feast Days are Appointed Times, but not all Appointed Times are Feast Days.

Much of what is listed in Scripture as part of these observances requires a temple and Levitical Priesthood. Since we do not have the Temple or the Priesthood, we cannot fully celebrate all of these dates. However, because we are commanded to memorialize them through all our generations and in all of our dwelling places, we can do our best to observe them and look forward to their second round of fulfillment when Yeshua returns. So let's dig in.

Most Believers celebrate Christmas and Easter. Catholics and some Protestants have Good Friday and other days as well. Are these Scriptural holidays? I hate to burst the bubble, but you will not find followers of Yeshua celebrating these days in Scripture. There is one caveat. Christians get resurrection celebration right when it happens to fall on the Sunday after Passover. It is a Scriptural command to bring a praise offering the day after the Sabbath during the Feast of Firstfruits (or on the first day of the week after Passover). This means you are to bring an offering and it is waved on the first day of the week, on Sunday. So, celebrating in church on the Sunday after Passover is actually a long-held act of obedience.

HOWEVER, the way we celebrate on this day is often not Scriptural at all, not to mention the date does not always align properly with Passover.

Many Believers think that only Jews celebrate the Mo-edim or Feast Days in Scripture and that they are either ONLY for Jews or not for anyone really and that it is odd that Jews do observe them. But Scripture has never approached G-d's Mo-edim this way.

Numbers 15:15 – 16 "The community is to have the same rules for you and for the alien living among you; this is a lasting ordinance FOR THE GENERATIONS TO COME. You and the alien shall be the SAME before the Lord. The SAME Laws and regulations will apply to both you and the alien living among you."

Here we see the nation of Israel being told that all the laws and ordinances were for ANYONE who had joined in the community. Every Law and Feast Day was for everyone for all the generations to come.

G-d's Laws are for all peoples. And of course they are, just as Yeshua is for all people. We are all called into familial relationship with our Creator, and His citizenry has equal and fair expectations. This is called justice. And Adonai is most certainly just.

Let's take a look at a short list of heavily held modern Christian observances versus the Mo-edim of Scripture.

Easter vs/Passover and Firstfruits

Easter — with its close ties to eggs and bunnies and ham — directly disregards the Scriptural decree by G-d to:

"utterly destroy all the places where the nations which you shall dispossess served their gods, on the high mountains and on the hills and under every green tree. And you shall destroy their altars, break their *sacred* pillars, and burn their wooden images with fire; you shall cut down the carved images of their gods and destroy their names from that place. You shall not worship the Lord your God *with* such *things.*" (Deuteronomy 12:2-4)

Some translations literally say something closer to, "You shall not worship the Lord your God the way the nations do."

The Easter traditions are mostly associated with the worship of other ancient gods and have no roots in Scripture. In fact, if you try to find these things in Scripture as tools for celebrating the Lord, you will find NO reference to them. Clearly, we have profaned the celebration of our Savior's resurrection on this day by mixing in pagan traditions.

Scripture DOES call us to praise, as the Resurrection is the day Yeshua rose from the grave, conquered death, and brought us life. He is our living sacrifice; a sacrifice that continues to do its work on our behalf because it has not stayed in the grave.

But we must begin our observance and celebration of the death, burial, and resurrection of Yeshua with the Biblically prescribed celebrations that imbue meaning to our story and G-d's redemption. When we begin this sacred time by celebrating Passover, we realize our connection with our spiritual ancestors — the Hebrews rescued by G-d from ancient Egypt.

They are our spiritual forefathers. We understand their suffering and bondage. We can then see how death passed over them because of their acceptance of the blood of a perfect lamb, tied to the death that passes over us because of the blood of Yeshua. And we celebrate renewal and salvation on the first day of the week after Passover because that is when the grave was discovered empty! We also understand Yeshua more deeply. What did He do? What did He fulfill? Who is He? The more we dig, the lovelier and more intricate the picture becomes. We are called to keep the Mo-Edim correctly, according to Scripture in order to more deeply understand our G-d.

The Feast of Unleavened Bread begins the day after Passover. During this time no leaven is eaten for a week. The first day of the week after Passover is the Feast of Firstfruits (this means it will fall on a Sunday) You may recall, Paul tells us that Yeshua is the "firstfruits" of a new life. He is the perfect man that Adam was not. He begins the spiritual seed that can enter into intimate relationship with G-d. Again, He is the Firstfruit. And here all the way back in Leviticus 23, we have the nation of Israel celebrating the Firstfruits, Yeshua!

Leviticus 23:14 "And ye shall eat neither bread, nor parched corn, nor green ears, until the selfsame day that ye have brought an offering unto your God: It shall be a statute FOREVER THROUGHOUT YOUR GENERATIONS IN ALL YOUR DWELLINGS."

It must be emphasized that the Appointed Times are not requests or options. They are statutes for G-d's people forever, no matter what generation and no matter where they live. And it makes sense, as thes holidays are something we CAN celebrate in any generation in any location.

Now we see why Jesus said, "I did not come to abolish the Law but to fulfill it." He meant He would fill it full of meaning, not rid us of it. While the nation of Israel had no idea what Firstfruits really meant, we do! Our joy is full! We see G-d in His cycles revealing and enacting His plan and His salvation.

Furthermore, we are shown the cycles of nature as a reflection of G-d's times. G-d has established His perfect plan right into the fields we plant. Yeshua is the seed of a new crop, an incorruptible seed. Unlike the seed of Adam, Yeshua can now produce a line of people who possess unfettered fellowship with the Father. All of this can be seen in the Feast of Firstfruits. How beautiful that the very first church had this knowledge but not yet fully. And how comforting to serve a G-d who historically wanted to make Himself so clear!

Passover = Christ's death, symbolized by the blood of the Passover lamb

Unleavened Bread = A time to recognize how impossible it is to get rid of all leaven, just like it is impossible to save ourselves. It is a time of recognizing our need for the Lord.

First Fruits = Christ's Resurrection and the planting of the seed (Word of G-d) into the very flesh of mankind, making us like Yeshua, High Priests of a personal heart-shaped temple.

Christmas VS. Sukkot

While these two holidays often come at pretty different times of the year, I think they hold a relationship in that it's far more plausible Yeshua was born during Sukkot than during Christmas. I don't want to spend too much time on this as we cannot prove for certain using Scripture alone, but it seems more likely given what I'm about to share. There are sensible reasons to believe Yeshua was born in the fall. Here we go…

The Bible tells us that John the Baptist was six months older than Christ and was born in the springtime. Six months after Spring (let's say April) puts Christ's birth sometime in the fall, much closer to the Feast of Sukkot (Tabernacles) than winter (Christmas time).

How do we know this?

Let's go to Luke 1 starting in verse 5: "In the days of Herod, king of Judea, there was a priest named Zechariah, of the division of Abijah. And he had a wife from the daughters of Aaron, and her name was Elizabeth. They were both righteous before God, walking blamelessly in all the Commandments and Statutes of the Lord. But they had no child, because Elizabeth was barren, and both were advanced in years. Now while he was serving as priest before God when his division was on duty, according to the custom of the priesthood, he was chosen by lot to enter the temple of the Lord and burn incense."

The story continues that Zechariah meets the angel, Gabriel as he is doing this incense service. Gabriel tells him that Elizabeth will bear a child, Zechariah questions this at first and is left unable to speak until John's birth.

> In verse 28 Luke tells us, "In the sixth month the angel Gabriel was sent from God to a city of Galilee named Nazareth to a virgin betrothed to a man whose name was Joseph, of the house of David. And the virgin's name was Mary… (Verse 36) "and behold, your relative Elizabeth in her old age has also conceived a son, and this is the sixth month with her who was called barren."

Now in order to know the timing of all of this, we simply must understand the timing of the division of Abijah since Elizabeth became pregnant with John around this division's temple service duties. Do we have that timing? Yes.

In 1 Chronicles 24 we see that King David organizes the priests into their divisions for service. Verse 10 "the seventh to Hakkoz, the eight to Abijah," So, now we know that Abijah's service timeframe was 8th.

With 24 divisions serving, each division would have served from Sabbath to Sabbath twice a year. So what part of the year was this?

In Exodus 12:2 G-d says, "This month (the Passover month) shall be for you the beginning of months. It shall be the first month of the year for you."

Ok, so, the first month is Nissan according to the Biblical Hebraic calendar. (Note, I'm showing a mix of Hebraic and Gregorian calendars here to help calculate) And Zechariah's service was 8th according to that calendar.

Nissan usually falls in March or April according to the Gregorian calendar.

Looking 8 courses later, Zechariah's temple service and encounter with Gabriel would have happened right around Pentecost. So he likely had to serve two weeks in a row, as this time of the year required all Priests to serve at the temple at once. After those days he goes home and conceives John with Elizabeth.

This conception then would have happened around May/June.

If Mary conceives during the 6th month that Elizabeth is carrying John, as Luke tells us, then Mary conceived around December. Likely at Hanukkah. (No coincidence there).

9 months after Hanukkuh, we have Sukkot, or the Feast of Tabernacles. And here is how we come to the opinion that Yeshua was likely born at this time, fall, and a Feast Day that aligns with Scripture. A day we are told that the G-d of the universe Tabernacles with us.

In the fall, we are commanded to celebrate Sukkot/Feast of Tabernacles. It is a picture of G-d tabernacling with us! During this time we are to create Sukas — little spaces outside with open roofs where we eat and spend time with each other. These temporary dwellings commemorate our time as Israel in the desert, dwelling in tents after the escape from Egypt and journeying to the Promised Land. G-d Himself dwelt among them and led them with fire and cloud, provided manna as food, and provided water through a rock. G-d among us, G-d tabernacling with us.

Is it any wonder Yeshua was born in more of an outdoor dwelling?

Other parts of the birth story align with the Sukkot timeframe. It is rational that a census would be taken at the same time that the Jews would be travelling to their cities of origin or Jerusalem. This travel is also associated with Sukkot. In fact, it is prophesied in Zechariah 14:16-17 that all the peoples of the earth will go up to Jerusalem to celebrate the Feast of Tabernacles:

> "Then the survivors of all the nations that have attacked Jerusalem will go up year after year to worship the King, The Lord Almighty and to celebrate the Feast of Tabernacles. If any of the peoples of the earth do not go up to Jerusalem to worship the King, the Lord Almighty, they will have no rain."

In the end, all people travel to Jerusalem to celebrate Sukkot! A wise Roman leader would have taken the census at this time, as it was a time when people travelled home to celebrate. Not proven, just sensible.

Jesus' parents made a journey to their home to stay in a temporary dwelling and welcome G-d entering earth to Tabernacle with us. Does this sound like Christ fulfilling the law? (Filling it full of meaning?) It sure does to me! Although we cannot prove this with 100% assurance, we have a treasure trove of historical and Biblical evidence including the convergence of planets in the sky to create a bright star at that time, and we know that John The Baptist was born in the spring. So it is far more likely that Christ was born in the fall and therefore a December birth date is truly a stretch.

So, who *was* born on December 25? I've asked many Christians this question. Most think that Jesus is the only deity, so to speak, who holds this date in the historical archives of religious celebration. But Dec. 25 is an important date for many ancient pagan gods, as was the general time of year. It shook me to my core to learn that:

- Mithra, the Persian god of light, was also celebrated at this time.
- Before 1000 B.C., the Egyptian Horus was believed to have been born Dec 25.
- Before the year 200 B.C., Heracles Dionysis, Tammuz, Adonis and others were also declared to have been born on December 25th
- Egyptain sun-god Ra was said to be born of a virgin on Dec 25.
- Horus was born of a virgin mother, Isis on Dec 25.
- Attis, a Greek god, was born of a virgin, Nana on Dec 25.
- Dionysus was born of the virgin, Persephone on Dec 25.

Mithra is a great example of the relationship between the Catholic Church's version of Christ and pagan god worship. Mithra, born on December 25, was the sun god, god of light. There have even been discoveries of an ancient temple dedicated to Mithra that was built to align with the rising sun on December 25th. Mithra's followers had midnight services (enter Catholic Christmas Eve Mass), had a virgin mother, and the sacred rock of Mithraism is Petra. The Catholic Church likely stole Petra and made it Peter, their "rock". Despite the fact that the Bible verse pertaining to the "rock" is actually talking about faith in Christ, not Peter, it was politically convenient to use some of Petra and the Bible story of Peter and mix them together to produce the version of Peter and holidays often promoted today.

Let's review those verses quickly before we move on. Lest you all take me to task for that claim.

In Matthew 16:15 "He said to **them**, 'But who do you say that I am?' Simon Peter replied, **'You are the Christ, the Son of the living God.'** And Jesus answered him, 'Blessed are you, Simon Bar-Jonah! For flesh and blood has not revealed this to you but my Father who is in Heaven. And I tell you, **you are Peter**, and on this rock I will build my church and the gates of hell shall not prevail against it. I will give you the keys of the kingdom of heaven and whatever you bind on earth shall be bound in heaven and whatever you loose on earth shall be loosed in Heaven.'"

Now, if this entire passage about keys, binding and loosing and the rock were all about Peter, then we would have a fairly short-lived faith and church existence. It would have died with Peter and the keys and binding and loosing would have gone with him.

Take a closer look. Peter declares who Yeshua IS. Then Yeshua declares back to him who Peter IS. "You are the Christ," and "You are Peter" are a call and response. Yeshua then declares that the revelation given by G-d the Father regarding Yeshua's Messiahship is the rock upon which His church is built. Going to the top of the section in verse 13, "Now when Jesus came into the district of Caesarea Philippi, he asked His disciples,"

Yeshua is talking to a group here, not just Peter. It is the royal "you" that is receiving the keys and the binding and the loosing. It is G-d's Church receiving this blessing after placing their faith in Yeshua.

We do not look to Peter as the founder of our faith. We look to our high priest, Yeshua, the only one who has the power to answer our prayers, the only one with the keys to death and Hades, the only one with the power to save. I do not pray to Peter. He was a man. However, the Catholic Church traditionally with their version of Petre does indeed pray to Peter and does indeed believe that Peter is the founder of the faith, stealing the power of the keys to the Kingdom of Heaven from the Bride of Christ, His Church.

Mithra originated in Indo-Persia. He was a mediator between god and man. The Persians and Romans adopted Mithraism whose worship dates back over 3500 years.

In Babylon, you find Mithra worship as the worship of Bel, a Mesopotamian and Canaanite sungod also called Marduk. He represented Jupiter and the sun. In Rome, Mithra was also Apollo.

Sometime after Christ, the Catholic Church decided to incorporate Christmas into the religious practices of Christianity. (Between 300 – 400AD)

According to History.com[xxiv]: "By holding Christmas at the same time as traditional Winter Solstice festivals, church leaders increased the chances that Christmas would be popularly embraced, but gave up the ability to dictate how it was celebrated. By the Middle Ages, Christianity had, for the most part, replaced pagan religion. On Christmas, believers attended church, then celebrated raucously in a drunken, carnival-like atmosphere similar to today's Mardi Gras. Each year, a beggar or student would be crowned the "lord of misrule" and eager celebrants played the part of his subjects. The poor would go to the houses of the rich and demand their best food and drink. If owners failed to comply, their visitors would most likely terrorize them with mischief. Christmas became the time of year when the upper classes could repay their real or imagined "debt" to society by entertaining less fortunate citizens."

Unsurprisingly, a winter solstice festival happened in December, as this is the time of the sun's return. Ancient peoples believed that the shortening of days pointed to a weakening of their sun god, and so when the shortness of days had reached its pinnacle and began to turn around, it would make sense to celebrate. For the ancient mind and many contemporary pagans, this is the celebration that summer is around the corner and crops and food will be planted and harvested. Sun god worship around December 21 – 25 is sensible to those who look to the created for sustenance.

I think I'd be suprirsed if the G-d who knew how humans would behave regarding the sun, moon, and stars, would put His holidays at the same time as the pagan gods' holidays!

The Bible says G-d's people are a holy people worshiping a holy G-d. Holy means "*set apart*". You cannot be set apart if you demand to sit at the same table of other gods and share their celebrations.

More than that, in Deuteronomy we are commanded not to mix pagan things with G-d's things. So why would G-d Himself do this?

The truth is, I don't believe He did. Christmas celebration is not found in Yeshua or His disciples afterward.

In this understanding of history we find, once again, the truth mixed in with lies. Not at all a surprise, given that the father of lies, Satan, has found that confusion is the best way to lead people astray. Not complete, bold-faced falsehood. Just a little bit of confusion here, a little mixing of gods and birthdays there, and voila! You have Jesus as Mithras. He isn't Jewish, he is a white Roman-looking fellow. He doesn't follow the Feast Days, he is part of many traditions that don't "have" to be Biblical.

Isn't this the pattern?

But during Sukkot, on the other hand, a tent is made, you eat and convene outside, the priests wave sheaves of grain, you wave the four branches called the lulav. You are called to ENJOY your time as you do this. It should be a wonderful time of celebration, just as when Yeshua tabernacled with us and will again in the future. It is a celebration of G-d journeying with the Hebrews in the desert, coming in the form of a man, and the future where Yeshua will reign on earth for 1,000 years. This is where Zechariah's prophecy takes place, during the 1,000 year reign of Yeshua on the earth. He will reign from Jerusalem and we will celebrate HIS Days.

Interesting that Zechariah doesn't mention Christmas anywhere. In fact, nobody in Scripture does. This red flag alone should leave the modern Christian at least wondering, where did we get Christmas? Is Jesus there, or is He somewhere else?

As a reminder, you may wonder at the lack of reference of Yeshua's birthdate in Scripture outside of the accounts of Zechariah. The ancient Hebrews did not celebrate birthdays. Plain and simple, it wasn't part of their culture. But in Yeshua, we know all the feast days are fulfilled or filled full of meaning. So Sukkot must be included in that fulfillment. Surely He did and surely He will again in His Second Coming.

My biggest problem with some of the religious holidays of the Christian Church is that I'm not sure we should be dedicating to Christ those things that may have been dedicated to other gods. Does our G-d desire those dedications? If He didn't ask for them in Scripture, are we bringing strange fire into his Holy presence?

Christmas is not like 4th of July. I don't dedicate the 4th of July to Christ or to His worship. It is a national holiday and so I treat it as such.

If we treated Christmas the same way, maybe it would be fine.

But we don't. We ascribe complete holiness to Christmas. And while I have no problem recognizing the birth of Yeshua much more than maybe we do, I'm concerned with ascribing something to G-d Almighty that I don't find Him giving in Scripture.

I'm not totally sure. But I think some of these historical questions are worth a look. You may want to keep looking yourself. As for me, I will continue to search for truth above sentiment. In our home, we do not celebrate Christmas.

Counting of the Omer/Shavuot or Pentecost

This is the time period between the Sunday grain offering during the Feast of Weeks, or Firstfruits, as previously discussed, leading up to Shavuot or Pentacost.

From the Feast of Firstfruits, this holiday counts out 49 days plus one to make 50 days. When the children of Israel left Egypt, it was 50 days until they received the Torah, or Instructions of G-d, at Mount Sinai. There, on the ancient Pentecost date (i.e. Shavuot) the word of the Lord came down the mountain and was given to them. It was considered an extraordinary gift to receive these Laws actually written out for the fledgling nation. And here we see the early mention of church in Scripture. In Greek, it is the word *ecclesia*. It means "the called out assembly". Certainly, this nation that was called out of Egypt was the church of Yeshua. The 49 days are days of preparation to receive this word from G-d.

An omer is a measure of grain. The Priest would wave a sheaf of grain from each farm one of each of the days. It welcomed in the eating of grain again from the new harvests. This waving grain is meant to symbolize the beautiful souls of G-d's people being waved before Him. It serves as a reminder that He collects a bountiful harvest from the First Fruit, Yeshua.

Shavuot is the goal of Passover and the Counting of the Omer. Deliverance was given so that the revelation of the Torah could take place.

There is a call during the Counting of the Omer to self-reflect, discover sin, and take action to return to the ways of G-d.

In this line up of holidays we are meant to experience the relational journey we take with Yeshua. He has removed our sin and revealed Himself. At Passover, he becomes the sacrifice we did not have, during Firstfruits he becomes the new man, conquering death and becoming a living sacrifice able to cover our sin forever, then on Pentecost (Shavuot) Yeshua reveals his Spirit to us (you can find Pentecost in the book of Acts. Note that the people gathered in Acts can speak in one another's languages and they are preaching the word of G-d to one another).

During this counting of the omer Yeshua appeared to others after He was raised from the dead. Forty days into the counting, Yeshua ascended to Heaven and instructed His followers to stay and receive the Holy Spirit on Shavuot.

You cannot see these sorts of patterns in the modern Christian/Catholic holidays. They do not hold the truths of Scripture, of Yeshua's fulfillment of prophecy, nor do they span the depths of meaning we find in our Creator's calendar.

YOM TERUAH

This is a day to rest and blast the trumpets or the Shofar! Teruah is translated as "shouting" or a "blast" or a "shout of joy!" Psalm 66:1 says, "Shout for joy to God, All the Earth!" Psalms has many of these calls to "shout". At Jericho, Israel and the people of Jericho experienced this same shouting and trumpet blast. This day also recalls a shout of war and of alarm. The same word, Teruah, is used in the referenced stories and verses below.

Again, we have prophecy about Yeshua in this celebration: the coming of the Lord a second time.

> As 1 Thessalonians 4:16 – 18 is written, "For the Lord Himself will descend from heaven with a 'SHOUT', with the voice of an archangel, and with the trumpet of God. And the dead of Christ will rise, and we who are alive and remain shall be caught up together with the Lord. Therefore, comfort one another with these words." [emphasis mine]

> Matthew 24 tells us that after the tribulation, "They will see the Son of Man coming on the clouds of heaven with power and great glory. And He will send his angels with a great sound of a TRUMPET, and they will gather together His elect from the four winds, from one end of heaven to the other." [emphasis mine]

This trumpet blast on Yom Teruah acts as an alarm for what is to come. Ten days after Yom Teruah is Yom Kippur, the Day of Atonement, or the Day of the Lord. (See Joel 2) This is the day in the future where G-d judges all people. The 10 days in between these holidays are called the Days of Awe and they are days of repentance. Yom Teruah is an alarm, a warning that Yom Kippur is coming, that repentance is at hand. It is a John the Baptist moment calling people to prepare themselves for the judgment of Yeshua. Just like in His ministry Yeshua judged the addition and misuse of Scripture by those in power, He will judge those who do not abide by G-d's heart-felt teachings and instructions. He will come again to judge the nations and individual souls. In this day we can look forward to the return of the King and prepare for His work and purpose after that return.

Yom Kippur

We observe this day as one of the Mo-edim, but it is NOT a FEAST. The Feast days we have learned so far are Passover/Unleavened Bread, Pentecost, and the Feast of Tabernacles (also called Sukkot).

We find some of our observance of Yom Kippur in Leviticus 23:26 – 32:

"And (Yahweh) the Lord spoke to Moses saying, "Now on the tenth day of the 7th month is the Day of Atonement. It shall be a time of holy convocation, and you shall afflict yourselves and present a food offering to Yahweh. And you shall not do any work on that very day, for it is a Day of Atonement, to make atonement for you before Yahweh your God. For whoever is not afflicted on that very day shall be cut off from his people. And whoever does any work on that very day, that person I will destroy from among his people. You shall not do any work. It is a statute **FOREVER throughout your generations** in ALL YOUR DWELLING PLACES. It shall be to you a Sabbath of solemn rest, and you shall afflict yourselves. On the ninth day of the month, beginning at evening from evening to evening shall you keep your Sabbath." [emphasis mine]

Again, it is to be obeyed forever no matter where we live. No work is to be done and it is a complete day and Sabbath day. And yes, "forever" here is the Hebrew word, olam. Where it is used it means perpetual, long, futurity, everlasting, etc. Forever means forever.

There is more of a description of this day in Numbers 29:1-6.

If you've noticed, all the information for each Appointed Time is not in one location. You find information in Exodus, Leviticus, Numbers, etc., on each of these days, each section giving more or different information.

We also see Paul and Luke recognizing 'The Fast' as some translations put it.

In the NIV Acts 27:9 says this,

> "Much time had been lost, and sailing had already become dangerous because by now it was after the Day of Atonement."

The Day of Atonement, Yom Kippur, is in the fall. After this time period the journey they were on would have indeed been perilous as the Mediterranean Sea would have been choppy and rough during that time of the year.

Why is Luke telling us this? I believe it is because we are supposed to understand this Feast Day, and its time of year. We are supposed to be observing this still.

Going back 10 days to Yom Teruah, we find the call to repentance. This call leads us up to Yom Kippur, The Day of Atonement. The name of this holiday is also Yom Ha-Kippurim. Kippurim has a root word of Kafar, which is related to cleansing. It is also akin to "Kofer", containing the idea of ransom. Reconciliation.

Yom Kippur was the only time the High Priest could enter the Holy of Holies to ask for reconciliation for the nation of Israel. During the time of the Levitical priesthood, a sacrificial animal was used and blood was sprinkled on the altar. On Yom Kippur, the high priest would sacrifice a bull for the misdeeds of the priests and those in their households.

Lots were drawn to select one of two goats to be a sin offering on behalf of the people. The priest would confess the sins upon the goat that was chosen and then the goat was sent into the wilderness. This was called the scapegoat.

Yeshua fills this holiday full with meaning. He offered his own blood in the Holy of Holies to be the sacrifice for sins so that we can be cleansed. Yom Kippur tells the story of Yeshua's atonement. He was the means for reconciliation for us. Yeshua entered the Holy of Holies, not on earth, but He entered it in Heaven with his own blood, once, to pay for our sins, once and for all. And as He came back to life, He fulfilled the need for a sacrifice for personal sins. He is a living sacrifice and continual testimony of our reconciliation.

We have what Jesus already did and then what He will come to do. There is a future Day of Judgment coming where G-d will judge all the people.

1 Peter 4:17 – 19: "For it is time for judgment to begin with the family of God; and if it begins with us, what will the outcome be for those who do not obey the gospel of God? And, 'if it is hard for the righteous to be saved, what will become of the ungodly and the sinner?' So then, those who suffer according to God's will should commit themselves to their faithful Creator and continue to do good."

Ecclesiastes 12:14: "For God will bring every deed into judgment, including every hidden thing, whether it is good or evil."

In these next verses, my thoughts are in italics.

2 Peter 3:10: "But the Day of the Lord (*Another name for Yom Kippur*) will come like a thief. The Heavens will disappear with a roar; the elements will be destroyed by fire, and the earth and everything done in it will be laid bare. *(The final Day of the Lord, or Day of Atonement, will see all things destroyed, revealed, and judged)* Since everything will be destroyed in this way, what kind of people ought you to be? You ought to live holy and Godly lives as you look forward to the day of God and speed of its coming. (*We are called to DO things that are holy. Not just feel them. This is*

about our hearts being in alignment with the Lord, producing good fruit) That day will bring about the destruction of the heavens by fire, and the elements will melt in the heat. But in keeping with His promise we are looking forward to a new heaven and a new earth, where righteousness dwells. So then dear friends, since you are looking forward to this, make every effort to be found spotless, blameless, and at peace with Him. *(If the Law of God is done away with, how could we possibly "make every effort" to be found "spotless, blameless and at peace"? Uh oh, sounds like works to me!)* Bear in mind that our Lord's patience means salvation, just as our dear brother Paul also wrote you with the wisdom that God gave him. He writes in the same way in all his letters, speaking in them of these matters. His letters contain some things that are hard to understand, which ignorant and unstable people distort, as they do the other Scriptures, to their own destruction. *(Many people throughout history will misinterpret Paul, claiming that he teaches against the Law of G-d. This will lead to destruction.)* Therefore, dear friends, since you have been forewarned, be on your guard so that you may not be carried away by the error of the **lawless** and fall from your secure position." *(Lawlessness means to be without the law. Without who's law? Of course, he means without the Law of G-d. The Torah. "Be on your guard so that you may not be carried away by the error of living without the Torah.")*

The judgment will begin with the people of G-d. Yom Kippur is a time to reflect on how we are following the Lord. Do we walk in His Torah? Do we do it with our hearts and bodies or just our mouths?

We see Yeshua acting out the Day of Atonement rituals before He is crucified. On the Day of Atonement, the high priest had to undergo ritual cleansing. The sacrifice also had to be declared perfect by a high priest. In Matthew 3, John, a high priest, declared that Yeshua was the perfect lamb and son of G-d and then he ritually cleanses Yeshua in the river through baptism. Yeshua received anointing by the Holy Spirit and headed into the wilderness to be tested. Once again, Yeshua embodied the Appointed Times. Each G-d-given celebration teaches us about our Creator, and Yeshua lives in them and can be understood through them.

THE FOOD LAWS

You will find the standards on food in Leviticus 11. Here, G-d tells us what is and is not food. Feel free to take a pass at reading Leviticus 11 and then let's dive in.

There are a few cultures globally who serve and eat almost anything — dogs, cats, living shrimp, bats, you name it, they will serve it up. But most Western countries have already designated some living beings as off limits. Why? This is an important question.

Why, for instance, in America do we not eat eagles, cats, horses, and dolphins? Certainly, something inside of us designates these animals as different than chickens or cows. Something innate tells us of their intelligence, their place in the ecosystem, their dignity.

But, for goodness sakes, why? For those who claim that G-d's food laws were abolished, why are you not willing to chop up a cat and fry it up later on tonight? What is it we inherently know that keeps us from crossing certain culinary boundaries?

In Western countries, we already have food laws. I would submit the Lord's food laws go just a bit further for reasons we can scientifically and religiously debate. Alongside health benefits, spiritual wisdom exists within the instructions on food. Spiritual principles we may not get to fully understand here on this earth. And while some cultures do indeed eat anything that crawls along the earth, many Western cultures were founded on Biblical principles; some that have continued to eek through despite our propensity to abandon them. The food laws are a great example.

But we don't completely have our palates aligned with Yeshua's just yet.

If I may interject a personal story here, it might be helpful. As I learn to follow the food laws, I notice more often the beautiful balance and eco-system G-d has granted humankind. While human life always comes first, I've also started to understand that humans weren't made to go around consuming anything and everything.

We are made to be caretakers of an amazing Earth that provides what we need. Each piece of creation is purposeful and meaningful. As I learned what animals G-d has said are not food, I've also learned where they are in the natural food chain of animals, why they are there, what they are there to do, and perhaps why we are not supposed to consume them. I find my love for science and nature increasing alongside my spiritual sensitivity to the Word of G-d and how He speaks through nature. I cannot make any grand absolute claims that this all came about because I began observing the food laws, but there is a connection that I cannot overlook. As I am changing how I nourish myself, other parts of me are changing that I did not anticipate, and that is a wonderful surprise.

Some may ask whether Yeshua and His disciples followed the food laws and/or upheld them. We can always go back to Yeshua stating, "I did not come to abolish the law but to fulfill it." He had to keep each law in order to be called the PERFECT sacrifice. Perfect according to who's standard? Ours or G-d's? Well, since Yehovah is the judge and He gave us the standards in His law, it follows that Yeshua had to keep the Law perfectly. That includes the food laws.

In order to properly understand what Scripture means whenever the word "food" comes up, we must understand Leviticus 11. You will note that the description of animals we are forbidden to eat describes them as "unclean for you." This phrase means that forbidden animals are not food for humans.

It is not that they are forbidden *foods*. According to Yeshua's word, they are NOT food for us at all. They are like rocks, or grass. They just aren't food. When Yeshua later discusses food, we have to take that definition with us.

So, what clues do we have that Yeshua recognized the food laws? In Mark, we have a pretty strange story where Yeshua heals a demon-possessed man and sends the demons into a herd of pigs. Here's Mark 5, beginning with verse 11:

> "A large herd of pigs was feeding on the nearby hillside. The demons begged Jesus, 'Send us among the pigs; allow us to go into them.' He gave them permission, and the impure spirits came out and went into the pigs. The herd, about two thousand in number, rushed down a steep bank into the lake and were drowned. Those tending the pigs ran off and reported this in the town and countryside, and the people went out to see what had happened. When they came to Jesus they saw the man who had been possessed by the legion of demons, sitting there, dressed and in his right mind; and they were afraid. Those who had seen it told the people what had happened to the demon-possessed man – and told about the pigs as well. Then the people began to plead with Jesus to leave their region."

It would have been against the nature of G-d and G-d's law to destroy another man's herd. A man's way of life was wrecked by Jesus in this tale. The entire herd drowned! But not just any herd, specifically, a herd of PIGS was destroyed.

Now, according to the Torah, is it lawful to herd pigs? Absolutely not. So here we are actually witnessing the fact that Yeshua had no issue allowing the herd of pigs to be destroyed, as keeping an unclean animal for food was in direct opposition to His law. Yeshua behaves with quite an obvious callousness to the outcome of the herdsmen. Likely because it was a sin to herd pigs.

There are other questions I have about this story. Why do the demons ask to go into a herd of unclean animals? Why does Yeshua seem to have mercy on them? Why not just destroy them? There is so much going on here, but it is no coincidence that a herd of pigs is destroyed by the actions of the Lord. It is such a destructive move, that the people of the town ask Yeshua and his party to leave!

Throughout the New Testament, we see Yeshua observing Passover and sharing the food involved in that feast. We watch him share fish and bread and make water into wine. He certainly eats and he certainly feeds people. And it is all food as defined in Leviticus. There is absolutely no place where our Rabbi, the one we are to follow, breaks the food laws.

Later in Mark, when Jesus is feeding the 5,000, he feeds them all with five loaves of bread and two fish. The symbolism in this story points us directly to the heart of Yeshua.

In Scripture, words and numbers always matter.

Five always harkens to the Torah and grace, as the Torah is comprised by the five books of Moses that G-d gave directly from his mouth. Yeshua feeds His people with the Torah.

The number two also has many meanings, but in this context I believe Yeshua was thinking of His two houses. The House of Judah and the House of Israel. The House of Judah was made up of the tribes of Judah and Benjamin. The House of Israel was made up of the other ten tribes. Those ten had been scattered all over the earth, having been conquered years earlier and carried off into other countries.

These two houses are prophesied to become one again. That G-d will re-gather his family from the farthest reaches of the earth. Jesus feeds His people the word of G-d and the prophecy of the two houses in the miracle of the bread and fish. It is fascinatingly deep, and also a recognition that Yeshua came to restore His people to Scripture, not take them away from it. He came to reignite our passion for His law, as it is like bread — filling, sustaining, and life giving. David calls the Law of G-d life and light. Surely it is. (More on this story in later Essays)

Consequently, when discussing food Laws, we must also address Peter's vision. It is really the catalyst for the changes in food laws among the early church, and Christians still today cite this passage as the reason they can eat whatever they want to.

I would encourage you to start by reading Acts 10 and 11. In this section of Scripture, you will see the entire picture of Peter's vision. Let's begin with, well, the beginning! And it doesn't start with Peter's vision. It actually starts with the vision of a man named Cornelius.

Cornelius was a devout Italian Centurion. Interestingly, he was NOT Jewish, but believed in Yeshua and followed Scripture. Not only that, but he gave generously, feared G-d, and remembered the poor. He walked with the Lord.

We must recognize that, at this time, it was not culturally acceptable for Jews and Gentiles (non-Jews) to be in the same home or eating together. According to the Pharisaic tradition, this activity made the Jew "common". And "common" in Scripture describes the act of coming into contact with something "unclean". The exposure to unclean things makes the exposed unclean as well.

While this concept applied to human beings is not Biblical, it was indeed cultural. There is no Biblical Law against eating with people of other nations or cultures, but due to fear of sin and adulteration, Jewish leadership added many cultural laws to G-d's commands.

Later, when Peter's dream is interpreted, G-d corrects his use of the word "common".

G-d granted Cornelius a vision that he should send for Peter. So, Cornelius sent two of his servants and a devout soldier to Joppa to call upon Peter. As they journeyed, Peter received his vision.

In the vision, a sheet comes down where clean (food) and unclean (not food) animals are all over each other. As previously referenced, the contact of clean animals with unclean would have rendered the clean (edible) animals, common. So, when G-d asks Peter to rise up, kill, and eat, Peter resists. Even the clean animals are not edible to him in this situation.

He states, "Not so, Lord, for I have never eaten anything that is common or unclean." (One interesting thing to note here is that Peter, even after Christ had ascended to Heaven, was STILL eating according to Leviticus 11! Surely Christ did not change the food laws after all.) Peter wrestles with the idea of eating unclean animals. Three times Peter and G-d go back and forth. Still Peter doubts what the dream means. G-d rebukes him saying, "What God hath cleansed, that call not thou common." Here we see G-d correct Peter's use of "common".

And, here we begin to understand where G-d is headed with this dream.

If the dream was about food, Peter would no doubt have understood it fully and immediately. I mean, a surface reading of this Scripture has given all Christendom the right to eat whatever they want. But Peter questions this interpretation. He wrestles with it and rightly so. It's the incorrect interpretation. Clearly, this dream is about something else.

Right after this vision, Cornelius's men show up. Sure enough, Peter actually agrees to go to Cornelius's home in violation of the cultural Jewish dictates. Upon arrival, Peter states, "Ye know how that it is an unlawful thing for a man that is a Jew to keep company, or come into one of another nation; but God hath shewed me that I should not call any man common or unclean."

Whoa there, buddy. We thought the dream was about food! But Peter continues, "Of a truth, I perceive that God is no respecter of persons."

The dream was about people.

Well, that's interesting. Peter does NOT go out and preach that Jews can eat whatever they want. In fact, he preaches that all people are considered fit and clean to enter the kingdom of Heaven and to sup with and commune with the Jew. Before G-d, we are neither Jew nor Greek, slave nor free, male nor female, as Paul puts it. This good news allows for Peter to see the Holy Spirit fill these non-Jews and testify of the gospel. What an incredible moment, and one that Peter would have missed had G-d not sent him the vision of the animals.

Most visions and dreams in Scripture are not literal. And once again, Peter's also is not literal. The animals represent peoples and nations. This isn't so far-fetched.

The United States is represented with an Eagle, the United Kingdom with a lion, and so on. It is a well-understood human practice throughout history to represent peoples with animals.

Likewise, this dream is representative of people. Not food. People. The Jews had been treating people the same way they treated animals and food. They had called people "common" and "unclean" when G-d had

NEVER defined people this way. They had forbidden eating with non-Jews despite there being no Law in the Torah requiring such a restriction!

G-d corrects this in Peter's vision, and through the preaching of Peter from that moment on. This essential moment shapes the ministry of Peter and the work of G-d's people for all time. It flew in the face of the traditions of men (not of G-d) in the Jewish culture, and helped return to the Jews who would spread the gospel the intentions G-d had for them in Exodus. Where both Egyptian and Jew came out into the desert together. It was a mixed multitude. Yet G-d treated them all the same. That is how G-d has always viewed people, equally.

We are not like the animals. We are separate. Special. And each can have a place in G-d's kingdom.

We have misinterpreted Peter's dream to our own destruction. Taking the power away from the message of renewal and unity and throwing it to the pigs, so to speak. (See what I did there?) Making his dream about food has trashed the real meaning and the beautiful message. We miss just how important this dream is to his ministry and to ours! Not to mention the tragedy of so many led astray into behavior that G-d has said is unacceptable. Food laws still exist. It's time to return to what G-d has commanded.

Let's take a look at a couple more verses. In Isaiah 66, there is a discussion about G-d bringing His people back together again in the end of all things. G-d rebukes those who are the enemy of His peoples. In verses 15-16, we hear:

> 15 For, behold, the Lord will come with fire, and with his chariots
> like a whirlwind, to render his anger with fury, and his
> rebuke with flames of fire.

16 For by fire and by his sword will the Lord plead with all flesh:
and the slain of the Lord shall be many.
17 They that sanctify themselves, and purify themselves in the gardens
behind one tree in the midst, **eating swine's flesh**, and the
abomination, and the mouse, shall be consumed together,
saith the Lord. [emphasis mine]

Here is a mention of the eating of pigs by those who practice empty religion. Swine's flesh is mentioned specifically. Those who preach that they love the Lord, but do not obey the Lord's Commands, are consumed by the fire of G-d. Rough. But we should heed this warning. Even in the end, G-d will be looking for those who have a care about what they put in their mouths.

One final concern over our lack of care for how we treat our bodies can be found within the idea that our bodies are a temple. 1 Cor. 6:19-20 states:

"Or do you not know that your body is a temple of the Holy Spirit within you, whom you have from God? You are not your own for you were bought with a price. So glorify God in your body."

Daniel 9 and Matthew 24 discuss the "abomination of desolation" that would happen both with Antiochus IV and in the end times with the antichrist. In 167 BC Antiochus IV tortured and oppressed the Jews and anyone who practiced clean eating or kept the Sabbath or Feast Days. He became a historical mini version of the Revelation Anti-Christ, desecrating the temple by sacrificing a pig on an altar to Zeus, and enacting the "abomination of desolation" we see mentioned in Daniel 9 and Matthew 24. His extreme tortures of the Jews lasted 3 and a-half years before the Jews stood up to Antiochus and were successful. He provides a picture of the coming Anti-Christ for the Believer.

If the Anti-Christ persona makes it his job to desecrate the temple, and one of the desecrations involves pig sacrifice, should we consider what a desecration of our bodies looks like? This personal connection I've made may not ring true in your mind and heart, but I'd prefer not be associated with historic OR future versions of Anti-Christ behavior, especially when it comes to the temple of the Holy Spirit!

YESHUA is Found in the Beginning

One of the inescapable, but ever so subtle, complications in the American Church's definition of Yeshua can be found in how He is or is not tied to the other personalities of this great G-d we see in Scripture. How do we connect Yeshua to the Father and the Holy Spirit? Does Yeshua exercise what was given at the beginning? Who is doing what and how can we test it?

Growing up, there was always this impression that the G-d of the Old Testament and the G-d of the New Testament were different. Somehow, G-d changed. He became nicer, less "judgy", squishier and more accessible. While accessibility certainly made a shift in the coming of Yeshua (instead of seeing G-d in plagues and parting of seas and only sometimes human — as in the encounters with Abraham — we see him in human form through the entirety of his embodied ministry), Jesus, if I may, is no departure at all from the G-d we see in the Old Testament. And He exhaustively proved that to us.

The characteristics of the Father are written on Christ. What is written on Christ is supposed to be replicated in us. We, the people of G-d, carry the DNA of our G-d.

I grew up immersed in a firm belief in G-d and in the Bible. I truly fell in love with Yahweh through nature far before I did through knowledge. I saw His handiwork and I relished in it. I'll never forget climbing an aspen tree in our backyard. It was fall and the leaves were each so brightly glowing. Up in the tree I was surrounded by gold, glittering as sunlight passed through it and I thanked G-d and wondered at the beautiful things He had made.

That magical and yet so tangible G-d was put into some finely tuned boxes for a time. Boxes that were built through a church history mingled with legends and pagan god mythology. The G-d of the Old Testament became rigid, judgmental, terrifying; requiring sacrifice and demanding behavioral adjustments. The G-d of the New Testament was our Savior. Yes, of course our Savior from sin, but also (as was always implied) our Savior from the terrifying G-d of the Old Testament. He saved us from judgment and legalism.

Now, maybe this is a harsh rendering of Christianity in the 1980s through today. But is it really that far off? The most misunderstood man in the Bible, Paul, is still quoted and misquoted enough to make us believe that at least the G-d of the Old Testament seemed less manageable. And Jesus seems much more approachable, much easier to work with.

And in one sense this isn't wrong. The humanness of Christ draws people to Himself. This all-powerful Being, shockingly, died for people. It is a strange story among the world religions. Most man-made deities would never deign to stoop so low for such unworthy creatures as humans. So yes, we have a very down-to-earth G-d. Legally, the only way we could have access to our eternal selves was to be reborn through a second, perfect Adam. Yeshua loved us enough to become human, conquer death, and remarry His bride.

But is Yeshua really a departure from the Old Testament? All the modern doctrinal talk about the first five books of the Bible being just a way to judge people, or simply a metaphor for what was to come, or even the idea that they are mythology and Jesus being the most important and real thing: could any of this be true?

As I grew up a bit and heard all the theories, I started to ask questions. Truly, I knew modern American Christianity fairly well. From kindergarten all through to high school graduation, I attended private Christian schools, listened to seminary teachers lead Bible classes, had weekly services at school and at church, attended Christian camps, and lived in a Christian home where we listened to Christian music and radio (the only departure being car rides with dad and his love of 70's rock music).

I've heard the same sermons preached hundreds of times. The same doctrines espoused thousands of times. And, attending a charismatic school for high school led me to all sorts of research of my own. No offense to Charismatics, but weekly sessions of speaking in tongues during our required school services always led to longer services, less class time, and no life change for those students afterwards.

To put it mildly, this was mostly a show.

And I'll never forget my first year at the school in 6th grade, heading right into the principal's office, Corinthians in my hand and the list of rules Paul gives for speaking in tongues during services. I was furious, and of course, not listened to.

However, the good research I had done helped me continue to discover my love of the Bible and my scrutiny of American Christianity. By 6th grade, I'd read through the Bible around seven times. I didn't understand a lot of it, but I loved it. The stories intrigued me, the language, the promises, the failures of people and faithfulness of God.

Speed ahead and young Rachel would not have recognized adult Rachel. My 20s were truly a disaster. I made every wrong decision based on the doctrines I'd learned in church, **not** the ones I'd read in my little pink Bible or fought so hard for at the principal's desk. In doctrinal and spiritual confusion, I crashed and burned, really, really hard.

I realized the Christ I'd met in the Aspen tree wasn't the one I heard about on Sunday mornings. There was not enough mystery or power or grounded-ness in the Yeshua who suddenly shifted everything in the 4th millenia. I wrecked my life, but for some reason, I couldn't shake the G-d of the Bible. Maybe, because I was still curious, maybe because I started asking G-d who He really was, for whatever reason, He was there when I called.

My redemption came in discovering that the G-d of the Bible answers questions, is not afraid of intellect, has no aversion to science, and He desires to be known and loved. Known deeply beyond surface interactions and blind assumptions, Yeshua desires relationship built on truth with the people He created from that truth. The G-d I actually had wanted and even more so, *needed,* to meet in my adult life emerged out from the fog of poor doctrine. He boldly broke through the lies I had believed.

He was the G-d my heart had met as a little girl. Not a G-d I could bend to my will. Not one I could make of my own psychological desires, this G-d had standards and boundaries and yet was like the wind moving over the earth, with mystery and power and hope. This G-d was the one I needed to know in order to truly change my life.

It's taken me until my…let's just say, mid-30s, to really see the Bible. But all those years of reading did not go to waste. And here I am with a new and more substantive picture of Christ and of salvation. A picture I feel called to share.

This sharing means I don't skirt uncomfortable discoveries. One cannot address modern church doctrine without tackling Paul. It feels necessary for the reader to first know that the New Testament is an 80% repeat of the Old. (See my Essay, *Righting Paul*)

This fact should help us understand why my favorite scholars follow a simple rule in understanding the New Testament. You must first define the words you are seeing in the New Testament by how they first appear in the *Old Testament*. It is essential to understand that the New Testament is simply a repetition and fulfillment of the cycles G-d set up in the Old Testament.

We have a foundation given to us where the definition of terms grants us the keys to understanding the rest of Scripture. One amazing image created by Christopher Harrison shows just how repetitious the Bible is, with more than 63,000 cross references in total.

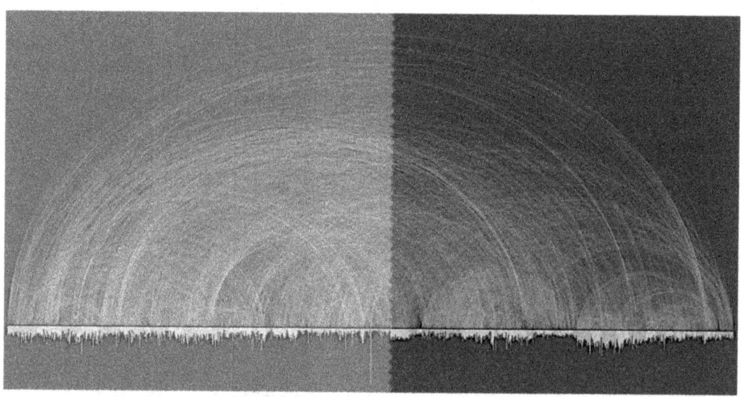

The New Testament repeats the Old in perfect patterns. Furthermore, just as Jesus is telling us that the Father is in Him, Paul is consistently telling us Messiah is in us. In fact, in the King James Bible, Paul says the phrase "In Christ" 83 times. What does "In Christ" mean? Let's look at the New Covenant.

Jeremiah 31:31: Behold, the days come, saith the Lord, that I will make a new covenant with the house of Israel, and with the house of Judah:

32 Not according to the covenant that I made with their fathers in the
day that I took them by the hand to bring them out of the land of
Egypt; which my covenant they brake, although I was an husband
unto them, saith the Lord:
33 But this shall be the covenant that I will make with the house of
Israel; After those days, saith the Lord, I will put my law in their
inward parts, and write it in their hearts; and will be their
God, and they shall be my people.
34 And they shall teach no more every man his neighbor, and every man
his brother, saying, Know the Lord: for they shall all know me, from
the least of them unto the greatest of them, saith the Lord: for I will
forgive their iniquity, and I will remember their sin no more."

First, the Lord tells us who He will make His New Covenant with. It is with the House of Judah and the House of Israel.

Not Christianity, not American churchgoers. It will be with His Church. And He defines His Church as these two houses, Judah and Israel.

We are grafted into His House, not the other way around. Next, let's look at what completes the process. "I will put my teaching within them." It will be different than the covenant with Israel when they came out of Egypt. The Bible uses the word "teaching" here. In the OT, the covenant G-d made with Israel is called the Law. But the Hebrew of this word for Law actually means **teaching and instruction**.

To "break the Law" meant that you missed the mark. You aimed improperly. We have a bow and an arrow pointed towards or away from the bullseye. When we point away, that is sin.

Paul explains that the New Covenant is a better covenant. Stone can be destroyed, but each of us carrying Torah on our Flesh is an unstoppable force. It cannot be easily forgotten or manipulated by pen, and it will spread to the entire world. If G-d's Laws become a part of us, we are now in relationship with the bullseye. Our aim improves.

When Paul tells us that we are no longer "under the Law" He is telling us that instead of being bound by it as an outsider (He calls the law a guardian), we are joined to the Body of Christ. We are part of Yeshua. We are His family. We are no longer outside of it. Yeshua will not be condemning His own body. We have taken on HIS DNA, HIS identity. And as mentioned in Galatians 3, we have taken on this identity through belief. We are "heirs to the promise" which could not be fulfilled through our bodily practice of the Law, but which could only be fulfilled through the work of G-d. To really understand Galatians 3 where "under the law" is mentioned, one must go back to the context which is the discussion starting in Galatians 2.

At the time of Paul's ministry there was incredible division between the orthodox Jews and Jews who believed in Messiah, etc. The greatest subject of division was circumcision. There is an obsession with this discussion in Paul's writings because many new Believers were also claiming that salvation and circumcision were necessarily linked. Paul preached against this misuse of the law of circumcision. This is the law discussed in Galatians 3, which is why he brings up Abraham! Abraham was not a Jew and when he was called to obedience to G-d, he was also not circumcised. Hence, Paul makes a beautiful point to the Jewish orthodoxy that circumcision and salvation are NOT linked. Even the founder of the faith was not circumcised when he was called into G-d's service. Notice Galatians 2:17:

"But if, in seeking to be justified in Christ, we Jews find ourselves also among the sinners, doesn't that mean that Christ promotes sin? Absolutely not! If I rebuild what I destroyed, then I really would be a lawbreaker."

Paul never promotes a change in the Law of G-d. Only that we understand that the only operating system that can grant us eternal life is in Yeshua's DNA and not in our own works. We cannot by our own hands save ourselves. He makes this point over and over again. Hence his reprimand, "You foolish Galatians... Did you receive the Spirit by the works of the law or by believing what you heard?" He basically asks, did you receive G-d's Spirit when you were circumcised, or when you believed in Yeshua? This of course extends to all the Law. You cannot come to the Father if you don't accept that His son is Yeshua and that He is the Law. (See much more on this in my Essay, *Righting Paul*)

You cannot come if you have not been reconciled to this perfection with a DNA you do not have access to without Him. He is the goal and aim. And any attempts at climbing into the sheepfold without going through Him as the gate will be unsuccessful.

This is not really so difficult to understand. "To love the Lord is to obey His Commands." This is repeated thoroughly throughout the New Testament through Yeshua, John and others. We know obedience reflects relationship. But it is not salvation. Simple.

There is also this to ponder. There are situations we come across daily where we may forget what G-d's Law even says or how to decide what G-d's law would be when presented with difficult decisions and we need the internal work of G-d to give us that direction and instruction as well as a deeper understanding of Scripture. I think divorce often falls into this category. There does seem to be Scriptural foundation for divorce. G-d Himself gave Israel a divorce. However, the details need deeper evaluation and reasons should be heavily weighed against the Scriptural love of marriage and covenant.

The Holy Spirit can reveal just how and when neglect, abuse, or adultery become enough to justify a divorce. This, of course, goes beyond a tertiary reading and keeping of G-d's Law. In some cases, G-d may ask an individual to stay in a marriage, even when the Law would allow for separation.

At times, the Believer has needed access to deeper Biblical understanding, something we often don't have on our own without the indwelling of G-d.

We cannot keep G-d's things perfectly without Christ's DNA. We just can't. Even if we did, the Law does not provide a route for salvation anyways! It just isn't there.

Let's return to the main point. Our DNA must be in Yeshua a DNA we are still working to understand. In Him we become "new".

So, let's go back to Paul's 83 mentions of being *In Christ.* (See Col 2:9-10, 1 Cor. 6:17, 1 Cor. 12:27, Gal. 3:27, Col 3:1-3 and so on)

Why does he say it so often? It seems quite possible that there becomes a link greater than most Believers understand to Yeshua as the Law. He was the "*Word* in the Beginning", and the prophecy states that in our times, He will write himself on our hearts. He will write His law on our hearts. Additionally, when Paul says He is in Christ, I think he is patterning his line of thought after Yeshua and Yeshua's unity with The Father.

Jesus consistently told us that He was in the Father. In my NIV Bible, in the book of John, Jesus says "My Father" or mentions He has come from the Father, or is in the Father, or does what the Father tells him to, or has approval from the Father, an enormous number of times. Out of the 391 verses in John where Jesus is speaking, 201 have him talking about the Father, the Father's Kingdom or praying to the Father. This comprises over half of the red words in the gospel of John!

Of all the things Jesus (and clearly John) wanted us to be sure about, He wanted us to know where He came from, who He came from, who's Word he was speaking, and who sent Him. There can be no doubt, Jesus and G-d the Father have the same goal, they are one, and they have one purpose. There is no division between the G-d we see in the Old Testament and the G-d we see in the New.

Yeshua was desperate for us to understand the unity He shares with the Father.

It is so plain, and yet we have often missed it. Replacing the G-d of the OT with some harsh, mythic far away G-d who couldn't possibly be real or kind, and making Jesus our squishy friend who we bring out of our pockets when we are having a tough day. Neither of these perspectives gives any credence or reality to the G-d of the Bible. The complete G-d of the Bible suffers no division from Genesis through Revelation.

He also wanted the Jews He was addressing to be well aware of His identity according to prophecy and their requirements of the Messiah. At the burning bush, Moses asked how the nation of Israel would know who he was. How would they know to follow him? G-d gave Moses signs to use so the people could trust they were following the right person.

Later, when G-d wrote the Torah, the people of G-d learned the Deuteronomy 13 test. This test defines a false prophet and clarifies how to deal with them. They are defined as those who lead people away from the G-d of the Torah into other practices.

I used to see Jesus as so judgmental and sarcastic when he would mention the people's need for signs. But perhaps, He was at times telling them He understood that G-d had always given them signs and tests to analyze the prophets who would come. And since He was the one who wrote the rules, He was going to abide by them and provide some signs so that they could be assured of His identity.

Furthermore, John tells us that Messiah IS the Torah. The New Covenant tells us that Torah is written on our flesh. Torah (Yeshuah) comes into our hearts. This is salvation. Did we know that we were asking for Torah to be written in our hearts? Do we understand that the covenant that Israel broke could only be fulfilled by a man who could keep the covenant perfectly? And now, through Yeshua's perfect Covenant keeping, G-d would see an unbroken covenant when He sees His followers. This can only be through the blood of Christ, which covers us and makes us perfect covenant keepers before the Lord. A broken covenant led to death. A restored covenant leads to life.

A man had to keep the covenant perfectly, die and defeat death in order to restore mankind to it's rightful, Garden of Eden state. We are not there yet. But now it is possible. Yeshua now holds the keys to death and Hades and will restore what was taken from Adam.

Because Yeshua provides a barrier, we can now have intimate relationship with G-d. And the process of the New Covenant is that we begin to keep G-d's things perfectly until we no longer have to teach each other. Until we all just know it in our hearts. We become "in Christ".

Because Yeshua kept His side and our side of the covenant for us, both sides of the covenant are fulfilled. His sacrifice doesn't get rid of the Law, it establishes the Law's perfection and that the Law becomes a part of our flesh because of the work of Christ. The covenant is now in our flesh, which means that we are "one with Christ". We are one with the bullseye.

So: Christ is in the Father and we are In Christ. The route to the Father across that broken covenant is Christ, and we have entered that space.

Does this sound like the Law has been done away with?

The parable of the seed can help us here. (Matthew 13) The seed is the Word. When it is planted in good ground, it produces fruit. Jesus is the Word, planted in the ground after His death and raised to life as the resurrection and the "first fruits of new life".

The *Word* is the Torah. It is planted in our hearts. It should produce fruit. Starting in John 12:20, Jesus talks about the kernel of wheat that falls to the ground.

> "Unless a kernel of wheat falls to the ground and dies, it remains only a single seed. But if it dies, it produces many seeds. The man who loves his life will lose it, while the man who hates his life in this life will keep it for eternal life. Whoever serves me must follow me; and where I am, my servant also will be. My Father will honor the one who serves me."

Yeshua is the Word, the seed that gets planted, and as He died we die to our old nature. This in order to take the Torah into our very flesh. We die to Adam, the old man. And we allow the seed of Christ to take root in us. We are "reborn".

Yeshua died and was put in the ground. Seeds fall to the ground and die. Then, suddenly, they break free to produce new life.

Paul calls Yeshua the firstfruits. Not only a reference to one of the feasts of the Old Testament, called the Feast of Firstfruits, which celebrates new life, but a reference to the new seed of the second Adam; the perfect, incorruptible seed, which could produce generations of incorruptible seed.

The Word written on our flesh should produce fruit. What is fruit? "You will know them by their fruit" is an important Biblical principle, but what does it mean?

Our fruit is what we do. Time and again the good fruit equates to acts of obedience to our Yeshua, who was the Word who produced the first fruit, the new Adam, so that many could come to Him.

Is it any wonder that as the New Testament writers talk about obedience, they were referencing Torah? Not just because the New Testament was being written as they were speaking (the only written word at the time was the Law, aka the first five books of the Old Testament, and the OT books of the Prophets!), but because the route to obedience can be found in G-d's teaching and instruction, the Torah. Obedience produces the fruit.

As Jesus told us, "Go and make disciples of all nations, teaching them to obey." OBEY! When you start hitting the mark, you have become a master marksman, able to discern and know what is good from evil and able to aim for the target and hit it more often. In the spiritual realm, this is maturity. And it produces life and fruit in abundance.

G-d's Laws From the Beginning til Now

Holocaust survivor and renowned writer Eli Wiesel famously stated, "G-d is G-d because He remembers." Learning, wisdom, knowledge, and even whole cultures can be lost, without correct memory. G-d has old memory. Every Covenant, every Promise, it is all before Him constantly. We forget.

His memory reaches before time.

In Genesis 26:5, the Bible tells us that Abraham kept the Torah. How could he have done that when it was not written down? Theories abound. But from Seth on, either the Laws of G-d that Adam and Eve had perhaps learned (consider that Cain and Abel knew they needed to bring an offering) spread through oral teaching, OR Abraham observed many of the Laws of God through observance of what he discovered in the natural world. Or perhaps Abraham heard the Lord directly and was willing to obey. Whether oral or inspired, or a mixture of both, oral tradition and a heart keenly listening to the Creator, the Law had not always been written down. Yet, people like Abraham still kept the heart of it!

Oral tradition was followed by the clarity of Law burned into stone. It's important to note that the day Moses was given the stone tablets was 50 days after the Hebrew people had left Egypt. This day was a Feast, or a religious holiday, that the Bible commands us to celebrate. It was Shavuot, what we now call Pentecost.

On that day of Shavuot, the Law was clarified by the fiery hand of G-d on stone tablets. In the New Testament, tongues of fire appear and people testify of G-d's Word to one another on Shavuot (Pentecost).

This was a new imprinting of the heart.

There is no coincidence here. As G-d's Law was written in fire onto stone on the day of Pentecost in the OT, it was subsequently written *in tongues of fire* on hearts on the day of Pentecost in the New Testament. Pentacost (Shavuot) fulfills the heart of the giving of the Torah at Sinai. And a miracle came with it to prove its uniqueness and prophetic importance: people could preach G-d's Word to one another in different languages they did not know.

Shavuot is the undoing of the tower of Babel. Where rebelliousness caused G-d to divide people, acceptance of Yeshua caused G-d to unite people. Praise Yehovah!

So, given this, what does Yeshua say about His role with the Torah?

> Matthew 5:17: Yeshua tells us, "Do not think that I have come to abolish the law and the prophets. I have not come to abolish but to fulfill them."

The word for fulfill in this verse is the Greek, "pleroo". According to Strong's Dictionary, this word means to furnish (or imbue, diffuse, influence), execute (an office), verify (or coincide with a prediction), etc.:--accomplish, fill (up), fulfil, (be, make) full (come), fully preach, perfect, supply.

The majority of the definition implies making **more full, fully preaching,** etc. Now, let's figure out what Jesus meant here.

First, we must note that his phrase "not to abolish but to fulfill" was a well-known Hebrew idiom. It was used to discern between correct and incorrect interpretation of the Torah. If you abolished the Torah, you had misinterpreted it, twisted it. Your teaching was unfounded and you had destroyed its meaning. If you had fulfilled the Torah, you had "fully preached" the truth perfectly.

We must take a moment to digest this. This wording was a well-known Hebrew phrase used by religious teachers in the ancient near east. This Hebrew idiom tells us the true meaning of "fulfill," or pleroo. It means to **correctly interpret**. To fill full of meaning. Jesus came to rightly teach us the Law and how it is properly applied.

However, let's pretend for just a second that pleroo means what the modern church has tried to make it mean. Let's say it means to "bring to completion" or to "end." If Jesus meant for fulfill to mean "end" or "complete," the phrase would read as such. "I did not come to abolish but to end the law and the prophets." In this reading, end and abolish mean the same thing. It makes no logical sense. This cannot be the correct interpretation.

Jesus must have meant that fulfill was to fully preach and to fill full of meaning. Kind of like asking for a refill on my delicious cup of coffee. Jesus filled the coffee cup full. So, what do I do with it then? Do I drink it, or do I throw it out? (If it's me, that thing is gonna get downed.)

Jesus was preaching that the Law and the Prophets would now be MORE meaningful, more full for us. We would now have a deeper understanding of the Law, and therefore MORE reason to follow it, not less.

> In Matthew 5 Jesus teaches, "For truly I tell you, until heaven and earth disappear, not the smallest letter, not the least stroke of a pen, will by any means disappear from the Law until everything is accomplished. Therefore, anyone who sets aside one of the least of these commands and teaches others accordingly will be called least in the kingdom of heaven, but whoever practices and teaches these commands will be called great in the kingdom of heaven. For I tell you that unless your righteousness surpasses that of the Pharisees and the teachers of the law, you will certainly not enter the kingdom of heaven."

Then Jesus tells them how to be better than the Pharisees:

> "You have heard that it was said to the people long ago, 'You shall not murder, and anyone who murders will be subject to judgment.' But I tell you that anyone who is angry with a brother or sister will be subject to judgment. Again, anyone who says to a brother or sister, 'Raca,' is answerable to the court. And anyone who says, 'You fool!' will be in danger of the fire of hell. Therefore, if you are offering your gift at the altar and there remember that your brother or sister has something against you, leave your gift there in front of the altar. First go and be reconciled to them; then come and offer your gift."

Jesus goes on about dealing with our brothers and sisters in obedience to Torah, and this is where He tells his audience to cut out their own eye before they let it cause them to sin. Better to have one less eye than to be thrown into hell. Jesus goes on to provide even more strict guidelines in order to produce righteousness.

> "Do not even look at a woman lustfully, do not give an oath, do not divorce, turn the other cheek, hand someone your coat if they want to sue you for your shirt, if someone forces you to go a mile with them go two instead, love your enemies and pray for those who persecute you."

JESUS IS TOUGH!!!! Remind you of anyone? (G-d of the OT anybody?!!)

Jesus takes the Law and *goes a step further.*

He goes straight to the heart. The amount of humility and tongue-biting, teeth-clenching, emotion-stuffing self-control it would take to do as Jesus asks is extraordinary. He says this is how you become better than the Pharisees and Sadducees. He isn't just talking about our actions now, He is talking about where the Law is about to be written. It's about to be written on your heart, and with that heart in alignment, you are perfect. You will not break the covenant or Torah. In fact, "In Christ" you will be better than physical enactors of G-d's Laws, you will be united to the Spirit of G-d's Laws. Your heart will be fully submitted.

He doesn't get rid of Torah, He points to the very place the Torah is going to be written — right on our hearts.

> In John 5:46, Jesus says, "If you believed Moses you would believe me for he wrote about me. But you didn't believe Moses, so how can you believe in me?"

Moses wrote the Torah. In these first five books, we find amazing teaching, salvation of a people, a call to repentance, and acceptance of covenant with the Lord. We must conclude that Yeshua is as John tells us. He is the Torah: the living, breathing Word of G-d.

Yeshua Used Numbers and Symbols to Teach Us

Scripture is replete with stories and numbers that point us to deeper meanings. How I wish we were taught how to pay attention to these clues in the Christian church, but since it seemed too "Jewish" at one point, these amazing concepts were thrown out of regular church doctrine. Despite that, the messages are still there, hidden in the stories. Jesus used numbers or "gematria" to communicate deeper meaning as He performed one of his most memorable miracles.

I've already mentioned this story of Yeshua feeding thousands with just five loaves of bread and two fish. Perhaps you know this story from your childhood.

The number "5" appears often and informs us that some deeper understanding is hidden in the text. Five always relates to the Torah (the first five books of the Old Testament). It is also often compared to the 10 Commandments, with five commands being about loving G-d, and five about loving others. We also know that 5 is associated with the concept of Grace.

In this particular miracle, Yeshua fed (grace) the masses the five loaves (the Torah), then told them He, Himself is "the bread of life." Bread is also Scripturally related to knowledge. As Jesus told Satan in the wilderness in Matthew 4, "Man cannot live on **bread** alone but on every **Word**..." Yeshua is the Torah and the Word. He is the Bread of life.

David understood this concept. When he set out to kill Goliath, he chose five smooth stones from a river. From living waters, he chose the Torah to slay the Giant. In essence, he takes Jesus to kill Goliath. (See more on this in my essay on Worship)

And what about the two fish? Fish represent life in the Bible. In the Biblical mediteranean culture, one would see a fish darting in the water and know life was in the water. The Hebrew letter Nun is used for fish.

That letter is sometimes inverted. The inverted noon meant more than just life. It meant *life from the dead.* Jesus fed the thousands with life, life that could even come back from the dead.

Two harkens to the two Houses, or groups of tribes of Israel. Before Jesus' time, the people of G-d were divided into a Northern Kingdom (House of Israel) and the Southern Kingdom (House of Judah). The Northern Kingdom had been scattered after being disobedient. They became so scattered that they forgot who they were. This is true to this day. But G-d intends to reunite His kingdom and the two houses, hence the parable of the prodigal son. Jesus fed the thousands his Torah and the promise of a reunited house. G-d is, we must be reminded, all about family.

The total food used for this miracle: five loaves and two fish. Or, seven items.

Seven corresponds to completion and creation. The creation was completed in seven days. So, in this miracle, Yeshua fed them Torah and Life from living waters which would bring reunification, recreation, completeness. Bread and water. Knowledge and baptism. Yeshua and Eternal Life. And feeding them these items gave them wholeness. Salvation. Restoration.

Jesus says, "You must eat of my body and drink of my blood in order to come into the kingdom of heaven." (John 6:53)

Yeshua = Bread = Torah
Yeshua = Blood = Water = Life

Jesus constantly references Moses and tells us that He is in the writings of Moses. Therefore, to believe in Yeshua in a literal way, one must accept Moses in a literal way. Yeshua's legitimacy comes from the beginning. He ruled there as He will rule the end.

Yeshua requests that we eat of His Word (Moses' writings) and drink waters of life (salvation) in order to understand the kingdom of Heaven.

This does not imply that salvation comes through works. It declares that we must believe what G-d wrote in order to accept His salvation.

Belief comes first.

If you don't believe something, you certainly won't act upon it. Moses must be believed to understand and follow Jesus, because Moses wrote about the character attributes of the one true G-d and the character requirements of the Messiah and His followers. These tenets are identified in the feeding of the 5,000. G-d's people needed restoration of Torah and the true understanding of Yeshua.

What we are really talking about here is the DNA of Christ. In Him are the characteristics of our G-d and the characteristics of the church body He is building.

In sharing just this one story where each word and number communicates precious information, I hope I've inspired you to better appreciate the miraculous and incomparable Bible. It is intricate, coded and filled with deeper meaning and psychology. It performs in a way other ancient texts cannot. There are material AND subliminal messages when you start to search it more deeply. Gematria is just the beginning.

This mystery and wonder applies to the science of the universe right down to the science of our bodies and how they connect to prove a flawless Creator.

OUR DNA REFLECTS YESHUA

I'm sure this chapter has brought a few pieces of obedience to the forefront that perhaps the reader was not aware are part of our walk with G-d. There are many more to dig into and many social issues that this book will attempt to thoughtfully cover.

But at this point in a chapter about the real Yeshua, I thought it appropriate to share the most tangible evidence I've found yet, of G-d's mastery over Creation and intricacy in weaving His Laws into what we can scientifically observe.

The unity that Yeshua has with the Father, as He makes clear in the book of John, cannot be overstated. And shockingly, you will find that unity is even reflected in our DNA. Let me show you how.

Physicist John Wheeler coined the term, "It from bit", ultimately positing that physics tells us matter starts with information. This simple scientific acknowledgement allows us to appreciate the Biblical creation story more deeply. Genesis tells us that G-d spoke (information), and *then* creation came into being. Information came before matter (science is just now beginning to discover that sound itself has matter).

If you manipulate the information, the outcome changes. Let's say you manipulate the DNA of a seed, it will produce a warped or mutated version of the original. If you manipulate human DNA, it can produce cancers and diseases and deformities. If you manipulate the DNA of Christ, it creates deformities and cancers in the "body" of Christ. Yeshua is constantly telling us that His DNA is that of the Father's. It is that of Torah. When we manipulate that message, we produce an unhealthy result.

One of my favorite Bible teachers is Brad Scott[xxv]. While he has recently passed away, his teachings will last in their profound and scientific depth. He keenly observed the natural world and its spiritual application. Knowing that the spiritual kingdom is "like a field" as Yeshua tells us in his many field parables, makes it that much easier to make inferences between the physical and spiritual dimensions. (See Matthew 13, 20 and 21)

G-d wants us to see His things when we walk out our front door, the basic things we can observe in creation. So, Scott always started at the beginning, creation. Many of the following ideas are inspired from or come directly from Scott's teachings. While G-d revealed a few to me, my next steps were to research what I had been told. In researching, Scott often had carefully laid out in advance what I thought was such a unique take. Look him up, it's worth the time. (Wildbranch Ministries)

In order to make a universe, you need energy, space, and matter. In the beginning, G-d (energy) created the heavens (space) and the earth (matter). (Whoever wrote the Torah must have been a lot smarter than we are.)

Without our scientific tools, the author knew the required building blocks thousands of years before modern science could explain it. Ancient Greek mythology poses that gods slept with each other to create each element. Chaos gave birth to Erebus (darkness) and Nyx (night). Etc. According to Brittanica, Pan Gu, an ancient Chinese Daoist figure of creation, came forth from an egg. One legend has him shaping the universe and the earth. The other has the universe coming from his corpse and that humans emerged from parasites that infected his body.

Ancient religions had all sorts of interesting ideas about the origins of everything but many of them lack scientific standing.

In contrast, the Bible has scientific order and structure to the creation of the universe. Many of the known laws of the universe were discovered by Christians who had avidly studied their Bibles, from Newton to

Kepler to Copernicus. Through revelation and observation, they found the Torah is literally true in addition to its other modes of meaning, like foreshadowing, analogy, and mystery.

In defense of its literal truth, let me pose a question. What are the chances of accurate fulfillment of 300 prophecies about a person given 250 years before that person's birth? Let me answer that for you: It's not possible. The chances of just 16 of these prophecies taking place is 10 to the 48th power. There is simply no way in the universe that even 16 prophecies would be fulfilled. And yet, the Old Testament has 300 prophecies given hundreds of years before Yeshua that He fulfilled. This is serious business here. We must take the Old Testament seriously, especially if we take Yeshua seriously. (Thank you to Brad Scott for this info!)

Colossians 1:16 – 17 tells us that, "By Him all things are held together. By Him all things consist." Let's break this down. "Consist" in Greek means that all things are stood up and held together. "Him" is referring to Jesus, or (as the apostle John so beautifully called him), "the Word."

If we check into the Hebrew. we see that "consist" is the word "tzav," which is related to or from the root of the word Mitzvah. A Mitzvah refers to one, or all, of the Commandments of G-d. So, the verse could also say, "**By Him all things are from the Word of God**." It is no wonder that God SPOKE creation into existence. He spoke His *Word.* His Torah. He had the information — like the DNA — and He used that Word (information) to bring creation into being.

How can words create something? We know that resonating frequencies in water can create the colors of the rainbow and can create light. But we still don't fully understand resonating frequencies. (We don't fully understand electricity, either.)

We know that the world is filled with things that are seen and unseen. It's physically possible that resonating frequencies can bring that which is unseen into the seen, and unknown into the known. With the recent discoveries that sound carries matter, many scientific questions arise. Yet the Bible has suggested a high level of power in the tongue.

> Proverbs 18:21 "Death and life are in the power of the tongue and those who love it will eat of its fruit."

> Romans 10:17 "So faith comes from what is heard and the message is heard through the word about Christ."

Salvation comes from "**hearing**" Our tongues direct the power of the sounds we make and the words we speak. G-d spoke the universe into existence and we resonate to that which was spoken from the beginning. Through the creation story, a deep spiritual and physical principle is revealed. "It from bit."

In drilling down to the building blocks of life as we know it, the Word reveals an important relationship between G-d, the Body of Christ, and the physical realities of our human bodies.

The idea of Torah is originally defined as teaching and "instructions." Scientists use the same word, "instruction" to describe what's written in our DNA. In fact, scientists will describe DNA as "instructions" for "building." The "bit" that inspires building blocks for spiritual and physical life has the same principles in this case.

Those DNA instructions form words, paragraphs, and sentences. DNA describes our biology using letters and it contains chromosomes wound up into genomes. These genomes are made up of three-letter combinations called codons. We call these "letter" combinations because they work just like language does to form information just like we form words. From Nature.com[xxvi] "The three-letter nature of codons means that the four nucleotides found in mRNA — **A, U, G, and C — can produce a total of 64 different combinations**. Of these 64 codons, 61 represent amino acids, and the remaining three represent stop signals, which trigger the end of protein synthesis."

Interestingly, the Hebrew language is based on 3-letter words that form the foundations for all the words in the Hebrew language. Hebrew root words are a lot like codons.

DNA is a long, unbroken string of codons, much like the ancient Torah scrolls, which had no breaks in them. Torah scrolls were at one time laid out in long lines of unbroken letters. Consistent with my theory, in our bodies entities called ribosomes must come along to read the long lines of DNA letters and break them into codons. Three-letter sections or *words*. When we break Hebrew down, we break it into three-letter roots that form words.

Additionally, DNA is built with four chemical bases. These bases have Hebraic language beginnings with meanings:

Thymine (T) - Hebrew word thumim = perfection
Cytosene (C) - Calla in Hebrew = Finish or complete
Guanine (G) - from Hebrew word Ganine = where things start
Adenine (A) - which comes from the word Eden = means pleases or satisfies.

When the genome sequence is read and broken into codons, thymine is broken up into uricil. Uricil means "lights". Thymine or "Perfection" is broken into Uricil or "Lights".

Matthew 5:48 says, "Be ye therefore perfect as my father in heaven is." The Father is like the Thymine. He never leaves the throne. But His essence and ideas take upon flesh and dwell among us as Yeshua, the "light" of the world. The Father sent His son to be the light of the world and to call us to be the same. We, each take on the light of Heaven when we follow Yeshua.

The cellular level of our existence resembles the macro spiritual and physical principles of the universe!

Isaiah 46:10 states, "Out of the beginning, God declares the things of the end." In Hebrew, it says that G-d declares "out of the beginning" the end.

Want to know the end? You must know the beginning.

The beginning was somewhat like a cell. Everything had to be there in order for anything to multiply after itself. Just as a cell has the information needed to build bigger things, so at the beginning, G-d had the information to build the universe.

Calal is the Hebrew word for cell, from Cala, which means bride. In the cell is the nucleus. And in that, the DNA.

The bride is a cell or body of cells with the DNA of Yeshua, who has the DNA of G-d the Father.

The Bride of Christ should contain the information needed, given by Yeshua and the Father, to build a body.

We now know that DNA holds the blueprint for life and for how a body is built. That information is embedded in the DNA and stays in the nucleus of the cell. It must stay there, safe, so that nothing can change or deform its perfect instructions.

Jesus said, "My WORDS are spirit and they are *life*." (John 6:63) [emphasis mine] The TORAH is teaching and INSTRUCTIONS, His WORDS spoken at the beginning. Yeshua's words are what gave the universe form and contained the directions for the *life* we see today.

The individual INSTRUCTIONS for your body are in the form of a molecule called DNA, which builds your you-ness and allows you to live. The individual instructions for life to even exist came from the Word given at the beginning, which is the DNA for all life.

DNA = Instructions
G-d's Word = Instructions

DNA builds a body = G-d's Word (Yeshua) builds a body
God's Word = Torah = DNA = Life

We look to G-d to build His church. Specifically Christ came that we may become part of the "body of Christ", the building of this body being essential to health for those in Yeshua. Son in Hebrew means "build", and it follows that son and building are related in the Hebrew language.

Yeshua = Builder = Blueprint = Instructions = Life

In order to produce the "body", something has to leave the nucleus. So, the DNA molecule untwists and then something called RNA (Messenger RNA or Servant RNA) takes on a copy of the DNA information. The DNA Is duplicated onto the RNA.

Now the RNA with that perfect instruction can leave the nucleus and transcribe the letters to build the body. If the son is the builder according to Scripture, RNA is the son. As the DNA strand unfolds, its letters line up all in a row. Here we have the picture of the OLD TORAH SCROLL lined up with no spaces.

Then, during transcription, the letters are divided in 3-letter roots. Divided into codons, amino acids, etc. Now it can produce different kinds of cells throughout the body. These letters make words and the words combined make sentences. Messenger RNA takes the message of the

DNA and translates it so the body can understand it. These sentences that are translated are called genes.

The Father = DNA
Jesus = Messenger = RNA

Roles and relationships are revealed at the cellular level. G-d the Father does not leave his Heavenly throne. He is the DNA, He holds the instructions for life. The DNA in our body is heavily protected. That information is too essential, and so it stays in the nucleus.

So, in order to build the body, the RNA comes in and makes a perfect copy of the DNA and takes it outside the cell to the body; the servant RNA or messenger RNA, the builder. Who is the builder of our church? Who came to give us the fullness of the message of the Father? Yeshua! Yeshua is the messenger RNA who leaves Heaven to come and build the body. The church body! How incredible that at the microscopic level of our existence, in our very cells we see a symbol of the unity of Christ with the Father. Hence Yeshua's insistance that we see He only obeys the instructions of the Father.

The perfect picture of a healthy body being built is RNA carrying the perfect instructions of DNA and translating that to create the body. The body of Christ is built like this as well.

So now we understand that the Word has to go out in order to continue to multiply, and it has to be translated to continue to produce like kind. The idea is to keep it as faithful to the original as possible. 1 Peter 1:23 tells us, "For you have been born again, not of perishable seed, but of imperishable, through the living and enduring *Word* of God."

We have been now born of the incorruptible seed, containing the DNA or information of Yeshua from the Father, who is the living and enduring WORD of God!

With this understanding of the importance of the DNA and RNA and body building mechanisms, we find that changing the meaning of G-d's word will corrupt the Church. It's like a recipe! If you want it to be correct or resemble the original, you cannot change the recipe. The Pharisees and Sadducees added to the Torah, changing the recipe and corrupting the message. Eventually, these inaccurate ingredients produce a mutation that multiples until it reaches the entire body of Christ. A cancer.

We cannot change G-d's DNA and expect a healthy body.

But Yeshua was the fullness of G-d, bodily. He became the imperishable, perfect, WORD that is the DNA of the new SEED, which is whole and healthy and a complete DNA copy. He can now get to REBUILDING the BODY with perfected DNA.

The body is continually building. Proteins eventually die off and the process of transcription and translation starts all over again. When Yeshua said, "It is finished" (John 19:28-30) He knew he had fulfilled all that the DNA had prescribed. NOW, it was time for the process to begin all over again through Yeshua's disciples.

Jordan Person, in his Youtube Biblical Series[xxvii] and Podcast, mentions a fascinating concept about the trajectory of Scripture and G-d's involvement in humanity. He notes growth of the body of Christ over time. G-d was very involved in human work at the beginning, interjecting and forcefully doing work to promote and encourage the movement towards relationship with humanity.

Then G-d came as a man and transformed the work of Believers, sending the Holy Spirit part of G-d to empower and comfort. At this point, the onus is on Believers who have the fullness of what G-d has taught through the Torah and the prophets. He said what He wanted to say. He gave us the tools we would need to become the presence of G-d on the earth. According to Peterson, the responsibility is now on US, the followers! And until Revelation, it is now human beings who are in charge of the major force for good on earth.

I wonder about this theory. We wish to see G-d show up at times the way He did in Exodus. We know He will again someday. But if we are comparing the work of G-d and the work of our bodies, we see that the transcription phase maybe has truly passed to us. As G-d writes His word on our hearts, we become like Yeshua. We become like the DNA of G-d. We literally carry the Teachings and Instructions in our hearts. The power is given to us through the Holy Spirit.

G-d may not show up like He did in Exodus again until His return because we are tasked with reading, understanding, and carrying His word so we can transcribe the information correctly. So, we "Go into all nations and baptize and steach others to obey…" In this, we assist in creating the body!

So, we see everything starts with information, an original source. In order to duplicate this perfection, copies are made and made carefully. The source information can NEVER change. Otherwise, the body cannot be built properly! If Yeshua changed the source information, He corrupted what the Father gave Him. But He tells us the opposite. He tells us that the Father sent Him and approves of Him, of His message and of His work. He is the perfect copy of the Father's information. Anything that veers from the information in Yeshua is not of the Father.

HEBREWS 4:15 states, "Do we have not a high priest? Who was in all points tempted but has not sin." Yeshua was tested when He left the throne room to come to earth. He was pushed to become corrupt, but He was incorruptible. He survived. The original message from the Father endured.

Returning to our cellular structure, we see that there is a "veil" between the nucleus and cytoplasm that is a double membrane. In the temple there was a double veil before the Holy of Holies — the most sacred place in the temple. And, during the time of Christ, there was an inner veil and an outer veil, which was twice the size of the inner veil. The inner veil was torn at the time of Messiah's death. Torn from top to bottom.

Yeshua's death granted access to the Father to all that are followers of what the RNA (Yeshua) told us. The instructions to build the body in perfect alignment with the DNA (G-d the Father) point us to perfect righteousness according to the Teaching and Instruction (Yeshua) and grants us a place in with the Father Himself. Now we can become the carbon copy of the Father. We can go directly to Him to receive instructions. We become like Christ. We become like RNA.

"No one comes to the Father except through me." (John 14:6) The instructions that Yeshua came with are the only way to the heart of G-d. Unity with the original DNA is health and life and a body built, and it only comes because of the original and perfect RNA.

G-d's designs are flawless and repeated in both the Heavenly and earthly realms. The pictures He gives us in nature that represent His spiritual principles. Yeshua and The Father, The New Testament and The Old are one, just as Yeshua, the Father, and the Holy Spirit are one. The beginning is one with us now.

The real Yeshua is just like the Father. He is the perfect representation of the Torah and the perfect interpretation of that DNA. He is forever and ever the Aleph and the Tav (Alpha and Omega), He IS the Beginning and the End! He was and embodies the G-d of the beginning. G-d's DNA can be uniquely understood in what was taught from the very beginning. Yeshua is the Law. The real Yeshua.

How does this change our worldview? Our following? Our understanding?

If you did not have this information already, it should change everything. Follow in the footsteps of the DNA of G-d. Learn what Yeshua knew and enacted, the Full Torah. His version should never be corrupted because mutations can only produce separation with the Father's character and intentions. To be "in Christ" means we have taken on His complete submission to the Father and unity with the one G-d who has not changed.

I've attempted here to detail some of the most notable Commands that have been overlooked. But there remain other Commands that Scripture prescribes to consider. The 10 Commandments (see next essay!), taking care of widows and orphans, how to treat the "stranger" or foreigner, and on and on. There are so many other Commands that would change how we interact with the world if we only took them seriously.

To clarify, this book will not detail all the Laws of G-d.

But if you're seeking clarity on what Laws we are to follow today in our location, I'd recommend the following resources:

119 Ministries (119ministries.com)
Lion and Lamb Ministries (lionandlambministries.org)
Wildbranch Ministry by Brad Scott (wildbranch.org)
Hebrew Roots Network (hebraicrootsnetwork.com)

There are extraordinary resources and teachers who can help you understand the Law from the Biblical perspective and correctly apply following Yeshua today!

Chapter 4

THE BIG TEN

I'VE READ A GREAT MANY COMMENTARIES about Hebraic understanding of the Commands of G-d, the Torah, these 613 instructions. It has taken me years to even begin to see how these Commands function, work with each other, and create a just and moral society. Just as archaeologists thousands of years from now may not understand our cultural norms (Facebook, football, etc.), we likely can't really fathom how religious a culture was the Biblical Jewish culture.

It was understood that all the Commands connect and join together at the top with the two big ones most Christians like to bring up. Like a family tree or a hierarchical chart, at the top you would have Love G-d and Love Others. Branching off these two are five of the Ten Commandments, and five on the other. Then, branching off of those, you would have all the rest of the Commands.

Years ago, G-d revealed to me how He put this organizational chart right on our body. We have two hands and 5 fingers hanging off of each. These two hands containing 10 fingers engage in the vast majority of working and loving and giving and creating that we do as human beings. The hands control everything from the food that goes to your mouth to the words you type on a page. And there, in them, is a reminder of G-d's gateway Commands into a life well lived.

This picture helps us visualize what G-d means when He tells us all the Commands "hang off of" or "can be summed up by" the top two. Loving G-d and Loving Others. Every single Command has love at its core and the Ten Commandments are the gateway into the rest of Torah. If you can understand the Ten Commandments, you can begin to understand how the 613 Laws, or Mitzvot, relate and interact.

I heard a **debate**[xxviii] recently between the prominent Canadian psychologist, Jordan Peterson, and noted philosopher and podcaster, Sam Harris. Harris made a point about the lack of explicit anti-slavery rhetoric in the Ten Commandments. As part of his larger argument that there are glaring omissions in all religious scriptures, Harris asked why the Ten Commandments don't ban slavery. Jordan didn't respond to that issue, which is unfortunate, because good answers actually exist for such a puzzling question.

And that is the good news. The Ten Commandments run very deep and wide, traversing large amounts of territory. They are broad enough and strong enough to support all the other Commands that are found in the Torah.

So what IS so great about the Ten Commandments that G-d gives us and why does it *seem* like big issues, such as slavery, aren't discussed specifically in these ten?

In fact, the story of the Ten Commandments really begins with the Hebrew people themselves enslaved by the Egyptians. (Fans of Charlton Heston, Yuel Brenner, and/or classic films will already know this.) For 400 years, the Egyptian regime oppressed and abused the Hebrew people through forced slave labor. With the leadership of Moses, G-d ultimately intervenes to rescue His people from bondage, punishing Egypt with ten plagues designed specifically to decimate the so-called "powers" of Egyptian gods.

Obviously, G-d is disgusted by the kind of chattel slavery that transpired between the Egyptians and Hebrew people, a monstrosity tragically similar to the heinous slave trade with which Americans are familiar.

But much of the slavery discussed in the Torah's legal structure is not that type of slave system. Rather, it is referencing something called "indentured servitude." In the ancient Hebrew culture, if you couldn't pay your debts or became homeless because of poverty, you could sell yourself as a servant to a master or family. In that home, you would have free room and board and would serve the family until your debts were paid. Instead of going to jail (as in, the way the IRS deals with people who have too many debts), you worked!

They did not have jails or holding facilities during this time period. Their judicial system had to work quite differently than ours.

Every seven years, all debts were supposed to be released and all servants set free. If you wanted to stay with your master/employer instead of taking your freedom, you would "bond" yourself to that person. Hence the term "bondservant." Paul uses this term often in the New Testament, stating that he is a "bondservant" of Christ. In other words, he has bound himself to serve G-d going forward. We explore this more later here in this chapter.

So, what is it about these Ten Commandments that illuminate the path to obedience and the heart of G-d?

The Big 10 are easy to understand and applicable across translations, cultures, locations, and peoples. This makes them a great starting point once you have grasped that all of G-d's commands are about loving G-d and loving others. Here with the Ten Commands we get to begin to delve into the specifics regarding G-d's definition of love, and as a great side addition, they are fascinating when you analyze their historical significance.

I cannot avoid references to Dennis Prager as we go through these. He has made many perceptive points about these Commands that have led me to comprehend them differently. If you want to read more of his commentaries and get the fullness of Prager's understanding, I'd highly **recommend his book on Exodus.**[xxix]

Before we dive in, it is important to take note of the events leading up to the revelation on Mt. Sinai and the writing of the Ten Commandments (and other Commands). In Exodus 19, G-d tells Moses to relate to the children of Israel that if they "hearken well" to Him and observe His "covenant" that they will be beloved to Him. They will be a "kingdom of ministers and a holy nation." He wants Israel to agree to take on this covenant He is about to give. It isn't forced upon them or coerced. After seeing His love for them in the Exodus from Egypt, this early church at Mt. Sinai would have been grateful and hopefully ready to respond to the salvation of the Lord.

In the same way, we are called to respond to the salvation of the Lord with an agreement to obedience. Salvation leads to a righteous walk. This is the pattern set up for us in Scripture. In Exodus 19:8, Scripture tells us "the entire people responded together and said, 'Everything that Hashem has spoken we shall do!' Moses brought back the words of the people to Hashem."

They had come to an agreement.

When we accept the salvation of Yeshua, we are also entering into a covenant. Called the "New Covenant," this deal ensures that G-d's ways will be written on our hearts. Written into our very flesh, that we may be "in Christ" and therefore not be judged as outsiders of the

Covenant of G-d. In our newness, our "reborn" state, we love G-d and His ways as David did. We are His people. His ways are not burdensome. We embrace each Command as rain from Heaven on parched land and a light unto our path out of desolate darkness.

It's a strange time to be writing this chapter. Coronavirus has taken over the globe. We are all huddled in our homes, watching the economy tank and hoping that our friends and family stay healthy. Deliverance feels so much closer as a concept, so much more important. I've had this feeling before personally, but never on such a large scale. Never have I looked and so often seen the same expression, in the eyes of friends, family, and even strangers covered in masks at the grocery store — so much uncertainty, fear, and discouragement.

What if all of a sudden, it all stopped? No new cases, all those with the disease were healed, freedom was upon us and all tyranny of both disease and human desire ended, and G-d spoke from the Heavens telling us that He had brought us out of the trial. If He promised that He would restore our economy, our jobs, and our health. What would our response be?

Would we answer as the nation of Israel did, recognizing the deliverance, the authority of G-d almighty, and would we agree to His terms?

Or how about when a lost soul finds the Lord? Enveloped in love and forgiveness, feeling the wash of cleansing pass over, melting away the burden of sin and death. Our soul responds, "Yes, Lord. I will go where you follow."

When the first sprout/root of the church was saved, they responded in kind. And G-d's answer of just HOW to follow and just WHERE to go was clear.

G-d began by speaking audibly to the entire people. No, Moses did not receive the Ten Commandments alone. Scripture (Exodus 19) tells us

G-d descended upon the mountain. There was lightning and thunder and the blowing of the shofar. Smoke and fire issued and G-d spoke in such a great voice that by the end of the Ten Commandments, the people begged Moses to have The Lord stop speaking to them directly.

They were terrified, believing if G-d continued, they would all die. However, each person heard the voice of the Lord speak the ten first Commands. It was not just through Moses that they were received. They were received into every individual who had experienced slavery and the sweet release into freedom. And they have traversed millennia, speaking to each individual who follows the G-d of Abraham, Isaac, and Jacob today. They are unchanged, foundational, exceptional in human history, and they produce a better society when pursued.

The 1st Command - You shall have no other gods besides ME.

Jews may often argue that the first Command actually starts a few verses before. These verses consist of a requirement of belief. It is more of an obvious statement that one must admit G-d exists before anything can follow. Belief must come first, otherwise, why read the rest? Either way, we must discuss having no other gods besides this One.

It is easy to think that 'gods' here means ancient deities, sun worship, idols, etc. But I believe strongly that anything that is FIRST in your life is a god. Dennis Prager, in his book *Exodus, The Rational Bible,* puts it quite well: "When anything is made an end in itself, rather than as a means to G-d and goodness, it is a false god."

This means that whatever your ideology is, there your god will be. If it's environmentalism, politics, atheism, climbing the ladder. If you spend your money, time, energy, or thought life on anything primarily, with that thing as the goal, that is where the ruler of your heart truly lies. G-d makes the point here that putting any of these things above Him is evil.

And it is quite easy to see why. Great evil is produced when G-d is not the point of one's efforts.

G-d designed us specifically and then gave us the corresponding Commands that would lead us to becoming better people and would create a better society. When we stray from making G-d the point and make, oh let's say, feminism the point, we can easily become inhumane in our pursuit of feminist ideals. Where G-d makes it clear that all human life is the highest priority, a feminist will make it clear that women must become the highest priority. At some point, if feminism is god, tradeoffs take place. That sort of 'job' can't exist anymore because it harms women if they are involved. That sort of 'activity' can't happen because men seem to do it more often. That child can’t exist because it is inconvenient for a woman. Etc. Etc.

I love women. They are beautiful, essential, equal, and wonderfully made in G-d’s image. But if feminism has replaced G-d in our hearts, we may end up replacing His commands with the demands of feminist ideology, to our own destruction.

The same can be said for political idolatry. For those who replace G-d with Trump or Obama or any number of leaders, blind following can create a cognitively dissonant nightmare. Political leadership MUST remain fallible and human in the minds of the public. If the people are to retain any power over leaders, they must be capable of critiquing poor policies, even if they voted for that individual. When leadership becomes an idol we degrade our intellectual honesty and trade it for blind worship. This is a poor trade and a platform for tyranny. We cannot worship a political system or politician.

We worship the Creator, not the created. Plain and simple.

The 2nd Command – You shall not make any Idols

This verse has always intrigued me, especially its chronological placement.

> Exodus 20:4 states, "You shall not make yourself a carved image or any likeness of that which is in the heavens above or on the earth below or in the water beneath the earth."

This seems to be a prohibition, first of all, to avoid creating an image of G-d Himself. It is, first off, troublesome to attempt depicting the G-d of the Universe in His omnipotence, power, presence, etc. G-d is described as a whirlwind (Zechariah 9:14), thunder (1 Samuel 7:10), lightning (Psalm 97:4), a consuming fire (Hebrews 12:29), and a huge range of other descriptions too numerous to name here. How in the world could you put that to a visual and not immediately limit His essence and expansiveness in the mind of the beholder?

Later on in Exodus, G-d is furious with the nation for making a golden calf. In the ancient world, the G-d of the Bible may have been represented as an ox. The paleo Hebrew symbol for the Hebrew letter, Aleph, was an ox-head and the Aleph (first letter of the Hebrew Aleph Bet) references the Father and the Oneness of G-d. The people may have essentially created an "image" of their G-d. Not necessarily a new god. They were making an "image" of their G-d as their mediator. Since Moses had gone up to talk solo with G-d, their first mediator had been missing on the mountain, and the nation of Israel stole a page from Egypt and made a new mediator: an image.

Worshiping an image, whether of Him or not, enraged G-d. He is not to be made into an image of any created thing. He is the Creator. We cannot force Him into a visual to worship or use.

But this is also a prohibition on making any image that you bow down to, pray to, believe in, etc. We see the Catholic Church replete with statues of Mary, Joseph, Jesus, Paul, the Saints, even their use of crosses feels a bit idolatrous. To pray to any of these statues goes directly against this prohibition. G-d has stated such beautification equates to idol worship. And take note! These are the 1st and 2nd Commandments — extremely important!

This Commandment continues by saying, "You shall not bow down to them or serve them For I the Lord your God am an impassioned God, visiting the guilt of the parents upon the children, upon the third and upon the fourth generations of those who reject Me."

I don't believe that God punishes generations unjustly. For a complete discussion on the word "visit," please read *Exodus* by Dennis Prager. In the meantime, it is of note that this word in Hebrew can also mean "take account of."

When we think about generations, we do see certain sins running through families. If the parents are alcoholics, it is often true that many of their children struggle with alcohol. If one parent is an atheist, you will hear the children espouse atheist beliefs. We pass our behavior on to our children because children are such magnificent sponges. It is why great parenting is so important and why a righteous walk will help preserve your children and their children and so on. It is just part of human nature. There are even studies showing that we **carry genetic memory**[xxx] of our parents and their lineage.

Good habits help create good habits in our kiddos. That's not rocket science, but it is important to remember.

I love that there is a good turn to this idea. In verse 6, G-d says, "but showing kindness to the thousandth generation of those who love Me and keep My commandments." The point here is how greatly G-d wants to reward goodness. He loves when His people behave righteously and He gets excited about giving to those who follow Him.

The 3rd Commandment – Do Not Take the Lord's Name in Vain

"Thou shall not take the name of the Lord thy God in vain; for the Lord will not hold him guiltless that taketh His name in vain."

As a child, I was always taught that this verse was about using bad language, and in particular using G-d's name to cuss. As I got older I began to wonder, as I learned the many names of God used in Scripture, from Yahweh to Yeshua, Hashem to YHVH, I almost never used these terms negatively. This Commandment seemed a bit like a joke.

But the Command is likely least about bad language or cussing. This Command is about doing evil in the name of G-d. Using G-d as an excuse or reason or accessory to sin and bad behavior. And wow, does that happen with mass casualty and destruction. A few examples come to mind:

- The misuse of certain verses to justify the abuse and control of women.

- The misuse and misinterpretation of scripture to justify the sort of slavery we saw here in the United States and around the world.

- The misuse and misinterpretation of scripture to justify anti-semitism. Specifically, the idea that because the Jews had Christ crucified, they deserve to be punished (see the history of the Catholic and Protestant churches for this scathing abuse of Scripture and direct disobedience to this command.)

Many more examples could be cited. Humans love to quote Scripture to support their own narrow and often incorrect interpretations and biases. Paul likely gets misquoted most of all. Being used abhorrently and often to condone sin, Paul's words have been twisted to fit every incarnation of religious interpretation, as Peter puts it, "To their own destruction" (2 Peter 3:16). And look at the destruction this causes! Not only to the people being violated, but to the spreading of the goodness of G-d and His ways, which is our greatest call!

I recently spoke with a man on FB who claimed the G-d of the Bible was bloodthirsty based on Yeshua's death and Old Testament sacrifices. He posted this twisted version of G-d for all to see. How many readers, ignorant of G-d and His Word, do these types of deceits lead astray? Is this not dragging G-d's name through the mud? And, of course, there was an angle to His post. The angle benefited his own rightness, while completely obliterating righteousness.

When Yeshua tells us to "go and make disciples of all nations, teaching them to obey all I have commanded,"(Matthew 28:19-20) and we teach falsehoods instead OR teach that obedience equates to abuse and mistreatment of our fellow man, we often do irreparable evil! This, of course, cannot be born by our Heavenly Father. Hence a wise prohibition with a punishment attached to its abuse.

Using the Bible and G-d to justify your bad behavior will not go well for you. As the Command continues to state, "for the Lord will not hold him guiltless that taketh His name in vain." G-d has no intention of letting this particular bad behavior go unresolved.

Dennis Prager interprets this as being an unforgivable sin. I disagree. Paul, in the New Testament, used G-d's name to put Stephen to death, and likely claimed Scripture forbids making false claims about a Messiah. These accusations against Stephen, were they true, carried the death penalty. But Stephen wasn't making false claims about the Messiah. Paul refused to see that. Stephen, who was a follower of Yeshua, was too much of a threat to the religious dictates of the day, according to Paul and his contemporaries.

So they used Scripture — G-d's word — to justify murder.

However, Paul meets Yeshua on the road to Damascus. In one instant, he is changed. AND forgiven. The blood of Yeshua covers all intentional sin, even Paul's sin of murder in the name of G-d.

Still, we cannot misquote Paul and his story by taking this grace too far. I would submit that G-d still hates the act of taking His name in vain. May we never excuse our sinful behavior or promote it using Scripture as a foundation. I love this quote from Prager: "No atheist activist is nearly as effective in alienating people from G-d and religion as are evil 'religious' people." (*Exodus, The Rational Bible*)

I have wondered about our innocence regarding this command here in America. Is the Church guilty of violating the 2nd Command?

Absolutely.

As we progress further into approving of LGBTQ leadership, calling it G-dly. As we continue to misinterpret Scriptures that keep women from teaching. I even recently saw a post from Beth Moore claiming that mask-wearing during the Covid pandemic is related to our Christian duty to love others! Too many use Scripture and G-d's name to promote activities of their own preference, claiming this is what the Bible teaches! And when science, or psychology or other understandings prove us wrong in our wrong-headed claims, we lose our testimony.

As for the first issue, I'm indebted to many ideas from **Brad Scott with Wildbranch Ministry.**[xxxi] G-d is quite clear that in the beginning He made MALE and FEMALE. He didn't make heterosexual and homosexual or even transexual.

There are instructions for how males and females are to behave. Those instructions include all sorts of things, like not committing murder, not coveting, not stealing, and so on. We all feel like gossiping, feel covetous or jealous. We all have moments of rage or we violate the Sabbath. This DOES NOT mean those things are no longer sin just because we feel like doing them.

Mankind has been leaning towards sin since Adam and Eve got kicked out of the garden. Does that mean we allow it and promote it, or do we treat it rightly, as damaging behavior that alienates us from Adonai? Well, anyone who has read their Bible would likely answer that we need to try to sin less, especially as people of G-d!

So why have so many Christians decided that homosexuality and gender confusion put into behavior isn't sin? I would argue because we have given in to our culture AND because we refuse to teach the Laws of G-d.

Much of today's LGBTQ community celebrates gender confusion. A lack of identity of gender is a wonderful, progressive thing to those who put gender-neutral children on the cover of magazines. But G-d makes things clear at the beginning. Defining the ocean from the land, the sky from the ground, the sun from the moon, and men from women. Distinguishing the Sabbath from the other days, good from evil, male from female.

Distinctions are one of G-d's specialties.

I believe a good father and a good mother in a home gives kids a better chance at psychological soundness, but also at understanding of the world! Roughly 50 percent of the world is male and 50 percent female. That means having both examples in the house gives you a better understanding of how 100 percent of the world, and your culture, operates.

And yet...

Despite the logic and clear directives from Creation and later on in Scripture, some churches claim that G-d wants us to embrace the lifestyle and teachings of the LGBTQ community. This violation of the 2nd Command is concerning, at the very least and far more damagaging than we are admitting. (see my essay on *The Family*)

On the other hand, this does not condone acts of wickedness or man-made justice carried out towards those who are in the midst of gender or identity confusion and disintigration. No doubt the church has attempted all sorts of unholy and unrighteous punishments for those they deemed "sinners" in the past. I've seen little, if any, evidence that those actions by the Church did not also amount to violations of the 2nd Command. Calling out sin and attempting righteous leadership in the Church is not the same thing as aggressively punishing or attempting harm against sinners. All love for G-d is grounded in humility. Congregants who prefer sin to G-d have made their choice. Leaders who prefer sin to G-d should step down from leadership. Before the Lord, you may choose death or life freely. You cannot, by force, bring people into alignment with the Lord. It must be of their own free will.

If we truly love our brothers and sisters on this planet, including the LGBTQ community, lying to them is not evidence of it. The kindest thing we can do is be personally kind to EVERYONE we encounter, spreading the love of G-d, while STILL teaching Scriptural dictates and definitions and protecting our children and our churches from wolves in sheep's clothing, otherwise known as false teachers.

Bring people to the love of G-d and then follow Yeshua's instruction to "teach them to obey all" that is commanded. We are to be teachers of

G-d's instructions. This blesses. When we use G-d's name to teach our own ideas and laws and instructions, we violate the 2nd commandment.

Additionally, many churches still prohibit female teachers and I do not believe that this is Scriptural. The dictates of the priesthood are clearly for the temple service (the tabernacle that the nation of Israel had). Are we in that tabernacle? No. Do we live in the land of Israel? No. Do we have a Levitical Priesthood? No.

To further the confusion, the New Testament has Paul teaching all sorts of things regarding women in the church and their behavior. But we, number one, often do not often have the context correct, and number two, do not know the questions that Paul is answering in his letters. Paul is directing these churches on how to keep order and teach truth while also bringing in men and women from pagan practices.

At the time Paul was writing, women were often not educated, (Paul encourages the church to educate them! This is meaningful!). They were used to having a say in the pagan worship settings they were in and they clearly were not controlled in their speaking and thinking. This means they were wreaking havoc on order, structure, and the focus of the communal gatherings. Moreover, they were likely teaching pagan ideas. This would need to be shut down immediately, as the Synagogue was devoted to teaching Scripture.

We know that the Lord believes in female leadership. The first judge that G-d appointed for the nation of Israel was a woman named, Deborah. She was also a warrior and led the armies of Israel into victorious battle. Clearly, G-d trusts good women in leadership.

Moses' sister, Miriam, was a prophet and also led the congregation in praise. She was considered an important leader during the Exodus story and was greatly mourned by the nation of Israel when she passed.

Josiah consults the Prophetess, Hulduh, regarding the finding of Scripture in the Temple and she declares a word from G-d in 2 Kings 22.

There is Anna in Luke 2 who is in constant prayer and fasting in the temple. She brings prophecies about Yeshua.

We see in Acts 18, Priscilla and Acquilla teaching higher truths to Apollos, who was already a strong man in the Lord. He learned from them and was able to teach more aptly.

In Romans 16, Phoebe is mentioned as a servant of the church.

In Acts 9, Tabitha is mentioned as doing good works and acts of charity.

In Philippians 3, Paul mentions women who have been working side by side with him to spread the gospel.

So many mentions of women who had a word from the Lord, a song from the Lord, or worked to spread the gospel! While it is often mentioned that women are to teach other women (this shouldn't be surprising — women still need older female mentors today!), we also see women's wisdom enriching men. We find men seeking out the counsel of women and we even see men following women into battle.

The church has badly mishandled the great gift of female teachers and leaders in community and churches and they have used the Lord's name to do it! While many churches have correctly interpreted Scripture in this regard, others still haven't come around.

Furthermore, because the church has often not advocated for women as intelligent and important voices in the church, abuse has been extended into homes where men for centuries have believed they are above and superior to their female counterparts. There has been great evil done in the name of Scripture regarding the treatment of women. In this way, we have broken the 2nd Commandment.

On the other side, Scripture is the source of the ideas that women are equal to men (see: the creation of Eve who G-d calls Adam's equal), the admiration for our spiritual heritage not just of men but of women like Sarah, Rachel, and Rebecca, and G-d's choice of Mary as the mother of Yeshua.

Paul tells us that G-d does not give preferential treatment to any of His children based on gender, race, ethnicity, or class. And although there are different rules for men and women in the Torah, as men and women ARE different (thank goodness), righteousness is the key component in all of them. We need to honor Scripture's insistence that women are wonderful teachers and that G-dly women are meant to infuse the church with their wisdom, just like men.

These are just a few of many areas where incorrect doctrine is taught as G-d given truth, creating injustice, chaos and evil. I submit this is what taking the Lord's name in vain really means. To cause harm in the name of Yahweh is a grievous action indeed and comes with a just penalty.

The 4th Commandment – Remember the Sabbath and Keep it Holy

This has become one of my very favorite commands of the Lord. I'll never forget the time period that G-d began to ask me to follow this command exactly as He describes it in Exodus.

My disappointment at the time must have hurt G-d.

But, I was a musician. The Biblical Sabbath is traditionally and has ALWAYS been kept from Friday night at sundown to Saturday night at sundown. (Scripture says G-d made "evening and morning, the first day," Genesis 1:5. The first 24-hour period in Scripture is defined as beginning at sundown. Moreover, the Bible describes Appointed Times

— in Hebrew called, Mo'edim — as beginning at sundown. The Sabbath is an appointed time. Not only is the beginning of the Sabbath at sundown, but it is and always has been designated as the 7th day of the week.)

With the specifics in hand, G-d asked me to NOT work from Friday evening to Saturday evening. But, weekends for a musician are essential! Without that Friday night gig, the Saturday afternoon festival, etc., honestly, I really thought I would lose most of my income. The Sabbath Command at first felt like assured death for our meager finances.

So, for a very long time I played around with this Command, to my great detriment. I made excuses about shows. I reasoned it wasn't really "work" for me or really anyone else. I mean, other people were enjoying what I was doing. Hey, maybe I could have them PayPal me on Monday instead? Who knows?

I attempted to lie to myself about the reality of G-d's request, racking up guilt and debts to my intellect and self-respect.

But G-d was persistent. He wouldn't let up. He harassed my conscience enough that I eventually (and begrudgingly) began to say no to Friday night gigs. I began to dedicate that 24-hour time period to The Lord. And, He did not disappoint.

Not only did G-d convene with me on a level I'd never had before, He began to prove to me that HE provides. It was never my Friday night gig that was paying the bills. In every case, it was The Lord. Within the year that I began dedicating Friday nights to Shabbat dinners and family, and most importantly to G-d, I started to see gigs on other days roll in. I started to get an increase in pay for those alternative gigs. And I started to wonder where else I had not surrendered my assumptions for G-d's provisions.

I made more money the last year I was a musician than the years previous. And on top of it, my relationship with the Lord grew exponentially. My trust grew. My faith grew. My knowledge grew. My mental health improved. My time with family became deeper. It was and has been extraordinary. Today, I wouldn't trade the Sabbath. You couldn't peel it out of my stubbornly clenched hands. It is my favorite day and I remember it every week by looking forward to it. I remember it is coming and I try to get all my work done beforehand so that I can honor it.

Our G-d is the only god that commands rest. Enjoyment, pleasure, time, sleep, family. And what a joy rest is!

There have been studies that have shown that people who work a 7-day work week produce LESS than those who work a 5-day work week. (American Journal of Epidemiology, Volume 169, Issue 5, 1 March 2009)[xxxii]

Want to know why?

People need REST! It is essential that we reinvigorate our minds and dedicate time to thinking outside of our jobs.

When we do it the way G-d asks us to, we get to show that we believe that G-d is the provider and that we are in His hands. Moving beyond just a productivity lesson, the Sabbath stands as a weekly opportunity to show G-d we actually love Him.

Even more important than just rest on the Sabbath is the Command to "keep it holy." The word, "holy", means set apart. We are to set apart this day as distinct from others. G-d loves distinctions, and even in our conception of time and dates G-d has called us to make distinctions.

Because Holiness is the highest calling of the day, Priests still run services on the Sabbath, songs are still sung, and even Yeshua healed on this day. You can save an animal in distress, and you can do good for people. In fact, it is good to do good on the Sabbath! When your work is related to making the day Holy, it is permitted. (So no, shopping at the mall, finishing your work project, or mowing the lawn are not acts that make the day holy).

I struggle with the concept that there is a Command to be IN church each week. There does seem to be a suggestion that we should be in a place of proper teaching and instruction. But is it a Command?

Woldn't that be horribly burdensome? If you were REQUIRED by G-d to be among people one day out of seven, how often would you be breaking that Command? Well, all the time really and beyond that, it would ensure that sick people, brand new babies, and the infirm would become a burden on each congregational service. While it is good and important to be in fellowship with Believers, I'm not certain we are Commanded to go each week.

Later on in Scripture the Sabbath is called a "holy convocation". Convocation is the Hebrew word, "miqra" which means "rehearsal". In practicing this day we are rehearsing for our future. In this regard I see great encouragement to be at a Bible teaching church, one where you are rehearsing for the future of G-d's Kingdom properly.

I wonder here if convocation could also mean that, in taking a Sabbath rest you ARE joining G-d's people, all over the world, in a dimension of time that G-d has set aside. I don't know how to avoid not driving 45 minutes to our Messianic Congregation at times of family illness, personal intrusion or just when we are taking a vacation.

However, there is no doubt that the Commandment to rest can be universally applied. Wherever you are, whatever generation or location, you can take this day and commit it to holiness and a departure from work. It is an easy Command to follow, and yet, we have made it so hard.

Here is the command in Exodus, worth reading in full:

"Remember the Sabbath and keep it Holy. Six days you shall labor and do all your work, but the seventh day is a Sabbath of the Lord your God: You shall not do any work – You, your son or daughter, your male or female slave, or your cattle, or the stranger who is within your settlements. For in six days the Lord made haven and earth and sea, and all that is in them, and He rested on the seventh day; therefore the Lord blessed the Sabbath day and hallowed it." (Exodus 20:8-11)

Each time we remember the Sabbath we are remembering that God is the Creator. That He completed His creation and then sat upon His throne as King. And it is a day when the Lord will meet with you.

The renowned Rabbi Abraham Heschel wrote the Sabbath "is not for the sake of the weekdays. The weekdays are for the sake of the Sabbath. It is not an interlude but the climax of living."

I love this. "Remember the Sabbath" is a call to prepare all week for a climax, a moment of rest and reflection. We work all week long so that we CAN observe the Sabbath and keep that Sabbath holy.

He also discussed that the Sabbath is a dimension. Part of G-d's time dimensions. G-d is building something with time we often don't recognize since we often see time as linear.

Heschel notes[xxxiii], "The danger begins, when in gaining power in the realm of space we forfeit all aspirations in the realm of time." In that realm, "the goal is not to have but to be, not to own but to give, not to control but to share, not to subdue but to be in accord."

Given the cyclical nature of Scripture, I often wonder if G-d is building something within time dimensions using His Appointed Times. Just as we know how to build with space, G-d knows how to build with time and we are asked to participate in that dimension in unity with His Kingdom.

I had a teacher (the dear, Marcel Murray at Messiah's New Life Tabernacle in Indiana) who told me that the Sabbath to him was a moment when our Father, G-d, set a table, a meal for us. And He waits for us to come and sup with Him. How distressing that our seat at the table has been empty so often because we do not observe His day. The Father looks down the table hoping to see our shining faces, but empty seats greet Him covered in lonely dust from long years absent.

The Chumash observes the following

"God blessed the Sabbath by providing a double portion of manna on Friday so that there would be food for the Sabbath, and He sanctified it by not giving manna on the Sabbath, so that no one would be forced to work to gather food. (Rashi) This is a lesson for all time: God provides for His children who observe the Sabbath."

"Prosperity does not come from work and intelligence; they are merely two of the tools that God gives us, but He is the Ultimate Provider. The blessing and sanctification refer to the individual Jew's heightened capacity to absorb more wisdom and insight on the Sabbath than on other days (Ibn Ezra). The Sabbath is blessed in that it is the source of blessing for the rest of the week, and it is sanctified because it draws its holiness from the higher spiritual spheres (Ramban). Indeed, in the literal sense of the verse: for six days – rather than in six – implies that God created the world to last for only six days plus the Sabbath. Then the Sabbath gives the world the spiritual energy to exist for another week, and the cycle goes on continuously."

The Sabbath contains the very energy we need for another week, it is the energy the universe needs to continue on. There is an important spiritual dimension to this day.

But we have perverted the Fourth Command to mean: "have a day off sometimes."

Yet, the Sabbath is not a day YOU get to choose.

We are called, every seven days, to honor the day the Lord G-d Almighty has said is holy. Not our own days, not our own ways.

It is a ritual, a discipline, a weekly surrender. It keeps us thoughtful and mindful of the time element G-d is working with and points us to the ultimate 7th day rest when Yeshua will reign on the earth.

Without its observance, we may think Yeshua's reign of rest could be just any millennia. But it cannot. It will be the seventh. We may think G-d could have rested from creation on any day. But He did not choose any day. He chose the seventh.

We need G-d's specific Sabbath rest to stay spiritually sharp, connected, and to participate in G-d's family time.

It is not a burden. It is a gift. We must rewire our hearts and minds to understand the freedom of the Sabbath day, the symbolism, and the importance to "keep it holy".

COMMANDMENT 5 – Honor Your Father and Your Mother

Exodus 20:12 states, "Honor your father and your mother, that you may long endure on the land that the Lord your God is assigning to you."

I am perennially reminding myself and others that G-d never asks us to do something we are not capable of doing. Can you imagine a good father asking his children to do something he KNOWS they cannot do? Then punishing them for it? That would be a truly cruel father. Yet, we have a loving Heavenly father. What He asks is possible AND it is good.

So, we must look at these Commandments specifically to find what exactly is being asked. How is the "yoke easy and the burden light" (Matthew 11) according to Yeshua?

In this case, a lot of people think that this Command is asking you to love, like, or obey your parents at all times. But this is not the case. The word used is "honor." Now, obedience and honor can often go hand in hand, but when your parent is asking you to do something that violates G-d's Law, in that case, you would need to be disobedient.

Therefore, you would be breaking a commandment of G-d IF He had used the word obey. But He didn't.

Honor, from the Hebrew word "Kavad," implies that you "give weight to" or "glorify." Dictionary.com describes this form of honor as "high respect, as for worth, merit or rank."

We are to give high respect and weight to the position of our parents. Through the story of Noah, we are taught not to embarrass or bring shame on one of our parents. We lift them up, appreciate their position, give weight to their years and keep them from dishonor. This is doable. Even if your parents are horrible, even if you cannot love them or always obey them, you can give them dignity in your heart in public and respect their position.

As previously mentioned, I believe G-d put the Ten Commandments right on our hands. When we look at our hands we can put our fingers together and they look a lot like tablets with five fingers on each hand representing five Commandments about loving G-d and five about loving others. That would mean the fifth Commandment is about loving G-d.

But how?

It is clear to me that honoring our parents teaches us to honor G-d. While G-d also asks us to love Him, He desires us to honor Him as well. Obedience and respect come along with that as we learn to always give deference and weight to the Word of G-d and to never bring shame to the Name of G-d or His things.

There is a promise attached to this command that we get to live long in the land our Father is giving us when we as a people honor our parents. This concept that peace and prosperity are the gift of inheritance that G-d provides reminds us that a well-operating family is a picture of Yahweh and His relationship with His children. The family is, as usual, a central tenet and the message is that healthy participants enjoy particular rewards.

We honor our parents when we take care of them, respect their position, and bring them dignity. In so doing we learn how to do the same of the Kingdom and the Kingdom's things. We do not always do it out of love, we may feel awful on certain days when we serve, but feelings are fair weather friends. It is what we do that matters, ESPECIALLY when we don't feel like it. We can learn all of this in the Fifth Commandment.

This respect for elders also brings sturdy structure and safety to society. A healthy understanding that wisdom often (not always) comes with age allows us to learn from our past, build on our parent's and grandparent's ample education, and not have to recreate the wheel with each generation. There is real societal value in respect for the older humans who happen to be your parents.

You may have a hard time loving your parents. You may have needed to walk away from your parent's ways. That does not mean you have violated this Command.

If you are careful in your speech, merciful in your judgments, and guarded about how you present your parents to the world, you are already exhibiting honor for them.

G-d does not ask us to do something we cannot. This Command is another proof of His excellent specificity.

The 6th Commandment – You Shall Not Murder

A very popular view of this Command (and one without nuance) asserts that killing and murder are equated. As I've been learning and hopefully sharing with you, each word G-d uses is intentional and actually MEANS something. Murder is the word used here and it is used on purpose. Murder is premeditated, planned, and results in the destruction of an innocent life. As we will see, G-d does not prohibit killing entirely. He prohibits the immoral premeditated ending of innocent life.

Self-defense, therefore, is not prohibited by this Command. If you kill someone in war, that is not the same as murder. If you kill someone to defend innocent lives, and especially if this is an unexpected situation, that is not murder.

Once again, the Ten Commandments prove to be nuanced and specific enough to deal with exactly the circumstance that G-d intends, but general enough to be applicable to all people at all times.

Premeditated murder of an innocent person is evil. It steals life and justice from the victim. Even if an individual feels the murder is justified, standards of justice outside of emotional outbursts are the way of Scripture. You cannot indiscriminately choose to end life in G-d's Kingdom. Without legal process, this kind of murder reduces the value of human life and justice to one's own personal moral code. It's a way of thinking that is too subjective to be useful in society.

The Bible sees killing differently than murder. Hence, the nation of Israel had many sanctioned wars. Killing an evil leader of a nation, for example, who may be torturing his citizens, would also not be considered murder. Why? Murder is also translated as the "immoral" ending of a human life.

Is the person innocent? A great example was the conspiracy to assassinate Hitler. Did G-d approve of this? Likely so. Hitler was the head of one of the greatest evils of the 20th century. Undeniably, had the assassination attempts been successful, rescue of many in the concentration camps could have happened earlier, saving the innocent. Assassinating Hitler would be considered a righteous killing, not the murder of an innocent.

Capturing and trying Hitler would have been the ideal.

Without a dictate from G-d, the process of justice is clearly Biblically preferred to vigilante killings, as Genesis through Deuteronomy describes detailed legal proceedings for evil actions.

G-d has not sanctioned a free-for-all, Wild West approach to punishment.

G-d hates murder, but does not prohibit killing. This nuance is important to understanding this Command.

Within this nuance, we are also able to observe the hierarchy of value in G-d's justice system. Life is always first. This is why so many killings in the Old Testament are considered righteous: because they were righteous preservations of life. From the wars Israel waged against Canaanite nations to Rahab's betrayal of her own people in favor of Israel and their G-d, there is evidence that G-d views the world from a long-term perspective. In the long run, how does life persist and thrive? How can righteousness and justice and the promulgation of Torah continue throughout the entire globe?

We cannot fully understand G-d's cosmic plans, but we can note from His own Word the perfect detail of His life-first system. He has preserved His Church and His Word exceedingly well so far. We must trust Him. I believe this Command is evidence that we CAN trust Him.

The 7th Commandment – You Shall Not Commit Adultery

The church in Scripture is called the "Bride of Christ." (Revelation 19:7, Ephesians 5:27, Hosea 2:16-23, etc.) This position can leave Yeshua's followers with no doubt of the intimacy and potency of Yeshua's love for us. The relationshp functions like a marriage where the example of a great husband is given in our Savior.

The nation of Israel consistently disobeyed G-d's commands throughout the Old Testament, and G-d was rightly angry. He called himself "jealous" at one point. This jealousy mirrors the way a husband would be dismayed and heartbroken over a wayward wife whom he loves.

The Biblical contractual relationship between G-d and His Church is the foundation for the stories themselves. (Exodus 19, Isaiah 24:5, Isaiah 8:1, Hebrews 8:9 and others). We have broken the contract, the marriage vows, the commitment we made. Hence, our need for restoration.

Over and over again, the nation of Israel broke its deal with G-d, but G-d pursued her. Eventually, He died for her. A man is called to love his wife the way Yeshua loves the church, sacrificially, humbly, and intentionally.

Deuteronomy 24:1-4 explains that once a divorce has taken place and one of the parties has remarried another, the two original spouses cannot remarry.

One is only free to get remarried if there is a death.

Now why is this? Well, if one of the marriage partners dies, then the other is no longer bound by the marriage contract. (Romans 7:1-4)

G-d gave the nation of Israel a certificate of divorce according to Jeremiah 3:8.

But then Yeshua came and DIED! He rose again, conquering death, yes, but even more than that.

His death allowed Him to remarry His Bride. She would be new and perfect because His blood would cover her iniquity. The marriage bond this time would not be breakable. For it would be written on her heart. The covenant of marriage would now span eternity.

Even in His death and resurrection, Yeshua was keeping the Torah.

And this beautiful image is supposed to be how we understand marriage. It is supposed to be an egalitarian relationship where commitment and covenant are honored. The husband sacrifices everything to bring wholeness to His bride and keep the covenant. The wife responds to the husband's love with respect and adoration. The two work together to co-create a universe, a space that belongs to the family, where each is safe and able to grow in health.

A stable family creates an environment for spiritual growth for children and for stability for the family's future. Stable families create a more reliable and honorable society.

Fatherlessness is one of the greatest issues our society faces. (See Essay on the Family)

So, anything that would break apart this family is obviously despised of G-d. The family is essential to understanding G-d and His character.

Yeshua does seem to give some reasons for divorce. Abuse, neglect, and adultery are three reasons I've come across in Scripture. Despite these being good enough reasons, G-d does not favor divorce.

If you've been divorced, you understand why: broken trust, broken faith in people, broken faith in future, a distorted version of marital bonds. The list goes on. Divorce shreds your soul no matter what the reason. And it becomes a distraction from raising G-dly children.

For children, it is a destabilizing event, an emotional trauma, a heart-wrenching experience where they feel they often are the reason for the divorce or must choose between their parents. This can create a web of negative coping mechanisms, developmental delays, and depression. Divorce destroys children.

And, adultery is one of the largest causes of divorces in society. Our high rates of divorce represent an inability to keep a covenant and to be disciplined in our choices. Adultery is a sign of a sickness in marriage. Needs not being met, brokenness never healed and selfishness on full display, adultery remains singular in its ability to reflect emotional damage.

In opposition to our beautiful destinies and giant souls, we seek physical affection instead of G-d's deliverance and comfort. We were made for more.

G-d did not design us for divorce.

As someone who has been there, let me advise. If you have good reason for divorce, don't commit adultery first. Don't double the pain for yourself.

If you can save your marriage, do so.

If your joy is stolen by your marriage, it's abusive, or untenable go ahead, get out.

But remember your children. Remember your character. Remember your G-d. And avoid breaking this command.

Commandment 8 – You Shall Not Steal

This Commandment has immediate applicability here in America, where a debate has erupted over what defines "stealing". Looters and violent protesters have taken to the streets alongside peaceful protesters, blurring the lines between the two groups, making it tough for the peaceful to continue to push for meaningful change. I've seen many posts on Facebook asserting that rioting is "peaceful" or that looting is necessary, and many more decrying that viewpoint.

On the other side are those advocating for Martin Luther King's style of peaceful but public displays of protest.

And why are we discussing this at all? In America, race relations remain perpetually tense in the public square and debates abound regarding reparations, Critical Race Theory, government programs, police reform, and so on. Some are wondering: Is it right for a movement to loot and steal to make up for the evils of slavery, even if they occurred over a hundred years ago?

Taking in the long view of human history, what is right? Can we find that ground here in the Big Ten?

Why do so many choose violence and theft to assuage pain or enact revenge?

Thou Shalt not Steal is deep. It goes way beyond just swiping some item at a store that you think you want or to get back at the oppressor. It is about a **misguided** desire for things that G-d has not given to you. What we have in life is either given by the Lord or it is earned and given/allowed by the Lord. We cannot have it any other way and maintain a dignified society.

But what is even stranger and more germane to the present moment is that this Command would have been understood by the ancient Hebrew nation to mean we are not to steal other PEOPLE.

It is the very Command that prohibits kidnapping and enslavement that is now being broken by those who are trying to find recompense for the kidnapping and slavery of the earliest Black Americans. We cannot steal other human beings. We cannot steal their bodies, their lives, or their livelihoods and expect G-dly approval. Here it is, right in the framework of G-d's Law.

The Command is simple. You shall not steal. In Exodus 21:16, the Command comes with a punishment. If you kidnap (The Torah actually uses the Hebrew word for "steal" here, not kidnap, despite the English translation) with the intention of selling someone into slavery, you "shall be put to death." In the eyes of the Lord, there is a severe punishment for those who steal a life. This, of course, means you cannot enslave someone else and be abiding by G-d's Kingdom principles. But why doesn't it just say, Thou Shalt Not Own Slaves?

Slavery can be defined as what the Egyptians did to the Jews, what happened in the United States and globally throughout the 1700 and 1800s, OR what the Bible describes as indentured servitude. There are varied and non-interchangeable meanings for the word "slavery." And what else could slavery come to mean in the long span of history? Are some jobs a bit like slavery? Do some employers use emotional trickery and abuse to get their employees to work, stay in line, stay competitive? Perhaps!

Some people could say they are slaves to their jobs, slaves to money, slaves to "the man," slaves to their debt. The idea of slavery is subjective. Therefore, it is not specific enough to be a FOUNDATIONAL principle that could be summed up in just ten commands. (See Dennis Prager's Commentary in Exodus for more on this.)

Despite the specifics being discussed later in the Torah (i.e., you cannot kill a slave or indentured servant, etc.), forced, abusive slavery CAN be defined as THEFT. You are stealing a life, a livelihood, and freedom from another human. Theft IS directly discussed in the Ten Commandments and can therefore be used as one of the big arguments against the concept of slavery we modern Westerners are usually referencing.

Dennis Prager points out that this Command also refers to stealing another person's dignity or reputation, including the use of gossip or libel. The Bible later talks about G-d's hatred for gossip. James 1:26 goes so far as to say, "Those who consider themselves religious and yet do not keep a tight rein on their tongues, deceive themselves, and their religion is worthless."

Proverbs is replete with warnings against the lying tongue. "Without wood a fire goes out, without gossip a quarrel dies down."

Believers have come across verse after verse about G-d's hatred for gossip and maybe have wondered, why is this not in the Ten Commandments? Well, here it is. You shall not steal ANOTHER PERSON'S REPUTATION! Intellectual property, dignity, story, trust, all these are included in Thou Shall Not Steal.

In Proverbs 3:27-28, we are encouraged to "not withhold good from those who deserve it, when it is in your power to act." This is another form of theft. If you are supposed to give something to someone else (payment, something you borrowed, an encouragement, whatnot), withholding this is theft. If it is owed to them, give it and give it immediately. Including what is owed to G-d. The seventh commandment goes far beyond not taking something from someone. The Bible also calls on us to give the good that is within our power to give. Do not be withholding of good. What a society we would create if we would do this!

In Exodus, The Rational Bible, Dennis Prager states, "Virtually every society in history, and most societies in the world today...were and are filled with corruption. People pay government officials for favors; government officials get rich selling state companies and contracts; individuals pay police or government officials to avoid prosecution; judges are bribed to twist verdicts (a practice specifically banned in the Torah – Exodus 23:8); schools and officials are bribed to get a son or daughter into a prestigious university; and so on. More than anything else, it is widespread corruption that makes it impossible for a society to progress politically, morally, or economically."

As Prager so deftly points out, all of the above are forms of theft. Theft of justice, theft of competition and fair trade, theft of a position in a school because of bribery: this is stealing! Prager is right. Theft is corrupting to society in all its forms. Theft of people, theft of things, theft of justice, and theft of dignity. "Thou Shalt not Steal" is one of the most profound Commands humanity has or ever will receive.

Commandment 9 – You shall Not Bear False Witness Against Your Neighbor

This Commandment deals with lying, specifically when testifying about another human being. It is not, however, telling us you cannot ever lie.

We must revisit the Torah's hierarchy of law. Life sits at the very top. It is easy to see throughout Scripture this pattern. Rahab lied to save Israelite spies. The Magi were not forthcoming to Herod with the location of Yeshua or their mission. Rachel is considered righteous despite deceiving her husband and switching Esau out for Jacob to receive the birthright. Life was going to come through Jacob's line, through the work of the Israeli spies and through Yeshua.

- The Egyptian midwives lying to Pharaoh to save the lives of Hebrew baby boys — a righteous act.
- Germans hiding Jews from the Nazis — a righteous act.
- Christians smuggling Bibles into China — a righteous act.

Lying is not what is being prohibited here. It is false testimony AGAINST your neighbor. Simple. To start, do not lie in court about whether or not someone committed a crime. If you know truth that will bring about JUSTICE, you are not to hide it or lie about it. Do not tell lies that are not about protecting or producing life. Do not be dishonest about others, especially if it is gossip.

If your lie is producing evil, death, pain, suffering, hardship, heartache, it is AGAINST your neighbor. Do not speak lies.

Tell the truth. Honesty is the best policy is a wonderful phrase, because as hard as the truth is to face, "The truth will set you free." Indeed, truthful knowledge that grows understanding leads to better outcomes and deeper and more trusting relationships. When we tell the truth, especially with sincerity (not malice or vengeance), we make the world a more just and stable place, in alignment with the truths of G-d and Scripture.

Lying against one another creates division and distrust, and it destabilizes the good among us. For instance, if many in America begin to lie about American history, spinning our founders into hysterical racists and bigots, how will we not demoralize the American public into hatred against America itself? If we can make people feel bitterness about our founding, that bitterness can be used to make the country open to all sorts of "new" directions — socialist, communist, even fascist.

On the other hand, what if we lift up our founders as gods, infallible and larger than life? We would be unable to separate their misdeeds from their ideas. The lie that perfection existed in any one of our founders would lead many to believe slave ownership would be acceptable under some circumstances. The Bible is not compatible with this view and many of our founders agreed. The result of believing these sorts of lies would be a renewal of great evil.

And that would be the ultimate end of the lies: destruction. Even if all intentions were good.

The media breaks this 9th Command on a daily basis. It is no wonder we are so divided, so prone to gossip, our hearts turned to hatred and our words turned to poison. We have allowed lies and turns of phrase to convince us that our brother is really not our brother, our sister is out to get us, our nation is 100 percent racist, 100 percent sexist, evil in 100 percent of its very heart. Or, that it is flawless, inerrant, and a cosmic good in all corners of its works. Both sides are lying.

The truth resides somewhere closer to what we know about the human heart. Both evil and unbelievable good exist there. It is what we feed that defines how we behave. When we feed honesty and trust, we build that into our homes and eventually our society. The opposite is also true.

This is a Command that needs a lot more attention today. Do not lie to make a point, to defend your ideas, to cover a misdeed, or to excoriate another. Tell the truth. The world needs the truth.

Commandment 10 – You Shall Not Covet

"You shall not covet your neighbor's house: you shall not covet your neighbor's wife, or his male or female slave, or his ox or his ass, or anything that is your neighbor's."

The word "covet" here is from the Hebrew verb "lachmod." This word means to desire to the point of seeking to take something that belongs to another. You desire that specific something or someone that does not belong to you.

This is an important distinction. One of my core beliefs is that G-d will never ask people to do something they are not capable of with His help. There is no Law too burdensome for a human to bear. Yeshua tells us that his "yoke is easy and burden is light." The Law of G-d is freeing and produces holiness.

It would be impossible for people avoid thinking, "Hey, I'd love to have a house like that someday." Or, "I can't wait to be married. They look so happy." Or, "I wish I was a better basketball player like those guys." It is human nature to look to things we want and have the desire to work towards them. In fact, if you are desirous of a better relationship with G-d, this is considered righteous!

This Command is not about wanting something more, it is about wanting the specific something someone else has to the point you would pursue getting that **specific** object. This type of covetousness leads to theft, adultery, murder, and lying. It produces the exact sins we see already delineated in the previous Ten Commands. And often, you can catch your mind heading down this path and cut it off, if you understand and are prepared.

Proverbs tells us, "Guard your heart for from it comes your life." What you keep inside you, what you meditate on, produces your very life. It will and can dictate your actions.

Yeshua expands on this idea in Matthew 5:28: "But I say to you that whosoever looketh on a woman to lust after her hath committed adultery with her already in his heart."

Are you imagining committing sins in your mind? It will lead you right to it.

Coveting also prevents you from having gratitude for what is already given to you. That particular thing or person that does not belong to you is not yours for a reason. You are given particular things that are there to edify and refine YOUR life. Sometimes you choose things that do not. Through carelessness, neglect, or evil action, we can acquire all sorts of things that will cause us harm. But in general, those of us who go to work, come home, try our best at what we are talented in, attempt to be great parents, and so on, have what we have for a reason.

Do not let covetousness muddy your view of what is right in front of you. Love what you have so you can expand into the next thing.

Gratitude leads to growth. It also keeps you from sin.

This chapter could be longer. No doubt, as you meditate on these Ten Commandments you will find more uses and places where they belong! G-d continues to reveal His goodness through His laws, guiding His children out of cages and into freedom. Moreover, all the rest of the Law hangs on these Commands, which come directly from the Big Two — Love G-d and Love Others.

Could you imagine a society, or even a church where just covetousness alone was abolished? We would likely wipe out a large portion of gossip, infighting, theft, infidelity, violence, greed, the list goes on.

Today, during a fairly chaotic moment in our history, the definition of love is being debated before our very eyes. "You're only a loving person if you support BLM the organization." "You're only a loving person if you support my right to choose an abortion." "You're only a loving person if you get the Covid Vaccine!" "You're hateful if you call out sin. How dare you! Who do you think you are!?"

Sound familiar? Now, I'll hedge a little here, we ALWAYS desparately need grace. The Savior's grace for us cost Him His life and bought us ours. We must have grace, especially for those who have not actually met this G-d yet!

But we cannot deny how the people of G-d have strayed from even the most basic of His commands. I aim this critique at those who truly know G-d or claim to. Repentance is the path to healing and redemption. Without it, we will distort G-d's truths and align ourselves with evil instead of good.

So, the question must be posed. Do we take the covering of Yeshua's blood and spill it on the ground? Do we "expand" grace as Paul puts it, by continuing in sin? Is our salvation from sin and death a waste of time if sin is never removed from our lives? What power does the cross hold if it cannot even compel us to obedience?

Are you confused about what love really is? John tells us that to love the Lord is to obey His commands (1 John 5:3). In John 21, Jesus says to Peter, "If you love me, feed my sheep." Feed them what? Physical food? Yes. AND spiritual food.

When we eat of Yeshua's bread, we connect to His Commandments.

And what is commanded?

The Laws of G-d. Here in this Law we find G-d's definition of love. Because G-d is a loving father, He did not leave us in blindness as to the specifics of love. He did not leave us without instruction or a map on loving, so to speak. Our Father made it perfectly clear. Obedience to His things IS love. G-d IS love. Yeshua IS love.

He cannot give ANYTHING BUT LOVE.

> "Dear children, do not let anyone lead you astray. The one who does what is righteous is righteous, just as He is righteous. The one who does what is sinful is of the devil, because the devil has been sinning from the beginning. The reason the Son of God appeared was to destroy the devil's work." (1 John 3:7-8)

Do not be caught up in the ways of the world but be "transformed" (Romans 12:2). Obedience to G-d's things is transformative. We will become the likeness of Yeshua, walking in His Commands, which produce fruit. We will be following our Rabbi.

Yeshua obeyed each of these Laws. If your goal is to "just follow Jesus," then you'd better know how He lived. This is how He lived, in obedience to every Law that G-d (He himself) gave. And those Laws produced evidence of the extraordinary love of G-d and the evidence of G-d's Kingdom come to earth.

The Ten Commandments are essential for the Follower of Yeshua.

Chapter 5

CHURCH HISTORY

Ecclesiastes 12:13 "Fear God and keep His Commandments,
for this is man's all"

ANYONE WHO HAS BEEN A PARENT for at least five years knows the value of consistency. It reigns when it comes to raising a disciplined and well-balanced child. Whether consistency of home life, and schedules or just consistency of rules and consequences, without that stability of daily contracts made between you and your child, your child will suffer and the potency of your parenting will dilute.

Younger children, who have no idea where the boundaries are, no idea if punishment will be in store, and no idea how far they can push back, will often cross appropriate boundaries. They will scream when they don't get what they want, throw temper tantrums publicly, and even resort to all out blackmail. I've heard of children who will hold their breath until they pass out if they don't get their way, scaring their parents into submission.

Over time inconsistent parenting produces more dangerous results. Children who grow up in broken homes, living in multiple locations, dealing with new dads and new moms, are far more likely to struggle in school, struggle with addiction and experience higher rates of disease when they are older. (See Essay on The Family) Lack of stability is an insidious and often underappreciated weapon against the tiny soul. (**Instability and Children**)[xxxiv]

Children need safety, stability, and boundaries. It helps them learn to trust, learn to self-regulate, and learn to love.

We see stability patterned in thoughtful homes where parents decide to be on the same page, set boundaries, and make clear rules for their children to follow with rewards built in. Maybe the kids don't turn out perfect. None of us do. But they do have a fighting chance. That's about the best we can give anyone, honestly.

For some reason, the church has decided that the G-d we serve, the one we call Father, decided not to give us a fighting chance from the very start. Somehow this Father changed the rules in the middle of the game and confused His intentions. Somehow He didn't see the future, didn't have a plan in place, and didn't know what He was doing when He gave the message of the gospel to Abraham. But Paul tells us in Galations 3:8 "Scripture foresaw that God would justify the Gentiles by faith, and announced the gospel in advance to Abraham: 'All nations will be blessed through you.'" This quote about blessing comes directly from Genesis 12:2-3

From Genesis, G-d made his plans quite clear. From Abraham, from before Israel fell, G-d had planned for all nations to be brought into understanding of G-d THROUGH Abraham and his offspring. This G-d did know exactly what He was doing. He mapped it out meticulously.

The promise of a family of Heavenly Citizens came to and through Abraham. Not Paul, not Timothy. Not your current Protestant Pastor or Catholic Priest. No fledgling congregations can claim this astounding blessing was first proclaimed to them. Yet, we all are still benefiting from it. G-d's plan is being brought into fruition and His faithfulness through all time being proved. The promise is old and long lasting, still happening to this very day.

And though Abraham was NOT a Jew, he spawned the beginnings of a Hebraic people, culminating in 12 Tribes that would adopt, not just the Hebrew, but the Gentile as well. Through Abraham, the world has been and will be blessed.

G-d knew. In Him there is no inconsistency.

Yet many proclaim even today that the SAME Father we assert is all-knowing and powerful *gave rules to people at the beginning that He intended to change in the end.*

Perhaps those first people were less mature than we are. I know many who think this. But a short glance at human history (the 20th century is a quick case study) doesn't really give us a lot of hope in that theory.

After all, humans are still bloodthirsty, addicted to pride, violent, greedy, and lost. The Gulag Archipelego details horrific, unthinkable atrocities committed under Stalin. I've only been able to read that book in small sections, stopping when overwhelmed by the depth of evil, insanity, and apathy of people who really existed in the 20th century.

America has her same issues. We are not evolved to a higher level of spirituality or morality than Abraham. We are just as chaotic, just as prone to divorce, and infidelity, and envy and wickedness. Maybe even moreso.

Stability, self-control, clear instruction and good fatherhood would offer a welcome respite. But Christianity often delivers the opposite. Perhaps we are reflecting a more and more fatherless society. At the very least, this propensity for random change doesn't seem like good fatherhood. Nor does it seem organized and filled with divine clarity. Instability, poor planning, new rules, or rules that only apply to a certain set of children, a gospel disconnected from its foundations, and a G-d that promises He doesn't change but then makes an about-face right at Matthew.

This seems like a recipe for a bloody mess. And sure enough, it has been.

When we look at the history of the modern-day church, we find exactly that — bloody mess after bloody mess. The gospel washed in the blood of martyrs and watered down by the edicts of politicians and whims of church leadership. The truth has been twisted by those who would mix G-d's things with mans, and those who would mix the wisdom of the Bible with the tree of the Knowledge of Good and Evil.

It can be surreal at times to face historical facts around this mixing. All the well-meaning, loving, and powerful churches and leaders that exist in modern-day Christianity make it difficult to divulge such hard-hitting claims. And truly, it isn't really their fault. In fact, many of them are doing amazing work!

The root of the problem is that people can only teach what they *know*. We share what has been shared with us. That's about the best we can do unless we are open to more truth than that. Until we are clued in that we may not have it all correct, we don't go looking for the correction. That is just our nature.

This leaves many well-meaning pastors across the country teaching the twisted and watered-down Bible to attract new believers and to stay "relevant." But there is a price to pay for this. And it is heavy.

A keen observation of the state of the church and society should be enough to know the truth of G-d's Word is not being preached fully.

The Bible says that G-d's people perish for lack of knowledge (Hosea 4:1). Are Biblical values and the people who are supposed to believe in them disappearing? Is our impact on culture diminishing? Is our energy zapped?

Indeed, here we are, faced with lack of knowledge and truth.

Revival has often come hand-in-hand with knowledge. In 2 Kings 22, we find Josiah discovering a Torah scroll. This discovery changes the King's course. He cleans house, bringing righteousness and repentance back to the people.

Yeshua did not just bring with him a loving nature and extra fish and bread for people. He *taught* them. He made claim to restoring Scriptural understanding and the intentions of G-d's Word. In His loving work on the cross, He infused the prophecies and Law with meaning. Through the disciples, armed with this life changing knowledge, Yeshua spawned the most profound revival and movement the world has ever seen!

It's time to bring Scriptural knowledge back to our people. So we can, as a Church, make a well-informed choice. Do we really believe Scripture? Or are we content with the lie that G-d has changed?

I believe wholeheartedly, that for the Believer, knowledge adds layers of power to their walk and ministry. Instead of shying away from G-d's truths, the one who loves the Lord considers them, and chooses life.

Modern Church Doctrine

For thousands of years, many have blindly believed that all the doctrine taught on Sunday mornings has come from credible sources taught by near-perfect Believers at seminary or a form of it. Surely, seminaries have all the knowledge that a pastor will need to properly teach their congregants! And I don't doubt, that much great teaching and thinking, as well as training, can be found in the halls of a good seminary school. (I haven't been to one but I've spoken to many who have.)

On the other hand, one of my best friends from high school attended seminary and she said it almost destroyed her faith. Another one of my mentors stopped one class short of graduating for the very same reason. I honestly have no idea why or how that can happen, but we know it does.

I wonder if perhaps it was because their seminaries weren't teaching any of the things that actually ignite and sustain the faithful. Knowing these two people very well, they are people of good conscience, careful faithfulness, and insistence on correct Scriptural understanding. Something about seminary just didn't jive with their commitment to Christ. I've always wanted to understand this.

That being said, I often get some wonderful teaching and ideas from modern, American pastors. You can tell when they are passionate about their work and truly desire to serve their congregations. They are looking for those lovely details and intimate treasures in Scripture that will assist their congregants in faithfully following Christ. So why, after so many teachings, so much "knowledge" available to us, so many children's programs and music programs and online streams and so, so, so much talking, why in the world is the Church diminishing in value and presence in culture? Maybe that was always going to take place? The Bible is certainly not always popular.

And yes, historically the truly faithful have been fewer than the culturally relevant. But in America, certain covenants with G-d were made and our founders were particularly interested in aligning interests with the G-d of the Bible. Our culture has been shaped differently because the seeds planted here contained some unique DNA.

So now in the face of information expansion, perhaps we are all only responsible for recognizing the signs of some the other seeds that were planted; seeds that have profoundly affected our modern affinity for culture over set apart-ness.

Perhaps no area better exemplifies the culture's effect on the modern church than how Sunday music has changed. Where once choirs (an incredibly inclusive, powerful, and unique form of musical expression) graced the stages, we now have bands. Bands that resemble the rock expressions of 80s and 90s music.

You know the usual set up: drummer, electric guitarist, acoustic guitar/vocalist, bass player. That's the foundation. Sometimes there is a keys player. That group complete, we have achieved "the band" formula used in radio music for decades.

The protestant church decided at some point that this was the best way to express itself musically. Sometimes, there are even light shows and smoke machines to go along with this "praise." Maybe even video is streaming, and of course, the lyrics are up on the screen accompanied by some backing video that is probably flowing in an eye-catching, hypnotic pattern.

As a worship leader in more churches than I can count at the moment, I've often been asked to adjust my performance to be more stage-like. More like a Friday night rock show. "People will love seeing you perform that way!" So the story goes. And I've always wondered if anybody asked G-d about me stealing a bit of the spotlight, maybe just sitting on His throne for a quick second. It's not Satanic if I don't mean anything by it, right? Perhaps G-d doesn't mind. I mean, in the face of "excellence," how can He possibly be offended if in hyping ourselves we hype Him?

As for me, I imagine that in the throne room of G-d, our light shows and sound systems would be noticed no more than a slight buzzing and flittering of a fly at Red Rocks.

The Bible tells us that the prayers of the Saints are like incense before the Lord. And how much prayer and authentic praise can take place when musicians are constantly trying to distract the congregants with their performance? I'm not sure, but I don't like the odds. (More on this in my essay on Worship)

In the meantime, for all the bands and fanfare, people still aren't attending church like they did even 20 years ago. A **Gallup poll**[xxxv] taken in 2019 found that only half of Americans are now church members. That's down around 70 percent from 1999. Church attendance was 70 percent or higher from the years 1937 – 1976. More than half of the current 70 percent decline has happened in the last decade alone.

The band isn't working.

But why would it? We took the idea from culture and decided it would be the foundation for building a deep and meaningful following. But, if someone walks into church and they are looking for a show that they could see on Friday night at a club or venue, then they aren't looking for G-d. Perhaps they want excellence. That's fine. Horrible music is horribly distracting. But what's the deeper search?

People searching for G-d are looking for something unique to their everyday experience. Their lives aren't enough. That band on Friday night didn't cut it. The fog machine and light shows and jumping musicians and stage sound just didn't fill that G-d-shaped hole. They are looking for more.

Now, I'm not saying that there aren't great worship leaders and bands that lead people into praise. I hope there are. I've led these bands for over a decade. Music is a powerful tool in the Believer's worship arsenal. If you want to change the tone of a room, if you want to refocus your mind, if you want to prepare your heart to listen to the Holy Spirit, music is a fabulous tool. Not to mention a commanded way to praise Yahweh! And there is nothing wrong with praising in a band. In fact, there is often everything right about it.

But I promise you, the band on stage is not a replacement for praise that happens alone, for quiet time in God's presence, for real teaching that assists people in understanding, and for community that could far more easily be built with a church choir or at least a focus on congregational voices.

Choir-like corporate praise is found in the very first song of Scripture. Moses' song, the song Israel sang after their Exodus from Egypt, was a choir. It was the nation singing as one. This is the first song in the Bible. This is a benchmark for communal praise.

Worship, Scripturally, is defined as bowing low, humbling one-self to the King. This sort of spiritual adoration of G-d doesn't come from cultural understandings of entertainment. It is, rather, uniquely built in acts of obedience and a tender heart that are neither seen nor oft praised.

It is literally the opposite of a band on stage. Worship is a ceremony of the heart.

But the church hardly allows even a minute for these moments to bow. Because the church believes that the culture knows better. *Entertain* people becomes the status quo.

Music is not the only place where culture has had enormous influence. In fact, the band choice in modern worship tends to be preferential, NOT sinful. But just observe the doctrinal belief shifts from just a few decades ago in areas with far greater spiritual degradation:

- Homosexuals in leadership
- Sex outside of marriage
- Television viewing habits (See My Essay on Technology)
- Drinking and drug use
- Remembering and keeping the Sabbath (See My Essay on the Big Ten)
- Materialism and the love of money
- Honoring your father and mother
- Abortion

Overall, the church seems to be blurring the lines or keeping silent on issues where it used to be adamantly clear. Self-control is no longer a Beattitude worth pursuing, despite it being the foundation for all obedience.

GRACE and LAW

Furthermore, current church doctrine has pitted grace against G-d's Laws. Somehow the Old Testament people HAD to keep all the Laws of G-d to receive grace, but the New Testament people now are free from this burden. A few questions may leave, even the most prestigious Biblical Scholar furiously turning Bible pages for answers:

- Where does G-d say that you have to keep the whole Law to receive salvation in the Old Testament?
- When Israel was saved from Egypt, was it because she was a perfect law keeper or because G-d had mercy and grace for her?
- Why did David receive grace and mercy?
- Why did Israel receive grace and mercy time and again?
- Why did the city of Nineveh receive mercy and grace?

Sadly, many don't understand that keeping the Law was NEVER a requirement for grace or salvation. In fact, without the law, we would not even have a definition for grace. *The Law makes grace a requirement for salvation*! Additionally, the number 5 in Scripture is a number representing grace and ALSO representing the Law, the Torah, the first 5 books of the Bible.

Grace and the Law are hand in hand. Not in opposition.

It was a blessing for the fledgling Church in Exodus to receive the Law at Sinai. It was gracious that G-d would desire to write His instructions down that all could share in them equally and become His people.

In fact, Israel had already disobeyed the Law egregiously by the time Moses came down Sinai with the Torah. Yet, G-d still kept them as His people. It took much longer for Him to divorce from them. Again and again and again He gave Israel mercy and grace with no requirement for perfection.

G-d was merciful and gracious from the beginning. His character does not change throughout all of Scripture.

Obedience is relational, grace is salvational.

G-d's people have never obeyed for salvation, they have obeyed because G-d, the G-d they love, told them to.

So how in the world did we lose this "first love," as Jesus in Revelation preaches?

The reasons are much older than the modern church. We have to go back further to understand the seed of all modern Christian church doctrine: Catholicism.

BEGINNINGS

Admittedly, even here at the emergence of Catholicism, we are not far enough back to see the seed of perversion of church doctrine. The first time we see the Church in Scripture is all the way back in Exodus. Church in Hebrew (Ecclesia in Greek) means "called out assembly." This assembly made of Israelites and Egyptians was the first church and there we have our first example of what church looks like. It is Jews and Gentiles called out of culture to be "separate and holy." Set apart to serve G-d's Kingdom.

This first church receives the first written teaching and instruction, the Laws given from Genesis through Deuteronomy. These are the first five books of the Bible, which are traditionally called the Torah.

We have to take a moment and consider what Laws of G-d this nation likely already knew. Cain and Abel understood the concepts of sacrifice, Abraham and Noah understood altars; there are many references to G-d's Laws being present in pre-Moses followers of G-d. Somehow, before the written Law, people knew some of the Commandments and followed them. Perhaps Adam and Eve learned them from Yeshua as they walked with Him in the Garden of Eden. What we do know is that some of the concepts that Moses brought down from Mount Sinai were already widely understood.

The giving of the written Law is an incredibly important moment in our church history. The nation of Israel was growing larger and had left Egypt with a contingent of non-Hebrew folk. Egyptians joined the nation in its Exodus from Egypt. This written Law would have been a gift in clarity for this nascent people, and to this fledgling church G-d gives the most foundational instruction for His Church for all time.

I liken this to parenting. When you have a 3-year-old, you want to make it clear that she doesn't run into a busy street. In order to get this message across, you tell her, "Don't run across the street! It's dangerous! Cars can hit you. You are too small. It is beyond your capacity to handle!" Etc. You don't go ahead and explain the intricacies of four-lane intersections, nor do you dissect how painful being hit by a car really is, or the procedures a doctor has to do to save your life if you do get hit. It's the beginning. You teach the most important part immediately. It's simple.

Do this, don't do that.

The first five books of the Bible ring that way at times. Here are the teachings and instructions of G-d. You can observe why and how they are beautiful and why they work. You can guess at all the reasons they are given and how that plays out in individuals and societies. G-d leaves much of that to the rest of Scripture and to us over time. Are the Laws of G-d good for people, for the nations that abide by them, for the people that hold to them?

These and others are helpful evaluation tools to analyze the truth and beauty of G-d's Law. But the analysis flows from first understanding the main idea: These are G-d's instructions for living in love to Him and to others.

He has laid out the essential instruction there in the Torah. Six hundred and thirteen positive and negative laws that would sustain the nation of Israel and would stand the test of time, being repeated throughout Scripture. In places like Daniel and Revelation, we even see prophecy about the final days and those who keep to G-d's first Commands. Here you will find how you avoid the spiritual and physical pitfalls and traps that exist on a fallen earth.

Here is how you walk like a citizen of Heaven.

On the day of Shavuot (Christians call it Pentecost), the early Church received these laws in written form. David calls them a blessing, wisdom, and priceless, and G-d calls them love. Yeshua says that all the Law and the prophets can be summed up in two ideas: Love the Lord and Love others (Matthew 22). Each and every law given is about love. The early church learned the rules of love and it kept them alive to this day, despite breaking them quite often.

After Exodus, Israel embarks on a journey of highs and lows in their relationship with the G-d of Abraham, Isaac and Jacob. The nation gains and loses the Promised Land. The dispersion of the Northern Kingdom, (which the Bible also calls the House of Israel), breaks apart the 12 Tribes. (The House of Judah, historically identified with the Southern Kingdom, is where modern-day Jews take their name.) The Church goes through massive hardship, and also loses much of its connection to the Torah.

Mixing in the practices of the nations it inhabits or outright rebelling against G-d are defining sins in the story of Israel. It is no wonder we see the same thing happen at the dawn of the Catholic Church. What happened during the time of Constantine was and is nothing new; however, it has been deemed as a great moment in church history and a new beginning for the church. Church doctrine has been taken from this time period and molded to fit evermore into our modern environment. Not enough of what was given to the early church in Exodus survived.

No, I'm not the biggest fan of the 300 AD Church history (or before or after for that matter) time period of the Church. Let me explain why.

Think about this. Before Matthew, the Bible stories up to that point were filled with the things of Yahweh. The Law was G-d's. It was all part of G-d and what G-d was doing. After Yeshua and the New Testament, many began to teach that the Law is a "Jewish" thing. It is no longer G-d's or belonging to G-d's people. To the peoples then and now, the Law is something that just the Jews do and even they don't realize that they shouldn't do them anymore.

What a strange transition.

Off-putting almost.

Out of context, inconsistent, abrupt and, oddly enough, not found in the actions or teachings of Yeshua at all!

We still have church leadership today discussing the "Jewishness" of the Old Testament. In a sermon given at Northpoint Church, GA, Andy Stanley stated, "First century Church leaders unhitched the church from the worldview, value system, and regulations of the Jewish Scriptures… Peter, James, Paul elected to unhitch the Christian faith from their Jewish scriptures, and my friends, we must as well."[xxxvi]

Jewish Scriptures? Does Yeshua talk about Jewish versus Gentile Scriptures? If He does, someone needs to show me.

So where did this doctrine begin, since it was obviously not with Yeshua?

Let me introduce a verse many Believers are unfamiliar with. It comes out of Daniel 7:25. In speaking about the 4th Beast and the work of the anti-christ, Daniel is told, "He will speak against the Most High and oppress His holy people and try to change the set times and the laws."

This word for "times" is Mo-edim which means G-d's appointed times. According to Scripture these times are the Feast Days and the Sabbath Day delineated in Exodus and Leviticus. The work of the anti-christ, according to Daniel, is to change G-d's times and G-d's laws.

Huh. So, the change is…

Satan's?

At the time of Daniel, the Law of G-d was found in the Torah — the first 5 books of the Bible.

According to Daniel, the Anti-Christ wants those things to be changed. Has he been successful?

When we read the book of Acts, we find that the early Church kept all of the Laws. They celebrated the original Sabbath day (Friday night to Saturday night), they celebrated the Feast Days, and they kept the dietary laws. The obedience mentioned about the church in Acts reflects the spirit of the early Church. They followed all, not some, of G-d's Commands. Not only did Yeshua not change his own Laws, but the church in Acts did not attempt to change the laws either. (Acts 2:1- Keeping of Pentecost which is known as Shavuot in the OT, Acts 12:3-4 Feasts of the Lord, Passover and Firstfruits, Acts 20:6 Days of Unleavened Bread, Acts 27:9 the "fast" is the Day of Atonement, Day of The Lord or Yom Kippur)

As to what exactly changed after Yeshua's resurrection Brad Scott of Wildbranch Ministry says this:

"It's not really that sacrifices and a priesthood and a temple ended. None of those things ended. It was 'who' was the sacrifice, 'who' was the priesthood, and 'who' was the temple now. And those are the three things that have to do with atonement for sin… All three of those things we are now a part of. Messiah became our eternal sacrifice, we are a temple of God and we are a royal Priesthood."

These shifts in location of roles do not nullify the rest of the Law. The location of some of the roles has shifted. This is a very different view from that occurring during the emergence of Catholicism.

Here we may begin a summary of the history of the Catholic Church's doctrinal teachings and influence, from Yeshua until now.

CATHOLIC CHURCH HISTORY

I will be blowing through a LOT of history in a short amount of time. You will find much of this from writers and historians like Cassius Dio, Jerome, the Talmud, and can also dig up quite a bit of this history in good old Encyclopedias.

In about 132 AD, the Roman Emperor, Hadrian, built a temple to Jupiter in Jerusalem and he renamed the city Aelia Capitolina. (**Hadrian**)[xxxvii] At this time, followers of Yeshua had named themselves The Way. A sect of Judaism, they faintly resembled the "Christians" that would emerge later, while also somewhat resembling traditional Jews. They existed as a blend of both believers in Yeshua and keepers of the Torah. Very much the position I find myself in often!

During this time, the Jews (not followers of the Way) were dismayed at what Rome was doing in Jerusalem as paganism crept into the Holy City's temples and practices.

There arose a revolt led by Simon Bar Kokhba against Rome, which the followers of The Way did not join. Denying that Yeshua was the Messiah, the Jews began to see Bar Kokhba as the Messianic savior. He was a strong military leader, which many Jews were expecting from the return of Yeshua.

But those of The Way knew better.

The revolt failed and out of this, more confusion and chaos ensued.

Suddenly, G-d's teachings, which The Way (also sometimes known as the Nazarenes), followed became "Jewish" things as more and more pagan and Roman influence poured in from the increasing Roman power. As the Gentiles came into the faith, they brought with them their celebratory days, ideas, foods, and traditions.

In the meantime, those keeping Torah were too often teaching that in order to be saved, everyone had to keep Torah perfectly. Paul's ministry was often centered around correcting this issue, but the confusion continued beyond Paul and the other disciples' ministries.

The Way was caught in the middle with Paul. Attempting to both keep G-d's Commandments and recognizing the need for Yeshua's gift of salvation through grace, The Way was a narrow path between the secular and the legalistic.

These divisions grew until about 300 AD.

Marcion of Pontus 85-160 AD

I'm often overwhelmed at how this one man's influence spread a particular view of Scripture that has stood the test of time so dutifully. How, in the face of all the Believers we have today, is Marcionism still so popular? His teachings that divide the Old and New Testament G-d into two idolatrous figures hold sway among American Believers in pews every Sunday. It seems unfair. But history is filled with these sorts of mistakes and diversions from truth.

According to Justin Martyr, by 150 AD Marcion's heresies had spread to the whole human race.

So, who was Marcion?

According to Brittanica (**Marcion of Pontus**)[xxxviii], he was well-known to church fathers, especially Tertullian, as a heretic. His teaching made a radical distinction between the god of The Old Testament (the creator) and Jesus (the god of love).

His principal Biblical direction came from the books that Paul wrote to the exclusion of context or other Biblical text.

One example that highlights the problematic instruction of Marcion is that Marcionism suggested that to be a true follower of Christ one must be celibate. Hence what we experience in Catholicism even today. But many other things were slowly adopted that twisted the original message of Yeshua and the Disciples' true teachings.

A few tenets of Marcionism included:

1. Christianity is distinct from and in opposition to Judaism
2. Rejection of the OT
3. Two different gods exist between the Old and New Testaments
4. Marcion gets credited with coining the terms Old Testament and New Testament

From the 2nd century on, Marcionism and Christianity were often considered one and the same.

According to Marcion himself, "The Jewish Christ was designated by the Creator solely to restore the Jewish people from the Diaspora; but our Christ (in Paul's writings) was commissioned by the good god of the NT to liberate all mankind."

The OT demiurge, according to Marcion, is not the same god we meet in the New Testament. The Old Testament god is mean, judgmental and ushered in the age of the "law". But the good god saves us from this Old Testament god and brings us grace.

Huh, in these exact words, most preachers would dare not tread. But certainly each Sunday we are taught that the Old Testament was a timeframe where people were "under the Law" and that the Law cursed people. Yeshua frees us from this, according to modern Christian doctrine. Somewhere in the middle of Scripture G-d changed.

It's almost as if He was a different being before Matthew, yes?

Is this not Marcionism?

Many ancient, respected church Fathers rejected Marcionism more forcefully and fluently than we ever attempt today.

Tertullian put it this way his book, *Against Marcion: Book 1*, "The separation of Law and Gospel is the primary and principal exploit of Marcion. His disciples cannot deny this, which stands at the head of their document, that document by which they are inducted, into and confirmed in this heresy. For such are Marcion's Anti-theses, or Contrary Oppositions, which are designed to show the conflict and disagreement of the Gospel and the Law, so that from the diversity of principles between those two documents they may argue further for a diversity of gods. Therefore, as it is precisely this separation of Law and Gospel which has suggested a god of the Gospel, other than and in opposition to the God of the Law, it is evident that before that separation was made."

Injected into Marcion's faulty philosophy history also offers ample evidence of his deep hatred of the Jews. His anti-semitic views of Scripture and G-d survive long after him as we will see later in studying the history of the Catholic Church as well as protestant leadership all the way through the 20th century.

Even certain books of the NT were too Jewish for Marcion. One of those books was the book of Acts. According to Marcion, there were too many Jewish things happening in Acts. Dietary laws, feast days, 12 disciples, on and on.

During this time, the Greek Bishop, Iranaeus also had a few critiques for the Marcionite trend. In *Adversus Haereses: Book IV*, Chapter 13 he stated, "And that the Lord did not abrogate the natural (precepts) of the law…For, it has been said to them of old time, Do not commit adultery. But I say unto you, that every one who hath looked upon a woman to lust after her, hath committed adultery with her already in his heart... For all these do not contain or imply an opposition to and an overturning of the (precepts) of the past, as Marcion's followers do strenuously maintain; but they exhibit a fulfilling and an extension of them."

He continues, "With regards to those (Marcionites) who allege that Paul alone knew the truth, and that to him the mystery was manifested by revelation, let Paul himself convict them, when he says, that one and the same God wrought in Peter for the apostolate of the circumcision, and in himself for the Gentiles. Peter therefore, was an apostle of that very God whose was also Paul; and Him whom Peter preached as God among those of the circumcision, and likewise the Son of God, did Paul (declare) also among the Gentiles."

Indeed, the overemphasis on Paul, (ahem... do we see that today?) came from Marcion. This obsession with using Paul to justify new doctrines cries out from the graves of thousands of ministers past. It is as old as Paul himself. (See my essay on Righting Paul)

Despite many admonitions of the church fathers of this time period and thereafter, efforts at tamping down such a deliciously responsibility-free version of G-d were unsuccessful. For the eager ears of Gnostic folly, ease and mystery abounded in the god of the New Testament, full of grace that rids us of his counterpart's burdensome obedience.

Marcion is an important figure defining the "how" behind the morphing and mixing of the Church after the disciples. It also reveals how rabid anti-Semitism in Christianity rose to popularity.

Many Christians began to (and still do) believe Marcion and they started to theorize that the OT Laws were only allegorical and they only represented spiritual principals, which was a theory founded in the popular Gnostic ideology of the day. By adopting this theory, they could state that we no longer need to follow any Torah Laws literally. Each Law simply represents some spiritual principal.

Sound familiar?

If not, perhaps you haven't been to enough contemporary church services. The church now states that G-d sees our hearts and judges our hearts through our INTENTIONS. If our heart intentions are pure, we don't have to worry about many of the Laws of G-d. Our hearts are the spiritual part of us, so they are all that really matter. Anything goes as long as "in our hearts" we meant well.

Or, if you are attending something more conservative, the Protestant and Catholic will burden you with many additional non-Biblical tasks, like Church attendance, confession, praying with beads or praying to Mary or other Saints. Ash Wednesday, Good Friday, Lent and the like are also especially signs of piety, though not Biblically dictated. They will tell you the 10 Commandments still apply. Still, the mix of pagan and Biblical is so chemically compounded that one may never know which thing is G-d's and which thing is just… well -- not.

One might ask, is the negligence that results in sin acceptable as long as we "meant well"?

I agree that G-d judges the heart. And in America, with all of our access to information and to G-d's Word, it is quite easy to see the "intentions" of too many in the Church. It is intended that we ignore the parts of Scripture that we do not immediately understand and completely change the ones we don't immediately *like.*

My question is: If your heart is for G-d, how can you be against His Word in the Old Testament? If your heart is for G-d, why are you not interested in learning His Law?

How did we get to so many principles and admonitions not found in Scripture and how do we so easily ignore the many that lay right there in the text? History helps us here.

Now enter the First Council of Nicea, around 325 AD. This council was convened to decide what doctrines the Church would agree to regarding Christ and which written things were acceptable to include in the Biblical canon. Information to note from this council:

No Jews or followers of The Way participated. This was only for Bishops invited by Constantine. After this council, Christianity became the official religion of the Roman State. But only a Christianity that is completely separate from the Jews or Way followers.

Constantine wrote that, "We should have nothing in common with the Jews." When joining the church, Jews had to renounce any OT Laws. No Feast Days, no Sabbath, no dietary laws.

Thus continued an ever-growing separation of Jews from Christians that spiraled into oppression of the Jews and anything that looked "Jewish." People were forced to be "Christians" to hold any sort of political office. Christmas and Easter became the official festivals of the church, replacing the Feast Days found in Leviticus. Christianity was infused with a Marcion-like obsession with Paul and destruction of too literal a view of the rest of Scripture.

The arts began to follow suit with paintings and drawings of images of Jews as devils with horns. The Jews were accused of being Christ haters, murderers, and worthy of punishment.

Christian theologians began spreading lies about the Jews.

For example, John Chrysostom, a famous preacher in Constantinople said about the Jews in the late 4th century, "They murder their offspring to worship the avenging devils who are foes of our life. The Jews are the most worthless of all men. They are lecherous, greedy, rapacious… For killing God there is no expiation possible… God always hated the Jews, it is incumbent upon all Christians to hate the Jews…"[xxxix] He continued on this theme in many writings discussing why the Jews would forever be persecuted and how to ensure they would be.

From 300 – 600 AD, discriminatory laws piled high. Under Emperor Justinian, the church law became state policy. We know it still today as the Justinian Code. The Jews were not allowed to hold high offices or pursue military careers, it became a capital offense to convert to Judaism, intermarriage between Jews and Christians could be punished by death, reading of the Torah in Hebrew was forbidden, Jews were only allowed certain sections of scriptures or prayers, circumcision was banned, and Jewish property was confiscated.

In 418 AD, Bishop Severus forced Jews to convert or die.

In 489 AD, a Christian mob set fire to a synagogue in Antioch and slain Jewish bodies were thrown into the fire.

In the 11th Century, Peter The Venerable (a Benedictine Abott) stated, "Truly I doubt whether a Jew could really be human… I bring thee forward you Jew, you brute beast, before all men." (**Against the Inveterate Obduracy of the Jews**)[xl]

And can we forget the Crusades? When the Crusaders arrived in Israel, they rallied around the synagogue, rounded up the Jews, threw them into the synagogue, and burned the building down while singing "Christ We Adore Thee."

At the church's 4th council in 1215, Pope Innocent III concluded by condemning the Jews to slavery. He stated, "Yet as wanderers they remain upon the earth and their countenance be filled with shame." Church doctrine continued after for thousands of years in eagerness to exterminate, enslave, persecute, and obliterate the Jews.

The Council's Cannon 68 stated that, "Jews must be distinguished from the Christian by a different dress, moreover during the last three days before Easter and especially on Good Friday they shall not go out in public at all."

In the Middle Ages, many Popes made decrees that were based upon what the early Catholic Church Fathers had taught. Church theology had been brutally changed from the days of the followers of the Way and the book of Acts. The continuation of hatred of all things that looked Jewish spawned the teachings that G-d started something new (and quite separate) after Christ.

During the Black Plague, the Jewish people remained faithful to the Laws of Scripture about quarantines, and how to care for the sick. Because of this Jews avoided the plague compared to their contemporaries. Given this miraculous health, a belief spread that Jews were poisoning the wells and were themselves the creators of the plague. Conspiracy theories provoking negative projections of Jews abounded. (I'll attempt no comparisons to Covid-19 here, but some smart person could make some good ones.)

Martin Luther himself was a rabid anti-semite. Yes, hard as it is to stomach, the venerated Church Father was quite the racist.

According to Luther, ***(The Jews and Their Lies***)[xli] "Therefore know, my dear Christians, that next to the Devil, you have no more bitter, more poisonous, more vehement an enemy than a real Jew who earnestly desires to be a Jew. There may be some among them who believe what the cow or the goose believes. But all of them are surrounded with their blood and circumcision. In history, therefore, they are often accused of poisoning wells, stealing children and mutilating them; as in Trent, Weszensee and the like. Of course, they deny this. Be it so or not, however, I know full well that the ready will is not lacking with them if they could only transform it into deeds, in secret or openly."

More Excerpts from Luther's Work:

"Their breath stinks for the gold and silver of the heathen; since no people under the sun always have been, still are, and always will remain more avaricious than they, as can be noticed in their cursed usury. They also find comfort with this: 'When the Messiah comes, He shall take all the gold and silver in the world and distribute it among the Jews.' Thus, wherever they can direct Scripture to their insatiable avarice, they wickedly do so."

"Moreover, they are nothing but thieves and robbers who daily eat no morsel and wear no thread of clothing which they have not stolen and pilfered from us by means of their accursed usury. Thus, they live from day to day, together with wife and child, by theft and robbery, as arch-thieves and robbers, in the most impenitent security."

"What shall we Christians do with this rejected and condemned people, the Jews? Let us apply the ordinary wisdom of other nations like France, Spain, Bohemia, et al., who made them give an account of what they had stolen through usury, and divided it evenly; but expelled them from their country; For as heard before, God's wrath is so great over them that through soft mercy they only become more wicked, through hard treatment, however, only a little better. Therefore, away with them!"

"Since they live among us, we dare not tolerate their conduct, now that we are aware of their lying and reviling and blaspheming. If we do, we become sharers in their lies, cursing and blasphemy. Thus, we cannot extinguish the unquenchable fire of divine wrath, of which the prophets speak, nor can we convert the Jews. With prayer and the fear of God we must practice a sharp mercy to see whether we might save at least a few from the glowing flames. We dare not avenge ourselves. Vengeance a thousand times worse than we could wish them already has them by the throat. I shall give you my sincere advice:

"First to set fire to their synagogues or schools and to bury and cover with dirt whatever will not burn, so that no man will ever again see a stone or cinder of them. This is to be done in honor of our Lord and of Christendom, so that God might see that we are Christians, and do not condone or knowingly tolerate such public lying, cursing, and blaspheming of his Son and of his Christians. For whatever we tolerated in the past unknowingly—and I myself was unaware of it—will be pardoned by God. But if we, now that we are informed, were to protect and shield such a house for the Jews, existing right before our very nose, in which they lie about, blaspheme, curse, vilify, and defame Christ and us (as was heard above), it would be the same as if we were doing all this and even worse ourselves, as we very well know.

"I advise that their houses also be razed and destroyed. For they pursue in them the same aims as in their synagogues. Instead they might be lodged under a roof or in a barn, like the gypsies. This will bring home to them that they are not masters in our country, as they boast, but that they are living in exile and in captivity, as they incessantly wail and lament about us before God."

"Third, I advise that all their prayer books and Talmudic writings, in which such idolatry, lies, cursing and blasphemy are taught, be taken from them."

"Fourth, I advise that their rabbis be forbidden to teach henceforth on pain of loss of life and limb. For they have justly forfeited the right to such an office by holding the poor Jews captive with the saying of Moses in which he commands them to obey their teachers on penalty of death, although Moses clearly adds: 'what they teach you in accord with the Law of the Lord.' Those villains ignore that. They wantonly employ the poor people's obedience contrary to the law of the Lord and infuse them with this poison, cursing, and blasphemy. In the same way the pope also held us captive with the declaration in Matthew 16 :18, 'You are Peter,' etc, inducing us to believe all the lies and deceptions that issued from his devilish mind. He did not teach in accord with the Word of God, and therefore he forfeited the right to teach."

"Fifth, I advise that safe-conduct on the highways be abolished completely for the Jews. For they have no business in the countryside, since they are not lords, officials, tradesmen, or the like. Let them stay at home... If you princes and nobles do not close the road legally to such exploiters, then some troop ought to ride against them, for they will learn from this pamphlet what the Jews are and how to handle them and that they ought not to be protected. You ought not, you cannot protect them, unless in the eyes of God you want to share all their abomination.

"Sixth, I advise that usury be prohibited to them, and that all cash and treasure of silver and gold be taken from them and put aside for safekeeping. The reason for such a measure is that, as said above, they have no other means of earning a livelihood than usury, and by it they have stolen and robbed from us all they possess. Such money should now be used in no other way than the following: Whenever a Jew is sincerely converted, he should be handed one hundred, two hundred, or three hundred florins, as personal circumstances may suggest. With this he could set himself up in some occupation for the support of his poor wife and children, and the maintenance of the old or feeble. For such evil gains are cursed if they are not put to use with God's blessing in a good and worthy cause.

"Seventh, I commend putting a flail, an ax, a hoe, a spade, a distaff, or a spindle into the hands of young, strong Jews and Jewesses and letting them earn their bread in the sweat of their brow, as was imposed on the children of Adam (Gen 3:19). For it is not fitting that they should let us accursed Goyim toil in the sweat of our faces while they, the holy people, idle away their time behind the stove, feasting and farting, and on top of all, boasting blasphemously of their lordship over the Christians by means of our sweat. No, one should toss out these lazy rogues by the seat of their pants."

I quote Luther extensively so that the reader may have no doubt. One of the Church's great heroes is one of history's most vocal anti-Semites. The writings of Luther are abhorrently hateful towards the Jews. He left the Catholic Church, but he certainly did not leave behind hatred of anything that looked "Jewish."

And so G-d's things were not fully restored by the Reformation.

These attitudes and political antics led to the abolishment of anything that resembled Judaism. Anything that comes from the Old Testament became greatly watered down or done away with altogether. The Catholic Church readily admits that it has taken steps to rid us of the Feasts of the Lord, change the Sabbath Day, and etc. The Protestant Reformation was just another sprout off of this Catholic idea that the Old Testament held little relevance compared to Paul and that the Law was nailed to the cross.

As history played out, thousands of Jews were killed during the Spanish Inquisition because, again, they would not comply with the Catholic culture. The Catholic Church portrayed the Jew as demonic and evil. Nothing new, the same evils and patterns continued.

During the Enlightenment, Jews were allowed to be a part of society once again, among their non-Jewish neighbors. Now, because there was opportunity, the Jews began to attend schools and mingle with non-

Jews more often, adopting the Gentile nations' ideas and religious philosophies. This time, the Jews gave over their beliefs voluntarily.

After the Enlightenment, anti-Semitism advanced again and Jews were once again targeted. In 1891, the Pogroms in Russia commenced and ignited the oppression, abuse, and murder of Jewish people. The year 1901 brought the Protocols of the Learned Elders of Zion. This book was published and it spoke about a secret Zionist conspiracy to rule the world.

Henry Ford would later reference this text in his own anti-Semitic booklet series called, ***The International Jew***[xlii], Ford used his own personal newspaper to lay out what he called, the "Jewish Menace."

Long history and powerful influences convinced millions of Christians to hate Jews. People believed Jews were of the devil or at the very least, Satanic in their business dealings. (Sound familiar?)

And centuries of this engrained hatred allowed for the Holocaust. What is crucial to note is the well-documented speeches in which Hitler exploited and used Martin Luther's anti-Semitic teachings to promote his murderous cause.

Dietrich Bonhoeffer, the famous German Theologian and Lutheran pastor, attempted to convince the German Church to join him in repudiating Hitler. On too many accounts, he failed. The church refused to join him early enough and the Catholic Church even came to an agreement with Hitler to support the Third Reich in return for less governmental controls over the church.

Today, the Catholic Church is well known for the vicious, hideous scandal of protecting priests who have sexually abused children. As history goes, this is just one of the church's great misdeeds. One of many.

It is difficult to face Catholic history, especially knowing the countless charities Catholic congregants support, and how many good people attend Catholic mass each weekend. They are our neighbors. In very fact, they are us! This is the seed of the Protestant church as well. Much of the rest of European and American Christianity has become a branch off of this foreign root. (Although letters from George Washington to Jewish Communities at the founding of our country show a very amiable relationship with our first President and the Jewish Community)

So, with honest love in my heart, let me clarify here, as I often do, that I do not intend to critique individuals. So many true Believers exist across all denominations.

But the institutions at the helm, the history, the documentation, the doctrines, these we must analyze.

There are good and G-dly people in all religions and walks of life. And it is our duty and call to love individuals whole-heartedly, while staunchly standing for truth and justice so that we may rightly serve our Creator.

But how can this be the history of the headship of the Catholic and Protestant Church? Where did they get this seed of anti-Semitism and anti-Biblical teaching?

One more history lesson will give us the answer.

Catholic Church History – Connections to BC era Doctrines

Let's start by observing that the Catholic Church claims it was founded by Jesus Christ. This would mean that its teachings and doctrine should all be derived from Scripture alone and no previous history outside the Bible should hold sway or influence.

And yet…

Christmas, Easter, Good Friday, the sainthood and worship of so many Biblical characters, including Mary and Peter, round wafers for communion, newborn baptism. Where did these things come from? You can't find them with Yeshua, nor in Scripture.

But these things were incorporated from practices that were centuries old. They were not new to the New Testament, as most Catholics believe. Some of these are old practices dating back to ancient Babylon. They are the practices of those who worshiped gods, not of the Bible, but of man's making. And somehow, they found their way into the seed of the church of the West.

CHRISTMAS

The most sentimental of all the holidays for believers, this one is a tough one to question, but question it we must. For it has nothing to do with Christ. (See Essay *The Real Jesus)* The facts are as follows:

- The ancient Hebrews and early Christians did not celebrate birthdays. They observed and tracked them, but they weren't attended with the magnificent festivity that today's birthdays often produce. Perhaps this is why the Bible is not explicit about the exact date of Christ's birth. The ancients did, however, celebrate deaths. They believed being born was not nearly as important as having lived a great life. Death was the weightier reflection on a life.

This is not to say celebrating birthdays is anti-Biblical. Unless your birthday is dedicated to G-d and staunchly part of your religious activity, celebrate away.

But Yeshua's birthday celebration isn't mentioned in Scripture for a reason. It wasn't celebrated in our way. It was perhaps hidden somewhere else.

- The shepherds watched their "flocks by night." Scripture describes Shepherds in their fields at night. December is rainy season in Israel. They would never have been out at night with their flocks in December. However, they did traditionally watch their flocks through the night in summer and fall, which makes it much more likely the Jesus was born in the fall.

- The Biblical fall festival of Sukkot is the "G-d With Us" celebration. It is a celebration of G-d tabernacle-ing with His people in the desert. Given that Christ came to fulfill all that was prophesied, if he was born during Sukkot then He would be "fulfilling" the meaning of this Festival by coming to "Tabernacle" with us during that time. This alignment gives more meaning and depth to the story of Christ's birth and lines up with many a historian's opinion of it. (More on this in The Real Jesus Essay)

- In the Roman world, Saturnalia was a time of merrymaking and gift-giving. December 25 was also chosen as the birthdate of the Iranian god, **Mithra**,[xliii] called the Sun of Righteousness. The Germans and Celts had Yule with yule logs, cakes, evergreen trees, and wreaths that all commemorated different aspects of the season. "Fires and lights, symbols of warmth and lasting life, have always been associated with winter festival, both pagan and Christian." (*Encyclopedia Britannica,* 15th ed., vol. II, p. 903)

Alright, so what's the big deal? Over time, after Christ, we stole a little bit here and there to create the marvelous religious traditions we have today, right?!

Let us remind ourselves of a few Bible verses about mixing pagan things with G-d's things. Jesus states in Matthew 15:9, "But in vain do they worship Me, teaching for doctrines the commandments of men." In Mark 7:9, "Full well you reject the commandment of God, that you may keep your own tradition". In 1 Corinthians 10:21, Paul tells us, "You cannot drink the cup of the Lord and the cup of demons too; you cannot have a part in both the Lord's table and the table of demons."

Deuteronomy 12:3-4 states, "Break down their altars, smash their sacred stones and burn their Asherah poles in the fire; cut down the idols of their gods and wipe out their names from those places. You must not worship the Lord your G-d in their way."

Leviticus 19:19: "Ye shall keep my statutes. Thou shalt not let thy cattle gender with a diverse kind: thou shalt not sow thy field with mingled seed: neither shall a garment mingled of linen and woolen come upon thee."

Deuteronomy 22:9-11: "Do not plant two kinds of seed in your vineyard; if you do, not only the crops you plant but also the fruit of the vineyard will be defiled. Do not plow with an ox and a donkey yoked together. Do not wear clothes of wool and linen woven together."

The last two sets of verses discuss not mixing *especially* where mixing produces weakness and rot to your product. In Deuteronomy, you see the concept of being unequally yoked that Paul brings up later in Scripture. (2 Cor. 6:14)

When it comes to seeds, are we not compared to a field and to plants and seeds? Are there not tares that grow among the wheat? Who planted those? It certainly wasn't Yeshua.

The spiritual principle of not mixing clearly applies to the Word of G-d as well. In one of Yeshua's parables, the seed is the Word of G-d (Luke 8). We cannot mix His Word with pagan religious ideology. That mixing of seeds produces defilement. And yet, the Church has done quite a bit of mixing of Word and world.

If Christmas and its rituals have been used to worship demons, is it not a violation of what Paul and Moses tell us? Have we not mixed the traditions of man with the ways of G-d? You cannot have both Christ and Satan at the same table. And yet, we have Christmas. Man-made worship mixed with worship of the Son of G-d. How can we believe a brilliantly wise G-d would in one moment tell us not to worship Him as other gods are worshiped and in the next breath allow for additional celebrations that belong to other traditions in His honor?

For those who may claim G-d wanted to snatch an extra holiday for Himself. (I can hear the logic now. "Why wouldn't G-d want to take this day from the Pagans or from the world?");

This would be a "new" holiday after the New Testament, yes? But did not Yeshua say, I did not come to abolish but to fulfill the Law and the Prophets? (Matthew 5:17) Which Law or Prophet is fulfilled in Yeshua claiming Christmas (or choose from any number of winter solstice names) for Himself? What precedent in Scripture is He filling full of meaning? We know that Matthew 5:17 is a Hebrew Idiom meaning you have either rightly interpreted Scripture (fulfilled) or you have wrongly interpreted Scripture (abolished). (See the Real Jesus Essay). We also know that "fulfill" is the Greek word, pleroo, which more closely means to "fill full of meaning".

What is Yeshua filling full of meaning by taking Christmas for Himself?

Additionally, if Yeshua did mean to give us a new holiday, then He disqualified Himself as Messiah AND as a true prophet. As Deuteronomy 13 explains, anything that leads people away from Torah is signpost for false prophecy. It is also a violation of Deuteronomy 4:2, which commands that we not add to or take away from the Law. To add a feast day dedicated to the Lord to what was given in Leviticus would mean

Yeshua violated His own Commands, disqualifying Himself from perfection and taking away His G-dhood.

We cannot make Scripture say what we want it to just because we like Christmas.

Many may claim Christmas as a cultural holiday and not a religious one. Or perhaps that they just want to "celebrate Yeshua's birthday, ok!?" Well, ok, maybe. I'm not totally certain, but consider this:

Doesn't the G-d of the Bible claim that His people will be peculiar, holy, set apart? If we are to celebrate the birth of Christ on the same day as the birth of pagan gods, or at the same time as a cultural holiday centered on Santa Claus, are we set apart? Are we peculiar? Are we holy?

No, we have become common, cultural and boring, offering nothing new or fresh and nothing to remind our brothers and sisters that our G-d is truly unique. And that seems to be the history of the church from all the way back in Exodus.

Rebellion against G-d through the adoption of cultural ideas about religion and theology permeates human history. We wonder at the church in Exodus, choosing a golden calf while Moses was receiving G-d's Law, and yet, here we are with our own golden calves, all the while pleading ignorance during the age of the largest access to Biblical knowledge in history. We, unfortunately, are without excuse.

One interesting thing to note about our own country's history: Easter and Christmas were much more popular with Catholics than Protestants in early America. Protestants regarded Easter and Christmas as non-Biblical and too involved in paganism to be celebrated.

Some historians believe that the first Thanksgiving with the Native American convert to Christianity, Squanto, and the Puritans was actually a Sukkot Festival, or Feast of Tabernacles. The Pilgrims were well aware of this Biblical holiday. According to Clifford Rieders, **writing in the *Times of Israel***[xliv]:

"There is plenty of evidence that the Pilgrims, devoutly familiar with the Bible, were imitating the Jewish celebration of Sukkot during the first celebration that became Thanksgiving. The Puritans fled England in 1620 on the Mayflower. As Bruce Feiler noted in his book *America's Prophet: Moses and the American Story*, the Puritans saw themselves as the New Israelites in the New Israel. The European refugee members of the North American continent read the Bible in its original Hebrew. There was even a proposal to make Hebrew the official language of the colonies!

The Continental community that defined the Puritans was taken directly from the Jewish concept of the Covenant at Mount Sinai. The Governor of the Massachusetts Bay Colony was John Winthrop. He said, 'We shall find that the God of Israel is among us, when ten of us shall be able to resist a thousand of our enemies; when he shall make us a praise and a glory, that men shall say of succeeding plantations, 'The Lord make it likely that of New England.' Winthrop borrowed heavily from the Hebrew Bible."

It is deep in our roots to question what is Biblical and what is not and choose the Biblical. In fact, it seems that two trees were planted at the beginning of the United States. The tree attached to G-d's roots and a tree foreign to the Lord, one belonging to ideas antithetical to G-d's ways. That battle has continued to rage here and around the globe.

EASTER

Before we dive into this section, I must revisit the *Real Jesus* Essay, which helps us understand holidays.

The Bible DOES prescribe a holiday for celebrating the resurrection. In fact in Exodus 34 and Leviticus 23 we find Passover and Feast of First Fruits, commanded holidays, that are the Biblical observance of Yeshua's death AND resurrection.

Paul calls Christ the Firstfruits in 1 Cor. 20:20-23. He is the first of a line of Believers with access to His DNA versus just Adam's fallen DNA. He overcame death that we might have access to that same life. This is the celebration of the Feast of Firstfruits in Leviticus.

We have our Resurrection celebration in Scripture, all the way back in Exodus and Leviticus. But no Easter will be found anywhere in Scripture (except in translations that added it later).

So where, did we get Easter?

The word "Easter" itself is a complicated word, filled with potential meanings. The word is eerily similar to Ishtar, Astarte, and Innana — pagan goddesses of Akkadia and Sumeria. Easter also can mean "spring" from the Anglo Saxon goddess, Eostra. However, do we really believe Easter simply means "spring?"

To Christians, Easter means the resurrection of Christ. Yet, we celebrate it in the strangest of ways. Short of the Biblical directive to bring in your offerings the day after the Sabbath (scripturally, this would be a Sunday) on the Day of Firstfruits, the church has some perplexing traditions regarding Easter celebrations. The spirit of Easter must be examined to understand the truth here.

How is Easter celebrated? What traditions do we attend to at this time of year? Upon examination of these activities, we will see how we have mixed the pagan with the sacred.

- Easter bunnies
- Colored Easter eggs

- Search for eggs and treats
- Church attendance on Sunday
- Celebration of rebirth and renewal
- Resurrection of Christ

Bunnies. Adorable. Prolific procreators. Fuzzy. Jesus? From the Cadbury bunny to the exorbitant numbers of stuffed bunnies given as gifts and set about as Easter décor, rabbits are an important part of Easter. The church has had no qualms about including bunnies in its religious repertoire. **Some historians**[xlv] say that German immigrants to America brought an "Osterhase" with them — an egg-laying hare. Thus, the Easter bunny myth was born in America.

Because rabbits are fantastic procreators, the Easter bunny has become the symbol of new life. And this is how it was attached to the church's resurrection tradition. It closely resembles the symbol of the egg.

Eggs are representative of renewal and new life. Jesus, egg, you get it.

A quick Google search calls up story after story of Christians suggesting these symbols are a beautiful part of Christian tradition.

But, that's not where they started. The American church adopted these traditions in the 1700s from German immigrants. And where did these immigrants get their traditions?

The origins of the Easter egg can be traced back to at least 13th-century Germany as part of the rituals connected to gods and goddesses of the culture.

Historians battle over the origins of Easter. But one thing we do know is that eggs were hugely symbolic to ancient pagan cultures. The Egyptian creation story uses an egg, the Romans used eggs as burial offerings, Hinduism connects eggs to the creation of the universe, the Zoroastrian religion uses eggs as a symbol of the universe, the list goes on and on. Take the Egyptian example: in Egyptian theology, Amen Ra is born from an egg. Or how about the Babylonian custom that the god, Tammuz, is reborn and emerges from an egg every year? Resurrection anyone?

Whether Christians adopted these things directly or not does not seem to matter. The resurrection and the egg predate Christ by many, many years.

Resurrection was also not a foreign idea in the ancient Hebrew mind. After all, the book of Job, considered the oldest in Scripture, mentions resurrection. "I know that my redeemer lives, and that in the end he will stand on the earth. And after my skin has been destroyed, yet in my flesh I will see God; I myself will see him with my own eyes – I, and not another." (Job 19:25-27). Scholars date Job to about 700 years after Noah.

Isaiah 53:10 – 11 prophecies about the Messiah, who would come, suffer, die, and raise up to new life.

How can we forget about Jonah in the belly of the whale 3 days and nights and restored to life to bring the Ninehvites into obedience to Yahweh?

The Old Testament is replete with resurrection. (Psalm 49:15, Isaiah 25:8, Ezek. 37:1-14, etc.)

And in Acts 23:8, Paul reveals that the Pharisees had professed resurrection as part of their teachings.

Resurrection has always been in Scripture and understood by Biblical devotees.

Egg symbolism has not.

Some people will take the fact that other cultures also celebrated resurrections as types and symbols of their gods and use that to discredit the

Biblical story. But that is not the move I intend to make, nor do I see that as founded in history or Biblical scholarship. In fact, while our celebration of Easter, Christmas, Good Friday, and other Catholic traditions provides proof of a break with the G-d of the Bible, the keeping of G-d's holy days easily proves God's mastery over history, human movement, and fulfillment of prophecy.

The ancients likely shared their religious stories and traditions and much was transferred culturally. Despite older religious philosophies, resurrection was not, for instance, admired or revered by Romans during the time of Christ. But the ancient near eastern mind knew about resurrection and spoke about it. The Bible speaks prophetically of resurrection as part of Messiah's work.

The idea floated around with some acceptance and some dismissal. As do many things on this earth.

Resurrection belongs to Messiah. Firstfruits is the holiday He prescribed for it. Firstfruits is tied to Passover and the Feast of Unleavened Bread. This is an 8-day time period according to Scripture. Not many 8-day holidays in modern Christian tradition.

But, then again, G-d's days have remained fairly unique throughout human history. Most Believers don't know the days that Yahweh commands us to celebrate, but a simple reading of the first five books of Scripture can change that. And, we know that Christ celebrated them as well. (See Essay on The Real Jesus)

GOOD FRIDAY

It seems fairly provable that Yeshua did not die on a Friday.

John 19:42 tells us that "…because it was the Jewish day of preparation," Yeshua had to be taken off the cross and buried immediately.

Ok, So, this could EITHER be a Friday OR another day of preparation before a Feast day. Now, Passover is a High Sabbath in that it is both a feast day AND a day of rest according to Scripture (Leviticus 23). Let's go back a bit…

John 19:31 states, "Now it was the day of preparation and the next day was to be a special Sabbath."

A **special** Sabbath. Interesting. Still Passover could be ON the Sabbath, yes? But was it?

Matthew 12:40 says, "For as Jonah was three days and three nights in the whale's belly, so shall the Son of Man be three days and three nights in the belly of the earth."

The reality is that Yeshua MUST have been crucified on either a Wednesday or a Thursday afternoon in order to be in the earth three days and three nights.

If he died on Friday and rose to life on a Sunday morning, the longest his burial could possibly have been is a day and a half.

The week of Yeshua's death, the High Sabbath Passover was likely on Wednesday or Thursday (giving Yeshua the opportunity to fulfill the prophecy about being the Passover Lamb as well as the prophecy comparing Him to Jonah). In this way, we find that there are two Sabbaths that happened before Mary discovers an empty tomb on the first day of the week (which was and still is Sunday).

Now, Yeshua could have risen from the grave the evening of Saturday night, since sundown is the Biblical start of a day, and therefore Sunday really begins at our Saturday night.

We don't know actually. Did he arise Saturday night or in the middle of the night or right before Mary arrives?

That, I cannot answer. But I can tell you, in order to fulfill the Passover Lamb and Jonah prophecies, he could not have died on a Friday.

Earliest dates of the celebration of Good Friday are around the time of the Council of Nicaea, again around 325 AD. This holiday pops up long after the disciples and Paul and the ministry of The Way. Good Friday is not a Scriptural dictate.

We have an observance of Yeshua's death that IS Scriptural. It is called Passover and for His resurrection, we recognize the Feast of Firstfruits.

We do not need additional man-made dates to observe and celebrate our Lord's act of sacrifice and defeat of death. Nor should we be replacing G-d's dates with our own.

COMMUNION

In Protestant churches, communion is often experienced with the breaking of bread into smaller pieces and tiny cups of grape juice. This tradition of a tiny "meal" also began during the time of Constantine. Before Constantine, smaller congregations met in homes and smaller buildings that allowed for a true Lord's Supper: a meal taken together that resembled the meal Yeshua ate with His disciples before going to the cross. This earlier tradition and the beautiful story of Yeshua's meal before His death have me convinced that G-d wanted us to remember Him each time we have a meal with our Spiritual family. The call is to eat in gratitude, remembering Yeshua's sacrifice and discussing the Lord as often as possible.

Additionally, now that we understand Yeshua is our Passover Lamb, at Passover as we eat unleavened bread and bitter herbs, we participate in memorializing both the rescue of Israel from Egypt and the redemption of our souls from sin and death.

However, over time this concept has been corporatized, codified, dwindled down and legalized into the small congregational moment we experience today. Our version comes directly from Catholic tradition, although without some of the symbolism and operative rites.

The Catholic Church believed and taught a concept called transubstantiation. For the early Catholic, the communion bread and wine really turned into the body and blood of Yeshua. A literal eating of His body.

Odd, in that if you know Torah, you know cannibalism is NOT Biblical. Scripture forbids it. But I digress…

In traditional Catholic services, a Monstrance is used to display the communion wafer. A round, golden sunburst with a handle, the monstrance — or ostensorium — is, by the Catholic Church's own admission, representative of the sun. The round wafer also echoes the sun, and these symbols were and still are often bowed to and venerated in worshipful manner.

Sun god worship. Ancient, pagan. NOT a meal shared with Christian family.

Luckily, most Protestant churches do not participate in quite this display. A mix between the Catholic version and Biblical version, Protestant churches tend to believe the wine and bread are representations and that communion is a sanctioned tenet of the faith. But, the idea that our version of Communion is somehow a Biblical law or Command cannot be backed up using Scripture. You will not find the command to have this version of Communion anywhere.

Furthermore, if Yeshua was giving a new command at the Last Supper, then He was most certainly "adding to" the Law (Deut. 12:32), which is forbidden. That would mean He was breaking His own Law and disqualifying Himself as a perfect man/G-d.

Once again, Yeshua does something that we have misinterpreted or twisted for the sake of staying relevant to Church customs. He was telling us to observe Passover and to remember Him at our meals together. But the meal remembrance is not a new Torah command. It is to help us understand what Passover means to the Believer, it is now not just about the Exodus from Egypt, now it is about Yeshua's path for us to have an exodus of our own; an exodus out of sin and death. The new type of love He mentions in John 13:34 calls us into an understanding of the New Covenant in which G-d's commands are established on our hearts.

Passover, however, is commanded. Leviticus 23 makes it quite clear that we are to observe this Feast. And no, not as a tiny bite once a month in your church. Passover is a Spring Feast Day that happens once a year (See Essay on The Real Jesus)

We could continue. So many of our man-made traditions are replacements for, not embodiments of, what is given in Scripture. And upon a closer look, they are sometimes the seeds of religions and superstitions that are antithetical to our G-d. Dig further and you will find the Catholic Church laying claims to the right to change the Sabbath Day to Sunday, to venerate human beings through worshipful activities, to coerce strange sorts of confessions and so on. There have been egregious departures from Scripture in Church history, the results of which linger with us throughout Christendom.

How To Move Forward

Upon discovery of the heinous acts of Church Fathers against the Jews, I straight up cried. My heart broke. I was overwhelmed, asking G-d to forgive us all, and help us to reunite with our brothers and sisters. G-d is already doing this wonderful, miraculous work. Praise Him!

The merciful G-d we serve knows how much and how little we know. No doubt He has looked upon all of our traditions with parental gentleness and patience. And yet, we still suffer from the absence of truth in our walk with Yeshua. In choosing superstitious traditions, we miss out on the power and education that G-d's cycles and pathways teach. We mix the pagan with the Holy. We water down our faith to include many paths to G-d, when only Yeshua can be the Way.

We are culturally relevant without spiritual impact.

In a time with limitless informational access, I fear we have chosen to learn how to improve ourselves WITHOUT attempting to improve our knowledge of the One we claim is King.

If our hearts are in the right place, then our actions should be towards time and study, unhindered by prideful sentimentality or a selfish need to justify our past religious activities.

For my part, I'll admit, my time online and in work and life is often more of a distraction from G-d than a pursuit of Him.

The disturbing realities of the history of our church are simply the realities of human nature. Israel adopted paganism throughout all of Scripture. Are we really shocked that we have done the same? Did we believe we were an improved version of humanity? In this our pride has sabotaged our access to the truth.

We are not better than Israel. We ARE Israel. And the G-d who has always brought us through is leading us to repentance and truth once again. Our Father has not changed. His faithfulness has continued and He will keep His promises.

When young King Josiah discovered the Laws of G-d, he immediately responded. His stance was repentance and change.

[11] When the king heard the words of the Book of the Law, he tore his robes. [12] He gave these orders to Hilkiah the priest, Ahikam son of Shaphan, Akbor son of Micaiah, Shaphan the secretary and Asaiah the king's attendant: [13] "Go and inquire of the LORD for me and for the people and for all Judah about what is written in this book that has been found. Great is the LORD's anger that burns against us because those who have gone before us have not obeyed the words of this book; they have not acted in accordance with all that is written there concerning us." (2 Kings 22:11-13)

In light of new knowledge, like Josiah, may we repent and embark upon lives that reject man-made religion for a life lived like Yeshua. He did not come to hand you another religion. He came to bring you life and life abundantly.

Deuteronomy 14:2 (Repeated in 1 Peter 4:9)
"For thou art an holy people unto the Lord thy God, and the Lord hath chosen thee to be a peculiar people unto Himself, above all the nations that are upon the earth."

Chapter 6

FAITH AND POLITICS

Faith and politics: a marriage made for conflict.

While everything we do has spiritual consequences, we often find ourselves splitting hairs in attempting to divide our political choices from our spiritual positions. Conversely, it's easy to forget that choosing a national or local leader is NOT choosing a god, the G-d. It is choosing the individual you think will most justly and rightly serve in that particular position, even if it is just that they will vote against abortion or Communism.

The problem lies in our idolization of political leadership. Their pedestal reaches high into the heavens while the citizenry look on in wonder. Abiding by a seemingly unique set of rules, those who hold positions of power enjoy extra freedoms. For instance, our Congress held onto their own healthcare plans when everyone else got Obamacare. Notoriously, some have lately been caught eating at fancy restaurants without masks while everyone else stayed cordoned off at home due to Covid lockdowns (see: Gavin Newsom). They get special tax breaks and head energy departments while owning millions in electric car companies (see: Jennifer Granholm, Energy Secretary for the Biden Admin.). And no, the corruption is not limited to Democrats. It's just egregiously obvious on that side at the moment of this writing.

Corruption amongst the power-hungry is to be expected. They follow up their corruption with dictates to the unwashed masses, informing us where to send our hard-earned tax dollars so they can get back to corrupting even more.

With looming issues like abortion and Communism pushing many Christians to vote conservatively (and rightly so), there still seems to be among the churched a desire to separate the political from the spiritual.

On the other side, the tendency of those who put their faith in atheistic views leans further left, unwaveringly and fearlessly politically intertwined with core beliefs.

You may be wondering why I point out abortion and Communism as specific reasons to vote for or against a candidate. Scripture declares the priceless nature of human life. People are made in G-d's image and He is responsible for our design. Abortion decimates G-d's handiwork.

Beyond that, we see time and again that life is paramount to Adonai. Above all other laws, giving life and protecting life is of the utmost importance. The first command given in Genesis instructs living creation — plants, animals, and people — to be fruitful and multiply. G-d intends for mankind to fill the earth and subdue it. From the first human family, mankind has today grown to over seven billion people.

Despite this outstanding growth, we were at our lowest levels of global poverty before Covid lockdowns hit. What extraordinary proof that G-d made the earth to expand to fit humanity and its fulfillment of the Creation command! Abortion is war against life and flies in the face of the first command, which is to be fruitful. Children are our most precious fruit and G-d blesses and expands the earth so that we can continue to be fruitful.

When it comes to Communism, Martin Luther King Jr. makes quite an eloquent argument. Communism and belief in the G-d of the Bible cannot go hand in hand. He admonished us, "Let me state clearly the basic premise of this sermon: Communism and Christianity are fundamentally incompatible. A true Christian cannot be a true Communist, for the two philosophies are antithetical and all the dialects of the logicians cannot reconcile them." *(Strength to Love, MLK Jr.)*[xlvi]

Why is this true? According to King:

"First, Communism is based on a materialistic and humanistic view of life and history…"

"Second, Communism is based on ethical relativism…"

"Third, Communism attributes ultimate value to the state."

I should let the reader know here, that a thorough read through of this 12th chapter in MLK's book, *Strength To Love,* will enable understanding regarding the Believers call to oppose Communism and Socialism that leads to it. At the very least, knowing that Marx dedicated much of his young works to Satanic ideals should raise at least a few red flags.

From his poem "The Fiddler," lines like this are a cold reminder of Karl Marx's mindset:

"See this sword
the Prince of darkness sold it to me."

<u>The Mises Institute</u>[xlvii] (School of Austrian Economics founded on the works of Austrian Liberal Economist and brilliant predictor of the disastrous outcomes of socialism and communism, Ludwig Von Mises)[xlviii] discusses one of Marx's pieces that poetically foreshadowed the great evil he would unleash upon the world.

"Particularly instructive is Marx's lengthy, unfinished poetic drama of his youthful period, "Oulanem, A Tragedy." In the course of this drama his hero, Oulanem, delivers a remarkable soliloquy, pouring out sustained invective, a hatred of the world and of mankind, a hatred of creation and a threat and vision of total world destruction. Thus Oulanem pours out his vials of wrath:

'… I shall howl gigantic curses on mankind:
Ha! Eternity! She is an eternal grief …
Ourselves being clockwork, blindly mechanical,
Made to be the foul-calendars of Time and Space,
Having no purpose save to happen, to be ruined,
So that there shall be something to ruin …
If there is a something which devours,
I'll leap within it, though I bring the world to ruins-
The world which bulks between me and the Abyss
I will smash to pieces with my enduring curses.
I'll throw my arms around its harsh reality:
Embracing me, the world will dumbly pass away,
And then sink down to utter nothingness,
Perished, with no existence — that would be really living!'"

Marx would indeed assist in carrying out his satanic agenda, as Communism, through the interpretations of Stalin, Mao, and others, brutally killed as many as 100 million people in the 20th century. And yet, even today after all that we have learned of such systems, Believers get caught up in these ideas antithetical to G-d, looking for worldly ways to bring His Kingdom to earth. Instead of looking to the Bible for Heavenly help the Believer is often tempted to look instead to politicians and ideologies. OR too many ignore politics altogether believing that human intervention in global events remains pointless.

Additional logical and Scriptural fallacies have recently become all the rage. I have seen images on social media lately using Yeshua to advocate for many anti-Biblical political ideals. One continuous example lies in the justification of violence and murder in the streets because Yeshua turned over tables in the Temple. The Temple that belonged to Him! These horrid abuses of Scripture to promote and rationalize violent activity in the name of Marxist ideology violate the Second Commandment, and what's worse, attempt to entangle the G-d of the universe with violence against precious humans.

Complexity floods discussions of politics and religion and where or whether they should and should not intersect. For some, our Founders are a group of old racists whose ideas need reimagining. For others, they are the flawed but brilliant constructors of the oldest still-used Constitution in existence today. Either way, we cannot escape the religious and Biblical convictions of the framers of our nation, nor can we escape their faults.

Our founders quoted the Bible and used its Laws as a foundation for discourse and creation of the law of the United States. Noting that G-d has a greater understanding of the character of man, and that the Bible contained great wisdom on how to live, they referenced Biblical principles for guidance and righteousness. But there is a careful line drawn between demanding that others follow the Bible, as opposed to using its time-tested truths to develop ideas that would justly rule the land. There is a dividing line between state-sanctioned religion and laws based in Biblical truths. Perhaps they understood what the modern American refuses to: the Bible doesn't dictate a religion. It dictates a way of living, one that produces life. It isn't so much a dogma as it is a handbook to elevating life on planet earth.

One does not have to search far to find mention of Scripture, G-d, and a Being greater than us in the writings of our founders. Quotes like these describe our founder's views:

John AdamsJ *(From a letter to Thomas Jefferson, June 28, 1813)*[xlix]

"Now I will avow, that I then believe, and now believe, that those general Principles of Christianity, are as eternal and immutable, as the Existence and Attributes of God; and that those Principles of Liberty, are as unalterable as human Nature and our terrestrial, mundane System."

Thomas Jefferson *(-Excerpted from multiple sources: "A Summary View of the Rights of British America," "Notes on the State of Virginia," "The Autobiography," letter to George Wythe (1790), letter to George Washington (1786).*[l]

"God who gave us life gave us liberty. And can the liberties of a nation be thought secure when we have removed their only firm basis, a conviction in the minds of the people that these liberties are of the Gift of God? That they are not to be violated but with His wrath? Indeed, I tremble for my country when I reflect that God is just; that His justice cannot sleep forever..."

James Madison *(Letter to William Bradford, Nov. 9, 1772)*[li]

"A watchful eye must be kept on ourselves lest while we are building ideal monuments of Renown and Bliss here we neglect to have our names enrolled in the Annals of Heaven."

Benjamin Rush *(From Essays, Literary, Moral, and Philosophical, 1798)*[lii]

"If moral precepts alone could have reformed mankind, the mission of the Son of God into all the world would have been unnecessary. The perfect morality of the gospel rests upon the doctrine which, though often controverted has never been refuted: I mean the vicarious life and death of the Son of God."

Alexander Hamilton *(America's God and Country)*[liii]

"I have carefully examined the evidences of the Christian religion, and if I was sitting as a juror upon its authenticity I would unhesitatingly give my verdict in its favor."

Patrick Henry (*Patrick Henry's Will*)

"I have now disposed of all my property to my family. There is one thing more I wish I could give them, and that is the Christian Religion. If they had that and I had not given them one shilling they would have been rich; and if they had not that and I had given them all the world, they would be poor."

The list of quotes could go on and on from John Jay to George Washington. The evidence our founders believed in G-d, or at least believed in the veracity and importance of the Bible and its precepts, is obvious to the honest historian.

How then can we have the audacity to depart from such logic? How often do Believers ignore the political, or get found in anti-Biblical territory when approaching politics?

This nation's very seed is set in principles that have stood for thousands of years and by which many live to this very day. Love thy neighbor. Pray for those who persecute you. Before the Lord there is no race, gender, or class. Give to the poor. Take care of the widow and orphan. Justice is blind. Do right, live justly, and walk humbly.

Our legal system and ideal of justice being blind, our ideas about freedom and liberty, and risk and reward, these all come from Scripture. But, just like the nation of Israel, there is no doubt that this relationship between politics and religion can become bastardized. Whether by a warped or deficient religious view in the polity (a lack of moral character in the people of the United States) or by an overzealous religious view that seeks to impose its outlook, wanted or not, upon the masses.

While we cannot ignore that some political systems are antithetical to Christianity (Communism being one), we also must be careful of what is produced in voting and living based on a bastardized version of Biblical truth. These twists and turns of political religiosity have devised a god in the image of the politician and are used as a political weapon.

Politics and religion have gone hand in hand since the beginning of time. The original set up for the early church of the Exodus was a Theocracy, headed by the Lord G-d Himself and distributed through Moses and Aaron. Eventually the people rejected this set up in favor of Judges and Kings, and G-d hesitantly granted their requests. And this came, of course, with its own set of consequences.

The pivot to a structure more in line with other nations was political in nature. It was also a lack of education that led them to such upheaval. In Judges we are told that after Joshua died,

> "10 After that whole generation had been gathered to their ancestors,
> another generation grew up who knew neither the Lord nor what he
> had done for Israel. 11 Then the Israelites did evil in the eyes of the
> Lord and served the Baals. 12 They forsook the Lord, the God of
> their ancestors, who had brought them out of Egypt. They followed
> and worshiped various gods of the peoples around them. They
> aroused the Lord's anger 13 because they forsook him and served
> Baal and the Ashtoreths. 14 In his anger against Israel the Lord gave
> them into the hands of raiders who plundered them. He sold them
> into the hands of their enemies all around, whom they were no
> longer able to resist. 15 Whenever Israel went out to fight, the hand of
> the Lord was against them to defeat them, just as he had sworn to
> them. They were in great distress.
> 16 Then the Lord raised up judges,[c] who saved them out of the hands of
> these raiders. 17 Yet they would not listen to their judges but prostituted
> themselves to other gods and worshiped them. They quickly turned
> from the ways of their ancestors, who had been obedient to the Lord's
> commands. 18 Whenever the Lord raised up a judge for them, he was

with the judge and saved them out of the hands of their enemies as
long as the judge lived; for the Lord relented because of their groaning
under those who oppressed and afflicted them. [19] But when the judge
died, the people returned to ways even more corrupt than those of their
ancestors, following other gods and serving and worshiping them. They
refused to give up their evil practices and stubborn ways.
[20] Therefore the Lord was very angry with Israel and said, "Because this
nation has violated the covenant I ordained for their ancestors and has
not listened to me, [21] I will no longer drive out before them any of the
nations Joshua left when he died. [22] I will use them to test Israel and see
whether they will keep the way of the Lord and walk in it as their
ancestors did."[23] The Lord had allowed those nations to remain; he did
not drive them out at once by giving them into the hands of Joshua."

The generation that rejected G-d's things "knew not" what G-d had done for them in the past. Nor did they care to learn it seems. Instead, they forsook the ways of G-d to follow other gods. They left the paths of righteousness for the secular and fallen ways of man.

This, simply put, is a perfect study in human history as a whole. Nations rise up in promise and hope, generations do great things, only to be followed by spoiled generations that forget the lessons learned in the past and who forsake the original ways. America is no different. Each new generation believing it is SO unique, SO important, SO special, and SO different, that the wisdom of old could not possibly apply!

The politicization of religion played a key role in shaping the church we see globally today. For the history of the Christian church, political entanglements have proved devastating to our doctrine and the health of the body. Examples abound upon study of Catholic Church and Protestant Church history.

The gruesome journey from Yeshua to our modern day church outlines political accommodation at its very worst. Without this understanding, we just can't properly analyze our current position. With each iteration of church ideology we have substituted one truth for another, often allowing for political aspirations to fill the gaps left by the theft of Scriptural understanding. We find ourselves in a state where gaining political points is considered storing up Heavenly treasures.

Even the most sincere of pastors often decide that there are a list of "untouchable" topics that they would rather not discuss from the pulpit, leaving the congregants to go out into the world and figure it out alone among the wolves.

Despite these troubling acts of cowardice, with correct knowledge we can know how to turn back to G-d even if the leadership will not. This is not a return to politics or religion, but to the Bible, a way of life, and the heart of our King.

Near the end of the first century, the Apostle, John, wrote Revelation and his gospel. Jerusalem had fallen and there was rampant confusion running through the Jewish community. Those who followed Jesus were called followers of "the Way" or Nazarenes. (They were NOT at first called, Christians). The church was still part of mainstream Judaism: a new sect who believed in the Messiah. They were hated, but they were still Jewish.

The council with James in Acts convened because debate arose about how to incorporate the Gentiles and teach them the root of the new faith they had come into, which is the Torah. At this time, some Jews taught a requirement of immediate circumcision in order to be saved. James and the apostles replied that even Abraham wasn't saved through circumcision. Why in the world would that be the standard for salvation? James reminded the church that we are saved by grace and we do good works *because* of our relationship with G-d.

This debate underscores the power of politics to influence G-d's people. Jewish believers who promoted a works-based salvation facing off with Gentiles, bringing in pagan ideas and grappling with the strangeness of Biblical Temple rules and life. (More on this in my essay on Paul)

Add in salvation through Yeshua by grace and expected chaos resulted! In the center, Paul and James and the rest of the apostles did their best to straighten out the crookedness of the times.

From the moment of Yeshua's transfiguration, people entangled political and religious philosophies. In essence, they messed it up. That's what we most often do.

Two thousand years later, Christianity and Judaism claim stark differences and worldviews that have grown exponentially apart since their debates on circumcision.

Ever encroaching political pressures have successfully changed and perverted church doctrine. Most seminary students today are not going to learn about the connection between the Laws and what Yeshua did, but will be taught more about how to divide Yeshua from His own Law.

This is unnerving at best. Because, for the Believer, a worldview that does not understand G-d's principles will most certainly allow for bends towards cultural versions of tolerance and social justice, with obvious negative outcomes that we are experiencing today.

MODERN POLITICIANS ARE NOT YESHUA

About our disconnection from truth, there should be no incredulous responses or shocked disbelief among those who understand church history. We are told to put on the Armor of G-d for a reason. Battle is upon us. Truth is under attack. It always has been.

The wedge between G-d the Father and the Son, between the Old Testament and the New, and between the G-d of the Bible and the god of the modern has ever been increasing the divide between truth and the average American church attendee.

I can say unswervingly that neither political party in America has a corner on G-dliness. I can say without a doubt that none of our recent presidents celebrate Passover, eat clean, keep the Sabbath, stay away from greed, consistently tell the truth, etc. Really, can you think of many presidents who have actually been G-dly?

Scandals, lies, gossip, slander, bitter words, violent actions. Until President Trump, almost every president in my lifetime had gotten us into some war or another globally. This often seemed to be to satiate the monetary needs of generals or the Military Industrial Complex. President Obama was so pro-abortion that he, as a Senator, had actually voted for partial birth abortion. Trump's Twitter feed was a full-on example of how NOT to use words as a Believer.

As we look to these people as political leaders, do we too often also hope they are spiritual leaders or maybe even gods?

Cringe along with me, but yes, I think we do.

It's time to let that go. G-dliness and political leadership are not often bedfellows or even acquaintances.

We are not wise to deify or ascribe righteous attributes to our leadership that they have not earned. It is, in fact, our duty to live justly and to seek truth, able to rightly discern righteousness from political power.

This means we must be able to divide the human from the idea and the ideal.

I've always found discussing ideas leads to excellent and deep conversation. Discussing people often leads to arguments.

The ideas our country was founded upon are far greater than their bearers. While our founders were flawed, many of their ideas have proven true and valuable. This is true most especially where we find their roots in Scripture.

The Bible firmly upholds the ideas of blind justice and a disciplined and honest judicial system. The Bible upholds the principles of freedom of speech, religion, and even the right to defend yourself or your family.

Yes, even self-defense finds its roots in Biblical precepts and characters.

When Lot and his family were kidnapped, Abraham and his many men armed themselves and went and fought to retrieve Lot. They were successful. (Genesis 14). He took a group of armed men to complete the task. Violence was at hand, defense of life and rescue of the kidnapped was a righteous act.

Additionally, consider verses like these:

> Exodus 22:2-3: "If a thief is caught in the act of breaking into a house and is struck and killed in the process, the person who killed the thief is not guilty of murder. But if it happens in daylight, the one who killed the thief is guilty of murder."

> Luke 22:35-37: "Then Jesus asked them, 'When I sent you out to preach the Good News and you did not have money, a traveler's bag,

or an extra pair of sandals, did you need anything?' 'No,' they replied. 'But now,' he said, 'take your money and a traveler's bag. And if you don't have a sword, sell your cloak and buy one! For the time has come for this prophecy about me to be fulfilled: 'He was counted among the rebels. Yes, everything written about me by the prophets will come true.'''

Luke 22:38-39: "'Look, Lord,'" they replied, 'we have two swords among us.' "'That's enough,' he said. Then, accompanied by the disciples, Jesus left the upstairs room and went as usual to the Mount of Olives."

Self-defense is Scriptural.

The pursuit of happiness, the pursuit of G-d, the pursuit of truth should never be hampered by any government. It is our duty as Believers to allow G-d to work through us, to bring His Heaven to earth. What is G-d's idea of Heaven? I believe it is free people who *choose* to live in love. Not forced against their will, not stolen from or lied to by coercive and oppressive power moves, no, to *choose* to do good is a Heavenly quality.

It is very hard to feed the poor when the government has taken all of your money or made you a slave to debt.

It is even harder to care for your neighbor when we have been taught by those in power to hate each other based on skin color, political ideology, financial prosperity, or medical choices.

The shrewd follower of Yeshua can see evidence for or lack of G-d's principles and evaluate presented ideologies based on Scripture and History. These observations do not necessarily categorize people into Democrat or Republican, but instead into G-d-centeredness or self – centeredness.

In a G-d-centered world we leave fear behind and embrace each other, allowing for each to decide which way he or she should go. We reform our own hearts and houses first and we call out evil when we see it.

In a self-centered world, we hate anyone who has what we want, we take those down who we disagree with, and we seek to remove the speck before examining our own plank.

At some point, if we remove the plank, we can finally help out with the speck. But no planks or specks get removed when we refuse to reform, first, our own hearts.

These Biblical views inform our political choices. But, is this righteous order of evaluation happening today or is it the other way around?

CONFUSING GOD DESTROYS GOOD CITIZENRY

Let's go back to the example of the image being shared on FB recently. Multiple people I knew, who claimed to be Believers, shared an image of Yeshua turning over tables in the temple. Their posts would read something like, "If Jesus could be violent to get his point across, why can't we?" Justification of murderous behavior, violence, theft and other degradations of the human soul being heaved upon the story of Yeshua clearing out His own house.

To the date of this writing, the riots of 2020 killed at least 32 people and caused billions of dollars in damage to businesses, public property and to police officers who were often the recipients of hysterical death threats by riotous protesters. The cities that proclaimed they would defund the police have seen such increases in crime that they are back to hiring police officers and attempting to expunge the violence they promoted.

On the surface, I wish I didn't have to explain how wrong this comparison of Christ to rioters is, but for the sake of thoroughness, here we go.

Yeshua was in His Father's temple, His temple. The House of The Lord. It belonged to Him and he had every right to, by force, remove anything He did not want there.

It remains a very singular moment of violence from Yeshua. Even when He is being arrested, He tells his followers to not react and heals a man's ear that was cut off.

Yeshua NEVER instructs his followers to use violence to advance their cause or to spread the gospel. In fact, in Scripture violence is only ever used in war or self-defense. It is never used as a tool to advance a purely **political** ideology. G-d is careful about the nations that are destroyed by Israel in the Old Testament. As an example, G-d gave the Canaanites 400 years to stop sacrificing their children to their gods. Four hundred years to stop being violent. Four hundred years to stop defiling their bodies and the land. It took Noah 100 years to build the ark. In that time, the people were duly warned that G-d would be coming to destroy everything. Unless G-d's instruction dictates it, we should be extraordinarily careful with violence and how and when it is used.

Finally, we can see G-d's intent through the actions of the disciples and Paul. Paul was imprisoned time and again. Every disciple besides John was martyred for spreading the gospel. They did not go to the world to use a physical sword, they went with a spiritual sword in the form of Scripture and with their feet shod with "the gospel of peace".

Peace can be incredibly potent. Take the world changing campaign of MLK. Peace and justice were the ideals that created a powerful movement. Clearly, MLK's followers had a righteous cause and they gained great political strides because so many could join their cause free of the guilt of violence.

How many would have joined if the movement tolerated lawlessness and lacked justice all in the name of promoting a change in the law? Probably far less.

The other problem with the imagery used in overly simplistic memes is that it does INDEED promote an idea that violence, theft, terrorizing the innocent (innocent business owners and residential areas) is right and just. And that somehow we can liken this behavior to Yeshua.

But it is not Christ-like. In fact, this behavior only degrades the individual, transforming them into the very thing they hate. Encouragement of this behavior compromises our destinies in Yeshua. Too many have made themselves into criminals for selfish gain that, in the end, has had no positive effect on a greater cause.

Worse, this behavior violates the commands of G-d. Love, justice, peace, mercy, thou shall not steal, thou shall not lie, thou shall not murder, thou shall not COVET anything that belongs to your neighbor. The unfortunate truth here is that a Marxist ideology of hatred towards generalized groups has seeped into many Believer's minds, defiling their behavior.

Because they do not have the foundation of Scripture, they lack the context of Yeshua's table turning, they do not understand the call of the Believer when facing trials, and many have been deceived.

Vengeance is not a Christ-like characteristic, and hatred is a tool of the enemy. The rise of Critical Race Theory, with its Marxist foundation, marches on in many churches. And I believe Heaven mourns the suffering that will come of it.

The Church cannot align with reckless, senseless violence, hatred, and racism while attempting alignment with the G-d of the Bible.

This is just one example happening in contemporary America. There are dozens more. They range from calling Yeshua a socialist to saying that G-d is always on our current President's side (whichever President we might have).

To these I scream internally: No!

The Bible's only **promoted** form of government was actually a theocracy (which we see before the Judges come) and then, of course, we are told to follow our Spiritual leaders in the New Testament as well as submit to authorities as part of our testimony. The Bible has very little to say about the Roman form of government, the Asian forms of government, G-d doesn't even really want to give Israel a King in the OT!

Among all forms of government there are a few instructions about honoring authorities. 1 Peter 2:13-17 states,

> [13] Submit yourselves for the Lord's sake to every human authority: whether to the emperor, as the supreme authority, [14] or to governors, who are sent by him to punish those who do wrong and to commend those who do right. [15] For it is God's will that by doing good you should silence the ignorant talk of foolish people. [16] Live as free people, but do not use your freedom as a cover-up for evil; live as God's slaves. [17] Show proper respect to everyone, love the family of Believers, fear God, honor the emperor."

This NIV translation closely resembles that of Strong's Concordance in which we find words like "submit" and "honor". The learned Believer will recognize these sorts of terms in the context of Paul's admonitions to submit to one another in love and to serve because it is a testimony of our righteousness and commitment to the love of G-d. Peter additionally reminds us that fearing G-d comes before honoring the Emperor. Fearing G-d will assist in the proper application of honoring an emperor, or a President, etc.

Lawless citizens are not going to have much of a testimony among their counterparts. The Bible encourages its Heavenly citizens to follow G-d first and foremost (see Daniel, Shadrach, Meshach, Abednego, Peter, Paul, Abraham and others for when and how to disobey the law of the day), while also living in peace as much as possible among our fellows on earth and in the cultures where we abide. Complete disobedience and disrespect for authority, especially where it violates Biblical Commands, does not engender trust or influence among global onlookers.

Mature Believers are called to have wisdom regarding civil disobedience. Most of us believe MLK's version was righteous AND worked well, a clear sign of Heavenly approval. Most of us believe the Founders had Heavenly help in their rebellion against Britain and the outcome that ensued produced blessings for a long time. Most of us consider the Germans who hid Jews in WWII and the Priests who claimed Christ as King in the face of a Soviet gun, righteous defenders of freedom.

Yet they did not "obey" the dictates of their leaders.

Can we decipher the wisdom in these rebellions versus that of random violence or disrespect? Are we mature enough to understand Moses' standing up to Pharoah versus rioters destroying businesses?

Sometimes I'm not sure. But we are certainly called to this level of discernment.

For the Believer, any act of rebellious political activity must be found in obedience and fear of the Lord first. Without the fear of G-d, we may find ourselves caught up in disobedience that honors nothing but our egos.

OR, we may find ourselves willing to obey authority without fear of G-d's reprisal. The German concentration camp authorities may have "just been following orders," but that does not excuse their offenses in G-d's courtroom.

Without Scriptural application, we have no rock to empower our footing. We must fear G-d's Laws first and in so doing, we will know where we are in violation or alignment.

May G-d grant us wisdom.

HEAVENLY ECONOMY VS DAMAGED HUMANITY

As economics goes, the Bible seems to be incredibly entrepreneurial — given to stories about farmers, cloth makers, the virtuous woman from Proverbs 31 who buys and sells land and tapestries, etc. David was a shepherd, the disciples were fishermen. The Biblical economy was based on individual laborers bringing their wares to the community. We can glean the tendency towards a free market and attempt extrapolation, but that does require more than a moment's thought.

It is left to us to look at what character traits the Bible wants to promote and to observe which forms of government and economy provide the best opportunities to encourage those traits along with promoting freedom and justice. Which ones promote life? What is the fruit of each form of government? Is it closer to Heaven or further away? Certainly, G-d, being on the side of life, would have something to say about that. Hence MLK's comments on Communism and Marxism.

Concurrently, the Bible is about an individual call. Not the call of a government or allegiance to a flag. It asks about your allegiance to the Creator.

So, why so much allegiance to a political party?

Politics has become a religion for so many in the United States. It has replaced G-d to the point that the big R or D next to a name can surely guarantee certain votes, even if the individual named does not align with the voter's political ideals! We have replaced reason and reasonability with Democrat, Socialist, or Republican. Blind to what is good or bad, we pledge our allegiance unwaveringly to flawed individuals who have stamped themselves with a political slogan and/or party, or to flawed policies just because, well, "we've always hated the other guy."

In the meantime, both Democrats and Republicans in power have been guilty of sexual trafficking, cronyism, corruptions, starting useless wars, recklessness with the American people's money, carelessness in signing legislation, failure to decrease poverty, and overreach against the individual American Citizenry. No party is guiltless.

So, how should all of this intersect for the Believer? Everything is Spiritual, including our political speech and actions or inaction. Many Believers today, emotionally rant and rave, descending into name-calling and ad-hominem attacks.

Others, so worried about offending, say nothing at all and choose to deny friends and society of education or wisdom.

There is no 11th Command to not offend people. Yeshua was absolutely offensive to certain listeners. If we think we get to escape that, are we following Yeshua or following culture?

Dietrich Bonhoeffer comes to mind here. The German pastor and theologian was a man who saw that the Third Reich was evil and was going to commit heinous acts, and he pleaded with the German Church to educate the congregants and to speak out against what was going on. Was he wrong? His faith certainly guided him in this regard, and yet he was outspoken and fearless in his messaging.

After reading much more of MLK, I'm convinced he never could have had any movement at all were it not for his deep abiding faith in the Lord and belief that G-d went with him in all that he did politically. He preached it, encouraging Believers to get up and get involved. Was he wrong?

Our Founders, should they not have included G-d and Scripture in their ideas about a nation? Should they not have argued and debated? Should they have put their reputation before their sincerest ideals and stayed silent?

Why are we so silent today? The church does not even have these discussions within its hallowed sanctuaries. No wonder Believers have nothing to say to the world. They say NOTHING to each other!

I recently posted a rebuttal to a claim that Critical Race Theory (a type of Marxism culturally popular right now) is just fine to teach to Federal employees. I made the simple comparison of Critical Race Theory to Marxism and the historical reasons why these teaching are dangerous and our tax dollars shouldn't go to it. It was my opinion, but well-founded and well-researched. I gave it honestly and bluntly with no name-calling or disservice to the other people commenting.

In return I was called a White Supremacist, a Racist, a supporter of fascists. I was told to keep my opinions to myself and asked a flurry of questions about Marxism from snarky individuals who thought I maybe hadn't done my research. They were wrong. But the nastiness was astonishing. My femaleness was thrown in my face as a reason I could not have an opinion, alongside my whiteness. As if these characteristics discredited the works of my mind.

As if those kinds of claims did not reveal the racism and sexism of the authors themselves.

I've realized in today's vernacular, this is the experience of so many. They want to have a rational discussion. They attempt to use proofs, history, texts, facts, and data. In return they are met with emotion, trauma, anger, bitterness, fear, and resentfulness.

We aren't emotionally healthy. We aren't grounded in reality. What has happened here in America?

The silenced Believer contributes to this problem. Too many church leaders have stayed pinned up, praying to the god of cultural relevance, and using kindness as a mask for cowardice. We have not stayed true to G-d's things and we have handed over our preaching against sin to preaching of tolerance of many evils, including political ones.

Where are the MLK's? Where are the fearless leaders preaching the truth and *educating* their congregants about how to defend that truth PROPERLY in our culture today? (To my dear pastors at the Church's I attend, you are excused from this particular lecture. You tell the truth quite well, hence my attendance.)

Their silence has left an uneducated and therefore unfruitful homogenized church polity. The close-mouthed, and the snarky abound in droves.

The well educated, honoring, thoughtful, perhaps humorous, but serious and intellectual Believer has gone missing.

And without these thoughtful discussions, challenges to belief and Biblical cultural applications, the Believer finds solace in pundits and politicians, assuring them of their voting ideals and correctness in religious idolatry of candidates.

We have a problem.

My answer is the answer to every problem posed in this chapter. Without the belief in something greater than one's self, the tendency will be towards narcissism and greed. These two traits feed off of fear and achievement, so much so, that in the face of all facts and analysis, they can defy logic by sheer force of conviction and emotion. There is no room for a loss. No place for a discussion. It's my way or the highway. For millions of Americans, politics has become religion, identity, and value. Without G-d this worship of the political is an easy leap to take.

No wonder the world worships the created and not the Creator!

SELF AS GOD LEADS TO POLITICAL TRAVESTY

Until the G-d of the universe has made us aware of our many faults and flaws, of how wrong we often are, of how little we know, why wouldn't we end up worshiping the political? Until wisdom challenges our beliefs, how can we be sure they have their proper place?

Ultimately, if G-d does not define value and worth outside of achievements, including political successes, achievements will be all that remains to define.

We kicked G-d out and we now have… drumroll please… SELF!

Self is the worst sort of god. It's probably better identified as an enemy. It finds you anywhere and everywhere. The inescapable terror of eternity enmeshed with the ever-present reality of the finite. Possessing a need for the infinite while attuned to a flawed, earthly vessel. Disconnected from soul, materialism and relativism are planted in friendly soil. What could possibly go wrong?!

Self attempts to achieve infinity from its own limited wisdom and experience. What frustration and utter devastation when Self fails at this time and again. The trauma of failure without a heavenly Father results in a hardness to life — an emotionally cemented heart, inaccessible to the conscious mind and devastating to the spirit.

These heavily burdened humans now run rampant in society. Because there is no G-d, there is nobody big enough to handle the burdens, nor an all-knowing Father to take our questions. So these devastated masses become the wall against which many well-meaning thinkers bang their heads with facts and data. The sincerest hopeful evangelist cannot overcome someone else's personal trauma and nauseating narcissism.

No logic can tear down the worshipped ego when the bearer sees it as their only line of defense.

The answer to a balance between political activity and faith is the humility to NEED G-d. Not even just assume that you know Him but to realize how little is known and how often we might get it wrong. The Catholic Church's history should be a lesson to ALL believers! The evils we do in the name of politicizing faith are unfathomable. (See my Essay on Church History)

When we do not align ourselves with Scripture but instead align with Self, we have the same problem the atheist does: We will need to be right. Even when we are wrong.

For millions with no belief in G-d, politics has become their religion. And what a horrific taskmaster it is. No human can replace G-d. So, in the attempt to make a political system or figure do so, they will twist and warp any action or fact that should offend to make it fit into the religious ideology of the party.

I once had a lady defend Bill Clinton's treatment of women and presence on Jeffrey Epstein's Island as perfectly innocent. Really. She really did.

And here we come to the biggest problem I find today. Politics has become a religion for both the Believer and non-Believer. It was easy for the non-Believer to fall into that trap, but those who claim to have met G-d should know better!

Yes, your faith should provide a wisdom that informs your voting choices and your political behavior. But it cannot be *the other way around.*

Politics should not be informing your faith.

G-d's Word stands alone and has stood the test of time through governments and countries and political movements and cultures. There is no substitute for, addition to, or taking away from what it states.

The Christ-follower stands on the truth of G-d's word and lets it inform decisions.

If we look to G-d for our faith, we also need NOT look to man to replace G-d.

No political figure will be perfect. THEY WILL BE FLAWED! They will be fallen.

It is not the idea of "choosing between the lesser of the two evils." It is the idea of choosing the BEST of the choices before you. At some point, everyone is evil. It is a Providential act to have a righteous leader. The question should always be, who will DO the most good and who most aligns with Biblical wisdom versus worldly worship of self.

SHORT AND SWEET ADVICE

Stop making political figures out to be religious symbols or Jesus replacements. Stop using hyperbole to describe them. Be specific.

Which policies are preferred and why? Who will enact the preferred policies?

If we would simplify, demystify, and bring unattached logic (a non-personalized analysis) to the discussions, I believe…

-We will remove the stress.

-We will bring truth to our conversations.

-We will not be ashamed of the gospel in the midst of our political proclamations.

-We will de-personify ideas so we can love the human being before us.

I don't believe that the follower of Christ is called to stay silent in the face of evil, both political and spiritual, because the political IS spiritual. I do, however, believe that the Christ Follower is called to tell the truth and to be the light.

The truth will set you free. Not your silence, not your acquiescence. Not your pandering. Not your anger. Not your emotion. Not your name-calling.

The truth alone. G-d's truth alone.

Tell the truth.

You have an armor that G-d has given you. A breastplate of righteousness (for those willing to be obedient to G-d), a helmet of salvation, the belt of TRUTH, and the sword of the Spirit, which is the WORD OF G-D.

If you know G-d's Word, you know the truth. And it will cut through all lies and deceptions. It will expose darkness and drive out evil.

Use it! There is nothing like quoting Scripture to bring thoughtfulness and blessing to a conversation.

It will also keep you from falling into the trap of pledging allegiance to a political ideology or person, instead of keeping your allegiance to Christ.

Had the church in the 1st- and 2nd-century kept the TRUTH, knowledge would not have been lost, Jewish persecution would not have taken root in the church, and the modern church would have a better handle on Scripture and the call of Christ. But they let the lies get entangled with the truth to appease politicians and powerful religious leaders.

We still do this today.

Let's stop.

Politics is the movement of power and people. G-d is therefore invested in politics. He is after all, political in His own way. "His Kingdom come, His will be done on earth." We bear that call. It is the call to bring His Kingdom into our world. That Kingdom call may often encumber us with what is, or what is perceived to be, a political message.

Our Allegiance remains to one King and His Kingdom principles.

Vote accordingly.

Isaiah 9:6-7
For to us a child is born,
to us a son is given,
and the government will be on his shoulders.
And he will be called
Wonderful Counselor, Mighty God,
Everlasting Father, Prince of Peace.
7 Of the greatness of his government and peace
there will be no end.
He will reign on David's throne
and over his kingdom,
establishing and upholding it
with justice and righteousness
from that time on and forever.
The zeal of the LORD Almighty
will accomplish this.

Yeshua is political, but His Kingdom principles are often in conflict with the world's.

One day His government will finally reign upon the earth. He will be the King and we, His people, will follow His Kingdom principles. In the here and now, we are bearers of His Kingdom within our hearts and, hopefully, in our actions, political and otherwise.

Get to know His Kingdom and you will know how to operate as a Believer in Babylon.

Until we are called out of it, we bear the responsibility to be the light in it.

Chapter 7

THE SIN OPERATION

There is a particularly damaging and sneaky sort of thinking that has existed in the Protestant and Catholic Churches for as long as I can remember attending. When pulled to the surface, it goes something like this: "You are truly awful, broken in fact, but don't worry, Jesus has got you covered."

You can find this doctrine undergirding Christian teachings, posts, and philosophy. One dear friend of mine who is a fellow worship leader recently posted on social media that he was so grateful for the grace of G-d because "we cannot please G-d."

We can't? Nothing we do pleases the Lord? Tested against Scripture, this idea fails the smell test, but yet it runs rampant throughout Christianity. The message is in countless worship songs and underpins the lion's share of sermons.

You are terribly marred. Sinful. Unlovable. Unable to please G-d by anything you do. Broken.

If I had a nickel for every time a Christian told me they were broken, I'd be quite a bit richer. Maybe not a millionaire, but several hundred bucks wealthier at the very least. And 'broken' in most contextx is not describing the usual trials and challenges of life. They use the term 'broken' as a replacement for 'sinful'. But it is not a good replacement as "I am broken" is very different than saying, "I am sinful". A wonderful example of how words matter.

In one form or another, this psychological tease has pervaded our Western culture with impressive longevity. Fire and brimstone preachers never ceased to expound on the horridness of our nature and the hell we deserve. The American preacher and philosophical theologian **Jonathan Edwards**[liv] even argued that the "*sight of hell torments will exalt the happiness of the saints forever. . .Can the believing father in Heaven be happy with his unbelieving children in Hell. . . I tell you, yea! Such will be his sense of justice that it will increase rather than diminish his bliss.*"

However he argued his way toward this view of a sadistic god is a mindset I'll likely never comprehend. Loving our own children gives us glimpses of the love of the Father for His creation, and the love He desires to put into us. We are prohibited from such vengeful perspectives.

Modern Christianity does not parrot Edwards. But the message is not so different as we might want to think. A 21st-century sermon rids itself of all the hellfire and invocations of terror; it softens the blow a bit.

Everybody sins. We're all just a boatload of brokenness. BUT…

"Who cares? Jesus died, so that old sin thing isn't a big deal!"

In fact, you can apparently just let your heart lead you. Obedience is based on what you hear from the Holy Spirit. It's subjective! It's a go with the flow sort of walk with Yeshua. Anything goes as long as you heard it from somewhere inside you when you prayed.

And what relief for the preacher who can now avoid the nasty, dark, difficult sections of Scripture called The Law. No need for weekly revivals. Hell may not even exist.

As far as we think the pendulum may have swung, both Edwards and Modern American Christianity base their beliefs on the same depressing idea: People are awful.

As an extension of this idea, there is, of course, no way for you to be perfected here on earth. You are too much of a mess. So Jesus' blood covers you. And once saved, when G-d looks down on you, He magically only sees Yeshua's blood of course, not all the brokenness and sinfulness you are apparently still living in. But even with that covering, you can never please Him. Or… something like that?

Untangling the subtle lies from the truth becomes quite the task when faced with hundreds of years of entwinement.

This is why, in the realm of psychologically destructive ideologies, I think this mindset has got to be one of the worst. A marvelous excuse for poor behavior and a convincing enticement to continue monetary gifts to expatiate sin. The "you're broken but Jesus covered it" idea makes for debauched Friday nights and expensive penitence. But it is not at all the fullness of Biblical truth and it works against soul restoration. Let's explore a few reasons why.

1. God doesn't create awful things.

2. God doesn't create broken things.

3. If you've been a Christian for a while and are still convinced you are broken, what steps have you taken to be made whole, and do you even believe G-d wants you to be made whole?

4. When you tell someone they are, of no fault of their own, intrinsically damaged, they no longer have any responsibility for their damaged behavior.

5. When you tell someone that all the awful is covered, then all need to reform is once and for all discarded.

Now, is this message a complete lie? Not in totality. That is why it is so pernicious. We do sin. We do need Yeshua. And we cannot become whole based on our own ideas of wholeness. However, G-d destines us for good things, calls us into righteousness, tells us we can follow Him (which means HE believes we CAN follow him and his Commands) and wants to make the blind man see in every metaphorical and literal way.

Here's where the idea that you are "**just a sinner** and G-d's got you covered" leads: **It leads to sin**.

I fell for it. Shredded within my own first marriage, and looking ahead at my own personal hell until "death do we part," I made a major error in judgment.

Yeah, my husband was behaving atrociously and burdened with his own iniquities, but that did not excuse my decision to have a weekend affair of my own.

I had rules. RULES, I say! But the rule I was taught by Christianity was that you could never get divorced. My parents forbade it, my friends would have abandoned me, and as a stay-at-home mom, financially it seemed like a quick trip to the poor house. So I abided by the rule that wasn't really a Command in exchange for breaking a rule that WAS.

In my mind, I was just a sinner. Jesus would forgive me, right? I was broken from my marriage and I wanted to pretend that I played no part in the outcome of that mess.

And it was a mess. A giant horrific mess.

In reality, had I NOT broken one of G-d's actual Commands, had I known G-d's Commands at all, I would have made a better choice. There was a way out, but I was convinced the only Scriptural route was the way through. And many suffered because of it.

Where was all of that so-called coverage I had always been promised? If I'm covered by "grace" and G-d only sees Yeshua when He looks at me, why in the world did I endure such hell after sinning? According to modern theology, I was broken long before I had an affair, and couldn't do anything on my own to repair myself afterwards either. Nothing could bring about my own righteousness. And heck, I had Jesus. Doesn't He MAKE me righteous? By extension, even in my sin, I'm saved by grace and righteous before the Lord, right?

If I can never please G-d, what does it matter if I sin or behave well? If Yeshua is the only pleasing thing to G-d and I have Yeshua, does behavior matter?

Do you see the problem here?

My doctrine failed me because, well, it's crap doctrine. Sometimes I wonder if the Catholic Church promoted this doctrine because of how enriched they became through indulgences. These literal monetary gifts to the church supposedly "covered" the sins of the congregants. Indulgences still exist in some forms in the Catholic Church today.

Money almost certainly motivated the teaching of this doctrine that you can't do anything about your sin. But hey, you can fork over some dough and the church has it covered! You're a wretch, but your money can make you a saint or at least get those pearly gates cracked for ya.

And Protestants hardly do much better. For too long the idea of a good Christian was someone who attended Church every weekend. That showing of face among the saints was enough to make a good man out of even the worst of sinners. Despite weekly Church attendance NOT being required in Scripture, somehow many of us grew up believing it was the one thing that could make us right with the Lord.

Unfortunately, these doctrines remain prevalent. We still need to free ourselves of our misconceptions of righteousness and sin, and their place in our lives as followers of Yeshua.

The psychology of "you're just horrible but G-d has you covered" is Satanic. And it produces death. Let me show you how else it works to produce a lazy and sinful body of Christ.

WHAT IS LOVE?

All Christians say they "love" G-d." It is a prerequisite and it is called for before sacrifice or obedience. Relationship is everything, and love is at the core of great relationship.

Most unofficial and official sources define love as an intense feeling. Here are three prominent definitions from Merriam-Webster's: "a quality or feeling of strong or constant affection for and dedication to another" or "attraction based on sexual desire : the strong affection and tenderness felt by lovers" or "warm attachment, enthusiasm, or devotion."

But what does the Bible say about the definition of love? Is it a feeling? As hard as this may be to stomach, I'd challenge you to go to Scripture and try to find how many feelings are actually even heavily discussed in Scripture. You're going to find it doesn't happen often.

Why? Why isn't the Bible talking about feelings? It seems to be so important, especially in our society today. Feelings rule the day.

You do you

Reality is relative

How does that make you feel?

It felt like the right thing to do

We have a way of looking at life through a lens of how life feels, not through a lens of what our lives produce. Are we happy? This is considered the ultimate question. "Do what makes you happy!" we are told. "Follow your passions" and "pursue your dreams." And again, nothing is so wrong with these admonitions. But when put into the context of Scripture, they aren't aimed properly.

The Bible seems far less interested in how you feel about something than it is interested in what that something produces. How often does the Bible tell us that obedience to G-d produces happiness? Was Abraham "happy" to leave his family to go somewhere he had never been? Did it make Moses "happy" to tell Pharaoh to let the Hebrew people go? How *un*happy was Jonah when he was told to go to Ninevah?

Paul's contentment in all situations and the joy experienced from Yeshua's miracles were an outcome of obedience, not an impetus for it. Scripture does not seem to give much weight to the emotions felt by the obedient. There are many reasons for this, so we will dig into just a few and then go back to the "love" question.

1. Hebrew is an active language. Unlike Greek and other Western languages, Hebrew doesn't describe what something looks like, but rather describes its purpose. Deepening the interpretation, every letter and word in Hebrew has extra meanings attached, as well as numerical significance. Additionally, many words have male or female assignment.

My favorite linguist teacher to date, **Brad Scott**[lv], often uses the following helpful examples when comparing Western languages to Hebrew:

If a Western mind wants to describe a pencil, they will say something like, "It's a long thin piece of wood with lead in it and a pink rubbery substance at the end." If an ancient near eastern (See Ch 1. Definitions for more on the Ancient Near East) mind went to describe a pencil, they would say, "I use it to write."

Or how about the word for anger in Hebrew? Translated literally, it means "flaring nostrils." You get the action of the angry person in the term for the feeling of anger itself. It is descriptive of the *activity* that anger produces in your body. This action-oriented worldview is buried into the very language of Scripture itself. Hebrew is an active language, meaning intention and feeling are not nearly as present as the activity that the intention or feeling may or may not produce. In the Bible, results matter.

2. From the very beginning of Scripture, G-d is active. He is creative and detailed, working six days and resting on the seventh. There is very little discussion (although there is some) about how G-d feels about this creativity. He tells us it is good (complete and fit for its purpose) and the Holy Spirit hovers with excitement over the waters before G-d forms the version of Earth we have now.

But most of the text recounts the activity of our G-d. Throughout the Old Testament, this continues to be the case as G-d sends Abraham out of his home, sends Jacob to the promised land, sends Joseph to save the world from starvation, intervenes on behalf of Israel to deliver them from Egypt, performs signs and miracles through prophets and Kings, helps David defeat Goliath, etc.

There is continued and active involvement in producing good results for His people.

Of course, we know that this all occurs because He loves us. But we must also note the active, not passive, proof of His love. The feeling promotes the activity, but the activity in and of itself must be good in order for love to be understood. And G-d shows us both. Love and the definition of love, which is: righteous *activity* on behalf of the loved.

There is no better example of this than Yeshua himself. Abandoning "feel good" activities for a servant-based life, Yeshua chose a cross over a longer ministry. He chose to wash feet over a few more drinks and laughs with his buddies. He chose service, feeding the hungry and healing, over a lifestyle dedicated to royal luxuries.

These actions are proof of the Father's love for us and a mirror for our definition of love today. Without G-d's actions, the word "love" is meaningless. We cannot escape how active G-d is in His love for us.

To the Lord, love is not just a feeling, but also correct behavior.

Obviously, love exists as both an emotion and an action. But for us, the wandering souls, we need also be always alert to that old adage: the road to hell is paved with good intentions.

Our feelings often lead us astray. Our feelings are often misplaced, and, worse, sometimes we "feel" like something is right, when the opposite is true.

Even the sinless Adam and Eve were deceived by desires that may, on the surface, seem good. In perfection, in the Garden of Eden, they wanted to be wise, to be "like" G-d! They wanted more knowledge and to improve their state of being. Those feelings/desires, in and of them selves, may not have been wholly wrong. Who doesn't want to improve their knowledge base and gain more understanding? But they allowed those feelings to lead them into disobedience.

Hell resulted.

They were aiming in the wrong direction. Their heart's desire was for something they "thought/felt" was good instead of their heart's desire being pointed towards obedience to God. These betrayals of the heart occur often enough that the Bible tells us our hearts are by their very nature "deceitful." (Jeremiah 17:9)

Out of this deceit, we can twist together truth and lies with ease. You can practically hear the hiss of hell as it whispers gentle reassurances of how the end justifies the means. If Adam and Eve could get this wrong, I guarantee we get it wrong consistently.

Our hearts are not trustworthy.

My fellow elder millennials may remember that DC Talk standby from 1992, "Luv Is A Verb." In John 14:15, Yeshua advises us that to love Him, you must keep His commands. The Lord Himself has instructed us this way from Genesis to Revelation.

If you love the Lord, you DO something GOOD with it. The Bible defines what is good, and you abide by THAT goodness, and abandon what goes against it.

So now, when we go back to the psychology of "you are horrible, but don't worry, God has got you covered," we can logically take issue with at least one part. We know G-d only has you covered if you love Yeshua. But if you love Yeshua, you obey His commands. And, if you are obeying His commands and living in righteousness, why are you still demanding that you are horrible and broken?

Now here, I can hear you all crying out, "But we are all sinners! Paul said so!"

Yes, we are. So let's dig into the word "sin," and see how the Bible defines that one.

In our Western mindset, sin is often correlated to our legal system. If you trespass the law, you will go to court where a judge sentences you to whatever is deemed legally fit.

But the word for sin in Hebrew and the understanding for it in the Ancient Near Eastern (Biblical Era) mind is more closely associated with "missing the mark."

You are shooting an arrow at a bulls-eye, but you have aimed improperly. Instead of aiming at following the heavenly Father, you are aiming at pleasing yourself.

In that framework, your next moment could be perfect without any mistakes in it. Your next moment could be whole and fit for its purpose (which is G-d's definition of good, by the way). In Genesis, when G-d says of His creation, "it was good," He is saying it is purposeful and can DO what it is intended to do.

At any given moment, you could aim straight for the bulls' eye. Living out G-d's Law is the central focus of our walk. If you aim there, you are aiming properly. This is why the Bible can call Abraham, Noah, and others righteous and/or perfect in the eyes of G-d. We are all sinners, yes, but we are all capable of completeness in obedience as well. This is a hard concept, but it is indeed Biblical. Check out Genesis 17:1: "When Abram was 99 years old, the Lord appeared to him... and said unto him, 'I am the Almighty God, walk before me and be thou perfect...'"

If G-d calls you to be perfect, He knows you can be. And remember, perfection doesn't mean you have the DNA within yourself to save yourself. You don't. Only Yeshua has that. It means you can be made whole and fit for your purpose. You can be made complete in the Lord. Your heart is *towards* obedience. You are being made to be the likeness and image of Yeshua. You can become obedient with the help of Yeshua.

A good father doesn't ask his children to do something they are not capable of.

(Even that does not and cannot produce your salvation, but it DOES produce proof of love and relationship.)

Obedience is evidence of whose you are.

Are you surprised to find that G-d has actually said completeness in obedience is possible?

Noah is also called "perfect in his generation" (Genesis 6:9). A further study of this verse reveals that, again, "perfect" means whole, and "generations" means *among his contemporaries.*

Noah lived in such an evil generation that his righteousness probably wasn't that of Abraham or other righteous men. Rather, among his contemporaries, G-d could call him whole and fit for his purpose. He was extraordinarily obedient to G-d, devoting 100 years to build an Ark for what his neighbors and community considered a fanciful future storm. He endured much to be obedient to the Lord. His perfection was in his heartfelt obedience. Thereby, he was perfect.

I doubt any of us can claim that level of obedience. Most of America can't even stand the thought of giving up a couple of food items for the Lord, let alone building a giant boat while enduring the mockery of our neighbors for 100 years.

So, do we love the Lord? How can we know? And yes, maybe we are broken. But do we want to be made whole, perfect, and useful for our purpose?

Many are going to hang onto the idea that one can never be perfect. It is because we continue to use the un-Biblical definition of that word. Perfection is completeness. Complete before the Lord means we have allowed Him to build us, we have submitted to His will, and even if we stumble, we stay to our purpose.

-It's not the fact that you cussed that one time when you dropped your coffee on your lap. That's not a sin according to the Torah.

-It's not the meeting you forgot about or when you took a job that seemed to waste some years of your life.

-It's not that you don't participate in every school fundraiser or make splendid dishes for Church lunches.

-It's not that you like to eat corn chips for lunch or drink more coffee than you do anything else. (Guilty as charged)

From a Biblical perspective, those things have nothing to do with perfection. And there are whole lists of ideas like this that we think are part of perfection. They're not.

Perfection is about G-d's destiny for you. You are called to be a Kingdom Citizen in a Kingdom with standards found in the Torah. Those standards are so much simpler than our fantasies about leading a "perfect" life. Perfection in Scripture is about alignment, submission, and yes, love. We are clay in the potter's hands. We allow G-d to mold and shape us to live like Yeshua lived and to love as He loves. We are humble.

His obedience is found in 613 positive and negative Commands found in the first 5 books of Scripture. Most will not even apply to you. They are simple, doable, applicable, and life-changing.

Anything beyond those is between you and G-d. But be careful that you have not put burdens upon yourself that do not belong. Man-made dictates become heavy yokes that turn into idols of their own.

Let go of the idea that you can't be obedient. It's not useful to your next step of obedience. Amen?

Hang onto the idea that you CAN be obedient WITH the Holy Spirit's direction and support.

If we could be made fit for G-d's purpose for our lives, then are we still broken? Or, are we actually in the process of becoming useful?

When you've received a large piece of furniture to put together or gathered wood to make a table, do you say the furniture is broken? Or, is the furniture being *built?*

We are compared to clay in the potter's hand for a reason (Jeremiah 18). The second we give our lives over to the Lord, he is a crafter, a builder, a restorer. When you see the clay in progress, it is not broken: it is *becoming.*

If you love the Lord and follow Him, you are not called to stay broken. You are being made.

And yes, sin still exists and plagues us. And yes, we still need the DNA of Yeshua in order to get to salvation.

We cannot achieve salvation on our own because we are not equipped for that purpose. Only G-d Himself was equipped for the purposes of becoming the perfect "Adam" who would bring about the spiritual DNA of G-d in people on earth. We cannot do this for ourselves because we come from the DNA of the first Adam. This DNA is fallen. We NEED the DNA of the second Adam, Yeshua.

On our own, we simply do not have the power to restore our DNA to its original intended purpose. When we try to do it on our own, it's like trying to use corrupted software to fix corrupted software. It won't work. We have to delete the former software and install the correct version. None of us carry the correct version when we are born.

However, with Yeshua's help and His DNA, we CAN walk in obedience. And just as Yeshua told us to follow Him, we must believe that we are able to walk after Him and live as He lived.

Now for the pesky back half of the "Don't worry, God has you covered" bit.

Don't worry, Jesus died, your responsibilities to G-d's teaching and instruction ended there.

Alrighty, so let's say you get married, maybe you're married already. The ceremony ends, reception party is a great time, and you head home with your spouse. Then you spend the next decade not talking to them, not asking questions, disinterested in their needs or point of view. The two of you live together, but that's about it. Maybe you date other people, use up all the money both of you make, assume your spouse will always clean up after you and serve you endlessly without anything in return.

Is this a relationship? Or, is this abuse?

Let's take a look at Hebrews 10:26-39:

For if we go on sinning deliberately after receiving the knowledge of the truth, there no longer remains a sacrifice for sins, but a fearful expectation of judgment, and a fury of fire that will consume the adversaries. Anyone who has set aside the law of Moses dies without mercy on the evidence of two or three witnesses. How much worse punishment, do you think, will be deserved by the one who has trampled underfoot the Son of God, and has profaned the blood of the covenant by which he was sanctified, and has outraged the Spirit of grace? For we know him who said, 'Vengeance is mine; I will repay.' And again, 'The Lord will judge his people.; It is a fearful thing to fall into the hands of the living God.

But recall the former days when, after you were enlightened, you endured a hard struggle with sufferings, sometimes being publicly exposed to reproach and affliction, and sometimes being partners with those so treated. For you had compassion on those in prison, and you joyfully accepted the plundering of your property, since you knew that you yourselves had a better possession and an abiding one. Therefore do not throw away your confidence, which has a great reward. For you have need of endurance, so that when you have done the will of God you may receive what is promised. For,

'Yet a little while,
and the coming one will come and will not delay;
but my righteous one shall live by faith,
and if he shrinks back,
my soul has no pleasure in him.'

But we are not of those who shrink back and are destroyed, but of those who have faith and preserve their souls."

"Outraged the Spirit of Grace." This stands out. If you treated your spouse the way I described, your spouse would be outraged. Perhaps you go into the world claiming you're married to this person, but you do not abide as if you have a marriage or relationship. More than that, you use that person up, trampling upon their grace.

Hebrews provides a Scriptural definition for this: a one-way relationship where we abuse G-d's grace, enraging the Spirit. It is a position deserving of judgment and Hebrews promises an unhappy verdict for those who treat G-d in this manner.

In Scripture, the people of G-d are always judged first. Our contemporary selves are no different. Hebrews describes here a moment of vengeance where those who abuse G-d's grace receive punishment. The writer then calls for the reader to recall days where they suffered for the sake of Christ, admonishing these believers to hold on in that faith, that suffering will bring about glory.

Obedience is not easy, but clearly it is possible.

Continued disobedience is an outrage to G-d.

In His love for His children, punishment can bring restoration.

The children of Israel were punished when they worshiped foreign gods. How much more do we deserve to be punished when we abuse the grace that came through the blood of Christ?

Why do we think G-d doesn't work this way? Do we not believe that G-d is the same yesterday, today, and tomorrow? Have we not seen what happened to Israel when they fell away? Time and again, punishment brought them back around to alignment with the Lord. Does not G-d "punish those whom He loves"? (Proverbs 3:12 and Hebrews 12:6)

Hebrews says, "For you have need of endurance for WHEN you have done the will of G-d..." There is an assumption here that obedience will take place. They will endure. They are going to accomplish G-d's will, even when it is hard. They are not going to live in disobedience.

Why don't we believe these Scriptures? Is it possible we have believed the terrible doctrine of "you're awful, but don't worry, G-d has you covered?"

Here is how Paul deals with this, from Romans 6: "What shall we say then? Are we to continue in sin that grace may abound? By no means! How can we who died to sin still live in it? Do you not know that all of us who have been baptized into Christ Jesus were baptized into his death, in order that, just as Christ was raised from the dead by the glory of the Father, we too might walk in newness of life.

For, if we have been united with him in a death like his, we shall certainly be united with him in a resurrection like his. We know that our old self was crucified with him in order that the body of sin might be brought to nothing, so that we would NO LONGER BE ENSLAVED TO SIN. For one who has died has been set free from sin. Now, if we have died with Christ, we believe that we will also live with him."

We are born into the world with the DNA of the first Adam in our souls: a fallen DNA. We cannot fix it. When we belong to Yeshua, that first Adam dies in us, and we are reborn into the spiritual DNA of the second Adam, Yeshua. Yeshua's DNA is FREE FROM SIN!

No, it doesn't mean you won't ever sin again, but it means you are CAPABLE now of fully following Yeshua. You are new and freed from sin. You were previously incapable. That cage SHOULD be gone.

If you are in Christ, you aren't "awful." Before you were in Christ, you weren't **made to be** awful. **You are made to become a new creation, crafted in the image of your Rabbi, Yeshua.**

To continue to sin is to deny the newness of life in your soul. To dismiss that sin as "covered by grace" with no responsibility attached is, well, as I put it before, Satanic.

Yeah, I said it. It's a bold claim. Here is why I make it.

The G-d of the universe says, "Come follow me and be like me."

Satan, or more often, your ego, comes along and says, "You can't."

Which one do you believe and what will it produce?

If Satan or that fallen inner voice convinces us that we cannot follow Yeshua, then I don't see how we could. Time will be spent avoiding knowledge of obedience because it will just remind us of how far from the bulls-eye we have aimed. The destiny of our ministries will suffer. We will not speak about G-d's things to others because we will be living too out of alignment to feel worthy of having a ministry at all.

Or, the ministry will be bastardized by excuses for sinfulness, encouraging a lackadaisical approach to restoration of the Spirit in others.

We will have a weak testimony because our lives will not look any different than those who do not proclaim to be Believers.

Is this weakness evident in the Western Church?

You better believe it.

In the Garden of Eden, Satan asked Eve, "Did G-d really say?" And now, he comes to us today with the same setup: "Did G-d really say you could follow Him? Or even that you should? Surely He doesn't mean it! I mean, you're a sinner, you're *Broken and irreparable.* You can't fully follow G-d and abide by His Law!"

If that's true, then what's the point? Many thoughtful believers will ask this question and it is in these "weeds" we find so many young people abandoning the Church. The doctrine is too vague. The call too lofty. And in a world bountiful with information, relying on subjective vague ideas of obedience becomes a burdensome task. One must constantly be looking and asking if something is good. Constantly burdened by the lack of direction from the pulpit on what Scripture says about job choices, or which ministry you are "supposed" to serve in.

But when we talk about obedience to Yeshua, I'm not usually talking about subjective directives or personal situational challenges. We are talking about obedience to G-d's Laws, His Torah. The objective starting place. If we aren't willing to do the first things in simplicity, we will never work out the more personal, subtle calls on our lives, because we lack foundation.

We must return to the rock of our salvation. The Yeshua whose specific calls to obedience are not burdensome. As of now, the ministry of Believers is so weak, helpless, full of sin and lies, and full of these intellectual holes, that huge numbers of people have fallen away or left the church. The current doctrine of irreparable awfulness inevitably ends with souls who never get freed from sin. That bondage destroys the power of the Spirit of G-d to change lives and innovate ministries.

That bondage is indeed awful. The cage keeps you from G-d's definition of "good." If good means "fit for its purpose," then living antithetical to good means you are missing your destiny. Worse, it could result in destruction instead of restoration.

Sin throws up roadblocks on the route to God's purpose for your life, and it offers up ample opportunity to construct roadblocks for others.

You cannot live the life G-d intends for you from a cage. This is why salvation is consistently described as freedom from Sin! Iniquity is a route to entrapment.

The scars of my past iniquities testify to sin's toll. Ask an alcoholic about cages. A drug addict. A porn addict. The one who worships money, or their job, or food, or even family. We know about cages. Why don't we just admit it?

Those task-masters keep you busy, keep you down, and keep you in bondage, as Paul tells us (Galatians 5:1, Romans 8:2).

And when we do sin, oh the shame! The shame that evil brings upon us. The shame we bring upon ourselves. We cannot help it. When we sin and live according to the first Adam, our sin mutates into a cage of endless self-destruction. Shame perverts our view of self so that, instead of seeking restoration, we seek the level we believe about ourselves. Shame calls us unredeemable.

This will only lead to a continuous cycle of sin.

When we believe we are NOT whole and fit for our purpose, we cannot live out our purpose. Shame is a natural result of sinning. But it is NOT G-d's will for our lives. G-d's grace exists for when we sin. His promise is that of blessing when we obey. Mercy and grace remain in our loving Heavenly Father. This mercy should draw us closer to Him and help us to fall more In LOVE with His ways!

G-d loves you right where you are, but He does not intend to *leave* you right where you are.

G-d's message has never been, "You're horrible, but I have you covered."

It has always been, "You are fearfully and wonderfully made" (Psalm 139:14).

"The path of the righteous is like the light of dawn which shines brighter and brighter until full day." (Proverbs 4:18)

"Let us be glad and rejoice and give Him glory, for the marriage of the Lamb has come, and His wife has made herself ready.' And to her it was granted to be arrayed in fine linen, clean and bright, for the fine linen is the **righteous acts** of the saints." (Revelation 19:7-8)

"In every nation, whoever fears Him and works righteousness is accepted by Him" (Acts 10:34-35)

You are not called to be continually dismayed over your sin! You are not called to stay broken! Clothed in white linen, which are the garments of righteousness, married to the groom, who is Yeshua, the follower of Christ is redeemed. "Broken" becomes egregious terminology in light of the power of the blood of the Lamb. You were once broken, but now you are being built. You were once lost, but NOW, you are found!

To be made whole and fit for a purpose is perfection.

When you accept Yeshua, you are His bride. Bright and beautiful and light and goodness. He releases you from the cage. He gives you His Spirit, an especially powerful tool that unlocks freedom. He promises to walk with you, climb with you, wade through crap with you. Just leave the cage, embark on the perilous journey, take interest in understanding the valley, and relish the mountaintop. Build your spiritual muscles and your wisdom. Increase your confidence and your courage.

See what G-d will do with an obedient heart!

He never says you can't, He offers His hand out, His heart for you, and says, "Come."

Yes. You. Can.

Sin is a tool of the enemy, a cage, a stepping-stone to a shame-filled existence. It is the world trying to keep you at home in it.

But in Yeshua, you are of another Kingdom. Be free.

John 8:10 – 11 "Woman, where are they? Has no one condemned you?
'No one sir,' she replied. 'Then neither do I condemn you.
Go, and sin no more."

Chapter 8

THE MONEY TRAP

I REMEMBER BEING 26 YEARS OLD. I had just had my first kiddo and was exhausted and overwhelmed getting used to the demands of working my tail off all for the little one while attempting a few side hustles, just so we could get by.

My husband at the time was a workaholic. Maybe he had to be. We could barely afford our mortgage each month, didn't take fancy trips or go out a lot. We made spaghetti, watched TV, and tried to improve our house so we could sell it. Then we attempted to sell it right as the 2008 housing market crash hit its peak.

I remember being lonely. Crazy lonely. Just my young boy and me, and, well, the dog. My husband was NEVER home. Teaching all day and sporting events at night, I remember watching TV and eating dinner by myself so many nights, even before our sweet kiddo was born.

It didn't feel like a marriage.

We thought we had everything we needed as we worked well over 40+ hours a week to keep the house, the cars, etc. But we were blind to the poverty that had struck within our home. We had very few shared interests. We didn't talk about anything important. When I would ask for us to pray together, he would almost always find a way out of it. We literally shared nothing except our son and the house we had moved into.

Though I'd eventually learned to adopt the American dream, my personal dreams had not always been to have a perfect house and a few kids. The realization of the American dream in practice depleted me. I couldn't fill the gaping holes in my heart with an empty but "good enough" middle class home or a perfectly fine dinner shared with a sweet baby. There was some spirit to those realized dreams that was just missing.

I hadn't learned yet how to allow G-d to fill those spaces. And even with G-d's help, facing rejection from a spouse who never wanted to be around would have been difficult.

For him, other distractions kept the holes from being obvious. He could laugh and happily attempt to fill his need for meaning with his job and friends and flirtations at work. Those were things he knew how to do and felt good at.

But at home, our relationship was falling apart. And for me, and I think for him too, the pursuit of career loomed larger and larger as a counterweight to this mismatched marriage.

As I look at our society, it seems that money has indeed been used to fill a lot of the voids. Want to feel like you're keeping up? A new car or house, no matter how much debt it takes, can really obviate that future mid-life crisis. Life is good. Need is low. Vulnerability is extinguished.

A shopping trip for easing the pain of relationships gone sour.

A work promotion for extinguishing our poor self-esteem.

A night on the town to make up for the loneliness at home.

Doesn't money make the world go around? And, of course, the most powerful people in the world are those with the most money. They wield influence above and beyond the everyday human. The more numerals to the left of the decimal, the higher the status elevation. Politicians bend to the will of those giant donations and behind closed doors they make deals that influence the poorer, less fortunate masses.

Wealth has always been a human pursuit, not just for the status, but for our very basic needs. We want our kids to eat, to have a bed and a roof. We don't want to burden them in our old age.

And, yeah, being able to pay your bills really lifts the stress. Believe me, I know. I've had times where I couldn't buy groceries or pay off my debt, and had no idea where my next job would come from. Pain produces fear, and fear produces a desperate need to make things safe and stable. Money seems like stability.

But is it?

Money is temporary, tied to the worldly system that is in place. You cannot take it when you die and you cannot even guarantee its worth when black swan events (see: Covid) shock the globe. It is no safe harbor for the security of your soul or your emotional wellbeing. Yet, how we use money can reveal our character and compose books and chapters of lives lived well, or lives lived selfishly.

In the church we often speak about money as if it is the only way G-d blesses us, the only way the Kingdom of G-d can expand, and the only route to seeing that G-d approves of our church services, buildings, and congregations. American churchgoers don't want to admit this. But…

If I say G-d wants to bless you, what is the first blessing you often imagine? Especially if you already have a spouse and kids, finances often rank as numero uno. Can you even prove it's G-d's blessing if it isn't in cold hard cash?

(Some of you sweet folks may have answered, "G-d wants to bless me with good relationships, or peace," etc. You know your stuff. And probably live better than most of us.)

But come on: for the average American, blessing means money, and with it, power, a higher position in life, sometimes fame.

Of course, monetary blessing does have a Biblical foundation! G-d blessed Solomon to be the richest man of his day after he asked for wisdom. But one has to ask, which came first: the wisdom or the money? Which one profited him for longer: the wisdom or the money? To this day most of us probably aren't carrying around physical treasure from Solomon's kingdom, but his proverbs live on and each one of us is RICHLY blessed by those teachings. The blessings of G-d outlasted the man through far more stable means than a worldly financial system.

I believe we have forgotten the many blessings of G-d — freedom, friends, healthy relationships, children, wisdom, peace, and Biblical knowledge. Because money seems to dictate so much, we are willing to overlook great evils in order to have just a little more, be just a little wealthier. And in the meantime, we abandon or forget so many of the other blessings G-d wants us to have.

We are no different than churches past in this regard. How many concessions have been made because money was at stake? In the great history of church attendance, filling the coffers has too often taken precedent over righteous teaching and Biblical behavior.

We must understand money and our interactions with it to move forward in the world as true followers of Yeshua.

MONEY AS god.

I heard a fascinating **podcast**[lvi] recently with Dinah Dye. She is an amazing author and speaker and I'd highly recommend seeking her out. In this particular podcast, Ryan White, the interviewer, brought up something I hadn't thought about deeply enough. I'd bounced around the idea but never taken it to its full meaning. Here's a paraphrase of White's question: "If our need for cheap clothing causes us to buy from people who are abusing and killing the poor in order to make it, have we committed murder according to the 10 Commandments?"

Dagger to the heart! The implications of our dependence on cheap, often exploitative labor practice overseas should provoke a profound sadness, and repentance, in us.

It reminds me of the story of Yeshua with the wealthy young man (Matthew 19:16-22). The man approaches Yeshua and asks what he must do to attain eternal life. Oddly enough, Yeshua answers him by telling him to follow the 10 Commandments, specifically the last ones, which have to do with how we treat other humans. The ruler says that he has done these already. Yeshua then says that he must sell his wealth and follow Him. At this, the young ruler turns away sorrowfully.

An examination of the monetary system of Yeshua's day provides an important and oft-missed context. The wealthy of that day had often gained their wealth through corrupt means. The poor were grossly taken advantage of in order for the wealthy to accrue more. I wonder if Yeshua, in asking him about the final few 10 Commandments, was really asking him to examine if he had noticed how his money had been attained. Was it ill-gotten gain? Did he need to sell it and give it to the poor because it had been taken through the unfair exploitation of the poor to begin with? Does the rich young ruler understand this and turn away sorrowful at his blatant sin? Even if it wasn't ill-gotten gain, we aren't sure if he went to sell it, or if he continued to serve money more than G-d.

It's worth considering how much we resemble the rich young ruler. And it's worth asking: which of us will turn away from our ill-gotten gain?

The horrific treatment of workers in China, India, and Africa amongh others — many of them children — who make and obtain everything from our clothing to the cobalt and lithium used in our iPhones and electric car batteries, is a regular subject in news headlines. How many have risked their lives for less than a day's wages so that we could have a cheap shirt or a new computer? And we buy it. We stand in line for it! We help increase the stock prices of the most vicious companies and exploitive leaders.

And though it doesn't take much effort to learn of the thousands of men, women, and **children**[lvii] who are stolen or drugged into sexual trafficking and used to make pornography, the church says so little about this moral catastrophe, our lack of stance is beginning to look like guilt. How many Americans view it, buy it, use it? Replacing real relationship and marital sexual relations with use and abuse of the least of these in our society, we take advantage of victims for our own pleasure or emotional need.

Are we not the rich young ruler?

And we tolerate all the gateways to these evils. From Christians' widespread love of *Game of Thrones* to our need for Nike shoes, we take small steps each day that prove our status as rich young rulers as well.

We don't call companies to task.

We don't switch brands.

We don't throw out our computers when someone is addicted to pornography.

We don't cancel our subscriptions.

We TOLERATE it.

And we aren't even as healthy as the rich young ruler. We aren't even sorrowful.

Or, perhaps we are. But not enough to repent.

Maybe we do care about it, but not enough to personally make sacrificial changes.

When asked how to attain eternity, would we really give everything up?

There is nothing wrong with money. But money that replaces G-d is money with no moral compass. It is ultimately destructive.

> Matthew 6:24 "No one can serve two masters. Either he will hate the one and love the other, or he will be devoted to the one and despise the other. You cannot serve both God and money."

The love of money produces a pursuit of it too easily attached to evil routes and moral compromises. We must be willing to give it up to reject hell and become truly useful to the Kingdom of Heaven.

This is not at all to say that the wealthy are evil or the poor are pure. Before the Lord, there is no class. But before the Lord there IS justice. Americans have become more and more aware of the way companies have provided us our goods and services, yet we seem to be less interested than ever in making the necessary sacrifices to change those practices. This should be a hard blow to the average American Christian. (I'm speaking to myself here as much as anyone.)

And yet, I know only a handful of Believers who don't give money to groups like Netflix who create shows like 365 (a gross piece of so-called "art" that glorifies sexual trafficking). Why don't we cancel? Can't you hear the rich young ruler now?

How will we be entertained? How will we keep ourselves occupied? How will we stay culturally relevant?

Putting it down on paper reveals the shallow, transient foolishness of those excuses. I'd hardly call it a ringing endorsement for our intellect, let alone our faith.

The weightier matters of justice and mercy — these are part of the currency of heaven. In all honesty, we are each likely guilty of murder to some degree. What have we been willing to buy for cheap, keep a year or two, and throw out that was created by hands and bodies and minds and hearts that were taken, exploited because of their poverty.

Released in 2015, the **documentary film *The True Cost***[lviii] unmasks the clothing industry, primarily the dark practices behind the rise of "fast fashion." This is the arm of the fashion industry geared towards creating as many cheap designer knockoffs as possible, that allows us to buy t-shirts and jeans at the rate we buy coffee. One argument of the titans of fashion is that, without them, the poor exploited workers in the film would have no jobs at all.

Well. For starters, I didn't realize the fashion industry was actually saving people! I had no idea that the industry was that altruistic. On the other hand…

Paying the lowest rate because no other competition even exists… Isn't this the definition of extortion?

Why can they do this?

Because Americans, millions of them Christian, buy it.

The second we stop, they would have to stop making their clothing that way.

The second we saved some extra bucks for our next purchases and decided to have five great outfits instead of 20 garbage ones, we would see a real change in the industry.

But for the rich young ruler, this seems like too much work.

Let us be frank that, yes, it takes effort to make sure you're a gift to the world and not a drain.

And sure, perhaps job growth hasn't matched inflation. Perhaps we have plenty of economically distressed individuals here as well that need clothing and phones too. Perhaps it is such a big problem that nobody even tries.

But this isn't fixed by some grand human savior. It is the work of each individual that will slowly change our cultural norms and what we will and won't tolerate. We must change the very way we evaluate our worth. The questions should not be about how you will change the world.

The real question for every believer is: WHO do you want to be in the world?

This will take the pressure off of what we cannot change and put it back on our CHARACTER, something we can control.

Yeshua was asking the rich young ruler to become a gift to the world. This young man was very good at the letter of the Law, but he did not ask any deeper questions about the spirit behind it. So, just how deep does the Law of G-d ask us to look?

Pretty deep.

If we reject the Law completely, we don't even begin to ask the right questions. At least the young ruler asked a question.

But if we want to know how to attain eternity, mankind must be our business (as Dickens would put it).

The curse of being constantly entertained and driven by the screens we hold in our hands is not only that we don't see the people in our immediate vicinity. We don't even think about the people who make all of our products so very far away. These very devices are designed to help us stop thinking.

But these that create our products are people, made by G-d. They ought to be the business of our spiritual lives, as treasures of the Kingdom and the creation of G-d Almighty.

I fear that money and entertainment will too often be the roadblock to discipleship. This is why it must be addressed in this most wealthy of countries.

ON THE FLIP SIDE…

We also don't want to see money in and of itself as an evil.

Yeshua gives us a parable in Matthew 25 about a master who gives his workers different amounts of "talents." These talents were considered a unit of currency.

The master returns to judge how the talents have been used. He is harsh with the servant who does not invest the talent to produce more, while he approves of the two servants who use their talents to create a profit.

There is both a physical and spiritual application to this parable. Investment and stewardship are G-dly characteristics. The ability to produce physically and spiritually speaks to wise entrepreneurship and wise investment into the Kingdom of Heaven.

So much for the "Jesus was a socialist" dogma. Yeshua seems to be anything but. He clearly believes that people are given gifts and abilities, which require proper caretaking and investment to develop. Comparison and competition are valuable tools that the parable exposes. The Master in the parable rewards competency and progress, which predict the ability to produce fruit. In vast contrast to the idea that society or government owes you something, G-d says go and *become* or *create* something of value. In bringing your destiny to society, you will gain far more than you could ever take.

I find some followers of Christ are often fearful of obtaining the sort of wealth that creates profitability. Even if it is based on their own merits or hard work, they are often fearful of teaching their children how to do the same. Instead we often parrot the dangerous philosophy that making money on earth doesn't matter at all, or worse, that it is evil.

Let me turn that on its head. It is the LOVE of money that is the root of all evil (1 Tim. 6:10). But the use of money to feed people, clothe people, and spread the gospel, well, wouldn't we all call that a vast good?

Nobody is better or worse spiritually for how much money they have, but certainly we are better or worse spiritually if we are too lazy to use our gifts and talents to take care of ourselves and others. If we refuse to put in the effort to grow the gifts that G-d has given us we refuse to correct and build our character. This is problematic, isn't it?

Alongside educational background and natural talent, an equally important predictor of success is one's determination or their ability to persevere. One of the most important lessons children need to understand to attain success is the ability to finish the job or work through difficulty. And what spiritual principles can be found within this lesson!

At the very least, perseverance is a better use of time than, say, complaining about life's difficulties.

What's even more apparent in Yeshua's parable is that the servant who did not invest the talent he received didn't just refuse to put it to work, he hid it away. The money didn't even go into the marketplace to be helpful or useful.

Money is not something you can take with you when you die. It can be made useful while you live. As Ebenezer Scrooge learned, much comfort and joy can be experienced in generosity of spirit. The generous wealthy often do great good.

Additionally, we cannot ignore that many of the OT patriarchs and matriarchs were incredibly wealthy.

Abraham owned loads of cattle, land, and goods.

Solomon, the wisest and also wealthiest of his time, built the first temple in Jerusalem. He spent money quite wisely (though he did not spend his relational life nearly as well).

Lydia is mentioned in the New Testament as a woman who knew how to create and sell, or trade, purple cloth. Her wealth helped to take care of the apostles' ministry. A truly wise investment indeed, and she was an entrepreneur to boot.

While not wealthy, Paul made tents (in Greek, this means he was making prayer shawls) to support his ministry. This entrepreneurial endeavor kept Paul from having to beg for money to support his work of sharing the Gospel.

The woman described in Proverbs 31 (presented as an ideal woman) had standing at the city gates. She bought and sold land, and did this from her own funds. She had goods that were valuable to others and invested wisely for her family.

Scripture overflows with examples of the value of entrepreneurial activity and how G-d approves of the wise use of money and goods in the caretaking of family and G-d's people.

Given this news, have the followers of Christ grossly mismanaged our understanding of money? With debt at all-time highs and church tithing at all-time lows, perhaps we are seeing the outcome of poor financial education. American Christians are not necessarily faring any better with money than their secular counterparts. Yet, we are called to do better.

When it comes to finances, perhaps we need to ask ourselves a few questions.

- **Do I spend my money on G-d's people and G-dly businesses?**
- **Am I involved in industries that exploit people, like pornography or child labor?**
- **Am I careful to buy products made humanely?**
- **Am I careful to buy food farmed humanely?**
- **Am I wisely investing my resources?**
- **Am I giving to the Lord and to others with my resources?**

This last deserves a section of it's own. And boy, is it a doozy.

Biblical Giving

What is Tithing According to Scripture?

The first idea of giving to the Lord happens far before any Scripture was written down. In Genesis 4, both Cain and Abel bring an offering to G-d. Cain brings an offering of vegetation. Abel brings the FIRST BORN of his flocks.

There is something special about bringing the first-born. And thus we have the foundational idea of bringing the first of what you have to the Lord. An offering is necessary, and it should be the first of what you receive, the best, the most honored, the most important portion.

Genesis 14 relates a fascinating exchange between Abram and a person called Melchizedek. The Bible says that Melchizedek was King of Salem and implies that he was also a Priest of G-d. In fact, the first use in Scripture of the word "priest" happens here, so there is certainly something important going on with this individual.

Later in Psalms 110 and in Hebrews 5, Yeshua is called a priest forever after the order of Melchizedek.

In Hebrews specifically, the author writes about the spiritual or heavenly temple (not only in Heaven, but also in our own hearts) and how Yeshua is the High Priest who enters those places, making sacrifices and prayers on our behalf. No earthly Priesthood can enter these sanctuaries. This is a spiritual order, a different priestly order than the earthly Levitical Priesthood.

With Abram, Melchizedek receives a tithe. Abram gives 10 percent of all he has to this Melchizedek.

In Jewish tradition, Melchizedek (Malki-Tzedek) was possibly Shem, the firstborn son of Noah.

Malki-Tzedek in Hebrew means "my king is righteous" OR "king of righteousness."

Some historians claim that Malki-Tzedek was a Canaanite King, but that would not preclude him from being one who had discovered the G-d of Abraham, Isaac, and Jacob. Clearly, he blesses Abram, and Abram gives 10 percent after having victory in rescuing his nephew Lot from an enemy.

This "gift" of gratitude given to Malki-Tzedek sets up a specific understanding of tithing. According to the Cain and Abel story, there is giving that is the first fruits of your labor. And here in Genesis 14, giving 10 percent is another part of a particular offering.

The word "tithe" in Hebrew is the word "Ma'aser" and it means, "tenth part." In the word itself we see that 10 percent is what is required to meet the qualifications of a tithe. Across the Old Testament, this word is used in relationship to different types of giving throughout the year. In Deuteronomy 14:22, a yearly tithe of all the yield of your seed from the field is given and it is eaten at the place that G-d chooses. Later on in that same chapter the third year special tithe is discussed, which should immediately go to the Levite, the stranger, the widow, and the orphan, so that they may eat until they are full.

There is great debate about how many tithes exist according to Scripture and how they should be applied. But it is crucial to note that there were two harvests in Israel, so tithing 10 percent of their increase at each harvest was likely, as well as a tithe for the poor listed in Deuteronomy 14. So at least three tithing periods are listed, even though one of them does not occur every year.

Because some of the tithe was only 10 percent of their increase (not 10 percent of what they made, but 10 percent of the *additional* food they took in compared to previous seasons OR 10 percent of the net profit), they likely ended up around 10 percent of total income or produce by the third year of giving.

No matter what view you take, 10 percent is the right starting place and it should be a gift to the Lord, as we cannot officially tithe exactly as the OT commands. There is no Levitical priesthood and no Temple, so we honor the Lord by giving to our church and to the orphans, widows, and needy among us. In this way, we observe what G-d has commanded to the best of our abilities and extend the tradition from Genesis when Cain and Abel were asked to give to the Lord.

However, when it comes to giving, we may conceive of it differently than the ancient mind.

In Exodus 30, a ransom was taken from each individual as part of a census. The ransom is very small so that the poor and rich alike can take part. It was to be used for the tabernacle they were building to the Lord in the desert.

Why would they want to take from the poor and rich alike?

This giving was considered an honor. *Each individual in Israel had the same ownership and influence over the building of the tabernacle.* It was a blessing for even the poor to have partnership of this place where they would honor the Lord as a society. The responsibility for spiritual health belongs to all in a society, not just the powerful.

The same thing happened in 2 Kings when Joash rebuilt the temple. A collection of all of Israel was taken. Giving was a communal effort and solidified the agreement they made with G-d.

To the ancient Hebrew, this ownership was a blessing and the giving was a joy. The temple centered their community and represented the greatness of their G-d and the covenantal relationship with His people. Communal giving meant the entire community had come together in one mind and purpose to honor something greater than each individual. The Church can still benefit from powerful, communal giving, especially when the giving is for a cause that is worthy of the sacrifice.

In Mark 12, Yeshua takes notice of a widow's offering. This section follows verses where Yeshua warns about the teachers of the law (note the lower case "L" in the word, 'law' here. likely teachers of the Talmud more than the Scripture), these were the Jewish political and religious leaders. He noted how they walked around in beautiful robes and had important seats at events and in the marketplace. He scorns them for "devouring widows houses" and making "lengthy prayers." They did not abide by the Biblical dictate to take care of widows and orphans, to give above and beyond the tithe.

Then, the widow approaches. She would have been coming to the Court of Women in the Tabernacle. In this court, there were 13 coin boxes with tubes that givers inserted coins into and the coins would travel down the tube clinking at the bottom. The wealthy, who gave much, would have made quite a racket with their giving. This woman brought just two small coins. They made little noise and likely garnered little attention.

Yet, her giving was esteemed by the Lord because it was a *sacrifice;* a costly gift that had a secretive element to it. She gave from what she could have rightfully kept. She gave because she knew the importance of Kingdom things above her own comforts, and maybe against sound financial advice.

Perhaps she knew the King of all things would be there that day. Either way, her giving was the richest.

Giving is not a burden. It is an honor bestowed upon those who have become part of a greater Kingdom. It is a way to participate in that Kingdom and become part of its economy.

Money, time, material goods and gifts are not something to hoard or worship. They are tools, and how we use them says a lot about whose kingdom we belong to.

Kingdom principle — Yeshua fed people physical food alongside the spiritual. Giving is our route to testimony and a good reputation.

Time and again, we see Yeshua healing people's physical bodies and feeding people physical food before, during, and after addressing the spiritual healing and food that we need. The physical has a spiritual counterpart, and vice versa.

We cannot expect to have Kingdom influence without addressing people's physical needs. Christ himself did not. Why should we?

Our testimony is one where we take care of our family and spiritual brothers and sisters, and then take care of our community and globe. In this way, we create communities that are enviable and lives that truly exemplify Christ's.

This means that when we see a need in our community, we do not shy away from being part of the solution and fulfillment of that need. In a digital world, we are often overwhelmed with need from all over the globe. The point here is not to save the world, but as a friend of mine puts it, "Save your corner." You have friends and family and a community. Improve your community. Start in your home. "Get your house in order," as Jordan Peterson advises in his book, *12 Rules for Life.*[lix] Then continue on to what you can do at work, at church, and especially amongst the followers of Yeshua, to take care of need.

The Bible has a lot to say about money because the way we use and abuse it says much about who we are. From hoarding and worshiping to giving and investing, money reveals our character, no words required. Are we wise investors, givers, and philanthropists? Or are we greedy, addicted, callous, and careless spenders? Your bank statements say more than words ever could.

For the follower of Yeshua, money is a tool for the Kingdom, not a pedestal for self-aggrandizement.

The World System

One final note here. I see real evidence that the history of our current monetary system and credit has produced a form of slavery and bondage that keeps people distracted by finances instead of creating generous contributors.

The operations of our central banking system, globalized currencies, gigantic interest rates, and levels of borrowing at historic highs all lead me to believe that the system we work within belongs to Satan.

I do not believe we were created to sit in a cubicle for 40 years working for someone else's dream while racking up debts and obligations whose absolutions rely solely upon employers who may or may not manage things well.

The Biblical system is entrepreneurial. Not only because it rescues us from boredom, but because it forces us to invest in our money, gifts **and** talents. What's more, it encourages family business where expertise gets passed down generationally.

Entrepreneurship also encourages healthy community. Believers absolutely SHOULD support other Believers in business. The love of our community is a testimony. If I can buy honey either from the grocery store or from my Christian buddy who raises bees, I'll go with my buddy. I trust him. I know the honey is real and not corn syrup mixed with dye. I want him to thrive because he gives back to my church and to the Kingdom of G-d.

The new American system is one where each generation is re-creating the wheel and communities are sometimes formed and destroyed in the matter of a decade. Our current system has its benefits; but, the downfalls are giant. Consider:

-Continual debt and borrowing. If businesses are not inherited, businesses are constantly being built from the ground up. This requires capital that most small business owners do not have, which makes most businesses a slave to the bank.

-Expertise is lost with each generation.

-Families have no unifying goal once children are grown. Disparate families make for lonely grandchildren who are often far away from their grandparents and aunts and uncles, who in previous eras would have provided important counterparts to parental figures.

-Christian led businesses have no Christian support.

-Christian community is more difficult to form and sustain.

-Talents that could be discovered and used for the Church are never exposed.

-Biblical concepts never reach the light of day in communities. Think: if most Believers work for someone else, they cannot dictate that the business is closed on the Sabbath and Feast Days, they cannot espouse ideas antithetical to the Business' goals, etc. A business in the community closed on G-d's Sabbath. Can you imagine what testimonies and conversations that could inspire?

Chick-fil-A provides a marvelous example of this. One of the most successful fast food restaurants on the planet is closed on Sundays. And while, I disagree with their version of the Sabbath day (Scripture puts it on Saturday) clearly G-d has honored the heart of the business dedicated to honoring Him. Not to mention the many discussions and debates that have arisen over their closed doors and grave disappointments to the palates that crave chicken on Sundays.

How we make our money, how we use our money, and how we define money is as spiritual as going to church.

While the system of the world may never change, our church community may be able to alleviate the burden of it. We each have a part to play. What is yours?

Chapter 9

WHAT IS THE HEART?

A YOUNGER VERSION OF ME WENT through two decades of life with almost complete conflict avoidance. Maneuvering my way through multiple challenges, I rarely voiced my opinions or disagreements with contemporaries and work colleagues. While life with my family of origin grew excruciatingly honest, I was too terrified of facing any more negative energy to buck social trends outside the house.

Some sort of crisis was definitely looming. Nobody benefits from this kind of conformity, and my spirit was exhausted from all the boundaries I had put up around it.

Luckily, during my divorce (one piece of the inevitable crisis) I found a truly brilliant therapist. The kind that pushes in just the right places, assists in healing, offers life skills and tools, studies all sorts of therapeutic options, and encourages a whole-body approach to healing. G-d was with me.

Somewhere along the line, I let my heart breathe again. I grew in my ability to be comfortable in healthy conflict and navigate even unhealthy conflict without wrecking myself (or, at least not as often). But this little gift does not come all at once.

A few years ago, I began working for a church in the production and worship department. Excited to bring to the table my years of experience in audio production and music, as well as video and creative work, I dived in uninhibited. I've always found I do better when my heart is in my work. So there it was, my heart on the table.

But I had failed to notice the group dynamics within some of the teams. Structures that were so set in stone and so resistant to new ideas that might challenge the norm that my enthusiasm was immediately deemed more of a threat than an asset. I immediately made enemies, and boy, did I pay the price.

There was not a Sunday when I was leading worship where some technical issue didn't ensue. I never sounded or felt like myself, because I was never allowed to. From the online live stream to the in-house monitors, my Sundays were filled with interpersonal tension and worship-fails worthy of online Instagram comedy. (Most of it rubbish, and all of it with embarrassing sound quality.)

I looked for small opportunities to encourage the team around me, and backed off of some of my requests for improvement or new structures. A few gifts purchased here and there. A few conversations where I tried to break the ice. It didn't work.

I was stuck. Attempting to sing on Sundays while being made to sound atrocious, and attempting to be worthy of a paycheck while my work life stalled.

We all encounter these situations. And it forces us to ask ourselves difficult, and sometimes not so encouraging, questions.

There is the possibility that, maybe, these people just don't like me as a human being. Maybe I've complained too much or I'm just not likable. Must I change to be acceptable in this environment? Is the change an improvement or a downgrade? Have I been kind? Am I wrong? If I cannot succeed here, will I succeed in the future? Why is this happening?

On paper, these things seem like quick and easy problems to work out. But in the real world, most of us discuss these kinds of issues at length, maybe on car rides, possibly out loud, with nobody but our iPhones and radios. We labor over how to become valuable in our fields and our relationships and in our own minds. And it is time consuming.

Alongside the sadness, pride, and frustration, other voices chime in; voices that desire to be in alignment with G-d's Kingdom. What is G-d doing in this situation? Is there good coming out of it? My ultimate goal was to serve the beautiful body of Yeshua's followers at church. If I serve the church better because of the tension, maybe it's good? In the long run, if I leave or if I stay and deal with the tension, which will produce the desired result?

And other, angrier voices also have a say. *Welp, feels like sexism has reared its ugly head once again.* Or, *nobody knows my resume, what I've done, how I know what I'm talking about!* Or how about simply, *I've been wronged!*

Battling emotions and warring thoughts clatter through my mind at these times. Attempts to listen for the Holy Spirit push me in one singular direction: speak and act in truth. What is true, and does it matter if there is an emotion attached to it?

But it is an exhausting task. It seems very likely that the average Western reader would say my heart and mind are having a battle. My logic and my emotions aren't getting along.

When I approached the Lord on this issue, He, as He often does, brought to mind a shocking, and seemingly off topic concept to assist my heart-broken state of mind.

Here is the idea that has changed my feelings about my church dilemma.

I'm not able to save people. Only G-d can do this.

Why did this idea make an impact? Because I can see how G-d is going to take care of His flock, if (or when) I fail. My job is to honor G-d and the role I've been given. If I sound horrendous every weekend, it may shatter my pride, but it will not shatter the Holy Spirit.

I can see how G-d is taking care of the people set so staunchly against me. I don't have to make them like me, because I'm not responsible for where they end up. They are G-d's. And so am I.

Nothing I do at the church can compare to what the Holy Spirit wants to do. I just have to be open to being used, and willing to submit to Yeshua's authority. Letting go of offense, fear, and emotions, if I take each step one at a time rightly…

I have no burden.

This letting go lies in the wisdom of loving others and handing them to G-d. Pray for your enemies and then let G-d take care of them.

This may mean you stay, it may mean you walk away. It doesn't steal the importance of sincere honesty or the drive that keeps you going.

What other people think of you is none of your business. What G-d thinks of you is all that matters.

These are all thoughts. Thoughts that have led to a "heart" change. My anxiety, fear, and sadness melted away as I thought through the awesomeness of G-d's power in my life and the lives of those around me. These thoughts are logical and full of meaning. But, it isn't always obvious how a thought actually affects the emotions of the heart the way that one thought alleviated mine. There is a relationship between the heart and mind that deserves some attention.

The first time we see the word "heart" in Scripture is the Hebrew word "Leb," in Genesis 6:5. "Then the Lord saw that the wickedness of man was great on the earth, and that every intent of the *thoughts* of his *heart* was only evil continually."

"The thoughts of his heart." The heart and the mind seem to be more interconnected here in this first use of the word.

Deuteronomy 6:5 states, "You shall love the Lord your God with all your heart (innermost man, or mind), and with all your soul (this word for soul is "naf shecha" and THIS actually more likely means what we think of when we think of heart, as it means your *passions* and *emotions*), and with all your strength."

As I look to Scripture for what the heart is, it actually seems to very much resemble our Western view of the mind. It is our thoughts and intellect, our reasoning and our worldview.

In the heart we find the seat of strength and decision-making. Proverbs admonishes us to, "Guard your heart for out of it are the issues of life." What you think about and spend your time on is what you create. So guard what is there, for it has the power to drive your life.

The heart is where your king sits. The ruler of your life has your heart (mind, thoughts, drivers of action). **If you choose to have Yeshua there, the petty and challenging issues of life meet a righteous King every time.**

THE SANCTUARY

A few weeks ago, I felt that G-d was asking me to study the physical heart in comparison to the physical sanctuary and temple in Scripture. As strange a request as this seemed, I could not believe how much the sanctuary in the desert resembles our physical heart and the work that

Yeshua does in our Spiritual heart. It is complex and yet so appropriate that, as usual, we find there is a physical representation of a spiritual reality, both in the nation of Israel and in our physical bodies.

Here are just a few (along many likely still undiscovered) similarities between the heart and the Tabernacle:

-The material commanded for the outer covering of tabernacle was red, blue, and purple, resembling the color of oxygenated and non-oxygenated blood in the heart. The two together would make a purple color.

-The material used here was to be smooth like "the skin of a porpoise." The outer layer of the heart is smooth, looking a lot like porpoise skin texturally. One of my favorite Torah Teachers, Rico Cortes, has listed this as badger skin.

-The layout is divided into chambers, in both the Tabernacle and the heart. (I'm currently exploring the idea of the three chambers plus Ark of the Covenant in the Tabernacle, equaling four. This would resemble the four chambers of our heart.)

-The Tabernacle was the seat of life for the community, and the heart is the seat of life for our body

-Blood sacrifices took place in the Tabernacle. Blood exchange takes place in the heart. Without blood, there is no life; and without the heart, the body cannot receive the blood. Without the Tabernacle, we cannot receive G-d. G-d dwelt in the Tabernacle and in the Ark of the Covenant with the people. This was where Holy exchanges between the people and the Lord took place.

-The heart is regulated by an electrical conduction system. The temple was regulated by the energy of the Spirit of G-d. It is His beat, His breath, His presence that brought the people of Israel to the Promised land.

-The heart is the new temple (Hebrews 10:16-22). We are told in Scripture that when we have accepted Christ, our bodies become temples that house the Holy Spirit (1 Cor. 6: 19-20). There, in our hearts our high priest Yeshua can do the work that the high priest on earth had done. His sacrifice is continually in our hearts, residing there as a living and continual atonement for our sin.

Monte Judah of Lion and Lamb Ministries provides a beautiful **teaching**[lx] wherein he discusses what happens when we truly enter the presence of G-d in prayer. We enter our heart space, the holy place, in the presence of the three pieces of furniture that resided in and behind the room just outside the Holy of Holies in the Tabernacle.

Here we would see on one side a Menorah. This seven-tiered lamp stand represents the seven spirits of G-d and the Holy Spirit. The Menorah has seven candleholders. In Revelation they are called lampstands.

"To the angel of the church in Sardis write: These are the words of Him who holds the ***seven spirits of God*** and the seven stars." Revelation 3:1

"From the throne came flashes of lightning rumblings and peals of thunder, Before the throne, seven lamps were blazing. These are the ***seven Spirits of God***." Revelation 4:5

> "Then I saw a Lamb, looking as if it has been slain, standing in the center of the throne, encircled by the four living creatures and the elders. He has seven horns and seven eyes, which are the seven Spirits of God sent out into all the earth." Revelation 5:6

We get the understanding of what these seven spirits represent in Isaiah, 11:1-3:

> "Then a shoot will spring from the stem of Jesse and a branch from his roots will bear fruit. The Spirit of the Lord will rest on Him, the Spirit of wisdom and understanding, the spirit of counsel and strength, the Spirit of knowledge and the fear of the Lord."

Here we see 6 different attributes coming out from the Lord Himself as the G-d who these "Spirits" inhabit. Therefore when looking at a 7 candle menorah, we see that the middle candle is the spirit of G-d. The two candles right next to the middle have a connection between them and they represent wisdom and understanding, the next two out are also connected, representing counsel and strength and then the outer candles are the knowledge and the fear of the Lord.

To our other side in our heart space, we have the showbread — twelve loaves shaped like the faces of mankind, representing the twelve tribes of Israel and the human form of Yeshua.

Before us, is the Ark of The Covenant representing G-d the Father, hidden behind a veil. We walk into the midst of these three symbols when we enter this space. And here, when G-d the Father sees us, to our left He sees the Holy Spirit, and to the right, He sees Yeshua. Each part of G-d looks at us and sees the other two parts. We are not alone.

When we are in right standing with the Lord, our prayer time is surrounded by the three parts of G-d that were present in the physical temple on earth. How can we not have communion when our hearts are set up in such a fashion?

We become like the priests in this space. Knowing that the sacrifice of Yeshua is constantly before us, we can point to this as our claim to salvation and petition the Lord because of the goodness He bestows and the work He has done on us here, in our hearts.

To the ancient person, the Tabernacle (or temple) to their god would be the heart of the community. Communal celebrations, feasts, and ceremonies would be centered around and in its structure. The ancient person believed that the life and death of the community was tied to the right worship of the god(s).

In the Bible, we see that the Tabernacle was indeed the heartbeat of the community. In Exodus 40, smoke fills the tabernacle, and G-d's glory is physically present in the space. The children of Israel were well aware that this G-d had brought them out of Egypt and was sustaining them on their journey. G-d was everything to their community, and the worship of a deity of some kind was so essential that many of the Israelites' problems actually stemmed from their straying to worship other gods.

The ancient Hebrew mind was consistently focused on worship of one god or another. G-d directs them not to worship Him "the way the nations worship their gods" (Deuteronomy 12) but in the ways that He requires. Despite straying time and again, we do understand that to the early Israelites, G-d and His house were the heart of their very existence.

The heart of a community produces its life, just as a human heartbeat is essential to life. Science has confirmed the heart's place of importance.

Modern science has also revealed the heart's physical structure. How interesting that our hearts are red and blue because of the color of oxygenated and non-oxygenated blood. And the cloth for the Tabernacle was made with red, blue and purple thread. Did G-d want to physically represent a heart and heartbeat right at the Tabernacle He commanded to be built to house His presence? I like to think so. G-d is intentional.

So, what can we understand about the worship that takes place in our hearts from the worship that took place in the Tabernacle?

It is Sacrificial. The Tabernacle and Temple were places of bowing low before the King of the universe. Sacrifices were brought in a timely and Biblical way. Each piece of temple service was carefully and painstakingly followed. (Leviticus 1-7, Leviticus 9, Numbers 18, etc.) Intention, humility, and holiness were rendered unto these acts of sacrifice.

Proverbs 4:23 tells us to guard our hearts. Is this not the same call that the Levitical Priesthood had? *Be careful!* This space is sacred ground that belongs to Yahweh. Do not defile it with evil thoughts, intentions, or behaviors. Do not bring into it "strange fire." Come before the Lord in an honoring way, ready to hand over sin, making it powerless because of the blood of the perfect Lamb. Bring something honoring when you enter the Tabernacle space.

It Is All Encompassing. The priestly services involved all five senses. Before entering the Holy of Holies, a high priest would wear bells at the bottom of his robes. You could hear him coming.

Incense would be burning, as well as the smell of a sacrifice wafting towards Heaven, whether from an animal or food offering on the altar.

The priests wore robes of pure white, stark and representative of perfection and holiness.

The heat of the burning coals from the altar could be felt on the Day of Atonement.

The Showbread in the temple was eaten by the priests at the end of each week, and new Showbread was provided.

Sound, smell, vision, touch, taste. Each sense was a part of the priestly service. In our bodies, each sense can be a witness and testimony to who holds the King-position in our hearts. We guard our eyes, limit our tongue so we can listen, attempt conscientiousness in clean eating, work lovingly with our hands, and produce a life that becomes a pleasant scent to the Lord. Our service to G-d encompasses each sensory aspect of our humanity.

It is Exclusive. Not just anyone could enter into the Holy of Holies. Likewise, in the space of your heart, only you can give access — either to the G-d of Abraham, Isaac, and Jacob, or instead to your own lesser gods. This place is exclusive to you, and only you can fully understand it.

When I give over my heart to communion with the Lord, my relationship with Him is almost ineffable. How can I explain the peace, joy, resilience, grace, and wholeness that I know in His presence? How can I possibly help people view the beautiful things that take place there? This space is mine and it is the Lord's. Your heart has a door that is shut to all but you and what you let in.

It is Life Giving. The heart is where we are promised the New Covenant will take its rightful place. G-d's word will no longer be written on stone, but now it will be written in our very flesh. (Jeremiah 31) We will take on the DNA of the second Adam, Yeshua. We are born into a new family, an eternal seed. No longer separated from the Lord by death, we are reunited in life through a DNA shift of the HEART.

This new heart dictates a whole new function for our bodies. We become ambassadors of the greater Kingdom and bring life to our communities through obedience to our King. Our hearts begin to beat in the Kingdom of Heaven. Just as there was evidence of G-d filling the Tabernacle as a cloud covered the first tent of meeting and the glory of the Lord filled the tabernacle in Exodus 40:34, we become evidence that G-d has filled our hearts. We become salt and light (Matthew 5:13-

16), preservers and visionaries. We produce fruit that fortifies and satisfies in our communities. We become Life.

FEELING VERSUS TRUTH

This worship can also be twisted, abdicated, undermined, and ultimately destroyed if we are not good caretakers of this heart space.

Being a musician for so much of my life has taught me how truly deceptive the heart can be, and how easy it is to replace G-d with something else. And yet, it still can "feel" magical and meaningful.

When you've played music to as many rooms as I have, you learn how quickly a song can change the mood of a space, how music manipulates humans with incredible efficiency. It can feel like a god exists in each note, communicating beyond words and enchanting the listener. Music has its own unexplainable qualities that I'll have to discuss in another book.

But it is fascinating how a concert by your favorite secular artist can give you the same high as a worship session. People discuss getting goose bumps listening to songs in both the religious and non-religious realms of music performance.

To the Christian, this poses a baffling problem.

Because of my experience, I understand it is just the power of music to speak to the human heart.

But, without fail, I find many Christians hang their hats on the idea that corporate singing is the height of worship, and that if music makes some people feel so good, then it must BE good.

And yet, if it is so good to be surrounded by praise music all the time, would not our culture and society and church witness be far more potent? We listen to and have access to more of this music today than anytime in human history. Wouldn't we be so filled with the Holy Spirit all the time that our testimony would be unstoppable?

Yet, we are becoming more and more morally and spiritually bankrupt as a society and, I would argue, as a church.

We have made a poor replacement. Worship based on its Scriptural definition is about bowing and obedience. But we have traded it for the pursuit of an emotional high through music. (More on this in my essay on worship)

We are not guarding our hearts.

We are pursuing lies in replacement of truth, and setting up gods of worship leaders and songs instead of focusing on the one true G-d.

Of course, I love worship music and I love worshiping with it. Who doesn't love the amazing feeling when a gorgeous song or melody hits you just right? Is there anything wrong with that? No. Can you use music to truly praise and give glory to our Creator? Yes! In fact, we are advised to praise Him with song by King David (Psalm 149). It is wonderful to give G-d glory with music and to allow that powerful tool to change our own hearts and minds. It can be quite a profound experience.

Is the high always from G-d?

Well, no.

This small example is just one instance of allowing emotions, or what we often mean when we say "heart," to lead us into faulty thinking. This is why G-d says He wants to be worshiped in Spirit AND in truth. It is easy to worship in spirit and lies. But much harder to pursue what G-d considers right worship with heart and accuracy.

The reality is, there is a battle over our hearts. I believe that the spiritual powers that war against G-d's kingdom have set up many traps for our hearts. From addiction to entertainment to the enticements of all those things that woo our brain and provide a dopamine hit. There is no end to what is able to replace the King on the throne of the human heart. Money and power may be the most obvious, but for the average American, it seems even emotional manipulation or musical obsession can distract us from obedience.

There are other distractions that keep our hearts from being holy spaces rightly served by Priestly behavior.

TIME DEFINES

How much time do we spend in silence away from technology? How much time in Scripture, or time in prayer?

Really, who has the time?

Filling up our time and being "busy" and successful has become a god in and of itself.

Do we know what we miss when work or social life takes too much precedence?

I think of the things I miss as a mother when I fill my time too heavily with work and other people's burdens. Time I cannot get back as I look into the faces of the ever-growing people G-d gave me. How dear and precious my time is with them.

Both my children are endlessly creative and they both write their own songs. I've sat outside their bedrooms doors smiling at or baffling over adorable and sweet, and often terribly honest songs they have written. To think, I may have missed those by just a brief moment of busyness.

I may have failed to walk by at that right moment, or failed to keep my ears open to their tender melodies.

Even moreso…

How dear and precious our time with the Lord! The Bible says our time is a vapor. (James 4:14) It rushes by, disappearing like smoke on the wind.

Our heart needs time and space in order to hear from, process, and have a relationship with the G-d of the universe; and yet, time seems to be racing away as technology progresses. We are packed with content, education, news, work, demands of friends, text messages, emails, not to mention grocery shopping, cleaning, caretaking of children, and animals, and all the other wonderful but expensive additions of living in the now. Tradeoffs must be made to accommodate time with the Lord.

And a single, hearty dose of emotion on Sunday morning isn't gonna cut it.

Daniel prayed to the Lord three times a day, at least. These were moments where he got on his knees. It wasn't just a casual convo in the car on the way to the kid's school. It wasn't a passing "Thanks, Jesus" before a meal. He went to a room and got on his knees in gratitude and in supplication for help. (Daniel 6:10-12)

This commitment to prayer, in a physical and set aside fashion, provides a guidepost for heartfelt relationship with the Lord.

Take the time. Carve it out. Don't compromise. It is a discipline as well as a relief. To head to your bedroom and get on your knees might feel like a respite on some days and an intrusion on others. Yet, just as we make time for our children and husbands and parents, our most important relationship requires making moments as well.

I have never regretted time spent in prayer.

I have often regretted time spent online.

Heartfelt devotion means mental commitment and in return there is a heartfelt reward. G-d loves time with us, just as we love that phone call from our kids, that moment when they run to us because their hearts are broken, the gifts they bring created from construction paper and markers. Precious time. And G-d responds as we do to our little ones and big ones. He reaches His arms around us and provides advice, comfort, and affirmation of our destiny.

The heart/mind of the follower of Yeshua focuses on walking in and with the Spirit of G-d and setting aside precious time for relationship with Him.

OBEDIENCE IS NOTHING WITHOUT HEART

We cannot dig into obedience to G-d without addressing the heart.

The heart of Mary when she anointed Jesus' feet with expensive perfume was the heart of a servant blessing and preparing a King.

The heart of David as he danced in public was the heart of a joyful worshiper. Putting all reservations aside, he was ready to dance and praise G-d with all his might.

The heart of Moses as he obeyed G-d was humility, a life laid down to follow the Lord.

In each of these cases and so many others, we see people acting in extraordinary ways with all their *heart*. Actions accompany a heart position before G-d. In fact, evidence of heart can often only be observed in action.

We see that Daniel, even in prayer, defied King Darius's ruling that prayer only belonged to the earthly king. (Daniel 6) Daniel, on his knees before a window, unconcerned with being caught praying and breaking the law, is a shining example of heartfelt obedience. Surely Daniel's prayers were heartfelt, but so were his actions. He boldly opened his windows, faced East, and got on his knees for all passersby to see that He belonged to the true King. His heart was to make it known.

Heart and obedience go hand in hand. From John 14: 15 – 30: "If you love me, you will obey what I command. And I will ask the Father, and he will give you another Counselor to be with you forever – The Spirit of Truth. The world cannot accept him because it neither sees him nor knows him. But you know him, for he lives with you and will be in you. I will not leave you as orphans; I will come to you. Before long, the world will not see me anymore, but you will see me. Because I live, you also will live. On that day you will realize that I am in my Father and you are in me, and I am in you. Whoever has my commands and obeys them, he is the one who loves me. He who loves me will be loved by my Father and I too will love him and show myself to him."

"Then Judas said, 'But Lord, why do you intend to show yourself to us and not to the world?"

"Jesus replied, 'If anyone loves me, he will obey my teaching. My father will love him and we will come to him and make our home with him. He who **does not love me will not obey my teaching**. These words you hear are not my own; they belong to the Father who sent me.

All this I have spoken while still with you. But the counselor, the Holy Spirit, whom the Father will send in my name, will teach you all things and will remind you of everything I have said to you. Peace I leave with you; my peace I give you. I do not give to you as the world gives. Do not let your hearts be troubled and do not be afraid.

You heard me say, 'I am going away and I am coming back to you.' If you loved me, you would be glad that I am going to the Father, for the Father is greater than I. I have told you now before it happens, so that when it does happen you will believe. I will not speak with you much longer, for the prince of this world is coming. He has no hold on me, but the world must learn that I love the Father and that I do exactly what my Father has commanded me.'"

A pointed passage. Often, pastors read this with ease, assuming "command" means to simply do whatever the Holy Spirit may ask on a whim. But according to Strong's Greek lexicon (A concordance of the Bible and original Greek words), the word for "Commandments" here relates to the word for Commandments that David uses in the Psalms. It is Mosaic in its seed. He is referencing the Commands that He gave to Moses. And our love for Him begins with the requirement to obey His Commands just as He obeyed His Father in Heaven. And certainly He did. He filled the Law full of meaning in living out each command and submitting Himself fully to it unto death.

Love and obedience. Obedience and love. Can we get around it really? There is no point of obedience if it is not for love. For in the end, it is because of our relationship with G-d, because of our heart condition, that we will enact G-d's requests. Our mindset directs our activity.

In reality, what is the point of taking a Sabbath if not for the love of G-d? Would you do it otherwise? It is a strange request and this is the only place we see a god require rest as part of worship and submission. It is out of the ordinary, and yet, those who love the Lord WILL do it BECAUSE they love Him. Because they want the fellowship they receive with Him on that day. We crave time with those we love, and the Sabbath is a vacation with the One we love the most. There is no reason to lean into that rest if we do not love the one who invited us to it.

Love is the HEART of obedience, and obedience to G-d is the heart of a follower of Yeshua.

"Hear O Israel, the Lord is One. You shall love the Lord with all your heart, with all your mind, and with all your strength."
(Deuteronomy 6:4)

The mind/heart of the believer is submitted to G-d's Laws out of a love for and relationship with our Creator.

The heart in Scripture encompasses your mind and thoughts. From these spaces our lives are created.

What we plant and allow in, we will enact and live out. This heart space is sacred and dedicated for the Lord's use and purpose. It's time to guard our hearts as the Levitical priest guarded his holiness. It's time to treat our hearts as the Levitical priests treated the Temple —with reverence, detailed focus, and increased care.

Only you can care for this space and bar imposters from degrading its sanctity. Give this space to the Lord that He may be what you encounter when you enter!

Chapter 10

WORSHIP

IN MY MANY YEARS LEADING WORSHIP, I cannot recall a year where I've been contacted by so many Believers who say they feel called back to Scripture, to repentance, AND to praise. It's a combination that seems to embody true *worship.* In my circles, this observable move of the Holy Spirit inspired me to dive deeper into my roots as a worship leader.

Often obfuscated, the true meaning of *worship* lies hidden beneath a lazy veneer of music. The first of the Ten Commandments insist that we love the Lord and worship Him only. But without definition, the church is left to vaguely describe worship as the short, and usually very generic, musical sessions happening at the beginning or ending of weekly church services. The depth of the terminology is missing. It's time to rediscover its true meaning.

From Abel to Yeshua, Scripture is filled with moments of worship before the Lord, tying together thousands of years of adoration of G-d. True worshipers throughout Scripture connect in both attitude and action. These leaders and their offerings beautifully intertwine with the work and message of the Messiah. But to truly see and understand this connection, we must rethink our views on worship.

The first time the word for *worship* appears in Scripture is in Genesis 18:2. The Hebrew word *Shechah* is used as Abraham is approached by three people outside his home. He goes out to them and "bows low."

This first mention and definition tells us what *worship* truly embodies: humble ACTION in the presence of a Holy G-d. It is submission, and acts of service towards a Being we recognize as above us. It is bowing, lowering, submitting.

Later, Abraham's action of taking Isaac to be sacrificed is also called *Shachah.*

In this way, worship is not just about musicianship. Rather, it is an attitude of humble recognition of G-d, of bowing low and lifting up. It is about obedience and allegiance. A wonderful teacher, **Rico Cortes**[lxi], often emphasizes that worship REALLY is "worth-ship." What worth do we bring to the Lord and His Kingdom? What of value are we offering? In our oath and pledge to Him, we are called to offer everything.

So, how does music fit in? Looking to Scripture, we discover some important music-filled inspiration. Interestingly, we even find Jesus with his disciples singing! Matthew 26:30: "And when they had sung a hymn, they went out to the Mount of Olives."

The word for *hymn* is from the Greek *hymneo,* and refers to what the Jews called "The Great Hallel," which comes from Psalms 113–118 and Psalm 136. Not surprisingly, they called upon David (our best guess as the writer here), the great songwriter and Psalmist, to provide their worship music.

While many Psalms were not necessarily written by David, over half were as far as we can tell. I consider David the go-to mentor and model for worship leadership. He wrote many of the Psalms, large odes dedicated to praise of the Lord, and he joyfully praised publicly with song and dance. He was an action-oriented worshiper — not fearing Goliath, nor shying away from battle, he understood worship is rooted in obedience. He desired to build the temple for G-d, although it was his son that did so. He had a true heart to obey, glorify, and love the Lord, as well as practice what that looked like in his life and his writings. David also loved G-d's Laws and obsessed over them throughout the Psalms.

His love of G-d's Law meant that David loved the words Moses wrote down. He was inspired and in submission to the Word that G-d Himself, through Moses, had given to Israel.

And, interestingly enough, in the Exodus story we find the first corporate praise moment recorded in Scripture. On the road to receiving the gift of G-d's Torah at Mt. Sinai, Moses' sister Miriam leads the nation of Israel in spontaneous song. This first song of the Biblical church is sung by the assembly/mixed multitude of G-d's people (considered by many to be the first church), which had just been delivered out of Egypt. After salvation, they spontaneously sang out, proclaiming the story of deliverance! Then Moses' sister Miriam grabbed a tambourine and led them in musical praise and dance.

This moment remains a testimony to the beauty and power of music as an expression of gratitude, and a powerful memory of G-d's salvation. (Not to mention evidence to advocate for female congregational leadership!)

Israel praised after they were saved by the grace of G-d from trial *(Egypt)*. Modern music follows this cue, as our praise often highlights salvation. This moment in Scripture, while more spontaneous and seemingly more miraculous, is the foundation and definition of the heart of worship through music today.

But there are aspects of this moment and the people involved that are worth digging into further.

What qualities does Moses bear that may be important to worshipfulness?

- Moses is considered by the Bible to be the most humble man in history. (Numbers 12:3)
- Moses wrote down G-d's Laws. (Exodus)
- Moses was the only man to meet with God face to face. (Deut. 34:10)

These are important ties to another previously mentioned star worship leader, King David.

Writer of the Psalms, player of the lyre, and therapist to King Saul, David must have been one heck of a creative talent, as his work remains heavily referenced to this day. Psalms is filled with treasures for all generations. Hidden in this amazing collection of songs are secrets to a worshipful heart. Here are a few of those secrets:

1. Devotion to and love for G-d's Laws.

In David's day, the Word included only the first five books of the Bible (and possibly some of Judges). David cannot speak highly enough about the Law of G-d and its perfection. Take Psalm 119:97-104 as one example:

"Oh how I love your Law! It is my meditation all the day. Your commandment makes me wiser than my enemies, for it is ever with me... Through your precepts I get understanding, therefore I hate every false way."

2. Honesty.

Whether he's asking for G-d's protection, crying out in desperation, or praising with all his heart, David is frank. He does not try to hide behind overwrought verbiage or hedging.

3. Persistant Attention to G-d's Details.

Psalm 119 has one section dedicated to each of the 22 letters of the Hebrew Alpha Bet, or Aleph Bet. Each letter in the Hebrew Aleph Bet has numerical and ideological meanings attached, making each section of David's song that much more interesting to ponder.

4. Vision.

David remembers to keep the main thing front and center: praise to G-d for His attributes. This vision is founded in His relationship with G-d. His walk with the Heavenly Father becomes evident when he defeats Goliath. We will visit this later.

In short, King David loved the Laws of G-d, which Moses had recorded.

Moses was humble, and Biblical worship requires humility or "bowing low." David exalted G-d above Himself, recognizing his need for salvation. Humility flows from a worshipful heart.

Moses saw G-d's face. David sought G-d's face. In Psalm 105:4, David says, "Seek the Lord and His strength, seek His face evermore." The pursuit of G-d makes for an honest worshiper. Finding G-d, even when he shatters our preconceived notions, proves our belief that He Is the Great I am. And that, well, "I" am not.

David understood that in the writings of Moses he would find the very heart of Yeshua. When we pursue G-d's ways, we seek His face. Justice, mercy, salvation, victory, authority, and praise are all key themes of David's writings as well as those of Moses, directing us to the position of a worshipful heart. G-d and His things are above all. G-d is a King with a Kingdom and terms for that Kingdom that David loved. He said yes to them, just as the nation of Israel did in the desert at Mt. Sinai under Moses' leadership.

In a climate becoming increasingly violent, hyperbolic, deceitful, and narcissistic, is there anything more needed than a humble return to G-d's ways as part of our worship?

This is echoed in the acts of worship that led to repentant humility and restoration in Scripture.

In Nehemiah 8, Ezra the Scribe read the Law to the people of Israel. As he did this, verse six records that the people lifted their hands and "bowed their heads and *worshiped* the Lord with their faces to the ground." The Law was then explained to the people. The response to understanding was followed by a renewal to keep G-d's laws, and the people celebrated and rejoiced! They repeated these humble actions again in Chapter 9.

Praising AND bowing, as parts of worship, have the power to lead us to truth, gratitude, obedience, and *change.*

Just as David pondered and admired G-d's Law as a part of his act of worship and just as Moses and Miriam led a congregation in praise after experiencing salvation, we too are called to return to truth and obedience with a heart of thanks and humility. G-d desires to be worshiped in Spirit AND in truth. True worship, the type we need today, does not shun the realities of Scripture or the Gospel of Yeshua!

We are to be salt and light. (Matthew 5:13-16) We are to PRESERVE the kingdom for the King. The King came to restore Himself and His things to us. By bowing, standing, and walking with the King according to His righteousness, we become the salt and light.

"Seek ye first the kingdom of G-d and His righteousness and all these things will be added unto you." (Matthew 6:33)

DAVID - Bowing, Standing, and Walking

My dear, Uncle Mark, brought a beautiful concept to my son's 13th birthday celebration, and I have pondered it time and again ever since. He shared that, "Each day we are to have three positions before the Lord. We are to bow to Him, stand by and for Him, and walk with Him."

These three positions reflect engagement throughout each portion of our days. There is not a moment where we are outside of G-d's purview, and each moment in the day is an opportunity to reflect relationship with the Creator.

Can we see these positions through the lens of worship? Does Scripture support these positions before the Lord and, if so, how would that change our behavior?

Romans 12:1-2 states: "I appeal to you therefore, brothers, by the mercies of God, to present your bodies as a living sacrifice, holy and acceptable to God, which is your ***spiritual worship***.[2] Do not be conformed to this world, but be transformed by the renewal of your mind, that by testing you may discern what is the will of God, what is good and acceptable and perfect."

As previously discussed, obedience and worship are interconnected. The physical aspect of our position before the Lord cannot be ignored. It is through our bodily acts of righteousness and our bowing, walking, and standing that we are living sacrifices to our G-d.

King David's story illuminates these positions. He understood that obedience was pertinent as a worship leader, and that is why he obsessed over it in his writings and songs. He consistently esteems G-d's Laws as perfect, as light and as life. We know David is referencing the first five books of the Bible because those were the only Biblical books, other than Judges, that had been written at the time David was writing.

David loved G-d's ways. The book of Psalms begins with him saying, "Blessed is the man who walketh not in the counsel of the ungodly, nor sits in the seat of scoffers, nor standeth in the way of sinners, but his delight is in the Law of the Lord and in His Law doth he meditate day and night."

In the very first Psalm we see *bowing, standing* and *walking*, uncle Mark's three positions.

We are not to walk in the counsel of the ungodly, but rather in the counsel of the godly, in the counsel of Christ. We are not to sit in the seat of scoffers, but to be laid low before the wisdom of the Almighty. We are not to stand in the way of sinners, but to stand in righteousness for the ways of our King.

Here at the very beginning of Psalms, worship is defined within what my uncle has also found to be true. We are first told where not to be, and then where we, as worshipers, belong. David teaches us to delight in the Law, which we know is Christ Himself. David understood my uncle's three concepts.

1. Bowing to G-d

I think about bowing as the idea of pledging allegiance. We have given our oath to something we believe is greater than we are and handed our hearts over to what we acknowledge as a greater King and Kingdom.

Psalm 119 is the longest Psalm. It contains 22 sections, each one dedicated to one letter of the Hebrew Aleph Bet. One section I'd like to highlight here is the 14th section, headed by the Hebrew letter "Nun." Psalms 119:105– 106 reads:

> "Your word is a lamp to my feet and a light for my path. I have taken an oath and confirmed it, that I will follow your righteous laws…"

The nun's shape, or orthography has an underlying meaning. Here is the ancient Hebrew letter, nun:

You can see here the bent-over nature of the letter. The letter takes a journey of humility and ends upright once again. It portrays the story of one who is HUMBLE before G-d, who will stand upright in the final day.

David speaks in this Nun section as having taken an oath, pledging allegiance not to himself or an earthly country, but instead to following the righteous Laws of G-d. This commitment certainly requires humility. We have to bow. We have to die to ourselves. We put ourselvs on the altar so that we die and Yeshua can live in us.

One of the greatest difficulties in teaching those who have fallen away from the faith, or those who grew up in the church but who do not have a relationship with Christ, is their insistence on judging G-d's actions in Scripture. Many come to G-d demanding that He behave as they would wish, forgetting that to come to G-d without humility will only lead to frustration.

The Bible tells us that G-d is not like us. His thoughts are not our thoughts. His righteous decisions and actions may not align with our human understanding or preferences. For all of David's mistakes and sins, he is wise enough to recognize that G-d is Holy, set apart, unique and uncompromising. If we come to G-d to judge Him, what can be learned? Nothing. We have already decided our ideas are better than the G-d of the Universe's. We have set ourselves in G-d's seat. We have become like Lucifer. This position will not end well for us. Humility is a position to take before the Lord to discover blessing and wisdom. The nun represents this beautifully.

Nun also relates to life. In Aramaic, "nun" means fish. Again, the shape of this letter early on looked like a kind of fish or something swimming.

Fish and life were interlinked for the Hebrew people of the BC era. If you looked into a river and saw a fish, you saw the hope of a future. Fish were a way of life and meant sustenance and survival. Food and water were everything. If there is life in the water, the water is healthy, the river is running, there is a continual cycle that ensures future generations. Fish, bread, water — these are particularly important for the society of David's time and are Scripturally laden with meaning.

The letter Nun even goes beyond just these first meanings. In Scripture, sometimes the letter Nun is turned backwards or inverted. When this happens, it connotes life *from the dead.*

Resurrection.

Miraculous life that once had no hope, now filled with eternity.

David made an oath, he bowed before a King and the King's precepts, and in this he saw life, even life from the dead. There is eternity about the King we bow to and His kingdom.

This is why we humble ourselves. This is the reason we are bent. It is for a king with the ultimate power even to bring life from the dead, a power so great that eternity lies in its catch. To become G-dly fishers of men, we must become bearers of resurrected life, lamps with the light of life burning in us.

David understood that in order to receive life, in the end one had to bow to the King of all. He knew that dying to one's self meant resurrection, eternal life, newness, and the promises of G-d fulfilled.

2. Standing WITH G-d and for G-d

Psalms 40 – The numbers four and 40 bear significant meaning throughout Scripture. Yeshua is nearby when these numbers show up. He arrived in human form in the 4th Millennia, spent 40 days fasting in the desert, 40 days of rain, which cleansed the earth. The 4th word of the Hebrew Bible is the Aleph-Tav (this is Yeshua). Yeshua is the 4th man in the book of Daniel's fiery furnace (the amazing story of Shadrach, Meshach and Abednego who were put into a furnace because they would not bow down to an image of King, Nebuchadnezzar. The King looks in and sees a 4th person in the furnace) There are four gospels.

Four and 40 are important. So Psalms 40 likely has something to tell us. By G-d's leading, I found it is right in the theme of standing with and for our Savior.

Psalms 40. Let's start at verse 6: "Sacrifice and offerings you did not desire, but my ears you have pierced."

So many times have I read through Psalm 40:6 and not understood this piercing David references. David is describing what Paul does later when he talks about being a bondservant of Christ. This piercing was part of the system of servant-hood (the Old Testament often uses the term "slave"). The system in place provided for a way out of debt for those who found themselves in trouble financially or criminally, and were without a route to pay someone back. It was also a system for those who owed a debt to society. You would become a servant of a master or family. Every seven years, the debtors were freed and debt was cancelled. However, if the servant loved their master or wanted to stay for some reason (perhaps he has married another servant who is staying, etc.), this person could decide to become a "bondservant."

The process for becoming a bondservant was public and slightly painful. The servant was taken to the gates of the city by their boss. At the gate, for all to see, the master would drive an awl through the ear of the servant. Now, everywhere that servant went there was physical evidence that he belonged to someone and had pledged his life to a master. He had chosen servant-hood instead of freedom. It was by choice.

David says here that he has become a bondservant to G-d. He is willing to make it obvious in the public square. Anyone that sees him will know WHO he belongs to.

> He goes on in verses 8-10: "I desire to do your will, O my God; your law is within my heart. I proclaim righteousness in the great assembly; I do not seal my lips, as you know, O Lord, I do not hide your righteousness in my heart; I speak of your faithfulness and salvation. I do not conceal your love and your truth from the great assembly."

David does not hide G-d's light under a bushel. He is interested in keeping things salty. He knows his worth-ship is tied to standing FOR the kingdom principles he has taken an oath to love and follow. He stands with G-d and for G-d in public and on purpose. His commitment is bold, unwavering, and unapologetic.

Much like the American Church? Just kidding.

Bold, unapologetic, unconcerned about judgment, fearless, brave. These words are often foreign in a mess of godless, hopeless, fearful, wavering, quivering church compromises.

How many times have I been told that the church needs to seem **kind and merciful,** so we must stay silent on anything that "feels" judgmental or legalistic.

Either they haven't thought that one through, or they are liars.

Where is the kindness for the pre-born?
Where is the kindness for the sexually trafficked?
Where is the kindness for the children of divorce?
Where is the mercy for the porn addict?
Where is the mercy for those stuck in sin?

In this author's view, kindness and mercy do not entail wholesale tolerance of the great evils of our day.

Mercy is helping people to become free from bondage.

Mercy is not ignoring sin.

Mercy is the route to **defeating** it.

King David stands in judgment upon our church leadership. Calling upon them to boldly preach eternal life and hope, and "teaching them to obey" all that G-d has commanded which will free people from sin.

The new life in Christ is not frail. It does not need to bow before sin as if that very sin has not already been conquered. What weakness we cast upon the cross when we daily forget what it actually freed us from! We weaken the power of the gospel when we tolerate evil in our communities.

We use poor doctrine and evil philosophies in our worship and we call G-d a liar when we say that preaching against sin is NOT "merciful."

What mercy is there that does not include freedom from sin?

What mercy is there that does not set the captive free from the hands of destruction?

What mercy is there that is not bent on bringing Heaven to earth and destroying the grasp of hell?

What mercy are we preaching? What love? Does a father leave his children to the gutter?

The father the American church preaches about is too often a wicked one. One who appeases the enemy as the evil of sin continues to rip apart and wreck the souls of the attendees.

A father who leaves the cage with the door closed, but promises eternal life once that body has died. A father who would rather avoid the difficulty of discussing the dirty clothing of his kids. Why wash, when you can stay filthy and be told you don't stink? The fabled emperor's clothes are nothing compared to the unwashed masses the church calls clean. We have denied the power of the gospel to bring people into righteousness and we have tolerated the wickedness of our culture to our own destruction.

The church preaches a weak father. And out of it, we respond in weak worship.

But it tickles the ears to tell people G-d loves them, without ever encroaching on that terribly offensive idea of repentance.

The road to hell is paved with good intentions and the path to getting and keeping butts and bucks in church pews is to make people feel good in their cages.

Standing with and for G-d means we worship the true Father in all that we say and do. To represent His household, we do not fall for the earthly version of mercy. We adjust our walk to be closer with the Lord so that we may preach obedience without hypocrisy, thereby avoiding the plank in our own eye problem.

Stop sinning. Then teach others to do the same. It is simple yet hard, but possible through our Savior. Stand for the truth so that others may experience the merciful freedom of our Savior and the beauty of bringing Heaven to earth.

If worship does not include humble submission to the terms of G-d's Kingdom, it is not worship of G-d. Perhaps we need to begin asking who we worship when we demand to live life on our own terms and attend church without reproach.

3. Walking with G-d

Here I must once again discuss the story of David and Goliath (1 Sam. 17). Yes, this story is one of my favorites. There is young David, who has already killed a lion and a bear with his own hands. David, decrying Israel's tolerance of Goliath in their midst, fearlessly asking why they aren't fighting Goliath and defeating their enemy.

The giant Goliath stands opposed to Israel, mocking both the nation and its G-d. In fact, the Bible tells us that "for 40 days the Philistine came forward every morning and evening and took his stand." (Forty. There is that number again. This will come up later.)

David knows exactly how to defeat this giant and win the battle.

It is not with the armor of men that Goliath will be defeated. David rejects Saul's armor.

He instead takes his shepherd staff in hand. In 1 Samuel 17:40, we are reminded that David is a shepherd. The verse about his weapons of choice begins with a simple symbol. He takes care of sheep. It is a staff that we see as we imagine this young man preparing to do the impossible. A staff that gently leads and rescues and helps him to walk. This staff defines his role, his place in the world, and his preparation for such a moment.

The shepherd then goes to living water — a river — and draws out five smooth stones. Stones that have been baptized. Stones that have been worn, that have stood the test of time and that have been immersed in life itself. We see here he chooses five stones, the number correlating with the Torah and also a number that, in Hebrew, represents grace.

David pulls G-d's Word and grace from the waters to carry with him into battle. He knew it would be by G-d's own mouth, by G-d's design, that Goliath would fall. The shepherd carries with him the Word of G-d from living waters to defend the sheep against the enemy. Can you see Christ? It is so obvious, and yet we have so often missed this.

And so important for us, David carried G-d's Law with him to defeat his enemy. He calls Goliath "uncircumcised," noting that Goliath represents sin: evil, a heart turned against G-d's ways and an ideology that stands against what David calls "the armies of the LIVING G-d." So, David takes with him what is alive and powerful. He takes G-d to battle with him.

Walking with G-d means we carry His things with us into every battle, into every meeting, into every situation. We don't go without G-d. We should not go without His Word.

We are confident that there is life in G-d's Word.

David is not the only one who defeats an enemy this way. Yeshua does the same.

In Matthew 3, Yeshua is baptized by John. As He is taken out of the water, G-d's voice speaks audibly saying, "This is my son, with whom I am well pleased." After Yeshua is baptized and drawn out of the water, he is led into the desert for 40 days and nights.

Yeshua, the living breathing Word of G-d, is baptized and then immediately approved of by G-d. And next, as we will see, Jesus is led into battle to contend with a spiritual giant. A spiritual enemy.

As he is fasting in the desert, Satan comes to him with three temptations. Yeshua responds with quotes from the Torah. In reply to Satan's first temptation to make stone into bread, Yeshua quotes Deuteronomy 8:3: "Man shall not live by bread alone but by every word that comes from the mouth of God." He speaks about the life in the Word of G-d. It is our sustenance and reason for being. Let's back up to give this verse fuller context and understand why Yeshua used it. From Deuteronomy 8:1-18:

"Every commandment which I command you today you must be careful to observe, that you may live and multiply, and go in and possess the land of which the Lord swore to your fathers. And you shall remember that the Lord your God led you all the way these forty years in the wilderness, to humble you *and* test you, to know what *was* in your heart, whether you would keep His commandments or not. So He humbled you, allowed you to hunger, and fed you with manna which you did not know nor did your fathers know, that He might make you know that **man shall not live by bread alone; but man lives by every *word* that proceeds from the mouth of the Lord**. Your garments did not wear out on you, nor did your foot swell these forty years. You should know in your heart that as a man chastens his son, *so* the Lord your God chastens you."

"Therefore you shall keep the commandments of the Lord your God, to walk in His ways and to fear Him. For the Lord your God is bringing you into a good land, a land of brooks of water, of fountains and springs, that flow out of valleys and hills; a land of wheat and barley, of vines and fig trees and pomegranates, a land of olive oil and honey; a land in which you will eat bread without scarcity, in which you will lack nothing; a land whose stones *are* iron and out of whose hills you can dig copper. When you have eaten and are full, then you shall bless the Lord your God for the good land which He has given you."

"Beware that you do not forget the Lord your God by not keeping His commandments, His judgments, and His statutes which I command you today, lest—when you have eaten and are full, and have built beautiful houses and dwell in them;and when your herds and your flocks multiply, and your silver and your gold are multiplied, and all that you have is multiplied; when your heart is lifted up, and you forget the Lord your God who brought you out of the land of Egypt, from the house of bondage; who led you through that great and terrible wilderness, in which were fiery serpents and scorpions and thirsty land where there was no water; who brought water for you out of the flinty rock;who fed you in the wilderness with manna, which your fathers did not know, that He might humble you and that He might test you, to do you good in the end—then you say in your heart, 'My power and the might of my hand have gained me this wealth.'"

"And you shall remember the Lord your God, for it is He who gives you power to get wealth, that He may establish His covenant which He swore to your fathers, as it is this day. Then it shall be, if you by any means forget the Lord your God, and follow other gods, and serve them and worship them, I testify against you this day that you shall surely perish. As the nations which the Lord destroys before you, so you shall perish, because you would not be obedient to the voice of the Lord your God."

This section of Scripture is about the wilderness. Forty years in the desert. Forty long days in which Goliath thought he would win. Forty moments of testing and trial, fear, and difficulty.

Yeshua is reliving what his ancestors did. Israel did not always do it well. They complained, they groaned, they wasted time due to sin. In contrast, Yeshua does the desert perfectly. When the tempter comes to him, he uses HIS own words written in the Torah to rebuff the advances of evil. He perfectly lives out the 40 days of desert, the lack, and the humility, as a sign to us. And he quotes a section of Scripture, pointedly telling us that we are no longer to rely on our own power to obey the Lord. Instead, it is through a heart position that we will not forget the Lord. We are to remember His ways and His covenant and live by those life-giving words. The "bread" of G-d is His Law. It is life.

For the next temptation, Satan tells Yeshua to throw himself off the temple that the angels may catch him. Yeshua replies, "It is written, do not put the Lord your G-d to the test."

So, where is that written? Also in Deuteronomy, chapter 6:

"**You shall not put the Lord your God to the test,** as you tested Him at Massah. You shall diligently keep the commandments of the Lord your God, and His provisions and His statutes, which He has commanded you. You shall do what is right and good in the sight of the Lord, so that it may go well for you and that you may go in and take possession of the good land which the Lord swore to give your fathers, by driving out all your enemies from you, as the Lord has spoken."

Do not test G-d. Stay faithful, and you can take possession of the good land. The Promised land. Eternity. Yeshua knows, because of His Word, that He must diligently keep to G-d's Laws and make a way for us to enter into the Promised Land, His eternity. By obedience, enemies flee and the follower of G-d can possess their rightful property. Yeshua knew how to make Satan flee. David knew how to defeat Goliath. It is by the Torah—by righteousness—that evil must flee.

Let's see if the third test bears this out.

As a final resort, Satan offers Yeshua an earthly kingdom. (Odd, truly, how can he do this? But this question is for another time.)

Yeshua responds, "Away from me Satan, for it is written; 'Worship the Lord your G-d and serve Him only!"

This is a direct quote from Deuteronomy 6:13, just before the verses previously mentioned regarding the second test of Satan.

Yeshua takes the Torah — smooth, sure, foundational, hardened, battle-worn, immersed in life — and he sends Satan away with those words. Shot from His mouth, these hardened weapons quickly did their work. King David understood and performed with G-d's Laws in mind. Yeshua filled this Law full of meaning rebuffing the spiritual Goliath.

The Torah is more than words. It is the foundation of truth, even to this moment. When we take G-d's Word into our lives, we carry Christ, the bread of life with us.

We cannot help but see these extraordinary symbols with Moses as well — the one who wrote the Torah from the mouth of G-d. Moses' name was Moshe, which means "waters." Moshe was pulled from the waters as a baby. This baptism ensured he survived the evil decree of Pharaoh to kill all the baby boys of his day. Through water his life was saved.

As the nation of Israel left Egypt, freed from the tribulation and bondage of trial, it walked through the Reed Sea between the waters. It was baptized into the life G-d desired for it to find. The same waters punished the Egyptian army and defeated it.

The same waters that brought life to Israel defeated Israel's enemies. This baptism led to the covenant at Mt. Sinai where G-d gave His Torah to His people. The Laws of G-d were given after salvation and baptism. The stone the Law was written on, contained both freedom and judgment.

Just as the stones David pulled from the river freed Israel and judged the Philistines.

The waters of the Reed Sea freed Israel and judged Egypt.

So, G-d's Law in Yeshua frees G-d's people and judges those outside of His redemption. Just as Paul describes.

We are given the right to conquer sin through the sacrifice of Yeshua. We are made new and able to live in righteousness. Without this gift, the Law is a judge. It only shows us our separation and with it, death. If we are not in Yeshua, we become like Goliath or the Egyptians. We are unable to enact the miracles of G-d. We are in opposition to His Kingdom.

Yet, through Christ, the waters of life from which G-d's Kingdom is pulled baptizes and releases us. We are allowed to abide in G-d's truth and love and adore His Kingdom principles. We are Israel, freed from Egypt. We are David, defeating Goliath. We are in Yeshua, conquering death.

How fascinating that water and blood came from Yeshua's side as He was pierced on the cross. The blood was the covering that brought "Yovel" or Jubilee, which meant freedom for slaves in the Hebrew nation throughout the Old Testament. Jubilee was a commanded time where all debt was released and freedom was proclaimed and granted. Additionally, land was returned to the original owners. Yeshua's blood is restoration to fullness of life, and the water is baptism. We are freed from sin, from Egypt, from Goliath, restored to our destiny in Yeshua, and baptized into new life. We are able to defeat Egypt, to defeat Goliath, to defeat sin, to conquer death.

The light of life is Yeshua and He is the embodiment of bread and water — the spiritual bread and water given to us as the very Word of G-d. We cannot come up with anything more powerful to defeat an enemy or more powerful to enact as worship. There is NOTHING that surpasses His Word. If Yeshua Himself used the highest and most powerful speech that He could to banish Satan from His presence, and that speech is from the Torah, why do we not do the same? Worship of G-d is founded in obedience to G-d's Kingdom principles. There is no other power that comes close. The power of our ministry finds its authority in G-d's ways. There is no righteousness without right standing in His ways.

And what about Noah? We usually apply this number 40 to the days and nights that the waters came and Noah was on the ark with his family and the animals. We learn from Scripture that Noah "*walked* with G-d" (Genesis 6:9). As the floods came the earth was baptized into new life, just as the nation of Israel was baptized through the Reed Sea. To dispel the great waters of the flood, a wind came to dry the land, just as a wind parted the waters for the nation of Israel fleeing Egypt. A dove brings back news to Noah that land and trees have finally emerged from this baptism, just as a dove appears when Yeshua is baptized. And of course, each of these people receives a covenant from G-d.

- Noahidic Covenant – the Covenant that G-d would never again destroy all life on earth. The sign of the rainbow is our continued assurance of this.
- Mosaic Covenant – the Covenant through the Law. This covenant is an agreement between G-d and His people regarding His Kingdom terms.
- Davidic Covenant – the Davidic Covenant promised that David would produce a House. That Yeshua would come through his line and establish a Kingdom forever.

- Yeshua – The New Covenant promises that the Laws of G-d will no longer be written on stone, but become part of our hearts. In individual, personal relationship we will be G-d's people and be grafted in as spiritual Israel. We will now become part of both the physical world AND the spiritual eternity, regaining access to both, just as Adam and Eve had in the Garden. Being born into a spiritual Kingdom, we now possess new spiritual DNA with access to eternity.

Noah, Moses, and David are often referred to as men who walked with G-d. They abided in his principles and attended to His things as a daily practice. Yeshua Himself walked out the principles of the Torah, proving his Almighty status and showing us the image of perfection in human form. The ultimate goal of all the stories and writings that had preceded Him, Yeshua is present in David, Moses, and Noah's stories. These are the ideal individuals to receive covenants, as covenant relationship requires continually walking with G-d and abiding in the covenant terms.

These men all understood. They were worship leaders.

You are called to be worship leaders. And to be like David, Noah, and Moses, we must be attending to more than music.

Song is a powerful tool, but song is meaningless if the position of our hearts is not correct. It is nothing if we are not rooted in obedience and if we are not more than admirers of the Torah – we must be doers. Singing is nothing if we separate Yeshua from His own Word and attempt to carry an idol of our own making into our ministry or into battle.

I want to encourage the Church to start by being salt and light and understanding *how we stay* salt and light. The position of leadership we have is undermined when we abandon sound doctrine and logic, when we stray from the path Yeshua laid before us. Our roles as worship leaders are meant to defeat giants, and yet we don't understand how easily we hand over our power when we tolerate evil by ignoring G-d's Laws.

If the Church worships a god separate from the Torah, it worships an idol. I fear I have led worship in many a church that did not worship the same god that I do. My G-d has not changed. My G-d is true from Genesis to Revelation and His ways are righteous from Adam to the ends of the universe.

It is time for the Church to pledge allegiance to the true King. Even if it means the world sees the awl piercing our ears. Our fear of being different has cut off our power. But we are CALLED to be different from the world! A holy, set apart people. We are not to approve of or ignore darkness.

David spoke differently than the average soldier of Israel. He spoke of defeating the giant. He spoke of the evil of the Philistines and the goodness of G-d. No fear held him back and no worry deformed his speech. He BELIEVED in the G-d of Abraham, Isaac, and Jacob. Among entire troops of the doubting he was willing to make the bold claim that G-d would defeat Goliath. Because of this holiness, he was useful in battle and useful in worship.

A light cannot help but change a dark room. It gives colors meaning and reveals shape and form. Light defines what is taking place in the spaces it enters. David defined the Spiritual reality. Goliath was nothing to the living G-d.

The American Church rarely defines evil or righteousness for people in our modern contexts. Little light is left to shine in the darkest corners where the masses stumble over the sharp edges of sin. We do not speak to the weapons of Goliath or the route to victory against spiritual enemies.

So, I guess the question is: are we the light? What do we bring to our earthly space? What is our *worth-ship* rooted in? If worship is living as a bodily sacrifice ready to carry the light wherever we go, then have we let our light go out? How can we fulfill our call as worshipers if we do not carry the light? Remember Romans 12:1: "Offer your bodies as living sacrifices holy and pleasing to God. This is your physical act of worship." But Romans 12:2 clarifies this even further: "Do not conform to the pattern of this world but be transformed by the renewing of your mind…" Paul then suggests all manner of ways to use our gifts for the Lord and His community, to serve each other in love, to honor one another and take care of each other. Action becomes worship of our G-d.

David worshiped G-d by admiring the Torah and lifting high the Lord for speaking the Torah to us. He recognized the gift, and mystery, power, and spiritual purpose of G-d's ways. He admired his King for creating such a beautiful Kingdom. He used the power of the Torah to defeat his enemies and spoke boldly of it in assemblies. He danced with joy before the Lord and wrote songs about the perfection of G-d's Law.

What would the world look like if we worshiped like David?

There is a strong tie between the obedient, humble, and action-oriented Fathers of our faith. Coincidence cannot easily explain the miraculous mastery of G-d's details binding Noah, Moses, and David (and surely others!) to Yeshua. G-d took pleasure in their obedience and laid out similarities to help us unite Yeshua to His law, His word, and His people.

Moses' writing defined Kingdom rules. David loved those rules. Yeshua IS those rules, the Torah itself. To worship the true G-d we must accept the true principles of His Kingdom. We must have the heart of David, loving the G-d who gave us such deep marvels to ponder and pore over, enveloping us in wonder.

What we often miss in the story of the Prodigal son is that to return to the Father he had to leave his destructive life. He pulled himself up from the pig-pen, put one step in front of the other until the city was behind him, and repentantly plodded to his Father's house ready to sacrifice his body in service to his dad.

Disobedience discourages relationship and praise of the Creator. Shame and guilt often make singing songs to G-d all but impossible. Not to mention, shame and guilt left to fester will build anger, confusion, and dissociation with G-d. While we still embrace the pigpen, we miss out on our dad's rich, loving house. Worship in Spirit and Truth pleads for a clean heart, a sound mind, and a face turned toward the light, not attempting to blend in the darkness here and there at the edges.

If we cannot accept a life submitted to G-d above ourselves, then we have not offered all of us. We are holding back. We are worshiping something else.

Do you see why singing some songs on Sundays falls hopelessly short of true worship and reverence? Where there is no respect for the Kingdom terms, there can be little admiration for the G-d who authored them.

While the Believer embraces the mercy and grace of a good Father, we must also not appease or approve of darkness. We are in that darkness to be the light. You cannot bring sin city with you into the throne room of G-d and expect blissful union. The Prodigal Son left his sin to enter into the presence of the Father. Spirit and Truth belong to those humble souls who are more interested in pleasing G-d than pleasing themselves. In humility, we discover the shape and texture of the House of the Lord. We admire the legal standards of the Heavenly Kingdom and adhere to its principles because of our love for its King. We know our

Father's house and rest in the peace and prosperity of its familial behaviors. Worship like David and Moses.

Modern Worship Music

The modern philosophy around this word, *worship,* is still applicable and important to address. What about music? What about our ritual behaviors towards G-d? Are we pleasing or missing the mark?

In doing some research on the largest producers of the modern worship song product, I came across some disturbing information. Places like Bethel Church obsess over the **Passion Translation**[lxii] of the Bible. This watered-down, man-made, Western-minded, weak translation could be called an interesting accompaniment to Scripture, but NEVER should be called Scripture itself. (**Alisa Childers**[lxiii] outlines a few of the problems the Brian Simmons translation presents.) The doctrinal underpinnings of churches who use translations like this, as if they are the inerrant word of G-d, should be suspect at the very least. Language matters, as we have seen in the stories of Moses, David, and Yeshua. Take away or change one small word — the number 40 for example — and all ties to antiquity, meaning, and the root of Yeshua can be lost.

Do not fall for the nonsense that "artists" often describe as "more relevant" interpretations. The English translation of the Bible already has enough problems of its own. Our modern pride does not need to add to them. (For example, while the ET, a Hebrew word meaning the Aleph and Tav or Alpha and Omega, and possibly referring to Yeshua Himself, shows up over 1,000 times in the Old Testament, our English Bible does not translate it as such. So, we miss Yeshua in much of our cursory readings of the OT) If people are ignorant about what words mean, teach them the meaning of words. To change G-d's word instead promotes intellectual laziness, already too common in our culture. The

American Christian should be the MOST educated person around, and if the church family is unwilling to educate its congregants, we will be found to be the most naïve. Naivety does not make for a strong Christian.

Bethel is not alone in the wandering of larger more influential churches. Throughout much of Christianity today, we elevate experience over truth and an emotional high over a solid foundation.

It is why modern worship music is so emotionally manipulative. Now, I love a good bridge that gets you singing. I'm a musician. This stuff is fun. It really is! But just because it feels good does not prove it IS good. Evil has crafted music to work people into exactly the same emotional frenzies. Is it any wonder Paul discusses orderly worship in his letters, especially to the Corinthians? The Romans also used music in their religious ceremonies for attaining a unity, for chaos, or for focus. Music is elemental for the spirit. Its power cannot be underscored enough. For good and for evil, music assists in changing the emotions of the listener.

Do you really believe you aren't manipulated by church music in this fashion?

And yet, how often do you analyze the ideas behind the music we sing as a congregation?

As a worship leader, I hate to admit it, but when asked to sing certain songs, I sometimes secretly change a lyric or two on the slides. I disdain the idea of people singing lies to the G-d of truth.

It happens more often than I would like to admit. But my reasons are fair. For instance, how many songs teach the pre-tribulation rapture? (A very debatable and, I would say, Scripturally not provable doctrine.)

How many teach that the church was started in Acts and not in Exodus? I know the wildly popular song "King of Kings" claims in their final verse that the church of Christ was "born" after Yeshua came. Well, this isn't exactly the case. G-d started His Church (His called out assembly) in Exodus. We are grafted into a root: a new root is not started mid-way through Scripture.

How many songs insist that we are broken pieces of garbage with no say in the darkness of the world? Am I being too harsh? Maybe. Okay, I'll tone it down.

Too much worship music is too weak and filled with inaccuracy to be any good for anything more than an emotional high.

But when I need something that grounds me, "Amazing Grace" is my go-to.

"I once was lost, but now am found, was blind but now I see." Yes, I once had no hope, but now, NOW, what am I? I am clay being formed, I am a home being built, I am a temple for a King. By grace I was brought out of darkness and into the light. I was pulled from the wreckage and made righteous.

I'm not garbage. I'm not destitute. I am a child of G-d. And I DO have a say in the matters of this world. It is my destiny to work in it, love on it, and make the difference I'm meant to. Salt and Light cannot help but be tasted and seen. It is the nature of these things to bring flavor and preservation, and to bring sight to the blind.

It is supposed to be our nature to want to be holy. So, what worship songs reflect King David's ideas about obedience and the love of G-d's laws?

Think for a moment. Which ones? Is anybody saying, "I delight in your Laws"? How about the ones discussing sinners being like chaff? Or consider "The Way of the Wicked Leads to Destruction," that age-old popular banger. (Just kidding.)

You get my point. Our songs resemble nothing of our greatest worship leaders' ideas or passions. We pick and choose the lines that make us feel likable, and we use the notes to do the rest of the work.

Yeshua Himself sang the Psalms. Yet we sing happy or dirgy emotionally charged numbers that may or may not be good for us, but certainly don't often contain the depth of saltiness or light that songs defining good and evil should possess.

(And credit where it's due, I'll admit I really like "Raise A Hallelujah" I love the story behind that one. I love "The Great I Am." I think that one is powerful. "Revelation Song" is unique in that it leads us straight to the awesomeness of G-d. There are some fine worship tunes out there.)

But the warning to you is this: worship to the G-d of the Bible is defined by allegiance. So, if our worship music never addresses the attributes of our King, if we are not admiring G-d's authority, defining the call of a bondservant, I'm not sure we should call it worship. We can call it praise. It often is very focused on praise, an incredibly important aspect of our relationship with G-d. We can call it good. Lots of Christian music is good and fun to listen to. But is it worship? Furthermore, G-d has said that He wishes to be worshiped in spirit AND in truth. If either is missing, we fall short.

How **true** and spirit-filled is our worship and praise?

The power of music elevates the ideas it embodies. What you sing becomes a part of you in a way so little else does. It forms a place in our brains and hearts that is easy to recall and even easier to stumble over. It is why I have grave concerns about the rise of artists like Cardi B, Katy Perry, Lady Gaga, or Little Nasx. Even country music is overwhelmed with break up, hook up and drinking songs.

What are we doing as a culture? Well, culture seems to belong to evil and evil will surely use the power of music to do its bidding. Make no mistake. Music is a great place to attack young hearts.

And to me, that evil is actively working in all aspects of the music business. Not just the secular part.

Proverbs tells us to guard our hearts for we create our lives from that space. Music seeks to hit at our hearts directly. Be on your guard about what you sing.

But do sing. The Bible also encourages us to praise G-d through music. Psalm 95:1: "Come let us sing praise to the Lord, let us shout aloud to the Rock of our salvation." Sing strong, beautiful music to the Lord, making sure you know what you are singing! And do not forget that obedience and truth are essential pieces in our worship arsenal. They are not sidebars. They are at the core of our worship existence.

G-d embodies the praises of His people. (Psalm 22:3) He is pleased when we praise Him with music, with our whole hearts, in truth. We are given this powerful tool of music to give our entire spirits over to His praise and worship.

Our understanding of Biblical worship is laid out in Scripture. Noah, Moses, David, and so many who loved Yeshua have all shown us that worship is the whole hearted embodiment of humility and righteous action.

Our bodies are living sacrifices. And obedience is our physical act of worship.

Chapter 11

TECHNOLOGY

I'M NOT A TECH GURU. I'm just an inquisitive person using her brain codifying observations after decades of time spent meeting people and talking after shows, before shows, in church services, and interviews.

I've spent extraordinary hours with people in person *and* interacting online, both as an artist and as someone deeply interested in politics and social issues. My work has kept me in the public eye enough to play shows and be on stages, but I'm not famous, so I often still have unpretentious, candid conversations with friends, family, fans, and strangers alike.

While I hold a college degree and other accreditations, I've coached singers and writers at UCD Denver and have run my own businesses, I cannot claim the opinions I share in this chapter should be taken as ultimate scientific truth. These are ideas and questions based on years of using the Internet and social media to share my art, business, and political views (and sometimes the random family moment). This essay is a platform for what I've observed, but may be used for you to mold your own family rules and theological perspectives around technology and its uses.

Let's just start by thinking. Together.

I've noticed a significant trend towards handing over power and independent thought to people we call experts. These know-it-alls may sometimes end up admitting fault, but it's often too long after the damage is done. (A few stellar current examples include the many politicians and elitists pushing one narrative about Covid and now getting proven wrong, but I digress.) These folks feel obligated to take strong public stances, yet they may possess no more knowledge or good council than you or me.

Our political and media economy seem to be more about the sales pitch than the reality, more about how many clicks it gets than how much truth it imparts. Since this is the game, the average individual is tasked to become a better thinker, or go on living as clueless as a newborn and hope that nothing disastrous comes of it. For the sake of our children, our culture, and our church, I believe critical thinking beats naivety every day of the week. If lack of knowledge can disintegrate the people of G-d, as the Bible suggests (Hosea 4:6), we are called to dig into Scripture and make keen observations about how to interact with a world growing ever more wolf-like.

I won't focus on all technological advances here. New discoveries exist in many fields in which the average person does not and will not engage regularly. The technology that exists in the average American home packs a significant spiritual punch and can be controlled by the average family. I highly doubt any of us will visit CERN and make or break any new development there. Neither will we be able to change what they do at CERN from our living rooms. (CERN is the European organization for nuclear research)

So, let's talk about our use of computers, televisions, phones, and the like. How are we engaging with these? How might these interactions contribute to or denigrate our ability to return to truth? What are the benefits and costs?

As someone who spent a small amount of time in the journalistic field, let me be clear. In my short years there, I saw too many underhanded deals, stories killed for political reasons, and plain old factual errors to ever again have faith in the average journalistic product. I lost my confidence in the idea that the media tells the truth. They lie and obfuscate.

That doesn't mean truth cannot be found.

But is it technology, in the end, that is our best bet to find the ultimate truth? Are the truths that really matter and that we will care about in our last breaths contained in the digital or analog realm? Physical truths feel often self-evident. They don't seem to need endless hours online, or computation.

Scripture tells us that we can learn of G-d in creation (Romans 1:20). Walk out your front door. Look at a blade of grass. Can man-made science produce on its own anything so lovely, so efficient, so perfectly crafted to continually produce without intervention? So far, no. There is much truth to be found in observing nature.

On the other hand, will you only find lies or deceptions in man-made technology? That likely is not accurate either. Technology may actually point us to some truth, may help us discover it, but truth is not embedded in the technology itself. Tech is just a tool, a tool with a bias towards the ones who create it. And I often wonder, who uses and manipulates that tool most? Is it a truth teller, or the father of lies?

I was recently reading Adam Smith with my 7th grade son. A hefty task, to say the least. Every other word was a piece of vocabulary lost to 21st-century society. And the ease with which Smith lays out his complex arguments took me back a bit.

Do people write like this anymore?

Without the Internet, nor a computer, thinker after thinker emerges throughout history to remind us of the extraordinary human mind. These minds existed and worked beautifully before the emergence of the modern computer. Brilliant writers and thinkers like Adam Smith, leaders like Abraham Lincoln and scientists like Isaac Newton did their work and made their marks long before screens became the go to educators.

The promise of technology and a computer in every home was that life and work would be easier and that we would progress. Have we? Is work easier? In all the ways we have progressed in knowledge, have we progressed in goodness?

While death rates have steadily declined over the last century, we still face massive health challenges. Rises of **heart disease, diabetes**[lxiv], and **cancers**[lxv] plague modern society at levels unseen before. Tradeoffs have been made to accommodate a workforce more likely to be in front of a screen, than out and about with people or doing physical labor. Perhaps we can argue for some of the tradeoffs, perhaps against others, but one thing is for sure: life is different.

Technological advancements and information are moving and growing at a lightning pace. It's dizzying to realize how much information we have added to the Internet year in and year out, or even how many technological advancements are taking place as I write. Two-and-a-half quintillion bytes of data are added to the Internet every day, a number impossible to grasp. Some advances, like AI or nanotechnology, don't even seem real. How are these things happening? I have not the time to research the science behind it all, yet there it is, raising my left eyebrow and inspiring my questions.

The world is so different than the one I grew up in — for better and worse. We are now so heavily reliant on technology for the very fabric of our Western society there is hardly room for much else. Surely, not as much time in silence or prayer now that every moment can be filled with an eye-popping story, a sonic escapade, a check-in on friends and strangers through FB, or a sarcastic quip on Twitter.

The current Covid-19 Pandemic and subsequent lockdowns have dramatically increased online activity. Reliance on technology seems to be at an all-time high.

However, evidence is strong that our humanity is suffering. **Depression and suicide rates skyrocketed**[lxvi] as the Internet became our only tool of connection during the lockdowns. This sobering fact should make tech companies nervous, although I doubt it does.

I have a handful of tech industry friends who obsess about the natural getaways they will be taking this weekend or summer; as long as no screens are involved, the more remote, the better. It is startling what people actually crave when queried about their dream vacations: a beach, camping, observing great architecture, the food in Italy, the wine in France, the Rocky Mountains, a Hawaiian sunset. With all the worlds we can visit online, we still choose an immersive full-body experience. Nobody wants to be taking vacation this summer sitting at home online.

We left our window open last night and I woke to birds chirping outside. It was the sweetest and most gentle moment I'd experienced in a long while. It meant spring was coming. Warmth would enter our little yard and grass would turn green. I could see it all in my mind, welcome and joyful and peaceful.

And not a computer in sight.

And, what's even better — I didn't choose that moment. I didn't design it. That moment came to me unannounced. While Facebook's metaverse promises a programmable perfect alternate reality, the real world is filled with unexpected ups and downs. It is up to our miraculous minds to solve unforeseen problems and bask in unexpected joys.

Throughout this past winter, all time seemed to be sucked up by discussions of pandemics and deaths. Deaths of people, deaths of society, of businesses. Deaths of freedom and religious activity. News, news, news, propaganda too.

But I had a real moment that morning hearing birds singing joyfully. I was reminded of life, real life, right outside my window, continuing to sing and communicate and survive. In spite of technological advances.

My heart yearns for an open space, a garden, a horseback ride through the country. Just get me out of this suburban, squashed, technologically advanced, monochromatic, safety-obsessed neighborhood. I want an adventure again. (Without a mask.) I want something real and tangible that grows and lives. Not this dirty piece of metal that is ancient in six months and requires my stationary and silent attention.

These tech devices inspire little integrated experience. It's just fingers tapping keys while my frame slumps towards it like an old sack of grain, bent and stagnant. The escape from technology offers freedom and health. The tie to technology feels burdensome and boring.

-The difference between a music concert online and one in real life? It's a canyon. A chasm so big, you cannot see across it. (And that's just from the musician's perspective here.)

-The difference between seeing flowers on a screen and smelling them in a field? It's watching someone eat a meal versus eating one yourself.

-The difference between an online call and a hug from a friend? It's longing versus communion.

We keep trying to make something that is better than life experienced with all five senses. But each attempt is fraudulent. There isn't anything more real than life lived outside of technology. Technology offers some ways to better that real life experience, alongside a deluge of attempts to replace that experience. One has been a tolerable and even beneficial complement, the other a complete failure.

Yeshua and technology. The two don't seem to go together. When we think about the operation of the early Church with its healings and miracles. And when we think about the Holy Spirit, the deep and abiding fellowship we have with our Creator out in nature, often times technology feels dead. There is no connection like the one G-d provides for His people, because a hunk of metal cannot contain G-d, no matter how vast the expanse of information it promises to provide. In fact, G-d's presence may be found in quite the opposite environment.

The whisper of G-d's voice in my life has almost never come with a screen attached to it. It is in quiet moments of meditation, an observation of human engagement, or an encounter with the beauty of nature. I cannot deny, there are so many amazing sermons and teachers online and, yes, I hear G-d speak through them on a weekly basis. However, if I lived in the location of these great teachers, I would attend their churches in person. My route to finding these teachers was word of mouth, not an Internet search. Still, I suppose I can vouch for some measure of the Internet on their behalf, while still wondering if it is the ideal.

The Internet has given me unlimited access to teachings. But it has not replaced the comfort and enlightenment of the Spirit as I read my Bible cuddled in a soft blanket in the crook of my couch on the Sabbath.

Many a person tells me they need teachers to understand Scripture. I agree with them in part. Making disciples requires leadership and without great leaders, the people perish, according to Scripture. On the other hand, the same Holy Spirit that walks with our great teachers is supposed to be with every true follower of Yeshua. Perhaps we give the Holy Spirit too little credit. No doubt, one way or another, G-d desires to open up His Word to each one who comes looking. When teachers are scarce, perhaps it is the layman's responsibility to go digging for truth. Perhaps it is our responsibility even in a wealth of teaching.

If we rely on one teacher or the Internet, are we in relationship with G-d or with that teacher or screen? Too heavy a reliance on someone else's interpretations of Scripture leads us to stay babies in the faith. At some point, perhaps we should grow up and open up the Word to see with our own eyes what it contains. And if we are to make disciples, don't we need to become better teachers ourselves?

To do so requires a connected and Biblically founded group of Believers. Reassuringly, it's not our job to oversee the managerial aspect of that. G-d Himself builds His church. It is our job to look, ask, seek, knock, pray, read, pursue, and teach. In that calling, how do we reconcile the Internet, technology, and entertainment with Yeshua? Where do we put these things that have now assumed so much of our time?

According to the **Washington Post**[lxvii], children ages 8-12 spend on average of four hours and 44 minutes on screens each day. Teens average seven hours and 22 minutes.

Seven and a half hours with a screen in front of your face.

Do we have an ADHD problem or a screen problem? A conversation for another book perhaps.

The amount of time spent with technology is literally taking over our every free minute. With this rise of use, there is a rise of other issues as well. Before accusing me of making an argument of correlation and not causation, let's just use our own brains for a second. Study after study has shown that social media use goes hand in hand with rising depression in individuals (**Healthline**[lxviii] **Sage**[lxix] ,**NBC**[lxx]). The promised connectivity of social media turned out to be a bust. Instead of promoting healthy community it has instead left the user feeling isolated, vulnerable, and subordinate among his/her peers.

Pew research[lxxi] shows that there was a 59 percent rise in depression among teens between 2007 and 2017. **Science Daily**[lxxii] reports that mental health issues over the last decade have greatly increased, especially among young adults. In 2017 – 2018, mental health issues in adults rose by 1.5 million people over the previous year's data sets.

Drug overdose deaths have more than tripled in the United States since 1990. We continue to have a well-documented opioid overdose crisis.

During the Covid lockdowns, binge drinking among adults also increased dramatically, according to a **Rand Study**[lxxiii].

Pornography addiction[lxxiv] also continues to rise. Currently, around **35 percent**[lxxv] of all Internet downloads are pornographic and there are continual increases in porn users reporting problems with family life, sexuality, and work.

Before we move into a closer look at the Internet regarding user behaviors like porn, I'd like to point out that it does not appear that a rise in Internet use has positively affected our mental wellbeing. Whatever extraneous reasons may exist, the fact remains that the more we have used technology, the more anxiety, depression, and addiction we are experiencing as a society. We face today a host of psychological disorders, addictions, and overall negative societal outcomes. More on that later.

Let's talk about porn

This is the uncomfortable, often shame-filled conversation that churches rarely have. We have got to take the shame out of it first. There has never been a time in human history when someone could get access to millions of images of sex at the touch of a button. This access makes it incredibly difficult for men and some women to keep their minds and hearts pure. It has often been called the most free, pervasive drug in human history. I'd agree with that.

If you fall into the category of someone who views porn, you are very much not alone. If you are addicted, you are very much not alone. We need to talk about it because of its spiritual ramifications and the offer of hope from the G-d of the Bible. Accountability might be a great place to start, alongside education. I find that there is a striking lack of knowledge in the general population about what pornography is, how it is made, and the identity of the people being viewed by so many millions of spectators.

Education directed at our youth about the characteristics of pornography and G-d's perspective could be the impetus for positive change and preventative behavior.

Porn itself has a shady history and an even nastier present. Some stats for you.

- 8 out of 10 people in pornographic material are there against their own will.
- 33 trillion pornographic images/ videos are VIEWED each year.
- Porn makes more money globally than Apple. By a lot.
- The majority of people that are in pornography are either drugged, sexually trafficked, or too poor and addicted to know

how to get out of it. These people are often victims of sexual abuse, both before entering the industry and during their time in it.

- The average person in pornography has thousands of sexual partners over the span of just a few years.
- The porn industry regularly uses sexually trafficked adults and children. These are slaves.
- Porn addicts need more and more outrageous material to satisfy sexual desire, which is why we see such a rise in violence and child pornography.
- 9 out of 10 people purchasing other humans for sex started by recreationally viewing pornography.
- Porn is the gateway to becoming a sexual trafficker.

This is not hyperbole. The United States makes up about 4 percent of the global population and yet is the number one purchaser of sexually trafficked individuals and, coincidentally, holds the **number one spot**[lxxvi] for pornography viewership, per capita.

The amount of money in and out of banks from the porn industry is astounding. With **estimates**[lxxvii] ranging on the low end of $6 billion to $97 Billion, porn likely does more business globally than Apple. Does our financial system want this to change? Does our population? Do we?

We have a porn problem. Nothing is viewed on the Internet more than pornography.

Does this change your view of the Internet? Perhaps not. Understandably, most people live in the tension of a fallen world where we often take the good with the bad.

But this isn't just bad. This is an egregious violation of human rights. This is evil behavior. It is catastrophic for a healthy society.

What if your dearest friend, family member, or child was taken and used in such a manner? Put a face to those people. Now, do you see the problem? I'm convinced G-d's heart breaks and His anger rages on behalf of the people bought and sold for sexual gratification of an over-entertained and bored US populace.

What do we do with this? What is the Internet to us? Do we care how we are using the Internet?

I'm convinced G-d cares.

I think I've mentioned this in a few of my essays already. But it's time to mention it again. Brad Scott has a wonderful **series**[lxxviii] expounding on the idea that the Internet is the modern-day Tree of the Knowledge of Good and Evil and that it also may end up being the Image of the Beast mentioned in Revelation. I tend to agree with him. Eve got sucked into the tree's temptation, lusting after the fruit that visually stimulated. But that fruit, that disobedience, held the DNA of death: soul crushing, hell producing, shame inducing, separation from eternal DNA. And she ate of the tree for all the reasons we do. She was promised extra wisdom and knowledge and a G-d-like ability to decipher right from wrong.

Why do we say we use the Internet again? Is it to gain knowledge, better workflow, more control over our lives, financial benefit? Are we Eve?

I don't know. I suppose it depends. There is no prohibition against using the Internet that I can find in Scripture. Yet, in Eve's story we see that the lust of the eyes and the desires of the flesh, when unquestioned and followed, lead to death.

How much of our time online is spurred by lust of the eyes or desires of the flesh?

The Internet can be so useful. In fact, it seems to be how we do everything; but, at what cost? Are there terrible traps that we may be toying with as our Internet use accelerates?

SEXUAL SLAVERY

Most people believe we ended slavery in this country some time after the Civil War.

Tragically, slavery is still very present —the sexual kind. Just as old, and more rampant than ever, this degradation of the human spirit is incredibly **prevalent in the United States**[lxxix].

This is not just men and women, it is children also, and it IS slavery.

According to the **anti-sex trafficking platform SHIFTai**[lxxx], almost all sex purchasers are porn users. And in 2019, there were around 33 trillion views of pornography globally. Yes, 33 TRILLION.

Pornography changes how people see others. It changes our view of humanity. Dehumanizing and separating soul from body, pornography forces us to think of people as parts without a whole. Instead of seeing integrated beings with soul, mind, and body as one, the porn viewer only sees a body. This is more than dehumanizing towards others, it forces a disconnection with one's own mind and spirit and changes the integration of sexuality from a fully unified experience to a merely physical one.

Moreover, it creates people willing to use abused, disadvantaged, orphaned, and trafficked people for their own sexual desire. Truth hits hard here. The very lowest lows of human nature are found in this sort of behavior. Many of the worst crimes in history have started with this kind of mental framework. To some, people they don't care about are less than human. Pornography treats all people in this dehumanized way and trains the user to think along those lines.

Sadly, most men have not been made aware of this horrific element of porn. And for many of them, they are already too addicted to end porn use on their own.

One of the main issues with our use of technology comes down to a misunderstanding of the Scriptural view of a human. The porn user has to live with an extreme dualistic view of him/herself.

In the history of Christianity, dualism is the idea that all of life can be separated into two different categories — either the sacred *or* the secular. This means that some activity is sacred and some is just regular worldly stuff. It also means that the spirit and body are two completely separate entities and that the eternity of the soul or spirit is more holy than the dirty, down-to-earth body. Dualism is an ancient idea, and is heavily embedded in religion and some denominations of Christianity.

But it is incorrect.

The food we eat, air we breathe, drugs we take, illnesses we get, exercise we engage in, sunshine we are exposed to, and so many other physical activities affect our mental well-being and, whether for good or ill, can become intertwined with our spiritual position. We are fully integrated beings with body, mind, and spirit intertwined. We cannot compartmentalize one or the other. **What we do is spiritual.**

Does not Scripture tell us to do everything to the best of our abilities as if doing it unto the Lord? (Col. 3:23) Does it not say to think on what is noble, right, true, lovely and admirable? (Philippians 4:8)

Why is Scripture so adamant that we protect our hearts? It is because through our minds we act, and through these actions we create our world. We co-create our lives with the Lord. For good or for evil.

As my mother always reminds me, the eyes are the window to the soul, and **that window goes both ways**. Your soul sees out into the world through your eyes, and the world also gains access to your soul through the same means. What you put in your mind affects your soul. What you do to your body affects your soul. We are sponges and we cannot escape that reality.

Body and mind are not separate. Body and spirit are not separate. How we use our bodies gives them purpose. If we are told our bodies are temples for the Lord, (1 Cor. 6:19-20), are not our bodies intended for holy purposes?

An end user's body enmeshed in pornographic exploration is not, in that moment, fit for temple use of a Holy G-d. It was made to be holy. But while it promotes, permits, and lives in evil, it is not able to attain the standard for which it was created. And we subject the Holy Spirit to great evil when we forget that it is unwillingly along for the ride.

Pornography degrades the very purpose of our bodies.

We know this because G-d is adamant throughout Scripture that His people stay away from the sexual nature of pagan god worship. The Bible discusses purity not just because sex is powerful for the individual and for relationship, but because illicit sexual activity, often using prostitutes, orgies, and the like were so often used in the worship of **pagan gods**[lxxxi]. Using sex as some sort of pathway to benefit the lives and livelihoods of nations, ancient religious practices often abused child and adult alike.

The very practice of treating sex this way likely mimics acts of worship of pagan gods. Which is, of course, at the very top of our Ten Commandments. There shall be no other gods before THE G-d.

Sexuality is spiritual, just as everything else, only it touches on something uniquely fundamental, something intrinsic to the very nature of our beings. Sexuality is deeply spiritually significant, reflecting oneness, life, relationship, wholeness, and a view of G-d-like unity.

When that picture is distorted and dismembered, we lose our understanding of healthy relationship not only with others, but also with the Lord.

How we interact with sex directly affects our souls. And who we have sex with leaves a lifelong impact. Healthy or unhealthy, we are formed by our first sexual experiences and have a heck of a time changing that formation (**First Sexual Experiences Determine Development**[lxxxii]).

Is it any wonder sexual acts are the most viewed thing on our screens? That smooth-faced box possesses a powerful draw, an addictive hit, and connects to our spiritual selves. Through just a video, the actors and director can strike the mind and spirit of the viewer in a foundational and life-altering way.

Our bodies can be offerings of worship of G-d OR worship of the world. What we do with our bodies and minds matters. It is why G-d advises us to be in right sexual relationship according to His standards.

I Corinthians 6:18: "Flee from sexual immorality. Every other sin a person commits is outside the body, but the sexually immoral person sins against his own body."

Matthew 5:28 "But I say to you that everyone who looks at a woman with lustful intent has committed adultery with her in his heart."

Matthew 5:29: "If your right eye causes you to sin, tear it out and throw it away. For it is better for you to lose one of your members, than that your whole body be thrown into hell."

Yeshua and the New Testament writers don't make this easy on us. How we use the Internet matters.

And it's not just sex.

BRAIN JUNK FOOD

Violence, immorality, propaganda. Our screens hold powerful messages that change how we view the world. And it's such an easy route, so different than reading or hearing the word of G-d spoken. Our eyes are often the quickest pathways to mental engagement.

> The Bible warns regarding this. I John 2:16 states, "For all that is in the world, the lust of the flesh and the lust of the eyes and the boastful pride of life is not from the Father, but is from the world."

What has social media, violent media, snarky propaganda, and negative news bias taught us? Lust of the flesh, lust of the eyes, boastfulness, envy, pride, pursuit of wealth, desensitization to human suffering, fear, disconnection, hopelessness, and how many other negatives?

Is it any wonder anxiety, depression, and mental illness are on the rise?

Is there any evidence that we are better off as humans, as a society, due to technological advancements that are used **11 to 19 hours/day**[lxxxiii]?

Surely, we can point to advancement in the sciences as helpful for humanity. Think surgeons or car safety.

But these advancements do not represent the majority of society-wide technological use. Despite communication being far quicker and easier, the majority of time spent with technology seems to be entertainment driven, with social media and programming at the top.

The good with the bad.

The Tree of the Knowledge of Good and Evil.

To get any of it, we get all of it. The same Internet I use to research this essay is being used to view illicit pornographic images, or launder money, or bully high-school kids, etc. It feels wrong, but so desperately difficult to get around.

What we view most definitely programs us. It is called "programming," after all.

I don't remember a lot from the time I spent earning a broadcast journalism major at CSU. But I will forever remember a class I took discussing the effect of media on the mind. We were forced (although I closed my eyes and tuned out through some of it) to watch some pretty dark and obviously mind-altering media to help prove a point. Study after study, even back in the early 2000s, showed major shifts in thinking and worldview based on what media a person consumed. Parts of our brain experience the videos we watch as personal bodily experiences. Without proper analysis, these traumas float around in our minds, desensitizing and morphing our thinking.

If the local news focuses on murders, you think there is a murderer around every corner.

If you've just watched a horror film, you are more likely to feel scared that night.

If you've viewed violent sex regularly, you are more likely to feel that sex and violence go together.

Interestingly, violence in film that is connected with a moral outcome affects the brain in a more complex manner. The moral lesson of the story gives context and meaning to the violence. Therefore, a giant difference exists between watching a WWII movie and playing violent video games that have no character development or distinctions between good and evil. What and how we consume matters. But no matter what…

Media changes you. It programs you. They knew this way back in the day when I went to college. And I believe we are witnessing the natural results of a millennial generation that has experienced an extensive amount of programming.

The game seems to go like this: create confusion, chaos, moral equivalencies, fear, anxiety, envy, and a victimhood worldview. Now we have created a hook (a powerful draw), tribes have been created and divides solidified. Now the human is more controllable.

This is a profitable game. Sexual confusion creates medical and therapeutic industry opportunities. A victimhood mindset opens the door to organization after organization committed to justice for the victims. Moral ambivalence means viewership for the next piece of garbage will remain high. Fear and anxiety promote dependence on information, like news, to satiate the void and justify fear-based behaviors.

The new and trendy Critical Race Theory plays with many of these emotions, creating victims and oppressors. Catalyzing enemies and fear-based belief systems, people become more prone to primal (emotion based response system) triggers. When people are emotionally driven, they are easier to deceive. Marxism is based on the idea that there is an oppressive "other." Critical Race Theory simply applies that to race, even where little evidence of such oppression exists.

This dividing of people who are all made in the image of G-d is the design of the enemy.

I would not even be aware of such theories of control were it not for screens, which seem to keep many locked in the matrix of propaganda.

Free and fearless people are not easy to control. People walking in the Holy Spirit often do things outside of the box. That means a healthy Believer must be willing to walk away from technology. Maybe not 100 percent of the time, but enough to know that the tech lords are not G-d and are terribly fallible as we all are, prone to greed and visions of power.

Adonai, the great I Am, is not a computerized G-d. He has existed long before our version of technology and will exist through every phase of advancement. HE will exist beyond and ahead of those advancements and yet is right next to us as we experience them. Is it hard to believe that one day He may ask us to leave the Internet behind altogether? For through it, we are subtly influenced to do all sorts of things, and we are relentlessly given information that affects our behavior. And perhaps G-d will not want us to be listening to that line of thinking forever. Perhaps He doesn't want us to be listening to it even now.

It's not just in America. Globally, cell phones are more prevalent than food in some places. The whole world possesses this connectivity and it could certainly be the route to the entire world following the Antichrist.

What cell phones do with connectivity does not, however, compare with the work of the Holy Spirit. That work does not just provide information; it sends us wisdom in dark places. The same wisdom that thousands of others may secretly be receiving in their hearts.

I have long thought that Satan was going after the Holy Spirit position now. After all, he tried to sit on the Father's throne. That didn't work.

He attempted to kill G-d's son, which failed miserably.

So, how can he possess more than one individual? How can he control in the way the Holy Spirit can? That kind of power would destroy all. It seems this is his new route to ultimate control over the earth.

And it likely won't stop with screens. To get into the mind of humans and maneuver like the Holy Spirit does may require more.

But it is this writer's theory that screens have been one obvious tool of the enemy for mind control.

THE GAME OF THRONES CONUNDRUM

If you missed the cultural phenomenon that was *Game of Thrones*, I must believe you have been living under a rock. People talked endlessly about the HBO show that originated with a book series. It came and went like a fiery comet. Here one second, and then out of the mind the next. (Although, unfortunately, a spinoff is apparently coming.)

But while it was, it was all encompassing.

I had many Christian friends who watched it, and who would discuss with great conviction that the perverse sexual nature of the show, along with the violence, was completely allowable due to the amazing storytelling. It was just so well written, and cast, and filmed. Too great a piece of art to pass up.

Convinced, my husband and I suffered through the first episode.

Now, I'm not attempting to assert spiritual superiority here. So far, you've likely discovered the great sinner I have the capacity to be. And no, I haven't kept myself prudishly pure when it comes to entertainment, although there are many days I wish I had. So, when I describe to you my thoughts about the first episode, please understand: I'm well versed in entertainment and not often prone to hyperbole in this arena. I love a good story.

But, come on. The first episode ends with a child plummeting to his death after seeing a set of twins from a rival family having sex with each other.

I not only didn't care about any other characters at that point besides this child, but I could see where the show was taking us. Soft-core porn to get a certain segment of the population actually addicted to the programming, followed by, well, I guess some sort of redemptive storytelling.

And THIS we call worthwhile art.

For who? For what? If we didn't demand to be entertained during all possibly "boring" moments of our existence, would a G-dly person attach themselves to this sort of a series?

Again, for who? For what purpose is this "good"? Do we even define "good" properly anymore? What is good? What is noble, just, true, pure, right?

Well, what is it?

Perhaps this is making my reader uncomfortable. Perhaps you loved *Game of Thrones*.

I think this book has likely made everyone uncomfortable in some way, so if it's your turn, so be it. Be uncomfortable.

In fact, push yourself into that discomfort and ask if the G-d of the universe enjoyed *Game of Thrones* as much as you did.

Why? For what purpose?

Is entertainment a good enough reason? Is it important enough, essential enough to our desitinies, to *view* garbage because it's seemingly creative and perhaps a good story? Really. Reeeaaally?

Perhaps I'm as upset with myself as I am with the Church for not addressing this. I watched an entire episode. What a waste. What filth I put in my mind because I was curious about this cultural phenomenon.

I knew better. I had studied media after all.

I still fell into the trap. Shame on me.

With that sort of programming becoming all the rage, is it any wonder that the Church feels like a giant mouth of hypocrisy? We cannot call the culture to become moral when we ourselves have an elephantine plank in our own eye. We worship at the feet of sexuality and violence, just the same as our cultural counterparts. We tolerate evil in our homes on a nightly basis with the programming we "entertain" ourselves with. We watch thousands of deaths on screen and call the Romans barbarians for watching dozens in their Coliseum.

I recall the line from *Gladiator*: "Are you not entertained?"

What value are we adding to society by promulgating these sorts of stories in the most graphic way, **visually**, into our minds?

I keep asking these questions because I want you to answer them, and then ask if the answers are good enough.

Where is the church different than culture? In what way?

Sure, we can point to individuals, friends, G-dly people in our circles who are walking the talk, but the church as a whole? As a body of Believers, where have we taken a strong stand that a public eye could look at and know well?

Could you imagine if every Believer could be heard telling friends and coworkers that they didn't watch *Game of Thrones* because they refused to compromise the life that G-d had given them to be entertained? What a testimony, and a simple one at that. Could we cause people to ask: what is it in this life that is so precious and bought with such a cost that even TV and entertainment are put aside to honor it?

A testimony is a life that is lived. A testimony exists in a person's moral structure, kept day-to-day, week-to-week, and year-to-year, and how it stands when compared to past behaviors and contemporary counterparts. What is our character like when we are alone, with technology in the room?

For many of us, the compromises we have individually made have shamed us into refusing to attempt a testimony or give G-d the glory for even our best behaviors. It is because we tolerate too many skeletons in the closet. Perhaps we know that underneath a shiny, smiling exterior, we fill our minds with garbage on a nightly basis. Or perhaps some of us claim to have that testimony, but often get found out and lose any ground we were gaining.

We must walk the talk, not just in one area, but many. It cannot be that we are well behaved on Sunday morning and evil in mind and spirit on Friday night. That is not a testimony. Our children know better, our spouses know, we know.

The Church can begin to get this right by calling its members to the life Yeshua called us to. "If you have even looked at a woman lustfully…"

Stop looking. Turn it off.

That opportunity has passed us by with *Game of Thrones.* But perhaps there will be another one. Tomorrow is a perfect day with no sins yet in it.

If guilt and shame are impediments to our public testimony, should we not take out our eye or cut off our hand to avoid what comes between us and our ministries? Drop the phone if that's what it takes. Put child guards on the television.

Cancel Netflix. Bring back DVDs.

Whatever it means to be like our Rabbi, Yeshua, that is the path. That is eternal. That is our call. And FYI, He did not watch TV.

THE VIDEO GAME

I'm sure you can anticipate by now where my mind resides regarding this part of our technological world.

It is said that as many as 12 percent of boys and 7 percent of girls are **addicted to video games**[lxxxiv].

Whether it's avatar-led imaginative worlds or violent war scenes, gaming has a huge footprint in our society.

Psychologists will tell you[lxxxv] that games like Fortnite seem to be the most addictive for young people. Because a game like Fortnite engages dopamine and other chemical signals, it can become as addictive as a drug. Parents report not being able to get their kids away from the screen or out of the basement. To which I have often replied, "If you have a trash receptacle, you have a solution."

And as often, I'm met with blank stares.

Most parents don't have the fortitude to throw the darn thing away. Perhaps the parents enjoy it as much as the kids do.

The same questions asked of Internet use, we must ask of gaming. Is it violent, is it sexual, is it addictive? And of course, is it true, noble, lovely?

Often "yes" to the first list, too often "no" to the second.

How many addictive games are based on Bible stories? How many teach humility versus ego, sacrifice versus greed, or peace over violence?

Those questions gave me a good laugh. Quite out loud actually, as I sit in my uncharacteristically quiet home.

Yeah, I'm not sure about these questions, but my gut tells me, not a lot of popular video games focus on the sorts of character traits G-d has laid out in Scripture.

Now, maybe I'm not totally against all video games. I did grow up sitting in a backseat playing Tetris while my parents looked for houses to buy or drove us to visit relatives. Some Mario here and there added a spicy change that kept us little munchkins livable in the car and out of the sort of trouble that found us pulled over on the side of the road.

We had fun with them.

I don't hear about Tetris or Mario Kart keeping the kiddos up at night while parents scratch their heads about how to teach balanced technology use. Well, at least I haven't heard that one just yet.

So, let's be reasonable. It matters very much what we choose to play, just like it matters very much what television programming we choose to watch.

The games aren't worth an addiction. They just aren't. A person who won't leave their house, get some sunshine, have a real social life or experience the joys and pains of real life is not really living. They are also not going to fulfill the destiny of the call of Christ.

We are called to go and make disciples. Leave your home, your basement, meet someone, teach them obedience to G-d. Obedience includes keeping the Sabbath, the feast days, feeding the poor. So many of G-d's commands include human interaction in a human framework.

You are not a fantasy, or an avatar. You are a priceless creature of a natural world. Your interaction is wanted, and hoped for by the people you will meet and the nature you will touch (caveat: this is when you are in alignment. There is no doubt many people do more damage than good when they are not following G-d's laws).

But your destiny is undeniable. You are made for goodness in a world of real souls, and human touch is one of the greatest contributors to health and wellbeing. We need hugs and handshakes and smiles and eye contact. The digital realm, as fun or real as it may seem, cannot and does not provide the framework for emotional and physical health. It does not replace soul-filled relationship. And it is not a good enough replacement for the call and purpose of your life, which is to follow G-d into adventures that demand the integration of mind, body and spirit.

SOCIAL MEDIA

As previously mentioned, the promised connectivity of being online with "real" friends has been a bust. It has devolved into the basest of human instincts. Upload the best of you. Put a filter on that pic. Slim your face, plump your lips, enlarge the eyes and breasts. Show a little more skin next time? Get the angles and the lighting right. Share the awesome trip, the job promotion, the cute girlfriend. Don't share the alcohol addiction, the screw up at work, the messy house, the screaming at the kids, or the speeding ticket.

Whatever connectivity we think we are getting, we are not seeing a whole picture. In fact, we may not even be seeing the truth.

Have you ever had that friend who uses all the face changing apps? You see a picture of them and it's so far from their natural face, you wonder if they got a facelift and lip injection? Only to see them for coffee and realize they have spent an awful lot of time adjusting their online persona.

We all want to do it. It's fun pretending we are perfect.

The problem is, we aren't.

The Social Dilemma[lxxxvi], one film of several, delineates the problems with social media amongst our youth. It is a place where kiddos are groomed by sexual predators, bullied by classmates, and pulled into a fake life not fit for even an emotionally well-adjusted adult. Not to mention, the thousands of opportunities to post mortifications that may prevent employers from hiring, or keep future love interests from going on that next date.

At the other end of these social platforms are tech gurus adjusting every ad and scroll to make your experience more addictive. Literally, a bunch of nerds trying to push a dopamine hit on your poor unsuspecting teen. Or on you.

Drug pushers.

This environment has not made us happier. It has made us lonelier and has stolen real human connection from us. I'm convinced that young people love to be around each other. Trying to replace that with social media produces a less intelligent, less keen, and less socially adept human.

Why?

In a person-to-person, non-screen environment, one has to come up with a response without thinking too long about it in advance. And without adjusting the lighting. We have to be able to communicate through sound, inflection, facial expression, AND verbiage right there in the moment. And we have to look imperfect, dare I say, even ridiculous at times to do so. Communicating well requires listening and focus. And listening.

Did I say *listening*?

A lot is lost in translation on FB or Instagram, and you must be fairly skilled with words to communicate properly there. This might be why people settle for a great picture and a stupid phrase about their vacation. It's too hard to only use a sentence or two to get anything of value communicated. Furthermore, how much listening is actually taking place on FB? When I attempt deeper communication on social media, I notice that most responses to my posts reveal the writer's tertiary reading of my post, if that! It's a one-sentence-world baby, but I'm not a "keep it simple, stupid" kind of girl. (At least, not most of the time.)

Social media tends to feed ego. Ego tends to need to be the best, to be right, and to have all the answers. There is no room for doubt or humility. There is no room to fully read someone's post, assume the best about their intentions, or ask questions about how they came to those conclusions. No, they are an image, an avatar, less than human, and perhaps competition. Who is getting the most likes? How are they getting them? Who is RIGHT? Who is POPULAR?

These become value judgments. We aren't interacting with our fellow man. We are competing for top dog position.

This environment was brought to you by a group of tech peeps. Mostly dudes. And boy, do they have us in a vice. Some call them Tech Bros — the "elite" few who control the time of the masses. We flock to their platforms and load up on content, then keep coming back for more pomp and more hype.

But I'm not the expert. I'm just one of millions of users reflecting on my experiences.

This discussion is fruitless if we do not look to Scripture to inform how we should and should not interact with these platforms and tools. Proverbs 6:16-19:

> "These six things doth the Lord hate: yea, seven are an abomination unto him: A proud look, a lying tongue, and hands that shed innocent

blood, An heart that deviseth wicked imaginations, feet that be swift in running to mischief, A false witness that speaketh lies, and he that soweth discord among brethren."

Pride, lies, wicked images and plans, running into mischief, false testimony, divisiveness. Even hands that shed innocent blood are at least tangentially implicated by social media. Have we not seen hatred towards other groups fomented online followed by murderous actions?

In scrolling through the imagery of TikTok or Instagram, through memes and posts on FB and Twitter, it is hard to avoid a slew of lies and propaganda. With divisiveness, pride, false testimony and discord being constantly sown, can we avoid the things G-d hates online?

And if we choose to be a participant in the gathering itself, it is possible we have silently agreed to overlook the major problems with our social media society. From viewing pornographic or sexually graphic material by accident on TikToK (**a regular occurrence**[lxxxvii]), and therefore participating in wicked imaginations, to reading memes that speak lies about people or sow discord, are we not heading to these sites voluntarily?

Ask yourself: would you come across this much garbage going about your everyday life away from social media?

I speak to myself in this. I have a particular penchant for politics, and often struggle to break away from a juicy, gossip-laden story. Too often for the sake of "education" I waste gobs of time on social media sites trying to glean more information. I understand the draw. Despite my head having the knowledge of the problem, other parts of me want to be educated on the latest outrageous or egregious scandal in the world. I often wonder: what can I do differently, how can I be better?

Jordan Peterson, well-known psychologist, author, and podcaster, offers the idea in his book, *12 Rules for Life,* of "cleaning up your room." The idea is to take care of your own life before going and fixing others. Do something that improves your life everyday, even if it is small, and in a year or two, your life may look totally different. This means you clean up the space you are currently in. The one you are actually in — not online space, but the physical realm in which you spend your time.

With distractions so readily available, just observing your actual surroundings could prove to be revolutionary.

Remove the plank in your own eye. Examine your life. Have you done all you can with what you have been given?

What would it mean to take the time I spend on social media and use it to clean up my own room instead? I don't know. (But I think it's worth a try and may inspire my next book!)

DEEPER SOCIAL CONSEQUENCES

Once again Jordan Peterson comes to the rescue as we identify problem areas of our social media and media engagement. One area of concern is **memory**[lxxxviii]. In a recent interview, Peterson states, "Forgetting and remembering are very sophisticated cognitive processes. Normally, what we do with an experience is we reduce it to its significance. Then we remember the significance and we let go of the details… We boil our lives down to the gist of the story and we remember that. And then we're not crushed by the detailed recollection." He says the purpose of memory is the extraction of wisdom. It is not to have a detailed recollection of everything that took place.

It is a great relief and grace that we are created to be able to put our past behind us.

The Internet does not allow for this. What you post lives somewhere out there forever. It is often easy to find and overanalyze by people who, most likely, don't know you at all.

This detailed record of foibles, misjudgments, or blatantly bad moments has become an excellent way to objectify and codify individuals into distinct homogenous classes.

"You like Jordan Peterson. You must be a sexist!"

"You voted for Biden. You must be a communist!"

"There's a picture of you looking drunk. You must be an alcoholic!"

"You were on the beach with thousands of people. You don't care about the people dying of Covid!"

You get the picture. No pun intended.

The dehumanization and denial of individualism is one thing. But how about a reputation that can last forever based on one mistaken photo or post? We are haunted by more detailed recollections of our past and, as such, society seems to be less and less gracious. Less and less we lean to forgiveness or the idea of redemption. What about transformation? Can someone change? What about potential? Are we fully realized or do we all still need a bit of work, maybe more than a bit?

It is a problem for Believers to interact with media this way. Not just for those who volunteer to be in the public eye or for those we have hired as politicians necessarily, but rather for regular people who also get caught up in the fray, with no escape.

There have a been a number of stories of late where someone was fired from their position as a writer, their books banned, their future crushed, due to misguided posts from high school. Or the public shaming of young people who say something out of turn at school that ends up getting posted online.

There is Alexi McCammond who was let go from Teen Vogue for tweets she put out in HIGHSCHOOL. Or Mimi Groves who was asked to disenroll from the University of Tennessee after a Black classmate found a video of her from high school saying the N-word. There were the Covington students who were incorrectly accused of disrespectful behavior towards a Native American at the Lincoln Memorial and so many others over the past number of years.

These people all suffered great consequences from youthful mistakes or inaccurate accusations based on video and social media posts.

My son had an embarrassing moment at school and multiple other students threatened to reach for their phones to film it and put it online for the world to laugh at. My sweet kiddo cried after school at just the thought of it.

It's ugly, and it's happening.

How many videos have we seen where violence breaks out, and there is clearly someone there taping the entire event to put up online or sell to a media outlet? Choosing to film a video instead of helping a human being.

Why is this footage so valuable? We are addicted to gossiping about the vulgar impulses in our fellow humans. And social media buffs know the benefit they will receive as that video endures in Internet eternity, to the great damage of those who suffer while others watch.

There are deeper questions we need to ask about societal degradation, as well as individual degradation. Of course, increased media use seems to be spurring both.

How violent would the BLM movement or Antifa or the Capital riot have been without media fomenting agitation and frustration and literally promoting violence against innocent people in the name of justice?

We have worshiped at the feet of social media darlings, celebrities, politicians and news stars because we feel like we know them. We have so much access to their information online. We trust them. They did somehow "make it big," after all. Surely anyone who has had that level of success is smarter, brighter, and wiser than us shmucks out here in regular old America.

We love King George in all his pomp and gold and money and power.

But we also feel the hypocrisy. The hypocritical elite telling those far poorer how big a carbon footprint they are making. How racist they are. How sexist they are. How horrible. To not have money and to purchase goods at Walmart, what savages!

I suspect Americans, just like our earlier counterparts, don't really love King George. They do, however, seem to wish they could BE King George.

And here, we find another stumbling block for the Believer: covetousness. In Proverbs, we are told not to be jealous of a wicked person (Proverbs 24:1). Do not envy their wealth, for they often got it through less-than-moral means. They often use it to oppress others. Giant corporations often use child and slave labor to make their products. The Hollywood Elite often live Sodom and Gomorrah lifestyles. News organizations often spread propaganda to elicit fear and addiction. Social media often limits free speech while enriching the wealthiest voices.

Do you really want that life? Maybe the money part. But to gain the whole world and lose your soul? This life is short. It is but a moment. Eternity awaits. We are told we must die to ourselves and give up our lives to gain eternity. We must be willing to be at the back of the line and to treat wealth and poverty with the same moral response. We have not been called to wealth. It can be a blessing, but it is not a calling. Your call is to pick up your cross and follow Yeshua. Perhaps you gain wealth; what do you do with it? Perhaps you are poor; how can you still be generous?

In a lovely discussion with friends, my husband noted the exceptional ability Mother Theresa had in making others uncomfortable, especially the wealthy influencers. In more than one speech, the small, unassuming woman fearlessly spoke against the evils of abortion, the darkness of poverty, and the suffering of orphans. She looked those monetary influencers straight in the eye. Her position in life did not affect her message. The status of her audience did not change the truth. She spoke boldly and, I believe, gained Heavenly reward.

So. What is technology? What is the Internet? In the presence of Mother Theresa or others of her rare moral quality, it is powerless. Despite the sway of the elite, the social media moguls, the barons of business and the political powerhouses, it is still the voices speaking the truth that deserve admiration and inspire hope. It is the whisper of G-d's voice, not the howling wind or roaring fire. This tiny spark that so quietly works in us, that takes some listening for and getting used to, is the place where so many find the strength to keep going.

For now, these platforms still carry voices like Jordan Peterson and Brad Scott. The freedom of speech that we still possess has provided opportunities for the Internet to offer up wonderful messaging. But it comes at a cost. Even the best-intentioned logon often degrades into blurry-eyed sleepless nights in front of a blue light screen that can never love you. The endless scrolling for information, either on friends' pages or world events, that flippant comment that you thought about for a good five minutes before making, the jealous anticipation of yet another peer succeeding where you did not.

That beautiful person who always looks stunning and has you running to spend your last dime on anti-aging creams — somehow, they always appear.

The pornographic imagery that provides no real satisfaction — just a click away.

The good and the evil are a package deal when it comes to the Internet.

The irreplaceable G-d will not be replaced by any conjuring of mankind. We are not satisfied or content, not more wise or intelligent. We are not mentally or physically better off for all our increasing tech use. There is only one G-d and He cannot be replaced.

SO HOW DO WE RESPOND

I don't know. This seems to me to be an individual decision. With the goal of keeping things true, lovely, pure and not selfish, I'd offer this advice: tread lightly when it comes to Internet use.

If we can master how we use the Internet, we truly will be masters of ourselves. If mastery requires purging social media, some websites and content, etc. from use, then so be it. Better to cut it off.

As I think on it, how difficult a task! Really, I've become so accustomed to some type of information pummeling my brain from my phone or computer.

But also, imagine the things I'll do!

Be careful of the messaging we blindly let in. It is often sneaky and unassuming, but in the long run can land an emotional blow.

Perhaps at the beginning, middle, and end of our days we could go before the Lord and ask Him: "What is it you want me to do today? How should I live? How should I be? How much media should I take in? Where should I spend my time?"

Sometimes, the answer comes quickly and succinctly. Sometimes, I get nothing but a general sense of the day. Sometimes, I'm too tired or disconnected to listen intently.

Almost always I'm reminded to find the time to be a present mother.

It is interesting how G-d responds when we ask questions and listen.

Take the Bible into the battle with you. If you have not already, do your best to memorize Scripture. Put it to music, or hang it on the bedroom wall. Put the Word of G-d on the desk where you work and in the room where you have the TV. Putting a physical reminder of what you truly desire in every space WILL make a difference. We are often so averse to physical reminders or things that feel like ritual, but good ritual is good habit, and good habits are life changing.

In Numbers 15 and Deuteronomy 22, tzitzit are proscribed for those of Israel. These intertwined blue and white strings were to be hung on the four corners of people's robes. They are reminders of the Torah. They are physical, visual elements that keep you aligned while proclaiming allegiance. I have tzitzit in my purse. Often in the search for car keys or chapstick, my fingers run across the small bits of yarn and I'm instantly reminded to spend the next moments, for as long as I can remember to, in obedience to G-d. I may eventually get to wearing them. Doing more study on that now.

These tzitzit are likely the "wings" mentioned in Malachi 4:2, which states: "But unto you that fear my name shall the Son of Righteousness arise with healing in his *wings*." It is likely the tzitzit of Yeshua that the woman touched to receive healing in Mark 5. The fulfillment of healing in His wings literally translated to just a touch of Yeshua's tzitzit.

Physical reminders can be powerful. Maybe buy some tzitzit.

Remember that you go nowhere without G-d's eyes. He knows all and desires to walk *with* you. Or rather, He desires that you would walk with Him.

Remember that your eyes are a two-way window. Your soul can see out and shifts according to what it sees.

I wonder if we all tried limiting media use, could we discuss what takes place? How does life change? Is the intention itself producing something?

For the readers that follow this and give it a try, save up your experiences. I'd love to hear them.

Chapter 12

RIGHTING PAUL

IF YOU'VE READ EACH OF MY ESSAYS to date, you may be able to write this one for me! Yet, I know that there is much we haven't discussed regarding one scriptural subject that will trouble us if left untouched.

Paul.

Poor, misunderstood, bastardized Paul.

Each time we see Yeshua following and defending G-d's Law, you can almost hear a pastor screeching out, unable to control the desperate defense of modern Christian doctrine: "But, Paul! But, Paul!"

BUT, PAUL.

We must deal with the common misinterpretations of this brilliant Pharisee in order to straighten out the doctrine prevalent today in most American churches. I believe this doctrine that G-d's Law has been changed, diminished, or done away with by the cross has caused most of the denominational splits in the church and has also stolen the power of the Christian testimony and walk.

Without G-d's instruction (which is how Law is defined for the writers of the Old Testament. Law = Instruction), how are we to know what it means to follow Yeshua?

How subjective is our walk with G-d?

Today, it is subjective enough to cause tens of thousands of denominational differences.

There aren't even tens of thousands of Biblical commands! There are precisely 613. And many of them only apply to the land of Israel, the temple, the Levitical Priesthood, etc.

Subjective legal frameworks have created a mess of doctrines and manmade laws, including but not limited to:

- Catholic Church indulgences
- Prohibitions on dancing
- Communion every Sunday or Communion once a year, once a month
- Good Friday, Ash Wednesday, imperative Sunday church attendance
- Sexual identity confusion
- Icon worship
- Baby baptism versus adult baptism
- Females prohibited from leadership
- Confusion on the commands about tithing and giving
- Prosperity Gospel
- Diminishing gifts of the Holy Spirit

You could probably add your own list of confusing differences between denominations.

How can this be when we all have one Scripture?

Many reasons no doubt contribute, but one inescapable figure often stands at the receiving end of pointed fingers and vehement arguments. In both defense of and subversion of Church doctrine, Paul is the central figure.

It is particularly his teachings about the Law (he speaks of many laws, we will discover this in a moment) that severs unity and encourages debate.

Does Paul teach that G-d's Laws (some or all) are done away with or not? We must finally answer this question. It is the underpinning for massive disruption and confusion among masses of Believers.

Many churches would say "not" yet do not teach the fullness of the Law to their congregants, adding to the mass confusion.

Paul has been used to redefine, undermine, and trash the Laws of G-d and the obedient Believer who follows them. I wonder what he would think about this disturbing trend. In a future life, perhaps we can all accost him with questions and plead for a response to his often, unwieldy writings. Until then, there are a few ways to untangle this doctrinal mess on your own.

- Read entire books at once. Never take one verse out without context and expand upon what you "think" Paul is saying. Paul was brilliant and his writings were complex. Without context, anything — but especially Paul — can be misinterpreted.
- Compare what you think Paul's doctrine is to what Yeshua teaches. If they are out of alignment, your interpretation of Paul is out of alignment. Go back and find out why.
- Make sure your interpretation of Paul is not adding to or taking away from the Laws of G-d. Deuteronomy 12:32 tells us that we are not to add to or take away from G-d's Law. If Paul added or took away from, he disobeyed a dictate that he would

> have been very familiar with. That is out of character for a man we esteem so highly and for a "Pharisee of Pharisees" (Acts 23:6), according to his own self-description.

And yes, in a moment we will dig deeper into these and other useful applications so I can show you what I mean.

First, why, oh why do we need to do this and do it regularly? In 2 Peter 3:16-17, Peter says this about Paul:

> "He writes the same way in all his letters, speaking in them of these matters. His letters contain some things that are hard to understand, which ignorant and unstable people distort, as they do the other Scriptures, to their own destruction. Therefore, dear friends, since you have been forewarned, be on your guard so that you may not be carried away by the error of the lawless and fall from your secure position."

We need humility when interpreting Paul. The brilliant Pharisee who likely had more Scripture memorized than we memorize ANYTHING probably didn't attempt to change G-d's Laws or introduce new doctrine that Yeshua did not.

If we think he is, WE are wrong. Not Paul, not Yeshua. According to Peter, any claim that Paul teaches against G-d's Laws is an "error of the lawless."

I fear we play around in this error quite a bit.

We are human. That's what we do: get things wrong. I do it, you do it, none of us is G-d, which is why we need each other and we need to TEST the Scriptures and spirit of the teachings we absorb.

One of the marvelous things about Scripture is you can dig into it like an archaeologist. You may have uncovered a dinosaur leg that you misidentify as an arm until you dig further to find more of the structure.

Perhaps it is a relief to find the full leg. Perhaps it is a horror. It does not change the fact that you are unearthing a leg, not an arm.

Dig further, find the structure. Even if it offends you, your pastor, or your parents, the truth is the truth whether we like it or not.

The Bible builds through time, understanding, story, and prophecy. The beginning is never going to be an unnecessary afterthought. It always provides definition and meaning for what comes later.

If our interpretations of Paul disregard or change the beginning, then WE are wrong. Not Paul.

Okay, I hear you screaming that you understand this concept. So, let's get into the nitty-gritty of modern Christian doctrine within a few helpful principles. In applying these principles we can better ensure we do not interpret Scripture with a mess of inconsistencies.

1. Anytime "Scriptures" or "Word of G-d" is used, it means the Old Testament

This one is simple. At the time of the writing of the NT, the full Canon of Scripture was not yet assembled. Only the OT existed. Please do not infer a historical inaccuracy when New Testament writers discuss G-d's Word. When any NT writer speaks of G-d's Word, they mean the OT. When John tells us Yeshua was the Word, it means He was the OT. This will be helpful. I promise.

2. The New Testament is an 80% Repeat of the Old

There is not a lot of New in the New Testament. From Yeshua to Paul, Old Testament writings are being used to define and discern present issues. Yeshua restores and imbues meaning to the OT, Paul uses it to confirm the gospel he is preaching. When you read and see quotations, or centered paragraphs, or all-capped phrases, or passages that seem like idioms, it is because they are quoting the Old Testament. As Paul states in 2 Tim. 3:16 – 17, "All Scripture is breathed out by God and profitable for teaching, for reproof, for correction and for training in righteousness, that the man of God may be complete, equipped for every good work."

Now, what do we know "Scripture" means here? (See the 1st principle.)

The OT is breathed by God and profitable for every use in our faith to equip the Believer for good works.

Yes, works. Still, Paul? Still? We're still on works?

If I could wink at you through the page, I would here.

All winking aside, remember: Paul teaches, as the rest of G-d's Word does, that salvation is by the grace of G-d alone, which cannot be earned. But relationship with the Lord is accompanied by obedience to His Law. We obey because of our relationship with Him, not FOR our relationship with Him. To follow Yeshua means to learn from His Word and to be equipped to bring light to the nations through our testimony. Our testimony is created in a life lived for the Lord.

What good is the word of our testimony if we accept Christ and then do nothing with it afterward? If our life does not change, there is no testimony.

Our lives will likely resemble that of our forefathers Abraham, Isaac, Jacob, and Joseph. We will be called into a different life, one that separates us, one where we are holy. There is nothing new in that. All of G-d's people in all times and places have been counter-cultural. We are STILL repeating the Old Testament. And when we quote the NT, we are often quoting the OT.

Walking with G-d IS our testimony and that obedience aligns with G-d's instructions from the beginning. This is NOT new.

I'd encourage you to go and look at this one on your own. You will be astonished at the repetition in Scripture. It speaks to the unity of the text and the miraculous nature of our Bible. Only G-d could orchestrate such perfect repetition throughout so many authors and such an expanse of time. We would expect nothing less of the G-d of the Universe.

3. Yeshua's Message went FIRST to the Jew, then to the Gentile

> Romans 1:16: "For I am not ashamed of the gospel, because it is the power of God that brings salvation to everyone who believes: first to the Jew, then to the Gentile."

The Jews had to receive the Messiah first because they were the ones looking for Him. In fact, they were the only ones who knew to and knew HOW to look for Him. Hundreds of prophecies existed in the Old Testament about Yeshua's coming. There was only one group of people who knew those prophecies, who could evaluate them in light of Yeshua, and only a Levitical Priest (John the Baptist) could proclaim that He was a perfect sacrifice.

What other people group could take the fullness of the gospel to the nations? Who else would even care that He had come?

The Roman Empire was polytheistic. In a culture cluttered with hundreds of gods, Yeshua could easily have just been added as one more. "Sure, you might be a god, there you get your own little statue."

Only a Jew would have known the Deuteronomy 13 test. Deuteronomy 13 delineates what makes a true or false prophet. Anyone who led the people away from the teachings of Moses would have been considered false. Yeshua never did this, hence many Jews, including Paul, followed Him.

If we now teach today that Yeshua changed the Law of Moses, or did away with any of it, we teach a Messiah who violates the very test He has to pass in order to be considered the Messiah.

Paul knew this. He knew that if he taught against the Law of Moses, he would immediately disqualify his own teachings and the Lordship of Yeshua. His ministry among the Jews would have ended quickly.

In fact, he is falsely accused of doing just this and takes the accusation quite seriously. In Acts 21:17-26, Paul arrives in Jerusalem and shares with his counterparts there all that he has been doing and teaching. They have relief hearing his faith and proclaim, "You see, brother, how many thousands of Jews have believed, and all of them are *zealous for the law* [Emphasis mine]. They have been informed that you teach all the Jews who live among the Gentiles to turn away from Moses, telling them not to circumcise their children or live according to our customs."

They go on to encourage Paul to join four men in taking a Nazarite vow, according to Numbers 6:1-21. By publicly taking this vow, Paul would be able to assure all that he did NOT teach against Moses' Law, but that he taught and lived by it.

Paul took the vow. He was eager to show that he believed the Law of Moses was still in effect. The educated Jews would have rejected his teachings otherwise. But Paul knew Scripture, he knew Deuteronomy. Moreover, he did NOT believe that Yeshua changed or did away with the Law!

Only the Jews would have traversed these arguments effectively, hammering them out using something like the Nazarite vow. It was essential that the Jews accept Yeshua as Messiah and Paul's teachings as valid.

If they believed Yeshua provided a route for our unification with G-d, not a route away from Torah, by whose authority do we now claim G-d's Law was made to have no effect at the cross? This is not what Paul taught. This is not what the Church in Acts taught. This is not what Peter taught.

We should not interpret the gospel differently than they did.

4. Scripture Does Not Contradict Itself

In researching this particular section, my heart regularly sank and my fingers itched to hammer out quick, heated responses to the many excruciating articles in places like **Bible.org**[lxxxix] and the **Christian Courier**[xc] that profaned Scripture and misinterpreted, even in obvious ways, what Paul discussed about G-d's Law. Alas, I decided to spend my time better. Just know, when you go to understand Paul online, you will be bombarded with doctrines proclaiming the ideas of "spiritual law," "moral law," and the "Law of God was nailed to the cross", "Noahide Law". Scripture does not support these ideas, even if it seems to do so on the surface.

Many doctrines have come and gone, but let's deal with what Scripture says, not man.

> Psalm 19:9-11: "God's laws are pure, eternal, just. They are more desirable than gold. They are sweeter than honey dripping from a honeycomb. For they warn us away from harm and give success to those who obey them."

> Psalm 119:44 – 48: "I will always obey Your Law for ever and ever, I will walk about in freedom for I have sought out your precepts. I will speak of Your statutes before kings and will not be put to shame, for I delight in Your commands because I love them. I reach out for Your commands which I love that I may meditate on Your decrees."

Leviticus 23:14: "It shall be a statute for you forever, throughout all your generations and in all your dwellings." (G-d says this about all of His Feast Days.)

Let's stop here for a moment. David uses the term "for ever" and Leviticus uses the term "forever." Both of these terms are the Hebrew word "olam." This word means (drum roll please): forever! These are eternal, never ending, never changing, permanent, and perpetual.

Even in English, the word "forever" gives us no excuse. G-d's Law, according to Moses and David, is eternal and unchanging. No, Paul does not have the authority to change or dismiss or twist these Laws.

In my essay on *The Real Jesus,* I discuss at length who Yeshua was and is and what He has taught from the beginning. You will find there the evidence that Yeshua also did NOT change, add to, or take away from any of the Torah.

If we teach that Paul created doctrines proclaiming the end of the Law of G-d, we pit David and Moses against Paul. This renders Scripture inconsistent. One theory has to go. You cannot have both Paul's view of a Law of G-d that changes alongside Moses and David's view of a Law of G-d that is eternally unchanging.

The struggle here is real and one of the most contested in American Christian doctrine.

Not to mention that we destroy any testimony of Yeshua's Messianic leadership with the Jewish people if we teach the modern American version of Him. Jews HAVE to reject this version of Christ and Paul as they become false prophets based on the Deuteronomy 13 test.

So, let's take our own Rabbi Yeshua's word for it, shall we? From Matthew 5:17-22, Jesus said:

"Do not think that I came to destroy the Law or the Prophets. I did not come to destroy but to fulfill. For assuredly, I say to you, till heaven and earth pass away, one jot or one tittle will by no means pass from the law till all is fulfilled. Whoever therefore breaks one of the least of these commandments, and teaches men so, shall be called least in the kingdom of Heaven; but whoever does and teaches *them,* he shall be called great in the kingdom of heaven. For I say to you, that unless your righteousness exceeds *the righteousness* of the scribes and Pharisees, you will by no means enter the kingdom of heaven. You have heard that it was said to those of old, *'You shall not murder,* and whoever murders will be in danger of the judgment.' But I say to you that whoever is angry with his brother without a cause shall be in danger of the judgment. And whoever says to his brother, 'Raca!' shall be in danger of the council. But whoever says, 'You fool!' shall be in danger of hell fire."

In Matthew 5, Yeshua calls Heaven and Earth and their existence as witnesses to the standing, lasting Law of G-d. (Deuteronomy 19:15 states that "according to two witnesses or according to three witnesses a matter shall stand." Heaven and Earth are the two witnesses here.) If Heaven and Earth are still in existence, then so is G-d's Law. Remember, the only Law written at the time Yeshua shared this was the Torah. There is no other Law in this moment. He is referencing G-d's instructions in the Torah.

Also, a reminder here that "fulfill" is the Greek word *pleroo*, which in context references filling full of meaning.

Additionally, the phrase "not to destroy the Law or the Prophets, but to fulfill" is taken from a Hebrew idiom. This phrase was used by Rabbis to judge whether their students had properly interpreted the Torah. If they had interpreted well, they had "fulfilled" Torah. If they had interpreted poorly, they had "abolished" Torah.

Yeshua himself says He came to fill the Torah full of right meaning and that not one dot of it will pass as long as Heaven and Earth stand as witnesses. He expands the reach of the Law, intimating the Covenant prophecy from Jeremiah 31, which promises that the Law is now moving off the stone tablets and into the hearts of those who love G-d. This new location is the new driver of righteous obedience. If your heart even hates your brother, you are at risk of hell.

If the Law is a bench press, **Yeshua just added 50 pounds to it**.

He not only did not take away from it, Yeshua stated that your heart must soften towards the Law enough that you submit to it. You will begin to embody His Law and will please the Spirit of G-d from the inside out.

G-d's instructions are not abolished. They stand today and they are being written on the hearts of His people.

Understanding this, we now have Paul pitted against Yeshua, according to modern church theology.

But, Yeshua has to win this one, right? To love the Lord, we must submit ALL other doctrine to what the Lord has taught. To believe Paul's teachings, it must align with what Yeshua taught.

So, what do we do with Matthew 5?

Conversely, what do we do with the idea that the Law no longer applies to us?

Are we really to believe that the G-d of all things came to earth and died so we could be unified with Him, but that He waited for new, important doctrines to be communicated through a later guy named Paul?

Are we really to believe the All-Knowing Being that lives outside of time messed up when He gave the "perfect" Laws to Israel and that those Laws really weren't "eternal," "forever," "perfect," "holy," or good instruction? (Psalm 119)

Were they less than perfect?

Did G-d give Israel bondage as the great gift in the desert after rescuing them by so many miracles?

These are valid questions. We must grapple with a G-d in the OT who gave burdensome Laws to His Holy People that He rescued at such cost and a G-d in the NT who frees His people from His own Laws. This is an inconsistent character.

What kind of All-Knowing Being makes such an egregious mistake?

And if those Laws don't apply to us today, what in the world is sin and what in the world are we freed from, according to modern Christian doctrine? If the Law of G-d died on the cross, we have no need of relationship with G-d to free us from sin. There is now nothing defining sin, from G-d's perspective. Sin can't exist. According to modern theology, the Law has no effect. This leaves us with an alignment with Yeshua that is now subjective to what *feels* right in the moment.

How to answer the question: What is sin? It cannot be as vague as "unkindness" or "selfishness." No earthly judge would rule based on such inexplicit terminology. For a judge to judge rightly there must be specific and delineated Law.

Our new rules (according to modern church theology) are subjective, to say the least. And a fair judge cannot use subjective rules to judge others. This is wholly unfair. How can G-d judge anyone if there is no Law to judge them by? If the Law is gone, judgment for anyone must also be gone with it.

Hence current Christianity has a grave problem. Without a clearly defined Law how can Believers ever claim anyone is out of alignment with

G-d or in need of G-d's gift of grace? Modern Christian doctrine on this MUST lead us to the idea that everyone after Yeshua is saved. Or at the very least that everyone after Yeshua is sinning less. If the Old Testament Law is done away with or replaced, then nobody can equitably be judged using terms like "generosity," "kindness," or ideas like church attendance and communion. These are not specific enough to catalyze relationship with G-d.

The Law is the only thing that defines our true nature. It is all we possess to assess whether someone is in relationship with the G-d of the Bible or not.

We also cannot pick and choose which Laws we like. They were all given in the same five books. The idea that some of them are "Mosaic" and some "moral" and some "ceremonial" is not found in Scripture, nor is it helpful to understanding the spiritual and physical purpose of each. The Church likes to point to the Ten Commandments, but it leaves out many other important instructions in the Torah, with absolutely no foundation for doing so.

I love the Ten Commandments. They really are the framework for the rest of the Law. In fact, I wrote an entire essay on them.

But, as previous essays have explicated, all the Law is summed up in two: "Love the Lord" and "love others." (Matt. 22:40)

All of the Law IS love.

So, why are we picking and choosing which ones we "think" are love, when G-d has already told us that ALL of them are love.

They are all of them moral and all written down by Moses. There is no Biblical delineation between "moral" and "Mosaic" here.

We come across this problem when we see the sacrifices of Cain and Abel and Abraham.

The Law was not written in those moments. It was not "Mosaic" or "Ceremonial" to offer a sacrifice to the Lord at that time.

It was just right. It was what G-d had instructed them to do. It was a relief for them to have a way to come close to G-d.

My point plain and simple is this: Following the Laws of G-d has ALWAYS been about being in relationship with G-d. The OT shows us how to be in RELATIONSHIP with this G-d. However, following the Law NEVER provided salvation for people. Adonai alone can save. Law keeping was not known as salvation in the Old Testament and it isn't today. We have had the wrong ideas about the relationship between Law keeping and salvation and it is time to bring them into alignment with Yeshua.

You will come across the idea of Moral Law versus Mosaic Law versus Ceremonial Laws. And while some authors handle it with care, others abuse these delineations to create a supposedly new Law consisting of pieces picked and chosen out of Moses according to, well, mostly Paul and the misinterpretation of Paul's discussions.

Yeshua doesn't distinguish between which Laws He thinks are right or not. He just says THE Law when He talks about it. We need to treat it as He did.

In one terrifying and clarifying moment, Yeshua looks to a future conversation with people who have fallen into this problematic modern church doctrine with disastrous results. From Matthew 7:22-23:

> "On that day many will say to me, 'Lord, Lord, did we not prophesy in your name, and cast out demons in your name, and do many mighty works in your name?' And then will I declare to them, 'I never knew you; depart from me, you workers of lawlessness.'"

Yeshua tells us He will judge in the end those who work "lawlessness." Those who do not live according to His Law have no place in His kingdom. With such a terrifying future judgment to look forward to, would you not expect Yeshua to be specific about WHICH Laws He will judge by?

But He isn't. Because all of the Law is His and none of it is extinguished.

He tells us quite plainly that He will judge relationship with Believers according to their works judged by the Law. You **cannot** earn salvation with your works, but if you are unwilling to submit your works to Yeshua, you are not in relationship with Him. You are not "in Him." You don't know Him. (John 1:12).

At the very end of time as we know it, the Law is still standing, still useful, still a part of the Believer's walk with G-d. This is according to our Rabbi, the One who died, the One with the power to open the scrolls of Heaven, the Lamb, The Almighty, The Creator, The King.

Yet, these principles Yeshua gives us are out of alignment with modern doctrines of Paul.

We now have Paul pitted against Moses, David, *and* Yeshua. Not a good matchup.

Luckily, Paul is not the problem. The real matchup exists in Moses, David, Yeshua, and Paul versus Modern Christian Doctrine.

Paul is not out of alignment. But we are.

Romans 7:12: "The Law is indeed holy, and the commandment holy and righteous and good."

Romans 3:31: "Are we, then, abolishing law through faith? May it never be! Rather, we are establishing law."

Paul seems to take every opportunity to confuse us. But think about the time period of Paul!

There was a rise in Greek and Roman god worship and a correlated rise in the number of their gods. All manner of religious ceremony and belief confused the message of this additional G-d, Yeshua.

Some of the Jews were skeptical of Paul's message. Desiring not to mix with the pagan religions of the day, they put up theological roadblocks to Paul. We benefit from those roadblocks as we read the debates today in Scripture and see how Paul was successful at convincing many of the most stubborn Jews to understand that Yeshua IS the Messiah.

Circumcision became perhaps THE great debate, as circumcision was political for the Romans and a difficult hurdle to cross for Gentiles coming into the faith. (More on this later.)

Not to mention, Paul had to help people understand WHAT EXACTLY Yeshua accomplished.

So, when we get to a chapter like Romans 7, boy do we have a lot to wade through. I'm going to use this chapter as an example for you. Read it alone first. Then come back and if you think you understand it perfectly, you can move on. But if you have some questions, great, so did I. Let's discuss.

Romans 7

In Deuteronomy 25, the Torah discusses the opportunity for a woman to remarry after the death of her husband. We see examples of this taking place in the lives of Ruth and Tamar. The Bible allowed for marriage after the loss of a spouse.

Here Paul talks about this. Why?

He is teaching one aspect of what Yeshua did on the cross.

The Nation of Israel had a covenant with the Lord until they cheated on Him with other gods to the extent that He gave them a divorce decree. Specifically, the ten tribes of Israel that are referenced in Jeremiah 3:

> "I gave faithless Israel her certificate of divorce, and sent her away because of all of her adulteries."

After this decree, G-d could not, according to His own Law, remarry Israel. From Deuteronomy 24:1-4:

> "If a man marries a woman who becomes displeasing to him because he finds something indecent about her, and he writes her a certificate of divorce, gives it to her and sends her from his house, and if after she leaves his house she becomes the wife of another man, and her second husband dislikes her and writes her a certificate of divorce, gives it to her and sends her from his house, or if he dies, then her first husband who divorced her, is not allowed to marry her again after she has been defiled. That would be detestable in the eyes of the Lord."

So, how could the bride of Christ be released from the law of marriage in Deuteronomy 24? The only way for reunification was through death.

We are Israel, divorced from G-d. In order to remarry, our husband had to die. This released us to be married anew to a risen Yeshua: the perfect Savior who had become man. And of course, this is what Yeshua did. He died and rose again.

Paul explains this through verse six.

And not only did Yeshua die, but we die to our old nature, our old selves when we unite with Yeshua. We are also made new, a shining bride for the groom. We die to the divorce we were bound to, where we were marrid to our idolatry and sin because of our wandering. In dying with Christ, we are now no longer bound to that life of death.

Yeshua's death filled the Law of G-d full of meaning in more ways than one. It even allowed us to follow the law of marriage perfectly. Praise Yahweh!

So, until these deaths took place, that divorce cut us off from unity with G-d. Before Yeshua, we were an adulteress people. Without Yeshua, the Law is outside of us and we cannot be unified with it the way Adam and Eve were in the Garden of Eden. In Yeshua, we are made like Him, as He IS the Torah, and we are able to produce fruit from this position. We are released from the first marriage that resulted in divorce, the one that held us captive to our adultery and kept us separated from Yeshua. We are released from the "law" that made us adulterers if we attempted reunification with Yeshua. We serve now, not from the flesh or the stone tablets, but from the Spirit, where G-d's Law is written in our hearts. The "old way" of relationship was Law abiding by stone tablets. The "new way" is Law abiding through G-d's Spirit within us.

Now onto verses 7-25

The only way sin can condemn us is if there is a Law that exists to define sin. Through that Law, we can be condemned. Without the definition of that Law, judgment cannot exist. It's actually the point I made earlier. The cross is confusing if there is nothing that reveals our separation from G-d. But the Law does reveal our iniquities, our inadequacies, and the great chasm between G-d and our fallen nature.

Because we know the Law, we are bombarded with every opportunity to understand our separation from it. We are in a state of continual awe at how often we violate its principles.

I liken it to the moment you realize sugar is bad for you and that it is in practically every product you buy. I often cringe as I read the labels on crackers and salad dressing at the grocery store, hoping sugar isn't an ingredient. But there it is, all the time, killing my hopes and dreams that some pre-made product might actually leave off the extra toxic calories. At times it feels like a terrible violation, at times disappointment, at times frustration. But now that I know, I don't buy the darn things as often. They are dead to me now, just like my hopes and dreams for sweet snacks without the consequences.

If I didn't read the label, I suppose I'd be blissfully ignorant. Still, I would violate my body with sugar excesses more often, but I wouldn't have the faintest clue why I felt so tired every day or why my workouts were a bit lackluster.

But the knowing has made me healthier. It is not the knowing about sugar that is dead to me, nor is it bad. It is the part of me that was free to eat it all the time that has died. The sobering, serious reality has made me healthier, but perhaps slightly more cautious and less prone to reckless abandon with my eating habits.

The labels and my knowledge of the ingredients have been a wonderful good that has helped me recognize the toxic from the nutritious.

Now, perhaps this isn't a perfect example, but I strongly believe this is close to Paul's utterly, devastatingly confusing argument in chapter seven. And it does make sense this way, doesn't it?

Through the end of the chapter, using our example, we could say that there is one part of us that wants to be completely healthy, always treating our bodies with decency and demanding that our palates behave.

And then there is a part of us that just wants a bowl of ice cream that tastes the way it did when we were children.

Of course, eating sugar, in and of itself, is not a sin. My example is light-hearted compared to the wreckage our sinful nature can cause us.

The reality is that our inner struggles are far more like war.

Knowledge of the Law of G-d increases our understanding of the battleground. With no knowledge, we do little fighting, because we do not see when we are in enemy territory. We have no boundaries!

With much knowledge, the boundaries are clearly defined and sometimes it's quite a struggle to stay within the boundaries of G-d versus the ones of the world. Yet, those boundaries keep us from the arrows of the enemy.

Paul ends the chapter by saying that the Spirit-led part of him is subservient to G-d's Law, but his Adamic nature serves the *law of sin.* The war is real.

This is not inconsistent with the rest of scripture. Yet if you do not understand the marital laws of Deuteronomy, or the separate law of sin, etc., you may find yourself believing Paul is battling with G-d's Laws here in Romans 7. You may think the Law of G-d oppresses you, or that its ability to produce increased knowledge that leads to guilt is a net negative. You may find yourself in the American Church Doctrine of Paul, which is inconsistent with itself and the rest of Scripture.

Like it is with sugar, knowledge of sin is not oppressive. In the long run, it is freeing. It produces health and life if we abide in that knowledge. If we do not, it produces guilt alongside the opposite of health and life. The Law and knowledge of it is not the problem. Our lack of obedience to it is the problem.

I suppose we can thank Paul for the mental workouts. No matter what, my encouragement to you is to tread carefully. If you find what seems an inconsistency between Paul and the rest of scripture, dig deeper.

5. Paul Discusses 7 Different Laws

As you read Paul's letters, you will come across different laws. Many conflate or package all the laws Paul is talking about into G-d's Law. This is a mistake and it is due to lack of context, which we will discuss later.

Let's go over all the laws Paul discusses.

-The Law of God (Romans 7:22 – 25): This is equated with Torah. "For I delight in the *law of God* in my inner being, but I see in my members another law waging war against the law of my mind and making me captive to the law of sin that dwells in my members."

-The Law of Sin (Romans 7:23): "…captive to the *law of sin*." This Law reveals that breaking G-d's Law equals sin.

-The Law of Sin and Death (Romans 8:2): "For the law of the Spirit of life has set you free in Christ Jesus from the law of sin and death." This law states that sin produces death.

-The Law of the Spirit of Life (Romans 8:2): See above verse. This law seems to be that Yeshua's work can set you free from the law of sin and death. By living according to the Spirit, we are set free from the death of living according to the flesh.

-The Law of Faith (Romans 3:27): "Then what becomes of our boasting? It is excluded. By what kind of law? By a law of works? No, but by the law of faith." We are justified by faith, not by works. We are given salvation through faith in Yeshua, not through our own doing.

-The Law of Righteousness (Romans 9): "But Israel that pursued a law that would lead to righteousness."

-The Law of Christ (1 Cor. 9:21): "To those outside the law I became as one outside the law (not being outside the law of God but under the law of Christ) that I might win those outside the law." This is essentially the law of G-d.

I'm grateful to 119 Ministries for first pointing these out to me. I find that it is incredibly helpful to determine which law Paul is discussing when he uses that term. A good way to describe the interaction of these laws is given by

119ministries.com , from *Pauline Paradox, transcript 4*[xci]:

"***The Law of God*** is our instructions from YHWH. Our flesh desires to not follow these instructions. This is defined as the ***Law of Sin***. Sin leads to death. We have all sinned. We all deserved death. This is known as the ***Law of Sin and Death***. While we are under the Law of Sin and Death, we are unknowingly in bondage and trapped in the promise of eternal death. The ***Spirit*** speaks truth to us, and points us to the everlasting ***life*** of the Word of God. In this, we realize that we are in bondage in the Law of Sin and Death. We realize that we must have ***faith*** in the Word of God by trusting and fully committing to the Word of God. This is a desire to follow the Word of God, characterized by a new desire that is contrary to the flesh that is against the Word of God. In this faith, we practice ***righteousness***. This righteousness is the same righteousness of our Messiah that he walked out in the faith. This is known as the ***Law of Christ***."

For some reason this explanation reminds me of the heavily debated movie, *The Matrix*. Depending on which pill you take, you either choose the awakening of the Holy Spirit or the continuation of ignorant existence that is, in reality, death. The Holy Spirit is the new and improved operating system, freeing you from the matrix, or *the law of sin and death*. With the new operating system of Yeshua, you are able to divide Scripture more rightly, live in more obedience and see the world as G-d sees it. It's not a perfect comparison by any means, but hopefully it is helpful.

When reading Paul, make sure you know what law He is talking about. It may not actually be the Torah!

6. Context Dictates Meaning

> Romans 6:14: "For sin will have no dominion over you,
> since you are not under law but under grace."

All on its own, this is quite a dangerous verse. Without context, here is what I used to take from it.

- Sin has no dominion over anyone in Christ. So, we shouldn't be sinning anymore!
- I don't have to worry about the law anymore. I now live in grace.
- Grace saved me from G-d's Laws.

HOWEVER, if we put it into context with the sections before and after, let's see what happens.

Right from the top, Romans 6 declares that we are not to continue in sin so that grace may abound. Paul clarifies that in being united to Yeshua in death, we are united with Him in resurrection — meaning our "old self," or Adamic nature, was crucified. It is gone. This creates a situation where we have traded enslavement to sin for a life lived for G-d. From Romans 6:12 – 14:

> "Let not sin therefore, reign in your mortal body, to make you obey its passions. Do not present your members to sin as instruments for unrighteousness, but present yourselves to God as those who have been brought from death to life, and your members to God as

instruments for righteousness. For sin will have no dominion over you, since you are not under law but under grace. What then? Are we to sin because we are not under law but under grace? By no means! Do you not know that if you present yourselves to anyone as obedient slaves, you are slaves of the one whom you obey, either of sin, which leads to death, or of obedience, which leads to righteousness? But thanks be to God that you who were once slaves of sin have become obedient from the heart to the standard of teaching to which you were committed, and, having been set free from sin, have become slaves of righteousness."

Paul goes on in this manner until the famed verse 23: "For the wages of sin is death, but the gift of God is eternal life in Christ Jesus our Lord."

Is it not the case that this entire section describes the position of being under the law of sin and death and transferred through the law of the Spirit of life to becoming slaves to the Law of G-d? Is he not stating that you will be obedient to one or the other, either obedient to sin or obedient to G-d? If you don't choose G-d, you are enslaved to the law of sin and death; but through the grace of G-d, "sin will have no dominion over you since you are not under the law."

The question must always be: which law, Paul? Which one are you talking about?

The answer can be found in the context. In this case, I believe he means the law of sin and death. You will find this same dichotomous discussion in Romans 5 before this, where Paul compares death in Adam to life in Christ — the Law of Sin and Death compared to grace and the Law of Christ.

There is another context that must be considered:

The Great Circumcision Debate

We discount how often Paul brings up circumcision and we misunderstand its importance during the first centuries of the Greco-Roman world.

This time period spans 332 BC to 395 AD. These years were an incredibly polytheistic time period. In fact, they were so polytheistic that the Jewish idea of monotheism was actually considered atheism at the time. One G-d was just not enough to make up a full religion. In *Christian Atheism and the Peace of the Roman Empire, Church History Vol. 42*[xcii], William Schoedel tells us, "To be an atheist was to deny the traditional state gods." Accusations of this specific form of "atheism" were launched at Christians during the reign of Domitian, although the vitriol found its roots much earlier. It was the denial of the many Roman gods that placed Christians in a position to be persecuted. And along with the Roman hatred of a monotheistic religion came a hatred of its laws.

According to Robert G. Hall in *Epispasm: Circumcision in Reverse from The Circumcision Reference Library, Aug. 1992*[xciii]:

"For centuries, Jewish boys have regularly been circumcised when they are eight days old (Genesis 17:12). An unusual challenge to circumcision developed, however, in the Hellenistic period (after about 133 B.C.E*). Hellenistic and Roman societies widely practiced public nakedness. But they abhorred baring the tip of the penis, called the glans. To expose the glans was considered vulgarly humorous, indecent, or both. This combination of attitudes could be—and often was—devastating for circumcised Jews. Enjoying oneself in a Greek *gymnasium* or Roman bath, where nudity was *de rigueur*, was a popular and stylish pastime. Here politics was discussed and business deals concluded. Athletic contests and exhibitions were also conducted in the nude. Participation in athletics was often a prerequisite for social advancement. Yet a circumcised penis effectively precluded this participation."

So great was the detestation of circumcision by the Greco-Roman society that many Jews refrained from circumcising their sons, or underwent a procedure to try to undo the circumcision.

Circumcised males were considered brutes, immoral, ungodly, mindless, and depraved. This resulted in stigmatization and eventually persecution. (But of course, the completely naked Romans were very moral as long as a tiny piece of skin covered their glans!)

In the midst of this Roman view of circumcision, there existed rabbis who were adamant that circumcision continue. So much so, that they tied salvation and faith to this one physical attribute.

To both the Romans and the legalistic Jews, circumcision in itself represented the decency, morality, and even salvation of the individual. The state of one's male genitalia was dictating quite a lot about that man's character and beliefs.

Paul stands in the middle of all of this chaos.

In Acts 15, Peter, Paul, Barnabas, James and others put circumcision in its proper place. It is an act of obedience to G-d, but it is not salvation. Just as Abraham was circumcised after he began following Yahweh, so those coming into the faith would eventually learn this as a part of their walk with G-d.

They instead define three to four beginning principles for the new Believer to immediately adopt. Acts 15:19-21 states: "Therefore my judgment is that we should not trouble those of the Gentiles who turn to God, but should write to them to abstain from the things polluted by idols, and from sexual immorality, and from what has been strangled, and from blood. **For from ancient generations Moses has had in**

every city those who proclaim him, for he is read every Sabbath in the synagogues."

I'll never forget having coffee with a pastor I worked for and questioning him about Acts 15:21. The clear meaning of this verse is that these early Church leaders will write to the churches to tell their new congregants to abstain from idol sacrifice rituals, from sexual immorality, and from unclean meat and from blood. And then new converts will learn the rest as they go to the synagogue and hear more of Moses' teachings.

The pastor told me that Acts 15:21 wasn't a verse in the Bible.

I protested, sincerely, thinking maybe he hadn't read it. The debate in Acts ends with Paul and Barnabas and the like agreeing that new Believers would learn the rest of the Torah when they went, on the Sabbath, to synagogue.

But this pastor said it couldn't possibly be there. It couldn't be true that the synagogues would be relied upon, and definitely not true that they were supposed to be learning the laws of Moses.

Ah, well.

How strange and strained it must be to hang so desperately to doctrines that proceeded from a compromised, often corrupted Catholic Church tradition rather than those of the Church found in scripture. Should you feel this verse doesn't exist, grab your Bible and take a peek. It won't take you long.

Nevertheless, here in Acts we see great import placed on circumcision, and knowing the cultural context, it is no wonder circumcision is a focal point of debate.

Circumcision was central to identifying the monotheist (then known as "atheist") in Greco-Roman culture.

With those glasses properly wiped and placed squarely before our logic, we can have sympathy for the adamant rabbis and teachers who demanded circumcision take place. They were wrong, but they were wrong for very good reasons.

It is clear Paul believed that circumcision was NOT salvation, and yet it had a purpose. In Acts 16, Paul circumcises Timothy because they were going to preach to Jews who were well aware that Timothy's father was Greek. This circumcision was an act of obedience to be in alignment with the Laws of Scripture so that Timothy could have good standing among the Jews.

If Paul did not believe in circumcision, he would likely have preached a message about its abolition to the Jews and Gentiles alike. But this is not the message he preaches, nor the action he takes. He simply straightens out the debate of the day.

Circumcision is not salvation. It is another act of obedience ONLY meaningful if the life of the circumcised is submitted to Yeshua out of love for Him. From Galatians 5:1-6:

> "It is for freedom that Christ has set us free. Stand firm, then, and do not let yourselves be burdened again by a yoke of slavery. Mark my words! I, Paul, tell you that if you let yourselves be circumcised, Christ will be of no value to you at all. Again I declare to every man who lets himself be circumcised that he is obligated to obey the whole law. You who are trying to be justified by the law have been alienated from Christ; you have fallen away from grace. For through the Spirit we eagerly await by faith the righteousness for which we hope. For in Christ Jesus neither circumcision nor uncircumcision has any value. The only thing that counts is faith expressing itself through love."

Paul is distressed that the Galatians have been giving in to what he calls the "circumcision party" in Galatians 2:12. Peter and Barnabas had been preaching and hanging out with the Gentiles until the circumcision party came along and then they quickly abandoned their new friends. Hypocrisy taking root, Paul rebukes them heartily, reminding them that the idea of circumcision for salvation can only lead to a belief system where you must follow the whole Law in order to receive salvation.

Yet, it must be love of Christ that comes first and inspires, not a fleshly following of the Law, but one of the Spirit of Yeshua.

The belief that circumcision was the key to Heaven was detrimental to the ministry of Peter and Barnabas and any others who would have adopted it.

What a mess was happening at the time of Paul and all over, not just in Jerusalem but in Galatia as well.

In this framework, if you read through Galatians you will understand the "different gospel" in 1:6 and those who "trouble you" in 1:7. You will begin to put the pieces together as to why Paul chronicles his history as a Pharisee, reminding them he himself was "zealous for the traditions of my fathers" in verse 14.

Paul is desperate to convince them that salvation is by faith in Yeshua alone—not the removal of a tiny piece of foreskin.

The rest of Galatians dives into this difference between walking in the flesh and walking in the Spirit. The difference between works-based salvation and grace-based salvation. He both begins and concludes with the circumcision party and its erroneous teachings.

Galatians reads like a well-written essay. He tells you at the beginning what it is about, expounds upon the concept, and concludes where he began.

Galatians is about circumcision. Consider Galatians 6:12 – 15:

"It is those who want to make a good showing in the flesh who would force you to be circumcised, and only in order that they may not be persecuted for the cross of Christ. For even those who are circumcised do not themselves keep the law, but they desire to have you circumcised that they may boast in your flesh. But far be it from me to boast except in the cross of our Lord Jesus Christ, by which the world has been crucified to me and I to the world. For neither circumcision counts for anything, nor uncircumcision, but a new creation."

Now, you must pardon me for my crudeness here, but can't you see why Paul is frustrated? Between the Romans judging based on penile features and the circumcision party judging based on penile features, Paul is dealing with a competition between two groups unduly obsessed with penises. Likely never in history have penises been compared more often. Paul calls it "boasting in the flesh."

You may call it what you will.

Whatever the correct terminology, this competition was frustrating indeed. And for those teaching that penis appearance had replaced the cross of Christ for salvation, Paul has some heavy rebukes.

Hopefully, Galatians reads like an entirely different book, making more sense in the light of scripture.

7. Paul Is Specific. Translators Were Not Always Specific

Paul deals in specifics, so I will attempt here to give you an example of why this is a rule to remember as you read Paul's letters.

Let's head to Ephesians, chapter 2:14 – 15: "For he himself is our peace, who has made us both one and has broken down in his flesh the dividing wall of hostility by abolishing the law of commandments expressed in ordinances, that he might create in himself one new man in place of the two, so making peace, and might reconcile us both to God in one body through the cross, thereby killing the hostility."

119 Ministries explains the 'dividing wall' in their *Pauline Paradox Series 5, Ephesians.* "The primary definition for the Greek word translated as 'abolished' in verse 15 means to render powerless, to deprive of strength and force, influence, and power."

We usually understand "abolish" to mean what **Merriam-Webster's** defines as "to completely do away with something." So, why didn't translators go with a different word? We cannot state for certain, but most translators are biased into believing that our Messiah did indeed "abolish" the law of God. However, the primary definition offers a slightly different spin on the particular Greek word used in Ephesians 2:15."

According to **Strongs Greek Lexicon**[xciv] - katargeō (The word "Abolish" in Greek) 1. to render idle, unemployed, inactive, inoperative A. to cause a person or thing to have no further efficiency B. to deprive of force, influence, power

And in case for some reason Strong's appears biased to you, consider how Thayer's Greek Lexicon defines katargeō: 1. to render idle, unemployed, inactive, inoperative, to deprive of its strength, make barren. To cause a person or a thing to have no further efficiency; to deprive of force, influence or power.

Basically, Thayer's backs up Strong's definition. Now, let's read Ephesians 2:14-15 again with this information:

'For he himself is our peace, who has made us both one and has broken down in his flesh the dividing wall of hostility rendering powerless the law of commandments expressed in ordinances, that he might create in himself one new man in place of the two, so making peace, and might reconcile us both to God in one body through the cross, thereby killing the hostility.'

Do you see how that fits? The law of G-d was not hostile to the Gentiles. The law of G-d is not hostile to those who come into the faith. Rather, the Messiah came to bring Jew and Gentile together. That was one purpose of our Messiah's coming! The Gentiles were not to be strangers or aliens or subject to the hostility of the Jews, but citizens of the commonwealth of Israel. They were to be made one together." (end quote)

Yeshua broke down the dividing wall of hostility that existed between Jew and Gentile. This hostility had rendered the Law powerless for the Gentiles.

We know in Greco-Roman culture that it wasn't just circumcision that formed a dividing wall between Jew and Gentile. There was an intense dislike of each other on both sides. Through Christ, this division is broken down so that the Law of G-d can be made powerful for the Gentile as it is for the Jew.

Here in Ephesians, we have a situation where the prevailing interpretation of Paul's writing would go against all other Scripture. But with some study, we see once again that Yeshua did not come to abolish the Law. He said that Himself.

In this case, we have been dealing with a translational issue.

We are downstream from the original language, and that sometimes means the meaning of a word is slightly, let's say, adjusted.

It doesn't happen often, but it does happen. The translators themselves may have been absolutely baffled by Paul's writings. I know I am at times.

So, we have to look at primary definitions and alignment and context (see applications 4 and 6).

Now, on to Paul's specificity in language and our ability to pay close attention. Tertiary readings of Paul have led us into all sorts of abolitions of Torah. Let's look at Colossians 2:13 – 14:

"And you, who were dead in your trespasses and the uncircumcision of your flesh, God made alive together with him having forgiven us all our trespasses, by canceling the record of debt that stood against us with its legal demands. This he set aside, nailing it to the cross."

What did he nail to the cross?

Go back read it again if you need to, and carefully answer.

Often Christian doctrine says he nailed the legal demands to the cross.

But, no. Grammatically, thematically: He nailed the record of debt to the cross.

He did not nail His own Torah to the cross. I suppose you could say He nailed Himself and He is the Torah. But then, He is resurrected which means that Torah is resurrected with Him and has a new place within our hearts.

Paul knew this. That's why Paul doesn't claim that the Law died that day. He claims that on that day, our debts were paid. Yeshua nailed our debt, our sin, our death to that tree. Perhaps it was the Law of Sin and Death and its demands that were nailed there that day!

And what a relief! Yeshua's death frees us from the entity that divides from G-d. It is not G-d's law that divides us from Him, but our sin that produces death.

I love this next part due to its ringing endorsement of a law-abiding Paul. Colossians 2:16-19:

"Therefore, let no one pass judgment on you in questions of food and drink, or with regard to a festival or a new moon or a Sabbath. These are a shadow of the things to come but the substance belongs to Christ. Let no one disqualify you, insisting on asceticism and worship of angels, going on in detail about visions, puffed up without reason by his sensuous mind, and not holding fast to the Head, from whom the whole body, nourished and knit together through its joints and ligaments, grows with a growth that is from God."

He tells them not to allow judgment for their observance of G-d's Mo'edim (feast days), which are aligned with new moons, nor to be judged for their observance of Sabbath or their clean eating. He says the substance of these observances belong to Christ.

Woo hoo! Thank you, Paul! Perhaps I'm onto something after all.

He then goes on to call out those who insist on "asceticism and worship of angels." Asceticism is severe religious self-denial. Monks and nuns and those who practice self-torture and religious veganism, etc., would probably, according to Paul, be practicing asceticism. Likewise, the worship of angels and similar practices are not helpful for the Believer. These, Paul tells us, are not to be added to the practices G-d has given.

For Paul, asceticism and idolatry are separate from the Head, separate from the roots of our faith. In the Torah, that sort of self-flagellation and extraneous worship is non-existent. He finishes with this Col 2:20-22:

"Why, as if you were still alive in the world, do you submit to regulations — 'do not handle, do not taste, do not touch' — according to *human* precepts and teachings? These have indeed an appearance of wisdom in promoting self-made religion and asceticism and severity to the body, but they are of no value in stopping the indulgence of the flesh."

Man-made human precepts attached to religion will not bring the freedom that simple Torah observance will. Veganism as part of religious practice, long dietary restrictions, extra-Biblical fasting, fish Fridays, body of Christ "hosts," vows of silence, vows of celibacy, etc.

While sometimes these practices may be good, and may even be of G-d in your personal walk with him, to turn them into part of your everyday doctrine in following Yeshua will do nothing for you. These are part of the "elemental spirits of the world," according to Paul.

Clean eating is NOT the same as veganism, extreme dieting, or fasting. While Leviticus 11 defines what G-d says IS food, it does not limit what you may eat as long as it IS food, according to G-d's definition. All fruits and vegetables and clean meats and fish are food, and are thereby edible according to the Lord.

To take foods off of that list or severely limit yourself at times of the year as part of a religious, faith-based act should be sincerely scrutinized.

I have fasted and prayed because I felt called to over many issues. G-d has blessed those times and those prayers.

But would I tell you that you must do the same exact fast that I did and at the same exact time that I did it? Should I do it each year at the same time attributing it to Biblical instruction? Should I become a vegan as part of my relationship with the Lord?

Paul says no. Follow G-d's Laws regarding celebrations and food and drink. Any additional religious asceticism is man-made and may lead to nothing.

This asceticism was specific to the first century as well. Catholic history is replete with it, and even today I find many who add laws to G-d's, making the faith burdensome and often lacking in joy. Paul is specific about these issues, proving the righteousness and productiveness of G-d's laws versus man-made ones.

Now, let's head to 1 Timothy 2 and a widely disputed passage. 1 Tim 2:11-15:

> "Let a woman learn quietly with all submissiveness. I do not permit a woman to teach or to exercise authority over a man; rather she is to remain quiet. For Adam was not formed first, then Eve; and Adam was not deceived, but the woman was deceived and became a transgressor. Yet she will be saved through childbearing — if they continue in faith and love and holiness, with self-control."

Um, hey Paul… Saved through child-bearing? Where is that Scripturally? Where is that prophetically? Looking, looking… Not finding.

How about Adam not being deceived… You sure? Pretty sure he was deceived by Eve. I mean, he ate the fruit. He bears no consequence whatsoever?

Women can't teach men? Can women teach males? What's happening here!!!?

Okay, I'm not trying to be disrespectful to Paul. In my cozy kitchen, I smirk a bit writing this, fully tongue in cheek, but with plentiful rage of the female advocate ready to pounce.

We must also remember these are letters to churches that we are reading. Churches with issues we don't know about exactly, and issues we may no longer have.

At the time of Paul, Gentiles were flooding into synagogues. In the Greco-Roman world, women were not as educated as men. They also often participated in anti-Biblical activities to their many gods, specifically in Ephesus to the god of Artemis.

Women were not great options for teachers or leaders, and likely were more of a disturbance when speaking in the synagogue than an asset. Luckily, Paul is an advocate of women learning at that time in history, albeit "quietly." He was not nearly as sexist as his cultural counterparts who did not educate women equally.

In Romans 16, Paul honors women ministers, apostles, deacons and servants by names: Phoebe, Prisca, Mary, Junia, Tryphaena, Tryphosa, and Julia.

So clearly, Paul is not against ALL Female instruction or leadership. But here he does seem to be. Complexity, context, and language might just be getting in the way of our understanding. We need to study all three, and luckily there are some marvelous teachings on this, including this **thought-provoking essay**[xcv] by theologian Marg Mowczko.

Additionally, the phrase in 1 Tim 2:11-15 "exercise" in the phrase "exercise authority" is best translated as "usurp." Women were not allowed to supplant Church leadership, this doesn't mean they were not allowed to BE church leaders.

And, perhaps the childbearing phrase is in regards to Mary bringing forth Yeshua.

So, we have a few options here to consider. Paul is either talking to a specific church at a specific time, the translation is horrific and unclear, Paul has lost his mind, this is not Paul writing, or a mix of some of these.

What we cannot sit easily with is a Paul contradicting all of the rest of Scripture.

What I do know is that this verse has been an extraordinary opportunity for men to sin against women throughout history. Taken out of context with no other testimony from Scripture backing those false interpretations, this remains a stumbling block for believers.

In this sense, Paul has been used for evil and this is why we MUST be careful with Paul.

As the above article by Mowczko describes, in the first chapter of 1Timothy, Paul talks about people teaching different doctrines, myths, and endless genealogies. It is quite possible the uneducated women in Ephesus were disturbing the knowledge and teaching of Scripture with myths, etc.

In fact, throughout much of 1Timothy, Paul seems to be concerned with false teachers. It sounds as if this church had a particular problem with non Biblical doctrine, and perhaps the women there were at the helm of the diversions, some of them likely sexual in nature.

In this case, Paul is right in refusing to allow the women to have an influential say. At this point, their doctrines were false but powerful enough to lead others astray.

(I find it telling that many progressive churches do not abide by this section of Paul's writing. They believe it is contextual. But the other verses about laws and abolishing laws aren't? Picking and choosing again, aren't we?

The Church seems too often to accept tertiary interpretations of Paul where it suits a seeker-friendly message. But where it may offend, oh no, Paul is simply hammering out a social issue of the day. Funny how that works.)

In Acts 2, we are told that in the last days G-d will pour out His Spirit and that sons AND daughters will prophecy. Women are not silent or excluded. In context, the concept that Paul teaches that women cannot teach just cannot be accurate.

Do you see the issues with rushing through Paul as if he is speaking to us, our culture, and our traditions? Or the problems with shallow interpretations and quick uses of single verses out of context?

Paul. Is. Difficult.

Much of Scripture was written FOR us, but not TO us. This distinction becomes essential when reading Paul.

As we read through his letters, it will help to apply these and other principles, so that we don't get led astray to our own destruction, as Peter warns.

In recent years, the Internet and access to Scripture has expanded so marvelously. Let us take this brief opportunity to reach further into our Scriptural understanding so that we may be prepared for the times to come. Get to know Paul and the Greco Roman world a bit better, and see how the Church in Acts likely greatly resembles much of the church today. **Out of confusion, may we be like Paul, desiring to set the record straight and wisely mediating between confounding doctrines and forces.**

I believe Satan only had to tell both Jew and Gentile one lie in order to forever split and steal power from G-d's Church: that Yeshua diminished G-d's Law.

This one lie makes it impossible for Gentiles to be fully obedient and impossible for the Jew to accept Yeshua as Messiah.

Dispelling this one lie will unify Believers and allow the Jews and Christians to see Yeshua as He really was and is — the Messiah, the Living Torah.

In this, we encounter the Unifier, the Refiner, the Rock that does not move.

In our Father's instruction, we can take full confidence that He has not changed and will not, and we have assurance that in Him we are set free and then set on the path of righteousness. No longer bound to death and lies, we live by the Spirit of Life accompanied by Holy Spirit empowerment for love, power, and self-control.

Your Heavenly Father generously offers you good instruction into the destiny He has designed for you.

The one lie of Satan has destroyed family, catalyzed chaos, confused G-d's Word, impeded deep relationship, and distracted from Yahweh's message.

But the truth will set you free. And beyond freedom, there awaits blessings we have not yet discovered when we engage in submissive obedience.

There is no division in G-d, and there is no division in His Word. May this miraculous fact unite His family and give us the strength for the days ahead, putting all hope in the fullness of the gospel and the Day when G-d will restore all things.

ABOUT THE AUTHOR

Rachel has been a worship leader in Denver, CO for over a decade. Her journalism degree and skillset pushed her to look further into Scriptural and doctrinal truth. Asking questions, and questioning the answers has become a pastime in the Amidei home and in Rachel's pursuit of Biblical understanding. She remains concerned first and foremost with the Biblical, academic and social education of her children and spends the majority of her time as a mother.

Rachel continues to lead worship and also record, write and produce for churches and artists throughout Colorado as well as playing live shows and events around the state and country. She is looking forward to a future of sharing Biblical knowledge and music more often and in more locations.

Thanks for reading! Please add a short review on Amazon and help the author and others know what you thought!

Rachela.substack.com

ACKNOWLEDGMENTS

I never thought I would release this to anyone but my family. But, I'm so glad that something spurred me on to let more people in on these discoveries. It has kept me humble and serious about every word. To G-d be the glory, for He is the author of each miraculous and unfathomably deep piece of the Torah and He has allowed me to know so much of it. I have had great teachers and great moments with the Holy Spirit through this process. It has been priceless. Thank you, Adonai.

I'm so grateful to my dear husband who encouraged every step, who never let me waiver for too long, and who has supported the time and space I've needed to complete this. Thank you, my dear! Each piece of feedback, each thought, each prayer has meant the world to me. How could I ever have found a man so willing to learn alongside me! You are evidence of mercy and Providence in my life.

To my children. You are the reason I have written this. You are the reason I will write more. I wish you never to be as bereft of understanding as I have been, nor as lost. But if you do lose your way, may good teachers find you, may G-d be merciful, and may you find in this book some things that have been lost that will forever change your life for the better. You are priceless, and the journey is worth the effort. Do not abandon the G-d of the Bible. He has never abandoned you. Fear not to question, or to search, fear not the difficulty that will come as a result of following Yeshua, fear only G-d and you will find the treasure you are seeking.

To my sister who I know has spent hours and hours editing and questioning so many of points. You have been exactly what I hoped in an editor! A beautiful writer, deep thinker, yet not attempting to change what I've put on the page, but to make sure it will make sense to the reader and will read rightly. Thank you! We are finally partnering, as we were destined to, and I just hope we get to do that more. You have been my best friend for almost my whole life. You are a blessing!

To my parents who introduced me to a big, mysterious, awesome, powerful and present G-d, I would not know Him without you. I know this is why, after all my prodigal journey, I returned to what was planted in me. You have supported my many creative endeavors and I hope they have produced beauty and truth more often than not. Thank you.

To Marcel Murray who first introduced me to the Bible in a way I'd never known it previous. I made every wrong decision at that time in my life, but one meeting was a seed planted in the midst of a very weedy garden. That seed took root while G-d burned off the rest of the chaff. As it grew in my heart, the rest of what I needed to change has slowly but steadily been leaving. I'm a changed person because of this work. And this seed of truth was first spoken into my life through your obedient teaching. Thank you.

To the many teachers I've had who I mention and don't in this book. Stu Fuhlendorf, Douglas Hamp, Dinah Dye and so many who have no idea just how much they have encouraged my boldness, or deepened my understanding. Thank you.

ENDNOTES

---

[i] ASPE Human Services Policy Staff, *Information on Poverty and Income Statistics: A Summary of 2012 Current Population Survey Data,* HHS, Sept. 11, 2012,

http://aspe.hhs.gov/reports/information-poverty-income-statistics-summary-2012-current-population-survey-data-0

[ii] US National Library of Medicine, National Institutes of Health, *The Risks of Not Breastfeeding for Mothers and Infants,* NCBI, 2009

https://www.ncbi.nlm.nih.gov/pmc/articles/PMC2812877/

[iii] US National Library of Medicine, National Institutes of Health, *Early Mother-Child Separation, Parenting and Childhood Well Being in Early Head Start Families.* NCBI, 2011

https://www.ncbi.nlm.nih.gov/pmc/articles/PMC3115616/

[iv] Babylon Bee, *Christian Looking Forward to 7th Season of Acting Like He Doesn't Watch Game of Thrones,* Babylonbee.com, 2017

https://babylonbee.com/news/christian-looking-forward-7th-season-acting-like-doesnt-watch-game-thrones

---

[v] Jennifer Graham, *The Case for Not Watching Game of Thrones on Sunday,* Deseret News, 2019

https://www.deseret.com/2019/4/10/20670515/the-case-for-not-watching-game-of-thrones-on-sunday

[vi] Gary Wilson, *The Great Porn Experiment,* Youtube.com, 2012

https://youtu.be/wSF82AwSDiU

[viii] *By the Numbers: Is the Porn Industry Connected to Sex Trafficking?,* Fight the New Drug, 2021

https://fightthenewdrug.org/by-the-numbers-porn-sex-trafficking-connected/

[ix] WND Staff, *Female Athletes Crushed by 'Women Who Were Once Men',* WND, 2017

https://www.wnd.com/2017/03/female-athletes-crushed-by-women-who-were-once-men/

[x] Jane Ridley, *Parents Speak Out About the Rush To Reassign the Gender of Their Kids,* The New York Post, June 30, 2021.

https://nypost.com/2021/06/30/inside-the-rush-to-reassign-the-genders-of-kids/

[xi] Rebecca Greenfield, *The Fashion Industry Suddenly Acknowledges its Anorexia Problem,* The Atlantic, 2012

https://www.theatlantic.com/technology/archive/2012/05/fashion-industry-suddenly-acknowledges-its-anorexia-problem/328533/)

[xii] Abigail Shrier, *Irreversible Damage,* Regnery Publishing, June 30, 2020

[xiii] Russel B. Toomey, PHD; Amy K. Syvertsen, PHD; Maura Shramko, MPP, *Transgender Adolescent Suicide Behavior,* American Academy of Pediatrics, 2018

https://publications.aap.org/pediatrics/article/142/4/e20174218/76767/Transgender-Adolescent-Suicide-Behavior?autologincheck=redirected

[xiv] Jordan Peterson, *Jordan Peterson on Constructing Your Identity, Chaos and Order, and the Ensuing Culture Wars,* Youtube.com, March 4, 2021

https://youtu.be/6_IGHMSsdD0

[xv] Alix Spiegel interviewing Dr. Ken Zucker, *Q&A: Therapists on Gender Identity Issues in Kids,* NPR, May 7, 2008

[xvi] Steve Doughty, *Women Who Have Abortions 'face double the risk of mental health problems',* Daily Mail, 2011.

https://www.dailymail.co.uk/health/article-2032431/Women-abortions-face-double-risk-mental-health-problems.html

[xvii] Roll Call Vote 108th Congress -1st Session, United States Senate, Partial Birth Abortion Ban Act, 2003

https://www.senate.gov/legislative/LIS/roll_call_lists/roll_call_vote_cfm.cfm?congress=108&session=1&vote=00402

[xviii] Lila Rose and Mary Davenport, *FACT: Late-Term Abortions are Never Medically Necessary,* The Federalist, 2019

https://thefederalist.com/2019/02/26/fact-late-term-abortions-never-medically-necessary/)

[xix] Post Editorial Board, *Planned Parenthood Finally Admits that its Founder was a Horrific Bigot,* New York Post, 2020

https://nypost.com/2020/07/22/planned-parenthood-finally-admits-that-its-founder-was-a-horrific-bigot/

[xx] *Maafa 21*, Life Dynamics, 2020

https://www.maafa21.com/

[xxi] Marist, *New Marist Poll: Americans Make Dramatic and Sudden Move Toward Pro-Life Label,* Knights of Columbus, Feb. 25, 2019.

https://www.kofc.org/en/news/polls/dramatic-shift-to-life.html

[xxii] Douglas Hamp, *Corrupting The Image: Hybrids, Hades, and The Mt. Hermon Connection,* Eskaton Media Group, April 8, 2021

[xxiii] Dr. Dinah Dye, *The Temple Revealed In Creation,* Foundations In Torah, 2016

[xxiv] History.com Editors, *History of Christmas,* History.com, Dec. 22, 2021**https://www.history.com/topics/christmas/history-of-christmas**

[xxv] Brad Scott, *Wildbranch Ministries,* **https://www.wildbranch.org/**

[xxvi] Scitable, *The Information in DNA Determines Cellular Function Via Translation,* Nature.com,

https://www.nature.com/scitable/topicpage/the-information-in-dna-determines-cellular-function-

6523228/#:~:text=The%20three%2Dletter%20nature%20of,the%20end%20of%20protein%20synthesis.

[xxvii] Jordan Peterson, *Biblical Series,* Youtube, 2017 – 2018

https://youtu.be/f-wWBGo6a2w

[xxviii] Sam Harris, *Sam Harris & Jordan Peterson in Vancouver 2018: With Brett Weinstein Moderating – Night One,* Youtube, Sept. 1, 2018

https://youtu.be/h1oaSt60b0o

[xxix] Dennis Prager, *The Rational Bible, Exodus: God, Slavery, and Freedom,* Regnery Faith, April 2, 2018.

https://www.amazon.com/Rational-Bible-Exodus-Dennis-Prager/dp/1621577724/ref=asc_df_1621577724/?tag=hyprod-20&linkCode=df0&hvadid=312143170987&hvpos=&hvnetw=g&hvrand=10546637273641952309&hvpone=&hvptwo=&hvqmt=&hvdev=c&hvdvcmdl=&hvlocint=&hvlocphy=9028741&hvtargid=pla-454106655563&psc=1

[xxx] Martha Henriques, *Can the Legacy of Trauma be Passed Down the Generations?,* BBC, March 20, 2019.

https://www.bbc.com/future/article/20190326-what-is-epigenetics

[xxxi] Brad Scott, *Frequently Asked Questions: What About Homosexuality?,* Wildbranch.org,

https://www.wildbranch.org/teachings/lessons/lesson75.html

[xxxii] Marianna Virtanen, Archana Singh-Manoux, Jane E. Ferrie, David Gimeno, Michael G. Marmot, Marko Elovainio, Markus Jokela, Jussi

Vahtera, Mika Kivimäki, *Long Working Hours and Cognitive Function, The Whitehall II Study, American Journal of Epidemiology*, Volume 169, Issue 5, 1 March 2009, Pages 596–605

[xxxiii] Abraham Joshua Heschel, *Essential Writings, Modern Spiritual Masters,* Orbis Books, May 15, 2011

https://www.amazon.com/Abraham-Joshua-Heschel-Essential-Spiritual/dp/1570759197

[xxxiv] Gina Adams, Lisa Dubay, *Explorying Instability and Children's Well-Being: Insights from a Dialogue Among Practitioners Policymakers and Researchers,* Urban Institute, July 22, 2014

https://www.urban.org/research/publication/exploring-instability-and-childrens-well-being-insights-dialogue-among-practitioners-policymakers-and-researchers

[xxxv] Jeffrey M. Jones, *U.S. Church Membership Falls Below Majority for the First Time,* Gallup, March 29, 2021

https://news.gallup.com/poll/341963/church-membership-falls-below-majority-first-time.aspx

[xxxvi] Andy Stanley, *Aftermath Part 3: Not Difficult*/Youtube.com, April 30, 2018

https://youtu.be/pShxFTNRCWI

[xxxvii] Joshua J. Mark, *Hadrian,* World History Encyclopedia, May 18, 2021,

https://www.worldhistory.org/hadrian/

[xxxviii] Editors of the Encyclopaedia Britannica, *Marcion of Pontus: Christian Theologian,* Britannica, January 9, 2022

https://www.britannica.com/biography/Marcion-of-Pontus

[xxxix] John Chrysostom, *Against the Jews: Homily 1,* Tertullian.org,

https://www.tertullian.org/fathers/chrysostom_adversus_judaeos_01_homily1.htm

[xl] Peter the Venerable, *Against the Inveterate Obduracy of the Jews,*

https://www.cuapress.org/9780813221304/against-the-inveterate-obduracy-of-the-jews/

[xli] *Anti-Semitism: Martin Luther – 'The Jews & Their Lies',* Jewish Virtual Library, 1543, https://www.jewishvirtuallibrary.org/martin-luther-quot-the-jews-and-their-lies-quot

[xlii] Henry Ford, *The International Jew,* Jewish Virtual Library, 1920,

https://www.jewishvirtuallibrary.org/quot-the-international-jew-quot

[xliii] The Editors of Encyclopaedia Britannica, *Mithra: Iranian god,* Britannica, April 26, 2018.

https://www.britannica.com/place/Capua-ancient-city-Italy

[xliii] Clifford Rieders, *Were the Pilgrims Celebrating Sukkot?,* Times of Israel, Nov. 20, 2018

https://blogs.timesofisrael.com/were-the-pilgrims-celebrating-sukkot/

[xliv] Clifford, Rieders, *Were the Pilgrims Celebrating Sukkot,* The Times of Israel, Nov. 20, 2018, **https://blogs.timesofisrael.com/were-the-pilgrims-celebrating-sukkot/**

[xlv] History.com Editors, *Easter Symbols and Traditions,* History.com, March 24, 2021 **https://www.history.com/topics/holidays/easter-symbols**

[xlvi] Martin Luther King Jr., *Strength to Love,* Fortress Press, MN, 1963

[xlvii] Erik von Kuehnelt-Leddihn, *Portrait of an Evil Man: Karl Marx,* The Mises Institute, July 21, 2021

https://mises.org/wire/portrait-evil-man-karl-marx

[xlix] John Adams, *John Adams to Thomas Jefferson, 28 June 1813,* Founders.archives.gov,

https://founders.archives.gov/documents/Jefferson/03-06-02-0208

[l] Thomas Jefferson, *Thomas Jefferson Memorial Inscriptions,* NPS.gov, Sept. 23, 1800

https://www.nps.gov/thje/learn/photosmultimedia/quotations.htm

[li] James Madison, *From James Madison to William Bradford, 9 November 1772,* founders.archives.gov,

https://founders.archives.gov/documents/Madison/01-01-02-0015

[lii] William J. Federer, *Benjamin Rush of Pennsylvania: Physician, United States Mint Treasurer, Continental Congress Member, Signer of the Declaration of Independence. Essay 56,* Constituting America,

https://constitutingamerica.org/90day-dcin-benjamin-rush-of-pennsylvania-physician-united-states-mint-treasurer-continental-congress-member-signer-declaration-of-independence-guest-essayist-william-j-federer/

[liii] Alexander Hamilton, *America's God and Country, Encyclopeidia of Quotations, Pg. 274*

[liv] Jonathan Edwards, *Punishment of the Wicked Eternal: A Sermon on Matt 25,* 1864

[lv] Brad Scott, Wildbranch Ministry, wildbranch.org

[lvi] Dr. Dinah Dye, Ryan White, *Parables of Unpredictable Coming, The Wicked Tenants and Two Sons,* Shifting Your Paradigm, Podcast, Feb. 28, 2021

https://www.audible.com/pd/Shifting-Your-Paradigm-Podcast/B08JJPRWVK

[lvii] *The Children of Pornhub,* NY Times, Dec. 4, 2020

https://www.nytimes.com/2020/12/04/opinion/sunday/pornhub-rape-trafficking.html

[lviii] Andrew Morgan, *The True Cost,* Untold Production, 2015

https://www.imdb.com/title/tt3162938/

[lix] Jordan Peterson, *12 Rules for Life,* Random House Canada, Penguin Allen Lane, UK, January 23, 2018

[lx] Monte Judah, *Torah is for All People: Episode 19,* Lion and Lamb Ministries, Youtube, Feb 20, 2021

https://youtu.be/kGu17R906CA

[lxi] Rico Cortes, *Wisdom In Torah,* wisdomintorah.com

[lxii] *The Passion Translation,*
https://www.thepassiontranslation.com/endorsements/

[lxiii] Alisa Childers, *Here is Why Christians Should Be Concerned About the Passion Translation of the Bible,* alisachilders.com, June 25, 2018.
https://www.alisachilders.com/blog/heres-why-christians-should-be-concerned-about-the-passion-translation-of-the-bi-ble?fbclid=IwAR10sDY098IaeXCNfWTVdJD24vuaxLX_LOo7WsPI8rqJe2HBSq76JVImLUo

[lxiv] Emilia J. Benjamin et al., *Heart Disease and Stroke Statistics 2019 Update: A Report from the American Heart Association,* AHA Journals Circulation, Jan 31, 2019, ahajournals.org

[lxv] Kimberly Drake, *Are Cancer Rates Really On The Rise Worldwide?,* Medical News Today, Feb. 24, 2022,
https://www.medicalnewstoday.com/articles/are-cancer-rates-really-on-the-rise-worldwide#What-forms-of-cancer-are-on-the-rise?

[lxvi] Mark E. Czeisler, *Mental Health, Substance Use, and Suicidal Ideation During the Covid-19 Pandemic,* CDC, Aug. 24, 2020, **https://www.cdc.gov/mmwr/volumes/69/wr/mm6932a1.htm**

[lxvii] Rachel Siegal, *Tweens, teens and screens: The average time kids spend watching online videos has doubled in 4 years,* The Washington Post, Oct. 29, 2019, **https://www.washingtonpost.com/technology/2019/10/29/survey-average-time-young-people-spend-watching-videos-mostly-youtube-has-doubled-since/**

[lxviii] Gigen Mammoser, *FOMO is Real: How Social Media Increases Depression and Loneliness,* Healthline, Dec. 9, 2018, **https://www.healthline.com/health-news/social-media-use-increases-depression-and-loneliness**

[lxix] Jean M. Twenge et al., *Increases In Depressive Symptoms, Suicide-Related Outcomes, and Suicide Rates Among U.S. Adolescnts after 2010 and Links to Increased New Media Screen Time,* Sage Journals, Nov 14, 2017, **https://journals.sagepub.com/doi/full/10.1177/2167702617723376**

[lxx] Japp Arriens, *Social Media Use Linked to Depression in Adults,* NBC News, Nov 23, 2021, **https://www.nbcnews.com/health/health-news/social-media-use-linked-depression-adults-rcna6445**

[lxxi] A.W. Geiger and Lesile Davis, *A Growing Number of American Teenagers – Particularly Girls – are Facing Depression,* Pew Research Center, July 12, 2019, **https://www.pewresearch.org/fact-tank/2019/07/12/a-growing-number-of-american-teenagers-particularly-girls-are-facing-depression/**

[lxxii] American Psychological Association, *Mental Health Issues Increaed Significantly in Young Adults Over Last Decade*, Science Daily, March 15, 2019, **https://www.sciencedaily.com/releases/2019/03/190315110908.htm**

[lxxiii] Michael S. Pollard, *Alcohol Consumption Rises Sharply During Pandemic Shutdown; Heavy Drinking by Women Rises 41%,* Rand Corporation, Sept. 29, 2020, **https://www.rand.org/news/press/2020/09/29.html**

[lxxiv] *Why Today's Internet Porn Is Unlike Anything the World Has Ever Seen,* Fight The New Drug, **https://fightthenewdrug.org/why-todays-internet-porn-is-unlike-anything-the-world-has-ever-seen/**

[lxxv] Robert Weiss PHD, LCSW, *The Prevalence of Porn: Americans Gone Wild,* Psych Central, May 22, 2013, **https://psychcentral.com/blog/sex/2013/05/the-prevalence-of-porn#1**

[lxxvi] Cory S. Carola, *Pornhub Released A Detailed Map of the World's Porn Interests,* Inverse, 2016, **https://www.inverse.com/article/26011-pornhub-post-popular-porn-report-2016**

[lxxvii] Ross Benes, *Porn Could Have A Bigger Economic Influence on the US Than Netflix,* Yahoo Finance, June 20, 2018, **https://finance.yahoo.com/news/porn-could-bigger-economic-influence-121524565.html?guccounter=1&guce_referrer=aHR0cHM6Ly93d3cuZ29vZ2xlLmNvbS8&guce_referrer_sig=AQAAAC219cj4r7qTPgHOxP4fZ3DhLIBeUqJAeh_tNcR_rvGIT9CTTLjrtbb8Xfl_mfpU3qOAH2Y1bl7q_0_XaCU44YouYfq5oGYcfd45mR8xtCKLLodHef**

VyC1cqdMmEbc45Kc4Imiu8VIkaoXzgS7e1cJLxIwI2ROf3av0KI NytjimB

[lxxviii] Brad Scott, Wildbranch.org

[lxxix] Cara Kelly, *13 Sex Trafficking Statistics that Explain the Enormity of the Global Sex Trade,* USA Today, July 29, 2019, **https://www.usatoday.com/story/news/investigations/2019/07/29/12-trafficking-statistics-enormity-global-sex-trade/1755192001/**

[lxxx] Shift AI, **https://shiftai.org/why-shiftai/**

[lxxxi] Rebecca Denova, *Prostitution in the Ancient Mediterranean,* World History Encyclopedia, July 19, 2021, **https://www.worldhistory.org/article/1797/prostitution-in-the-ancient-mediterranean/**

[lxxxii] Gonzalo R Quintana et al., *First Sexual Experiences Determine the Development of Conditioned Ejaculatory Preference in male rats,* Pubmed, NCBI, NIH, Sept. 17, 2018, **https://pubmed.ncbi.nlm.nih.gov/30224555/**

[lxxxiii] Andrew Perrin and Sara Atske, *About Three-in-Ten U.S. Adults Say They Are Almost Constantly Online,* Pew Research Center, March, 26, 2021, **https://www.pewresearch.org/fact-tank/2019/07/25/americans-going-online-almost-constantly/**

[lxxxiv] Kabir L, *Video Game Addiction Statistics 2021: Is the World Addicted to Video Games?,* Healthy Gamer, 2021, **https://www.healthygamer.gg/blog/video-game-addiction-statistics**

[lxxxv] Chris Littlechild, *Research Psychologists Report Fortnite is as Addictive as Certain Drugs,* The Gamer, Oct 1, 2018, **https://www.thegamer.com/fortnite-addictive-drugs/#:~:text=Research%20Psychologists%20Report%20Fortnite%20Is%20As%20Addictive%20As%20Certain%20Drugs,-By%20Chris%20Littlechild&text=If%20you've%20found%20yourself,in%20the%20world%20right%20now**.

[lxxxvi] **https://www.thesocialdilemma.com/**

[lxxxvii] Rob Barry et al., *How Tik Tok Serves up Sex and Drug Videos to Minors,* The Wall Street Journal, Sept. 8, 2021, **https://www.wsj.com/articles/tiktok-algorithm-sex-drugs-minors-11631052944**

[lxxxviii] Jordan B Peterson and Maja Djikic, *You Can Neither Remember nor Forget What You do Not Understand,* Research Gate, December, 2003, **https://www.researchgate.net/publication/242697022_You_can_neither_remember_nor_forget_what_you_do_not_understand**

[lxxxix] James M. Arlandson, *The Language of Law in Paul,* Bible.org, **https://bible.org/article/language-law-paul**

[xc] Wayne Jackson, *Did the Law of Moses Continue Until A.D. 70?,* Christian Courier, **https://www.christiancourier.com/articles/1096-did-the-law-of-moses-continue-until-a-d-70**

[xci] 119 Ministries, *Pauline Paradox Part 4: Which Law Paul?,* 119 Ministries, Dec. 21, 2021, **https://www.119ministries.com/teachings/video-teachings/detail/pauline-paradox-part-4-which-law-paul/**

[xcii] William Schoedel, *Christian Atheism and the Peace of the Roman Empire, Church History Vol. 42,* Cambridge, 1973

[xciii] Robert G. Hall, *Epispasm: Circumcision in Reverse from The Circumcision Reference Library*, Aug. 1992, Pages 52-57

[xciv] **https://www.blueletterbible.org/lexicon/g2673/kjv/tr/0-1/**

[xcv] Marg Mowczko, *The Consensus and Context of 1 Tim. 2:12,* From Live Talks June 28, 2014, July 2, 2014, **https://margmowczko.com/the-consensus-and-context-of-1-timothy-212/**

CPSIA information can be obtained
at www.ICGtesting.com
Printed in the USA
BVHW052322170722
642384BV00004B/100